AGRICULTURE AND ECONOMIC GROWTH: JAPAN'S EXPERIENCE

Edited by

Kazushi OHKAWA
Bruce F. JOHNSTON
Hiromitsu KANEDA

Princeton University Press
University of Tokyo Press
1970

Copublished by
PRINCETON UNIVERSITY PRESS
and
UNIVERSITY OF TOKYO PRESS
Library of Congress Catalogue Card No. 73-106422
SBN 691-04195-4

EDITORS' PREFACE

The chapters in this volume are the final version of a set of papers that were examined critically at the International Conference on Agriculture and Economic Development—A Symposium on Japan's Experience, which was held in Tokyo, July 3–7, 1967. The objective of the Conference was to make a comprehensive reappraisal of Japan's agricultural development and its relevance to economic growth over the last 100 years. The advance that has been made in the past decade, centering on our group study on this subject encouraged us to hold the first conference of this kind in Japan with an international group of participants. The Conference placed emphasis on the long-term view in analyzing Japan's agricultural development, with the historical scope being set as the century following the Meiji Restoration of 1868 to the postwar years, but in view of the importance of the pattern of the initial development of Japan's agriculture and its contribution to economic growth, consideration was also given to the Meiji Era, 1868–1912.

The Nippon Agricultural Research Institute, a private organization founded in 1942, was the Conference's sponsor. Mr. Einosuke Ishii, chief director, represented the Institute. An organizing committee prepared for the symposium in collaboration with Director Ishii. The committee consisted of Professors Kazushi Ohkawa, Shigeto Kawano (co-chairmen), Yuzuru Kato, Kenzo Hemmi, Yujiro Hayami and Saburo Yamada. Professor Bruce F. Johnston was of assistance regarding international affairs. While the symposium was in progress, the organizing committee, headed by Professor Yujiro Hayami, functioned as a management committee to ensure a successful meeting.

To facilitate a productive and intensive exchange of views, participants were kept to the modest number of 31, comprised of 19 Japanese and 12 foreign scholars. English was adopted as the conference language with provision for occasional interpretation into Japanese when necessary. The papers were not read at the Conference, but circulated beforehand. Each author gave a brief summary of his paper. The discussants for each paper were asked to prepare written comments in advance to review the assigned paper and open the discussion on it. The session was then opened for general discussions and questions from the floor, the author being given an opportunity to reply. The program of the Symposium appears at the end of this volume.

Following the Conference an editorial committee was established, the members of which were Professors Bruce F. Johnston and Hiromitsu Kaneda in addition to the above-mentioned members of the organizing committee. The Editorial Committee agreed to publish both an English and Japanese version of the proceedings. Professors Ohkawa, Johnston and Kaneda were asked to be co-editors of the English version and Professors Kawano and Kato were asked to serve as co-editors of the Japanese version. The committee agreed in principle to include all the papers presented to the Conference in this volume subject to the revisions suggested in the comments by the assigned discussants, comments from the floor, and changes recommended by the editors. The editors gratefully acknowledge the contributions of the discussants, which have led to improvements in the papers as published in this volume, although the written comments could not be included.

Yuize's conference paper, "An Econometric Model of Agriculture in Japan," is not included. It is the most ambitious attempt of this kind ever tried in Japan. The committee agreed with the author's view that it is in the preliminary stage and needs further work. (The paper appeared in a brief form in *Keizai Kenkyu,* XVIII, October 4, 1967, in Japanese.) On the other hand, the committee decided to include three papers which were not presented to the Symposium by Professors Gustav Ranis, Arlon R. Tussing, and Ryoshin Minami. These papers are closely related to our group study and the committee believes that their inclusion is highly desirable. We are grateful to have both the cooperation of these authors and the generous permission of the *Economic History Review,* the *Journal of Economic History* and the *Quarterly Journal of Economics* to include these in this volume.

The committee expresses its sincere thanks to Mr. Bernard Key for his major contribution to the task of editing the papers and to the NARI staff for local arrangements. The committee would also like to express its appreciation to the Ford Foundation and the Asia

Foundation for their financial support which enabled the foreign participants to take part in the Conference. Finally, the committee is deeply indebted to Professor T. W. Schultz for accepting our invitation to contribute a Foreword to this volume based on his participation at the Conference.

The selected papers are arranged in four parts. Part I, with three papers, gives overall analyses of the significance of Japan's experience in different dimensions; Part II consists of three papers which deal with productivity growth and technological progress; five papers are included in Part III which treats the agricultural population and the labor force; Part IV includes a set of papers which deal with exports of primary products, credit and financial institutions, farm-household savings, the impact of the Land Reform, and food consumption patterns.

Part I begins with Ohkawa's identification of three historical phases of the agricultural development in Japan. In so doing, Ohkawa attempts to give a comprehensive exposition of Japan's longterm experience. Taking up agriculture from the viewpoint of general economic growth, Ranis discusses the crucial role played by agriculture in financing the initial economic development of Japan— a controversial and important issue. Johnston then treats the international significance of Japan's model to the development strategy of currently developing countries, especially in Southeast Asia.

Part II begins with an attempt to reappraise the statistical documentation of the Meiji agriculture with respect to output and productivity growth measurement, another controversial issue. Hayami and Yamada, on the basis of their newly-estimated data, confirm the validity of the widely-accepted view in favor of the "concurrent growth thesis." It is followed by Sawada's longer-term analysis of the effects of the technological changes using the production function approach. Here, Sawada discovers three phases of technical changes in agriculture. Next, the impressive progress of small-scale mechanization in postwar agriculture is taken up specifically by Tsuchiya using an econometric approach, and a widely prevailing view that emphasizes non-economic motives of mechanization is challenged. Tsuchiya identifies distinct effects of substitution of power-tillers for labor, the price of which has drastically risen.

Part III begins with Umemura's paper, which characterizes Japan's demographic transition internationally and clarifies the pattern and causes of changes in labor force distribution between agricultural and non-agricultural employment. Here, Umemura reveals vividly the features of two historical phases: a labor growth-dominant and a productivity growth-dominant pattern in Japan's prewar economic development. To compensate for the paucity of data for the whole country, we have presented next Tussing's detailed quantitative study of Yamanashi prefecture, for which special surveys are available, on the labor employment and input distribution among major industries, particularly related to agriculture. Tussing suggests that it is important to make a distinction between labor's marginal contribution and the earnings of workers in the early years of economic development. This is followed by the papers of Masui and Misawa, both of which deal with the labor and related problems of the farm economy. Focusing on a farm-household basis instead of an individual basis, Masui attempts to identify various supply prices of farm workers of different categories, aiming at clarifying particularly the differences in the pattern of labor movement as seen between the pre- and postwar periods, whereas Misawa concentrates on the postwar farm economy, clarifying the causes of the remarkable increase in part-time farming. Last, Minami's long-term analysis of labor supply from agriculture to non-agriculture is presented to conclude Part III. Here, Minami places the turning point (in W. A. Lewis' sense) of the Japanese economy in the 1950's, not at the end of World War I as suggested by others.

Part IV begins with a problem of international trade. It is widely known that silk exports made a large and sustained contribution to foreign exchange earnings. Hemmi attempts to reveal the causes and significance for its early economic development; satisfactory financing of capital to silk industry and technological progress realized in sericulture, among others, are identified as the major causes. The problems of providing the developing agriculture with credit is further described historically by Kato with reference to government-administered long-term credit; functions of the Hypothec Bank and other special banks are clarified. An analysis of farmers' savings behavior is directed to the postwar experience because of data limitations for the prewar years. Next, Noda tries to apply a special device to measure the savings function of farm households in order to clarify the effects of increases in non-farm incomes such as wages and salaries. The impact of the Land Reform, which was undertaken immediately after the war, is then taken up in by Kawano. The treatment of the subject does not try to deal with the difficult problem of assessing the output-productivity effects of land reform; the analysis is focused on the positive impact on the farm economy, particularly on the increase in both consumption and investment of the farmers who became owner-cultivators in the postwar period. In Chapter 1, however, brief comments are made on the probable effects of the Land Reform on incentives and output, and it is also suggested, that as a result of the remarkable change in the structure of the Japanese economy that has occurred in the postwar period, the Land Reform restraints such as maximum farm size have now become negative factors impeding necessary structural adjustments within Japanese agriculture. Finally, Kaneda has reappraised Japan's distinctive food consumption pattern with respect to the demand for farm products. Kanada's analysis, based on new long-term data, found that income elasticity of food demand remained low throughout the prewar period whereas it increased substantially in the postwar years. He concludes that the process of the slow change in food consumption patterns in the prewar period contributed to the development of the Japanese economy by freeing foreign exchange that might have been required to finance food imports, for other resources.

We believe that the major objective of the Symposium was achieved. In fact, the participants found a great deal of broad agreement in most of the empirical findings and their interpretation. In particular, they agreed that the Symposium established a broad generalization that Japan's experience of agricultural development does not present a simple, unchanging pattern over a century; instead it contains three historical phases, including both rapid growth and stagnation. Throughout the discussions, however, not a small number of important points were raised and directed for further study. In regard to our analytical approach as a whole, apart from the individual papers, we would like to mention the following points in particular:

Although the organizing committee had intended to cover all the important topics of agricultural development relating to Japan's economic growth, some topics were missing from the conference program. For instance, no paper dealt with the long-run behavior of commodity prices or the sectoral flow of savings-investment. Such gaps were intended to be filled partly by Chapter 1 and by the inclusion of the three papers not presented to the Conference. Yet a gap remains. The main reason for this deficiency is incompleteness of data. The data limitation is also true for the selected topics to a certain extent and attention is called in Ohkawa's paper to each particular point. Many papers depended upon the volumes of the *Estimates of Long-Term Economic Statistics of Japan Since 1868,* edited by K. Ohkawa, M. Shinohara and M. Umemura (Tokyo: Tōyō Keizai Shinpōsha, 1965—), referred to in this volume as *LTES*. Particularly useful was the volume, by M. Umemura, S. Yamada, Y. Hayami, N. Takamatsu and M. Kumazaki, *Nōringyō (Agriculture and Forestry)* (1966) referred to in this volume as *LTES,* IX. The new estimates contained in these volumes contributed greatly to furthering the quantitative analysis of Japan's experience. Although some of the papers are the results of efforts at original data preparation, some others are not satisfactory in this respect. Further efforts are called for in preparing a more consistent body of data. This is particularly urgent for the early Meiji years before 1885, for which the Symposium could not reach agreement with respect to output-productivity performance of agriculture.

Also affected by later limitations were analyses of major substantive issues such as the concurrent growth vs. the preconditions thesis; different interpretations of the significance and of the transferability of Japan's experience to currently developing countries; different ways of approaching the study of productivity growth in agriculture. Much more relevant, however, are the theoretical frameworks. The organizing committee intended that the conference papers and discussions should concentrate on "economic analysis" using modern theoretical concepts and tools. This was largely successful in that emphasis was on examining testable hypotheses against the complex historical realities and in avoiding empty topics. Despite a broad agreement among the participants with respect to this methodological approach, some disagreement was felt and a fuller exchange of views to ascertain issues would have been desirable. We believe this was mostly related to the basic problem we face in analyzing the process of modernzing agriculture: the historical vs. an analytical approach. Not a small number of papers described the historical patterns exclusively while others adopted a functional approach with econometric tools. Those in favor of the latter approach criticized the former for its weak "analytical results," whereas those in favor of the former expressed dissatisfaction with the latter approach for parting from the "realities." Through discussion, mutual understanding was promoted to a considerable extent as far as the individual problems were concerned. However, some disagreement remained explicitly and probably more implicitly through various sessions. Finally, a basic theoretical problem was raised by Professor Schultz in the last session: what is "productivity increase"? or what is "technological change"? As explained in his Foreword, he proposed "a more complete input and capital accounting method based on the concept of the rate of return on "investment." In view of the use of the "conventional" productivity concept in many papers presented to the Conference, there was stimulating discussion of opposing views, and several participants defended the useful aspects of the "residual" approach. Further theoretical studies are thus strongly encouraged by this disagreement.

Kazushi Ohkawa
Bruce F. Johnston
Hiromitsu Kaneda

LIST OF PARTICIPANTS

Hayami, Yujiro	Associate Professor, Faculty of Economics, Tokyo Metropolitan University, Japan
Hemmi, Kenzo	Associate Professor, Faculty of Agriculture, University of Tokyo, Japan
Hsieh, S. C.	Director, Economic and Technical Assistance Division, Asian Development Bank, Philippines
Ishikawa, Shigeru	Professor, Institute of Economic Research, Hitotsubashi University, Japan
Janlekha, Kamol C.	Ministry of Agriculture, Thailand
Johnston, Bruce F.	Professor, Food Research Institute, Stanford University, U.S.A.
Kato, Yuzuru	Professor, Faculty of Agriculture, University of Tokyo, Japan
Kaneda, Hiromitsu	Associate Professor, Department of Economics, University of California, Davis, U.S.A.
Kawano, Shigeto	Professor, Institute of Oriental Culture, University of Tokyo, Japan
Maruyama, Yoshihiro	Associate Professor, Faculty of Agriculture, Kyoto University, Japan
Masui, Yukio	Assistant Professor, Faculty of Agriculture, Hokkaido University, Japan
Misawa, Takeo	Professor, Faculty of Agriculture, Tokyo University of Education, Japan
Nakajima, Chihiro	Professor, Faculty of Agriculture, Kyoto University, Japan
Nakamura, James I.	Associate Professor, East Asian Institute, Columbia University, U.S.A.
Noda, Tsutomu	Senior Research Officer, Economic Research Institute, Economic Planning Agency, Japan
Ohkawa, Kazushi	Professor, Institute of Economic Research, Hitotsubashi University, Japan
Park, J. H.	Professor, College of Agriculture, Seoul National University, South Korea

Ruttan, Vernon W.	Professor, Department of Agricultural Economics, University of Minnesota, U.S.A.
Sacay, O.	Agricultural Development Council, Rizal, Philippines
Sawada, Shujiro	Professor, Faculty of Agriculture, Kyushu University, Japan
Shinohara, Miyohei	Professor, Institute of Economic Research, Hitotsubashi University, Japan
Shinohara, Taizo	Professor, Faculty of Agriculture, University of Tokyo, Japan
Schultz, T. W.	Professor, Department of Economics, University of Chicago, U.S.A.
Tanaka, Osamu	Professor, Faculty of Economics, Kobe University, Japan
Tang, Anthony M.	Professor, Department of Economics, Vanderbilt University, U.S.A.
Tolley, George S.	Professor, Department of Economics, University of Chicago, U.S.A.
Tsuchiya, Keizo	Associate Professor, Faculty of Agriculture, Kyushu University, Japan
Umemura, Mataji	Professor, Institute of Economic Research, Hitotsubashi University, Japan
Wang, Y. T.	Joint Commission on Rural Reconstruction, Taiwan
Yamada, Saburo	Assistant Professor, Faculty of Agriculture, University of Tokyo, Japan
Yuize, Yasuhiko	National Research Institute of Agriculture, Ministry of Agriculture and Forestry, Japan

Special Contributors:

Minami, Ryoshin	Associate Professor, Institute of Economic Research, Hitotsubashi University, Japan
Ranis, Gustav	Professor, Economic Growth Center, Yale University, U.S.A.
Tussing, Arlon R.	Associate Professor, Department of Economics, University of Alaska, U.S.A.

FOREWORD

We have here the core of the best International Conference I have had the privilege to attend. It is most assuredly a landmark. The topics, the approach, and the analysis, both theoretical and empirical in solving real problems, make it quite valuable to economists. It adds depth to our understanding of the modernization of agriculture and economic growth. Those who planned the program and those who prepared the main papers that we discussed at the Conference avoided the many empty topics which have been so fashionable in recent years. The economic perversity of farmers is not here —thank goodness! Nor are the papers burdened with backward sloping supply curves. Resource allocation is not wholly determined culturally, labor is not to be had at zero marginal cost, and the modernization of agriculture is not dependent upon gigantic farms. Above all else, the Conference papers do not exclude changes in the relative prices of products and factors.

Instead, the Conference set the stage for a series of meaningful dialogues. It came to grips with consumer behavior as it is revealed in food consumption, with savings and capital formation in agriculture, with land reforms, with the population transition, the labor market and the supply price of labor, and with small farms and part-time farming in terms of economic efficiency and in adjusting to the requirements of economic growth. In treating these topics, the advance in knowledge is a joint product of economic theory and empirical analysis. These papers are not a mere display of ever more economic models or an appeal to more history without theory.

What emerges clearly and cogently is that remarkable *Japanese Invention* of a modern agriculture under Asian conditions. Japanese agriculture is technically in the vanguard and efficient in its economic performance. Although the farms are very small, they have successfully demonstrated that they have the capability of using a wide array of complex, modern inputs including mechanization. Although the area of farm land is exceedingly small by any relevant standards, Japanese agriculture has taken this limitation in stride. This Japanese Invention has to its credit three achievements in which Japan excels Western countries. One of them is the rise and success of part-time farming. In schooling and improvements in the quality of farm labor and its utilization, Japan also appears to excel; and not least, is the extent to which Japan is avoiding the burden of severe depressed areas in agriculture, areas such as Appalachia in the United States and the agriculture, for example, of southern Italy and France.

Doubts were expressed at the Conference with respect to the views of some American economists that Japanese farmers not only financed the modernization of agriculture in Japan but also supplied much of the capital for the industrialization of Japan. I share these doubts. The capital accounting of all private and public capital formation appears vulnerable for reasons of omission. (The Ranis paper was not on the agenda of the Conference and I have not had an opportunity to read it.)

Turning to agriculture's part in the economic growth of a country and how this part of growth can best be optimized, under the conditions that characterize Asia, I confess to a long-standing belief, namely, that the successful Japanese experience can teach us much more on this score than we can learn from the economic history of the United States. I am of this view still, although these papers convince me that the underlying and as yet unsolved analytical problems are precisely the same in Japan as in the United States. Farms, undoubtedly, differ but not the state of economics. In our studies of economic growth, we are up against the same puzzles.

Professor Ohkawa's paper gives us the long view covering virtually a century. I know of no comparable analysis of agriculture for the United States which covers the period since our Civil War. Ohkawa's approach is akin to the scholarship of Simon Kuznets from whom we also have learned much about our economy. But the economic growth from our agriculture has not been analyzed in depth along these lines over so long a period. Professor Ohkawa identifies three distinctive sub-periods (his phases I, II and III). They emerge clearly from his data. They, also, characterize the economic history of agriculture in Taiwan judging from the recent study by Yih-Min Ho.[1] Professor Ohkawa analyzes changes over time in inputs and in productivity. The distinction between inputs that

---

[1] Yih-Min Ho. *Agricultural Development of Taiwan 1903–1960* (Nashville: Vanderbilt University Press, 1966).

originate from within agriculture and the inputs that are acquired from the non-agricultural sectors represents a marked advance analytically. Transforming the inputs that are reproducible and that become a part of the resources in agriculture into stocks of capital is another step in his analysis. The apparent constancy over many decades of the scale of the farm-firm greatly simplifies the analytical problem. His concepts of complementarity between and among the changing pattern of inputs is surely relevant.

It is beyond my competence to evaluate the adequacy of the underlying data. Professor Ohkawa with much care, again and again, throughout the paper calls attention to some omissions and to other data limitations. I would presume that the estimates of agricultural output are in good repair but that the estimates of inputs are necessarily much less satisfactory. Even for land and labor they are hard to ascertain. For the other inputs, whether purchased by farmers from year to year and used currently or transformed into reproducible stocks of agricultural capital, the measurement problems are beset by many difficulties. These difficulties, so it seems to me, take us to the heart of the unsolved analytical problems in determining agriculture's contributions to economic growth and in discovering how to achieve this growth efficiently.

Despite the difficulties of which I speak, there are many policy lessons at hand from these studies. But since the conference was not policy oriented, I shall not elaborate on these lessons. Instead, let me turn to a consideration of analytical difficulties, not that I have solutions, but to help clarify the problems that await solution.

1. What is the economic meaning of an index of productivity? Leave aside any particular factor productivity indexes, that is for land or labor, and consider only an index of the productivity of total inputs used by a sector, or the economy as a whole. Suppose such a sectoral index shows a gain in agricultural productivity between two periods, namely, that measured output increases more than the measured aggregate of inputs, what economic inferences are permissable from these measurements? The implication would seem to be that the economic value of the output has increased more than the economic value of the inputs over such a period. If so, to farmer-entrepreneurs in the second period would presumably accrue a

windfall gain relative to the profitability of farming in the first period. Suppose, however, that the agricultural sector were in equilibrium in each of these two periods and that profits were normal and identical, the economic value of the output in each period would be equal to the value of the productive services of the inputs plus normal profits during each of the two periods. In this sense, an index of total factor (inputs) productivity is an anomaly; it is inconsistent with economic theory.

Thus, we cannot infer from a gain in productivity which is revealed by such an index that farming has become more profitable, that the value of output exceeds the value of the productive services of the inputs, that the increase in output attributed to the gain in productivity was obtained at no cost or relatively cheaply, or that the investment in achieving the additional outputs was in accordance with priorities set by the relative rates of return. I wish to suggest that such an index of productivity is a proxy for an *economic unknown*. This troublesome unknown is presumably hidden somewhere in what we are treating as inputs.

2. Can this problem be solved by introducing an adjustment for technical change? The productivity index can be transformed into shifts of the production function using Professor Solow's 1957 approach (See Professor Sawada's paper). But it is no solution; it merely provides another name for the troublesome unknown lurking among the inputs. The specific inputs that account for what we loosely call "technical change" are quite elusive. How can they be identified? Acceptable answers are not at hand. Is technical change a matter of definition or of evidence? The distinction between solutions of this problem that depend on definitions and those that rely on evidence is, so it seems to me, a relevant distinction.[2] Turning to the *embodiment hypothesis,* Professor Jorgenson has advanced and clarified this distinction in his argument that "one can never distinguish a model of embodied technical change from a model of disembodied technical change on the basis of factual evidence."[3] Here we are at one of the frontiers of economic growth theory and

---

[2] I draw here on my paper, "The Rate of Return in Allocating Investment Resources to Education," *The Journal of Human Resources,* II, No. 3 (Summer, 1967).

the terrain is still far from settled. In treating the sources of economic growth at the macro-level, I doubt that the vintage or the embodiment conception of technical change is likely to prove rewarding. It should be noted that at the micro level, as many studies in agricultural economics have shown, a new input, for example the tractor (tiller), can be handled straightaway and its economic effects analyzed.

3. Why not treat the productivity index as one would any other partial productivity index? We do this for land and also for labor. Such an index is of some use and we are not misled into drawing unwarranted inferences from gains in productivity revealed by such an index. The advantage of this approach lies in the fact that we serve notice on ourselves at the outset that we are not taking all of the inputs into account. It, also, alerts us to the analytical importance of continuing our search for an all-inclusive specification of inputs.

4. Is the solution in devising a more complete input and capital accounting method? The advance in reducing this unknown that Professor Griliches has achieved using this approach, in the case of U.S. agriculture, is noteworthy.[4] It entails a specification of additional identifiable productive services from different forms of material and human capital in an accounting framework from which refutable hypotheses can be derived.[5] These hypotheses can then be put to test by confronting the data. It is an approach that requires additional information.

Although the challenge which arose out of the observed increases

---

[3] Dale W. Jorgenson, "The Embodiment Hypothesis," *Journal of Political Economy,* LXXIV (February, 1966), pp. 1–17. I am indebted to Jorgenson for this distinction. This distinction is somewhat too strong if one were to say the embodiment approach solves the problem wholly by definition. It, too, leads to an appeal to data but in a manner and under what seems to be implausible assumptions, e.g., that there is a constant relationship between the rate of technical progress and the rate of investment.

[4] Zvi Griliches, "Estimates of Aggregate Agricultural Production Function from Cross-Sectional Data," *Journal of Farm Economics,* XLV (May, 1963), pp. 419–28; "The Sources of Measured Productivity Growth: United States Agriculture, 1940–60," *Journal of Political Economy,* LXXI (August, 1963), pp. 331–346; "Research Expenditure, Education and the Aggregate Agricultural Production Function," *American Economic Review,* LIV (December, 1964), pp. 961–974.

in output exceeding the observed increases in inputs—the residual, the productivity index attributed to aggregate inputs, the troublesome unknown—has led to many false starts, it has opened new analytical doors. The one which seems most promising, so it seems to me, is an all-inclusive concept of capital. I turned to it in my "Reflections on Investment in Man."[6] It is at the heart of the Jorgenson-Griliches approach to the U.S. private domestic economy in which they proceed to a specification and measurement of improvements in the quality of both human and non-human capital, and succeed in their growth accounting to explain the increases in macro production without an appeal to technical change.[7] Also relevant here is the formulation advanced by Professor Johnson, his "generalized capital accumulation approach to economic development."[8]

I close by listing some of the unfinished work implied by the all-inclusive concept of capital approach. In our endeavor to provide knowledge for improving economic decisions "the central concept in capital theory should be the *rate of return on investment*"[9] and investment resources should be allocated in accordance with priorities set by the relative rates of return on alternative investment opportuni-

[5] Despite my strong inclination to rely on "refutable hypotheses," I realize that Solow can point out that not all of the observable total factor productivity may be of this sort. A part of it may still prove to be a "residual," whether it is labelled a "return to scale" or something else. Thus it may be that a part of it may not be imputable to any resource cost, or that whoever makes such a residual technical change is unable to collect the return. While the capital accounting approach is a way of identifying and measuring new forms of capital, it is not possible empirically to account for all of it, and the notion of a once and for all refutable hypothesis settling the measurement problem is too strong. As Zvi Griliches has taught me, his approach to input and capital accounting succeeds in reducing the unaccounted part.

[6] Theodore W. Schultz, "Reflections on Investment in Man," *Journal of Political Economy,* Supplement (October, 1962), pp. 1–8; also in *Transforming Traditional Agriculture* (New Haven: Yale University Press, 1964).

[7] D. W. Jorgenson and Z. Griliches, "The Explanation of Productivity Change," *The Review of Economic Studies,* XXXIV (3), No. 99 (1967), pp. 249–283.

[8] See Harry G. Johnson's comment on this approach in *The Residual Factor and Economic Growth* (Paris, OECD, 1964), pp. 219–25.

[9] Robert M. Solow, *Capital Theory and the Rate of Return* (Amsterdam: North-Holland Publishing Co., 1963).

ties. My short list is as follows: (1) treat organized agricultural research as a production activity and determine the rate of return on investment in this activity; (2) treat human agents as human capital and ascertain the rates of return on investing in different types and levels of schooling; (3) attempt to analyze the cost and returns associated with agricultural extension activities; and (4) treat new agricultural inputs in the same manner.

Lastly, I wish to express once again the high value to us professionally of this remarkable Conference.

July 29, 1968

Theodore W. Schultz
The University of Chicago

CONTENTS

PART I

PART I

CHAPTER 1

PHASES OF AGRICULTURAL DEVELOPMENT AND ECONOMIC GROWTH[†]

KAZUSHI OHKAWA

Introduction

All the papers presented in this volume analyze specific topics, selected individually by each author, contributing much to our further understanding of various aspects of agricultural development and its relation to economic growth in Japan. Taken together, they seem to cover adequately, if not completely, all the important aspects of our subject. The purpose of this chapter is, therefore, not to analyze an additional topic, but to present a summary discussion. Although such a summary discussion could have been presented as a comprehensive account of the findings of the individual papers, I have instead attempted to describe historically the overall picture of Japan's agricultural development in terms of "growth phases." I believe this will "complement" other chapters.

Although this is not the place to enter into a detailed discussion of the concept of growth phases, a brief explanation is in order. In our conceptual framework, a growth phase is a distinct time segment of long-term growth, the unique characteristics of which can be identified by certain indicators. I might remark here that the criteria for these indicators can vary according to the purpose of the analysis one has in mind. Although this concept has previously been applied to the aggregate growth of the economy in order to avoid use of the much more rigid concept of "stages,"[1] I believe it can also be used for certain sectoral analyses. In the discussions that follow, the major criterion for the phases of agriculture will be the growth

---

[†] I would like to acknowledge the valuable comments received at the conference and Mr. N. Takamatsu's work on the statistical data.

[1] For a more detailed description see Ohkawa and Rosovsky (1965).

3

pattern of output and input. The dating, identification and interpretation of the phases thus defined will be attempted first and then their relationship to other aspects of the economy will follow, in reference to three interrelated problems:

1. To what extent can we agree in recognizing and appraising the growth pattern of Japan's agriculture—an experience which now extends over a century since the Meiji Restoration?

2. Both in the output and input approaches, what further research is specifically called for to fill the important gaps in our present knowledge?

3. In order to arrive at a more consistent interpretation of the long-term growth pattern of Japan's agriculture and its relation to economic growth, what analytical approach seems most desirable at the present stage of our knowledge?

I. Long-Range Growth Pattern of Agriculture: A Statistical View

Let us begin our investigation of growth phases by presenting a general picture of the long-range output growth pattern of Japanese agriculture based on the latest data which are available continuously for the entire period under consideration (hereafter referred to as Yamada-Hayami or Y-H Series; Umemura et al., pp. 182, 226–27, hereafter referred to as *LTES*, IX). In Figure 1, two kinds of output data are shown, both in a smoothed series of 1934–36 prices: *A*—farm value of production and *B*—value added gross of depreciation. Series *A* and *B* suggest four broad observations: (1) From the mid-1870's to World War I, Japanese agriculture shows a continuous, unretarded growth. (2) From that time until the thirties, it entered a period of prolonged retardation; it is clear that the growth rate during this interval became much smaller than that of the preceding period. (3) Even more obvious is the dislocation caused by World War II. During and immediately after the war, agricultural output tended to decline towards an abnormal low: its average of 1946–50 fell to pre-World War I levels. (4) Postwar agriculture has grown at an unprecedentedly high pace, especially in Series *A*. However, the prewar annual peak, reached in about 1938–39, was not attained again until 1954–55 in Series *B*. The extrapolated position of the trend line passing through 1919 and 1938 has only recently been attained.

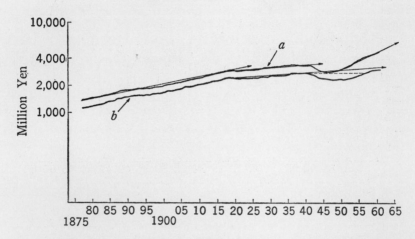

FIGURE 1
Output of Agriculture in Seven-Year
Moving Averages in 1934-36 Prices*

* Data from Hayami and Yamada, *LTES*, IX, pp. 182, 226-227. These figures are for the most part estimates which are a revised version of the often-used estimates contained in Ohkawa et al., *The Growth Rate of the Japanese Economy since 1878* (hereafter referred to as *GRJE*).
a) Farm value of production in 1934-36 prices, gross of both intermediate goods and of capital depreciation. In the Y-H series, two kinds of value added series are presented in real terms: one is estimated directly by using 1934-36 prices and the other estimated by deflating by price indexes. The former is used in Figure 1 simply because the latter is not available for 1941-50.
b) Value added gross of depreciation.

In Figure 2 the average annual rate of farm output (Series *A*) is shown in two forms: Series I simply depicts year-to-year changes in seven-year moving averages, while Series II shows those annual rates smoothed by a five-year moving average. The seven-year moving average of the original data is intended primarily to eliminate the effects of crop fluctuations. Since this is close to the average duration of the business cycle of the prewar Japanese economy, we can also expect its effect, if any, to be eliminated. Annual fluctuations, however, still remain large in Series I, so that Series II is added to give an indication of the long swing pattern.

FIGURE 2

Average Annual Rates of Growth of Farm Value
of Production in 1934-36 Prices*

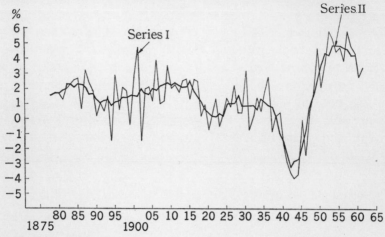

* Data from *LTES*, IX.

TABLE 1

Trend Changes in Terms of Average Annual Rates of Growth*

(Unit: %)

	(A) Farm value of production	(B) Value added
1877–1919	1.78	1.80
1919–1938	0.77	0.46
1877–1938	1.46	1.39
1919–1960	1.16	0.51
1877–1960	1.48	1.17

* Data from *LTES*, IX, pp. 192, 226–227.
a) All figures from seven-year moving averages.

Let us calculate average annual growth rates for selected intervals to show trend changes (Table 1). If we take the longest interval,
1877–1960 (83 years), the growth rate is 1.48 per cent *(A)* and
1.17 per cent *(B)*; this provides the simplest indicator of the pace
of Japan's agricultural development. It is difficult to offer an international comparison here because of limited information; nevertheless, Japan's average rate of long-run growth can probably be ap-
praised as moderate. What appears to be striking are the changes
which appear in the general trend over time. During the years of

early development previous to 1919, the rate was 1.8 per cent, a high even by international standards, whereas during 1919–38 it dropped to a low 0.77 per cent *(A)* and 0.46 per cent *(B)*. The prewar period as a whole (1877–1938) thus records 1.46 per cent *(A)* and 1.39 per cent *(B)*, the former being very close to that of 1877–1960 and the latter higher than that of 1877–1960. This implies that the 1960 level in terms of value added was still a bit under the long-term prewar trend. Furthermore, the figures for 1919–1960 are 1.16 per cent *(A)* and 0.5 per cent *(B)*, so that if we discuss Japan's experience of agricultural development for the period since World War I, its growth rate would be said to have been very slow, particularly in terms of value added.

TABLE 2

Output-Input Relations in Terms of Average Annual Rate of Growth*

(Unit: %)

	Output index[a]	Input index[b]	Productivity index[c]	Gross added value	
				(1)[d]	(2)[e]
(1) 1877–85	2.18	0.03	2.03	2.43	2.36
(2) 1885–94	1.67	0.05	1.50	1.57	1.49
(3) 1894–1905	1.85	0.19	1.43	1.45	1.73
(4) 1905–19	2.24	0.74	1.48	1.73	1.78
(5) 1919–31	0.95	0.45	0.50	0.63	0.52
(6) 1931–38	0.95	0.47	0.56	0.61	0.63
(7) 1938–54	0.54	0.81	−0.32	−0.07	−0.45
(8) 1954–61	4.26	2.13	2.51	2.13	2.46
(9) 1885–1919	1.96	0.49	1.47	1.60	1.69
(10) 1919–1954	0.70	0.56	0.14	0.31	0.17

* Data from *LTES*, IX, pp. 222–223, 224.
a) Linked of several indexes of different weights valued at constant (i.e., 1934–36) prices.
b) Ibid.
c) Output index/input index.
d) In 1934–36 prices obtained by using linked deflators.
e) Directly valued in 1934–36 prices.

These observations may lead to a number of questions and suggestions. Among them, the following are most relevant here: First, does it suggest that in Japan's century of growth there are contained not only elements of growth acceleration but also of deceleration? If the answer is affirmative, what approach can insure a consistent interpretation of both growth and retardation? The conventional approach to answering these questions is to make use of output-input analysis. The Y-H Series are shown in Table 2 in terms of average annual rates of growth for selected intervals, the choice of which will be explained later. The corresponding figures for value added are provided for reference.

Changes in the rate of output growth show the swings previously observed, whereas the rate of increase in the input index presents a conspicuous pattern. It is extremely low during the initial years of development, periods (1) and (2), and accelerates rapidly from period (3) to period (4). After showing a moderate rate of increase during periods (6) and (7), it jumps to an unprecedentedly high rate exceeding 2 per cent. A combined result of these output and input movements is seen in the pattern of productivity growth. Until period (4) high rates of more than 1.4 per cent are sustained, but from period (5) the rate of growth drops to as low as 0.5 per cent. Furthermore, the rate for period (7), which includes the war and reconstruction years, even shows a negative value. The highest rate of productivity increase, attained during period (8), is a result of an unprecedentedly high rate of output growth combined with the highest rate of input increases. Thus a more or less similar pattern is suggested by the two series of gross value added.

These findings lead to the following important propositions. The entire process of agricultural development can broadly be divided into three long periods: first, from (1) to (4), i.e., the period ending in 1919; second, from (5) to (7), the interwar, war, and immediate postwar period; third, (8), the postwar period. The first is characterized by a high rate of output growth despite a low rate of increase in input. The second is characterized by a low rate of output growth despite a slightly higher rate of input increase. The postwar period is marked by a combination of the highest rates of both output and input growth, although its duration is still too short to be comparable with the other periods. The figures for periods (9), (10) and (8) in the table offer us a good basis for marking growth phases. The characteristics of each period seem to be distinct enough to be demarcated from other periods in terms of our criteria of output-input relationship. Of course final identification of these phases can be given later because we do not have sufficient knowledge as yet about the factors responsible for characterizing these different periods. As an operational assumption, therefore, let us call these time segments Phase I, Phase II, and Phase III. We have following questions: How could output increase so fast despite a very slow increase in input during Phase I? Why did the rate of input increase slow down and why did the rate of output growth decelerate with the level of input increases during Phase II? Why was the postwar spurt possible in Phase III following the long retardation of the interwar period and wartime years?

II. Long-Term Performance of Various Inputs to Agriculture

The performance of inputs and relevant factors such as technological progress and changes in incentives for farmers must be examined. Two preliminary remarks, however, are necessary: one concerning the problem of reliability of the basic statistics and the other, the method of approach.

Since the publication of the GRJE series, the method to be used to revise the possible underestimation of agricultural output data for the early Meiji years has become an important problem. Our research group made serious efforts to carry out this difficult task. The result is the Y-H Series on which the previous observations have depended entirely. James Nakamura contends that the question raised above with respect to Phase I is largely a statistical illusion caused by the understimation of the output level for these early years. He believes that such a rapid growth did not occur in Phase I. To confirm the underestimation of the official statistics for the period in question is one thing. To make an appropriate adjustment for them is another. While I appreciate his work on the former, I cannot share his view with respect to the latter. The Hayami-Yamada paper appearing in this volume seems to confirm the reliability of their output estimates, and largely share their views. Nobody can be perfect, however, in pursuing such a task and there still seem to remain some doubtful points in the Y-H Series for the

---

[2] For example, the year 1885 appears to be a peak of the first swing as is seen in Figure 2. In the *GRJE* series it was a trough; the Y-H series shows no retardation for the years immediately before 1905 which was witnessed in the *GRJE* series.

very early Meiji years.[2] In the following discussion, an acceleration in output growth in Phase I is found *not* to be a mere statistical illusion.

Agricultural development depends upon a complex of various inputs. Because the required data, as well as our analytical tools, are still limited, the questions previously posed cannot be answered comprehensively in a rigorous way, at least at this stage of our knowledge. Recent model analysis, for example, appears to have been successful in long-term analysis only when the relevant factors have been narrowly specified. The discussion that follows, therefore, is intended as a first step toward clarifying the broad historical pattern of changes in various inputs in terms of the three growth phases. Sawada attempts a production function analysis in his article in this volume. This is one of the most ambitious approaches for clarifying the long-term pattern of Japanese agricultural production. I believe that the results he presents are complementary to a considerable extent with my historical analysis that follows.

To facilitate the discussion, two assumptions are made. First, changes in inputs take place due to two major factors: one, the potential of technological progress to be applied to agriculture and, the other, the incentives for farmers. Each of the above factors is complex, and it may be too simple to treat them in such a framework. Furthermore, other factors than these two are often relevant to the input changes in agriculture. Yet I believe this framework will serve as a useful convention. Secondly, inputs can best be classified into two categories: one, the internal (or of agricultural origin) and the other, the external (or of non-agricultural origin). This distinction is useful not only in clarifying the pattern of sectoral inter-dependence through the flow of inputs, but also in dealing with the relationship of technological progress between agriculture and industry.

Let us begin with the internal input which has labor and land as its two basic items. In Table 3 average annual rates of change in land and labor and their related terms are shown in the same periodization as Table 2. Unlike Western farming, the area of arable land, i.e., the sum of paddy and upland fields, can approximate the land stock, because pastures are insignificant in Japanese farming. Modern economic growth in Japan has been characterized historically by the initial condition of an unfavorable land-man ratio (the reciprocal of the more conventional term, man-land ratio). In 1877 the total arable land is estimated at 4,624,000 chō (a chō is approximately equal to a hectare), which, together with 14,773,000 gainful workers in agriculture, gives a land-man ratio of 0.32 chō per worker—an extremely low ratio even by Asian standards. There remained only a little room to expand the area of arable land. Under such conditions which prevailed in subsequent yeais, any change in the ratio, even though slight, must be a good indicator of the farmers' attitudes toward farming: when incentives were favorable they made great efforts to expand the area of cultivation. In Table 3 we see that the average annual rate of increase in arable land was continuously accelerated from period (1) through period (4) and since then became more or less stagnant. This performance coincides with our tentative phasing. No index of change in the rate of land utilization is available so that a supplementary indicator is provided by changes in the area of the second crop of paddy fields, which show the farmer's marginal activity. The cultivated area of barley

TABLE 3

Changes in Land and Labor and Related Terms: Average Annual Rate*

(Unit: %)

	Arable land	Labor	Land/ Labor	Land productivity		Labor productivity	
				(1)	(2)	(1)	(2)
(1) 1877–85	0.37	−0.24	0.61	1.81	1.99	2.60	2.42
(2) 1885–94	0.42	−0.19	0.61	1.26	1.07	1.68	1.86
(3) 1894–1905	0.55	−0.08	0.63	1.30	1.18	1.81	1.93
(4) 1905–19	0.80	−0.08	0.88	1.44	0.98	1.86	2.32
(5) 1919–31	0.09	−0.03	0.12	0.86	0.43	0.55	0.99
(6) 1931–38	0.28	−0.25	0.53	0.67	0.35	0.88	1.20
(7) 1938–54	−0.41	0.55	−0.96	0.95	−0.03	−1.00	0.99
(8) 1954–61	0.30	−2.74	2.44	3.96	2.16	5.20	7.00
(9) 1885–1919	0.62	−0.03	0.65	1.34	1.07	1.72	1.98
(10) 1919–1954	0.00	0.25	−0.25	0.70	0.17	−0.08	0.45

* Data from *LTES*, IX, pp. 182, 216, 226.

a) All land (in area of arable land) and labor (in number of gainfully employed workers) figures are in terms of seven-year moving averages except for 1961 which is in terms of five-year moving averages.

b) (1) and (2) under land and labor productivities correspond to (1) and (2) of gross added value in Table 2.

and wheat crops was 524,000 chō in 1889, the first year for which nationwide official statistics are available. It continuously increased until 1919, reaching some 730,000 chō, but declined during the twenties. Double cropping is a traditional method of fuller utilization of paddy fields; it prevailed even before the Meiji Restoration. The improvements in water-control facilities and in cultivating methods during these years undoubtedly supported its expansion. Thus the attitude toward fuller utilization of land shows a distinct change by about 1919; it was positive during Phase I and turned out to be the opposite during Phase II. In Phase III, because of food shortages immediately after the war, enormous efforts were made to expand arable land, but the prewar levels were barely recovered due mainly to the limitation of natural resources.

The number of people "gainfully occupied" in agriculture is shown as "labor" in the table. The figures are based on Minami's recent estimates (*LTES,* IX) which are in turn the revision of previous ones including estimates by both Ohkawa and Hemmi. Not only the paucity of basic data, but also the insufficient knowledge regarding the actual working situation in the rural community make it difficult to apply the more appropriate concept of "labor input" with quality adjustment to the prewar Japanese agriculture. The articles contained in this volume by Umemura and Tussing contribute much to clarifying the early situation in this and other respects. But still further study is needed.[3] The figures in the table are, therefore, approximate. Yet we believe they can indicate a broad trend. The number of laborers had continuously decreased, although very slowly and with some fluctuations, during the entire prewar period. This trend was interrupted by a great increase immediately after the war due to the large number of people repatriated from

---

[3] The lack of a continuous series of labor input data (i.e., man hours) in agriculture as well as in non-agriculture is a great handicap. Tussing's regional analysis in his paper contained in this volume is illuminating concerning this point. I share the view that the attitude toward fuller utilization of resources in Phase I mentioned here might also have been accompanied by a fuller utilization of existing labor. Illustrative of this attitude regarding farming we have the expansion of second crops, introduction of summer-autumn cocoon crops and increased production of farm-supplied fertilizers. Further studies will be necessary, however, before we can reach any quantitative conclusions on this point.

abroad and the abnormally weakened power of industry to absorb labor. Its peak was reached in 1951, amounting to 15,734,000 in the smoothed series, an increase of some 2 million as compared with 1938. From 1951 on a rapid decrease set in, which has continued up to the pre sent: the average annual rate of decrease for 1954–61 is 2.74 per cent—a percentage close to those of Western countries —and the rate of decrease has been even higher since 1961. Thus, Phase III is characterized by a distinct declining trend in the number of workers; no such distinction can be made between Phases I and II.

A combined result of these two patterns is shown in Table 3 by the average annual rate of change in the land-labor ratio. During Phase I it had increased at a sizable pace of 0.6–0.9 per cent; during Phase II it slowed down, and at the time of World War II it even became negative. The postwar phase is marked by an unprecedentedly high rate, simply described by a comparison of the figures for periods (9), (10) and (8) in the table. The partial productivities with respect to land and labor are also shown in Table 3. Their annual rates of increase show broadly the same three-phase pattern. No further explanation would be required except to point out that during the postwar phase the increases of both productivities are large and the rise of labor productivity is particularly spectacular because of the decrease in the number of workers in agriculture. Granted that these can only be a crude measure, they seem to serve as broad indicators for our purpose. The pattern of land-labor input together with that of their partial productivities fit well into our tentative phasing.

How about the other internal inputs? Some parts of capital formation represented by increases in the stock of trees, shrubs and livestock as well as inputs of intermediate goods of agricultural origin are of importance as internal inputs. For the sake of convenience of description, however, they will be dealt with later in relation to the external inputs. Let us now take up the strategic indicator of technological potential: supplies of improved varieties (seeds, silkworm eggs, etc.) included in the input of internal origin valued at market prices. I share the view that the development of improved varieties of various crops together with related methods of cultivation can represent the technological potential previously referred to; their diffusion can then explain a good part of output and productivity increases in agriculture. Johnston's article contained in this volume is particularly illuminating in this respect. This must have been especially eminent in rice cultivation during Phase I. By contrast, the relative retardation during Phase II must be relevant to the tendency of such technological potential to fade away. The renewed spurt in Phase III can be explained substantially by the emergence and diffusion of new technological potentials based on scientific research. This may be too brief a description to weigh appropriately the importance of the subject, but both the factual evidence and the analytical results in this regard have been widely accepted and need not be repeated here.[4]

In summing up the foregoing discussion, what specifically concerns us is the general growth potential within agriculture. A backlog of technological knowledge about agriculture and the capacity of the farming community to absorb it, which involves farmers' attitudes and institutional factors—these two are the main determinants of the growth potential. The performance of inputs of internal origin and the realized pattern and speed of technological progress —these two major phenomena discussed above provide us with knowledge about the historical changes in the growth potentials within agriculture and help to confirm the appropriateness of our phasing.

The three phases are dated as follows: Phase I, 1885 – 1919; Phase II, 1919 – 1954; and Phase III, 1954–? A brief explanation is needed with respect to the above periodization. First, our periodization is based on a smoothed series so that instead of single year points in time they relate to broad demarcations, i.e., bands of years. Second, the very early years before 1885 are excluded for a reason to be mentioned later. Third, although World War II years and the subsequent period of rehabilitation are included in Phase II, these years could have been omitted from our phasing because of the abnormalities involved. However, agriculture suffered least from direct war damage; from the standpoint of growth potential, I believe, they are better included in our phasing. I have chosen to set

---

[4] For a recent representative work see Hayami and Yamada.

the beginning of Phase III from the point where the rehabilitation process more or less ends. As is shown in Figure 1, the level of value added reached the 1938–39 prewar peak in about 1954, and the labor force in agriculture began to decrease steadily from around this year. We would not deny that some of the effects of war dislocation continued to be felt even after 1954. For example, the once swollen agricultural population must have contributed to accelerating the rate of its decrease during the subsequent years. The fact that until about 1960 the agricultural output growth followed the long-term prewar trend may also be indicative of possible recovery factors. Even so, the inclusion of these years in Phase II would serve our purpose. Last, according to our criteria, Phase III seems to be continuing and at present we have no knowledge about its end.

We should reiterate here that our technique of phasing is based tentatively on observations of output-input relations in terms of growth rates and then confirmed by observing the pattern of internal inputs, the criteria being the growth potentials within agriculture. Furthermore, this technique assumes long-lasting distinctions, instead of short-term changes, in the growth potential in the century

FIGURE 3
Current Inputs to Agriculture*

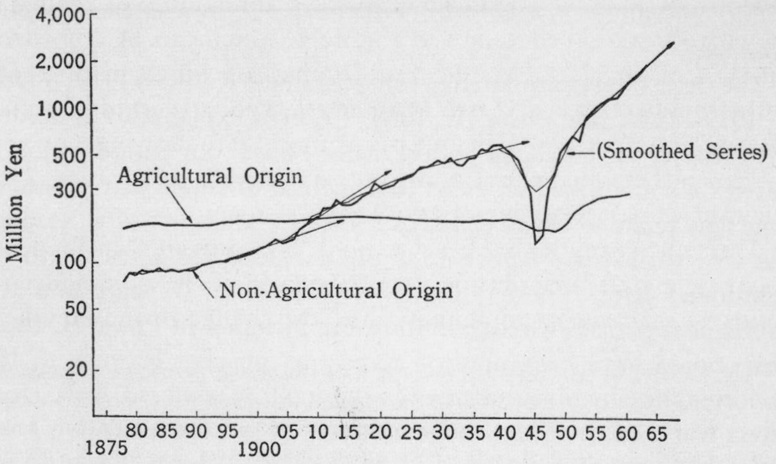

* Data from *LTES*, IX, p. 185.

of development of Japan's agriculture. It should be added, however, that we have, as yet, said almost nothing about the relationship of the agricultural with the non-agricultural sector. One of the important characteristics of Japan's agricultural development is that it took place concurrently with the growth of industry and that the pattern of sectoral interdependence is particularly crucial for understanding its performance. Without entering into a detailed discussion of this aspect,[5] let us take up inputs of external origin as a representative indicator for our present purpose and look at their performance in the light of the above phasing.

Figure 3 gives a general picture of current inputs to agriculture based on the Y-H data of seven-year moving averages in 1934–36 prices. We can see here a sharp contrast between the two series: inputs of external origin show a rapidly increasing trend except for the period of World War II and its aftermath, whereas the changes in inputs of internal origin show a very moderate trend. The estimates of the latter series are less reliable and do not include manures produced on farms except for green manures mostly produced as a second paddy-field crop. Increases in inputs of manure seem to be more important as we go back to earlier years, so that a considerable reservation must be made here. Yet it is intuitively obvious that the changes in the total current inputs were caused mostly by the changes in inputs of external origin. Their average annual rate of change is shown with smoothed values in Figure 4, which can be compared with that of output in Figure 2. Our comparison will be made essentially from two aspects: First, from the viewpoint of swings, unlike the case of output, a trough appears around 1885, showing a reverse movement between output and input during the early years. This might be explained in one of two ways:

1) The short swing with a peak around 1885 presented in Figure 2 might be a statistical illusion; or 2) because of the dominance of inputs of internal origin at that time, the change in the inputs of

---

[5] The concept of concurrent growth is first developed in Ohkawa (1964). In denying the thesis of preconditions, the Hayami-Yamada paper presented here takes a similar view and supports the concurrent growth thesis with convincing data. In order to establish this thesis more firmly, it is desirable to have a quantitative identification of a distinct kink in the growth curve of agriculture which marks a change between the Tokugawa and Meiji Era.

external origin was insignificant. In any event it is clear that further work is needed before any firm conclusion can be reached on this point. This is the reason why the years before 1885 have been excluded from our phasing. The exclusion may not be a serious defect historically because, in our view, modern economic growth started in about 1885 and the excluded years belong to the "transition" phase (Ohkawa and Rosovsky). Secondly, the entire prewar period, broadly speaking, is divided into two segments demarcated at about 1908 into a period of acceleration and a period of deceleration which roughly corresponds to the performance of the rate of output growth. Third, the sharp drop during the World War II years and the rapid recovery during the rehabilitation period again correspond to the output performance.

FIGURE 4
Current Inputs of Non-Agricultural Origin:
Average Annual Rates of Change*

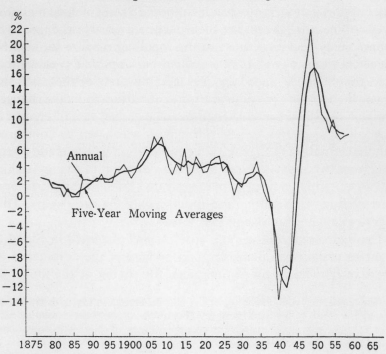

* Data from *LTES*, IX, pp. 183-4.

Looking at the level of average rate of input growth, the following three points are noted: First, during the period of acceleration it jumped to a high of 6 per cent from a very low level, but before around 1905 it was still largely under 4 per cent, a rate which was more or less sustained through the twenties. The stagnation of output growth during Phase II cannot therefore be explained by a low rate of input increase. On the other hand, a comparatively high rate of output growth during Phase I cannot fully be explained by a high rate of current input increases. Second, the sharp drop in the growth rate of inputs during World War II must have been the main factor responsible for the drop in output increases, as Japanese agriculture at that time depended heavily upon inputs of external origin. Third, the postwar level of the growth rate of inputs is unprecedentedly high. Although it falls following the rehabilitation period, its normal rate is more than 8 per cent—distinctly higher than the highest prewar level which reached its peak in about 1908. It goes without saying that this pattern corresponds to the high rates of output growth. During Phase III the degree of dependence on external inputs becomes much heavier because of the rapid increases in the input of chemical sprays as well as other chemicals, imported livestock feed, etc., in addition to fertilizers. In order to quantify these observations, the average annual growth rate of current inputs is shown in

TABLE 4

Changes in the Current Inputs to Agriculture:
Average Annual Rate of Increase*

(Unit: %)

	Total	External origin	Internal origin
(1) 1877–85	1.03	1.62	0.73
(2) 1885–94	0.35	1.50	0.19
(3) 1894–1905	1.46	3.20	0.04
(4) 1905–19	2.74	4.97	0.52
(5) 1919–31	2.36	3.67	−0.53
(6) 1931–38	1.93	2.54	0.38
(7) 1938–54	2.86	3.24	1.68
(8) 1954–61	8.16	9.55	1.90
(9) 1885–1919	1.76	3.47	0.29
(10) 1919–1954	2.43	3.22	0.68

* Data from *LTES*, IX, pp. 183–4.

Table 4 for selected intervals. The selection of the demarcating years is the same as in previous tables. No further explanation will be needed except on one important point. We have shown in Table 4 the total current inputs of external and internal origin. Even with the reservation made previously regarding the statistical reliability of the internal series together with the reservation mentioned in the footnote,[6] it is to be understood that the rate of increase in current inputs was generally higher for Phase II than for Phase I, except for the period 1905–19.

In interpreting the effects of current inputs on output, the widely prevailing view both in Japan and abroad maintains that the rapid increase in the fertilizer input played the greatest role in raising output and productivity in Japanese agriculture. Recent econometric studies have confirmed this.[7] It is also the consensus that seed improvements which produced varieties with greater capacity to respond to fertilizer and related progress in cultivation practices in farming have a technical complementarity with increases in fertilizer input. In terms of our framework, this can be called an important technological linkage between the growth potential within agriculture and current inputs of external origin, i.e., a carrier of the technical advance in industry. From this particular point of view, let us finally observe the pattern of each phase.

Beginning with Phase II, we observe that the conditions in agriculture in this phase (except the World War II period) were much more favorable than during Phase I regarding current inputs of external origin. For example, we see here an increased supply of fertilizers as a result of the development of the modern chemical industry, which also helped to increase demand for fertilizers by lowering their prices. And yet the subsequent decline in the rate of output growth in agriculture must be explained mainly by the decline in growth potentials within agriculture—a fact suggested previously—is more firmly recognized here.[8] Next, for Phase I, the

---

[6] The greater rate of increase in the inputs of agricultural origin during periods (7) and (8) was caused by a postwar increase in forage crops which was accompanied by the development of livestock farming. This point should be taken into account when comparing the figures of periods (9) and (10).

[7] See Hayami (1964, 1967).

[8] It should be noted, however, that external factors—notably the increase in

period of 1905–19 deserves special attention. The growth potentials in agriculture were found previously to be still sustained towards the end of this period. In addition, the accelerated growth rate of current inputs coincided with the spurt of the modern industries of the Japanese economy. Although the causes of associated movements of the two should be explored further, it is clear that the two-fold effects combined must be the cause for the high rate of agricultural growth during this period. It is interesting to note that the year 1905 is identified also as the beginning point of an investment spurt, indicating the independent growth of the modern sectors in Japan. By contrast, the experience during 1931–38 draws special attention. Unlike in 1905–19, agriculture did not show a high rate of growth despite a big spurt in investment and output of the industrial sector. As is shown in Figure 4, toward the end of the twenties the rate of current inputs of external origin began to show a sign of increase but this did not continue, due to the lack of growth potentials in agriculture at that time. Secondly, how about the early years before 1905? We have some difficulty in interpreting a relatively high rate of output growth during this period. The twofold effect mentioned above could not be expected as current inputs of external origin at that time were mostly the product of traditional industries, whose weight in the total current inputs was small. As has previously been mentioned, under the existence of growth potentials the main driving force had been a nationwide diffusion of improved traditional varieties combined with an improved method of cultivation, both of which took place with increasing returns to current inputs. However, to obtain more convincing evidence, further research seems to be needed with respect to other relevant factors, some of which will be discussed later. Last, with respect to Phase III, there is no particular difficulty in interpreting its characteristics. This subject will be taken up in the next section because

---

imports of cheap rice from Korea and Taiwan (discussed in the following section) and the slowing of the growth of the non-farm labor demand—meant that Japan's farmers faced less favorable demand conditions which reduced the incentive to introduce output-increasing innovations and made it difficult to reduce farm labor inputs.

agriculture came to depend more heavily upon industry, and the different nature of technological advance raises different problems.

III. Relationship between the Phases of Agriculture and the Pattern of Economic Growth

In the previous section three phases of agricultural development have been identified, and suggestions were made in order to arrive at a consistent interpretation of Japan's experience in the light of that framework. In so doing, attention has solely been concentrated on the peculiar characteristics of this particular sector of the economy. This kind of approach, though it appears too narrow, is specifically intended to clarify the peculiar nature of agricultural development, which the usual approach of the macro-type would be likely to miss. However, agriculture does possess, to a certain extent, characteristics in common with other sectors of the economy and this aspect becomes more important as the economy grows. In posing the problem of agricultural development in relation to other sectors of the economy, therefore, common terms of growth analysis are indispensable. This section attempts to discuss several topics selected from this viewpoint: capital formation and its related problems, commodity prices and trade, demand for farm products and income formation in agriculture. Except for the first topic, discussion will be brief as they are specifically dealt with in other papers in this volume.

Beginning with capital formation, the general picture is as follows: In 1881, from which time smoothed series are available, the existing total gross fixed capital stock, residential buildings excluded, was distributed 72.4 per cent and 27.6 per cent, respectively, between primary and non-primary sectors. Although the former includes forestry and fishery, agriculture constitutes the major component. In 1937, the last year representing normal prewar economic activities, the existing gross capital stock was distributed 18.9 per cent in the primary sector vs. 81.1 per cent in the non-primary sector. These figures emphasize quite dramatically the extent to which capital formation was concentrated in the non-agricultural sector. Two particular points, among others, are implied. First, it makes clear that, at the beginning of modern economic growth, the major portion of capital stock had been accumulated in agriculture. In fact, gross capital stock per gainful worker in the primary sector was at a level of 62 per cent that of the non-primary sector, indicating that capital intensity of agriculture was comparatively not so low. This in turn implies that a certain amount of capital was indispensable even for farming of the traditional type—a fact which has often not been adequately recognized. In 1885 the breakdown by type of capital goods in agriculture was: producers' durable equipment, 13.4 per cent; non-residential buildings, 68.5 per cent; and livestock, trees, and shrubs, 18.1 per cent. Secondly, as will be shown shortly, it nevertheless suggests a fact often referred to roughly as the function of "capital-saving" in agriculture.

With these preliminaries, let us observe the time pattern of capital formation. Table 5 shows the data in terms of average rates of annual growth. Total capital stock in agriculture increased at a very slow pace during the entire prewar period, the highest rate being 0.72 per cent. This is largely due to a slight increase in the level of non-residential buildings on the farm. However, it is noted that the

TABLE 5

Gross Capital Stock in Agriculture and Related Terms:

Average Annual Rates^a of Changes*

(Unit: %)

	Total	Livestock	Trees, shrubs	Equipment	Capital intensity^b
(1) 1877–85	0.24	0.30	1.56	0.77	0.48
(2) 1885–94	0.34	0.45	2.43	0.73	0.48
(3) 1894–1905	0.48	0.26	2.26	1.26	0.56
(4) 1905–19	0.72	0.84	1.93	2.10	0.80
(5) 1919–31	0.70	1.26	0.87	2.03	0.73
(6) 1931–38	0.24	0.85	0.03	1.49	0.49
(7) 1938–54	0.60	1.81	−2.51	1.03	0.05
(8) 1954–61	3.18	3.52	5.25	8.63	5.92
(9) 1885–1919	0.54	0.52	2.17	1.45	0.57
(10) 1919–1954	0.54	1.38	0.83	1.48	0.29

*   Data from Ohkawa et al., *Capital Stock,* III, *Long-Term Economic Statistics of Japan since 1868* (hereafter referred to as *LTES,* III), p. 154 and *LTES,* IX, p. 226.

a)   All figures taken from five-year moving averages.

b)   Capital intensity based on capital stock/labor.

rate of increase is somewhat accelerated through periods (1) to (4). Since no acceleration occurred following period (4), these years can be grouped as one phase, a pattern which conforms exactly with the previous phasing, noting at the same time the remarkably high rate of growth that characterizes the postwar years. The movement appears similarly in capital intensity except for period (7) whose exceptionally low rate is caused by an abnormal increase in the labor force in agriculture following the end of World War II. These provide a general picture of the fixed capital movement in agriculture together with the figures for longer periods (9) and (10).

Regarding the performance of components, the importance of equipment or producers' durables is stressed as a representative indicator of capital formation of external origin. Its rate of increase is distinctly accelerated through period (4) and then decelerates to period (7). Its postwar rate is as high as 8.6 per cent, showing a rapid process of mechanization. The pattern of equipment thus broadly coincides with that of current inputs of external origin and suggests an operation of common factors. As a matter of fact, it consists of agricultural tools and equipment of small size designed to fit the traditional production organization of small-scale farming. Their function must have been complementary to, instead of substitutable for, the other inputs as well as the labor (except for the case of threshing). Particular attention is drawn to the fact that the rate of increase in these capital goods shows a distinct kink around 1905, coinciding with the investment spurt of the non-agricultural sector. The performance of capital stock largely of internal origin is briefly seen as follows. Trees and shrubs increased at a rather rapid pace during Phase I while the rate of increase in livestock appears larger for Phase II. The former, including a rapid expansion of mulberry cultivation, gives further evidence for the growth potentials that existed in agriculture during Phase II. The latter seems to be caused by changes in the demand pattern. The postwar rate of increase in both livestock and trees and shrubs is considerably accelerated and this indicates that Japan's agriculture is undergoing a rapid diversification for the first time after a century of development.

Statistical estimation and valuation of capital stock in traditional agriculture is a hazardous task. The data used above are based on a number of assumptions; they call for careful reservations depending upon the purpose for which they are used. Yet the above observations, I believe, could give us a generally correct picture of the capital formation performance in agriculture except for one important point that concerns infrastructure, particularly land improvement and water control facilities. Because of the difficulty of obtaining continuous data, these are not included in our series of capital stock and this is a serious omission. To fill the gap, I would like to mention here a hypothetical proposition that capital formation for infrastructure must have been carried out at a faster pace during Phase I than during the pre-modern epoch. This is intended to reject a widely accepted view that the infrastructure, particularly for water control, in agriculture had already been established during the Tokugawa Era to the extent that no sizable investment was needed during Phase I. Admittedly, the bulk of paddy fields was created before the Meiji Era and official records tell us that during early years of development the government investment rather aimed at improving riparian works; irrigation and drainage works of large scale (over 500 chō) do not show an acceleration of the pace of capital formation of this kind. However, scattered regional records suggest that a number of small-scale works were vigorously carried out, as is logically expected, in connection with introducing improved cultivation practices and better varieties of rice. A large labor input, with use of considerable construction materials largely of internal origin, seems to have taken place for the maintenance and improvement of the old facilities. It goes without saying that the public investments in riparian works must have contributed much indirectly, if not directly, to improving these facilities for agricultural use. My proposition thus implies that unless we assume that substantial investments of this nature were made, the relatively high rate of output growth realized in Phase I cannot be interpreted satisfactorily. This calls for further study and the figures in Table 5 are subject to possible revision as a result of it.

Now our concluding remarks on the discussion of capital formation can best be given by observing a trend in capital-output ratios. The relevant series are presented in Table 6. In column (1) we note the following: The capital-output ratio for agriculture had a relatively large value at the outset and tended to decline during Phase I. During Phase II the ratio remained unchanged or showed a slight increase; from 1954 on definite rises were observed. The ratio excluding non-residential buildings is presented separately in column (2) in order to check the effect of possible statistical biases of estimating non-residential buildings. It shows a similar pattern. The figures in columns (3) and (4) are presented for further reference. The movement of ratios in (3) does not contradict the above findings. It is important to note that the ratio of the non-primary sector shows a trend of reverse movement, increasing during Phase I and then decreasing during Phase II until the thirties. Combining the two counter-balancing tendencies, one in the primary and the other in the non-primary sector, the capital-output ratio of the prewar Japanese economy had been maintained more or less unchanged on a macro-level.

TABLE 6

Capital-Output Ratios[a] for Selected Years: Long-Term Changes*

	Agriculture		Non-primary sector
	(1)	(2)[b]	(3)[c]
1885	3.40	1.05	1.90
1894	3.13	1.06	2.11
1905	2.71	1.02	2.30
1919	2.30	1.00	2.33
1931	2.35	1.10	2.56
1938	2.31	1.13	2.38
1945	2.37	1.04	
1954	2.63	1.19	2.18[d]
1961	2.91	1.60	1.54[d]

* Agriculture data from *LTES*, IX. Non-primary sector data from *LTES*, III, p. 230. Both are in five-year moving averages.

a) All ratios are in gross terms for both capital and output in 1934–36 prices.

b) Non-residential construction is excluded.

c) (3) is based on other kinds of output estimates; for 1945 comparable data are lacking.

d) In 1960 prices and not directly comparable with other ratios.

Because of technical difficulty all the social overhead capital is included in the non-primary sector. There is possible underestimation of capital stock in agriculture for the reason mentioned previously. Admittedly these and possibly other statistical deficiencies may have distorted the above findings. And yet, I believe that their broad pattern is likely to be sustained by future revisions: to be most conservative, the capital-output ratio of agriculture did not rise in Phase I. If this is correct, the findings are of great significance, not only because they fit well into our phasing but, what is more important, because they give evidence for the "capital-saving" nature of agricultural development during Phase I. I say "capital-saving" here not as a rigorous definition of the type of technological progress. It is almost impossible to test the bias of technological progress in such a traditional agriculture. It is sufficient to note that it made it possible to raise output continuously without requiring the increase of fixed capital, at least at a greater pace than output. This was particularly crucial because the capital-output ratio tended to increase in the non-agricultural sector during Phase I. Ranis' article in this volume is closely relevant to this point. No further explanation will be needed for Phase II. A remarkable rise in the capital-output ratio of agriculture in Phase III, however, is to be noted, particularly in contrast to its relative decline in the non-primary sector.[9] The situation is now reversed and agriculture has become a sector which requires more capital per unit of output as it grows.

One comment is required before closing the discussion on capital. All the above descriptions have been based on physical stock data, and neither investment nor monetary financial flow data have been used. This is not to deprecate the importance of a flow approach. Instead it is simply because of a lack of continuous data. With respect to the financial aspect, Kato's article contained in this volume clarifies some important historical and institutional problems, although it is confined to specific aspects of the subject. Long-term analysis of investment in agriculture, based on both physical and monetary data, is one of the unexplored areas relevant to our study.

Turning to other aspects, let us begin with the price-cost relationships. An "inflationary growth" is one of the characteristics of Japan's economic growth. It implies that there was an inflationary

---

[9] Despite the remark in the footnotes on Table 6, it is safe to say that a tendency of increase in the capital-output ratio in agriculture did exist whereas the capital-output ratio in non-primary sector tended to decrease considerably during the postwar investment spurt.

trend, a sustained rise in the general price level as a result of investment increase over saving *ex ante* and that it was unavoidable in order for the Japanese economy to maintain its comparatively high rate of growth (See also Chapter 3). From the end of the well-known Matsukata deflation, which had succeeded in curbing the initial inflation by 1885, Japan was on the road toward modern economic growth. Since then the general price level approximately tripled until 1935 (an average annual rate of increase of 2.2 per cent). This threefold rise appears much larger than the 150 per cent rise of the corresponding indicator of either the U.S.A. or the U.K. during the comparable period. Domestically, the average annual price rise of 2.2 per cent is also strongly indicative of inflationary growth when compared to the 4 per cent average rate of increase in real GNP. Japan started with an exchange rate of 1 yen=1 dollar in its initial period. In 1897, when the gold standard was established, the value of the yen had already dropped by about half. For a time its value was more or less maintained, but again tended to drop. By 1940 the subsequent decrease had reduced the value of 100 yen to 23.4 dollars. Such a record implies also continuous foreign payment deficits almost throughout the entire prewar years despite the big contribution of sericultural development to accelerating silk exports, the analysis of which can be found in Hemmi's article in this volume. The only exception occurred during World War I when Japan enjoyed a bonanza in exports.

Inflationary growth was, in general, favorable to agricultural development. The following points are of particular interest: First, a distinct feature is discernible with respect to the differentials of price rises by industrial sector: relative prices of the modern sectors' output tended to decrease while those of the traditional sectors' output tended to increase. For example, during the long prewar period mentioned above, the prices of manufactured goods increased 2.6 times while the prices of agricultural products increased 3.4 times. The differential is substantial. The postwar pattern appears to be essentially the same, and in recent years the relative prices of farm products have noticeably risen, supported by the government policy. Many factors are intermingled to cause such a differential in the trends of sectoral prices, but the major factors are found in the gap between the sectoral rates of technological progress and those of demand increase for the products.

FIGURE 5

Price Indexes of Output and Input in Agriculture*

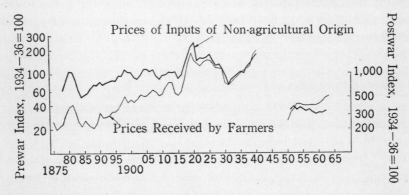

* Data from *LTES*, IX, pp. 164, 190-191.

Second, what further concerns us is the fact that the relative price of inputs of external origin has tended to decline substantially relative to the prices of farm products. With regard to this trend, however, we must note that the situation changed to a considerable extent during the long process under review, as shown in Figure 5. During Phase I prices received by farmers tended to increase almost continuously. In Phase II they tended to decrease until the beginning of the thirties when they again showed a tendency to increase. In fact, changes in the prices reached hyper-inflation proportions (excluded in the graph) during years of the war and immediately thereafter. In the beginning of Phase III output prices were rather stable, but again have begun to increase in recent years. In comparison with these, we see the trend of relative fall of input prices in Figure 5. Simple indicators are given in Table 7 in the form of an index of relative prices of farm products to those of inputs of non-agricultural origin. A relative increase in output prices is conspicuous, and particularly for Phases I (except for period (2)) and III. Undoubtedly for these phases, the price mechanism worked favorably for agricultural development by providing positive incentives for farmers. During the twenties the situation was quite different:

the general price level as well as the prices of farm products continued to decline and the index shown in Table 7 moved less favorably to farmers. Greater imports of rice from colonies aggravated the unsettled situation of Japan's agriculture toward the beginning of the thirties by pushing down rice prices. Thus, the unfavorable price incentives must have been one of the major causes of agricultural retardation during Phase II.

TABLE 7

Relative Price Index of Farm Product to Current Input to Agriculture*

	Index^a	Average annual rate of change (%)	
1877	37.2	(1) 1877–85	2.33
1885	43.6	(2) 1885–94	−0.93
1894	40.1	(3) 1894–1905	1.78
1905	48.7	(4) 1905–19	3.03
1919	73.4	(5) 1919–31	1.75
1931	91.1	(6) 1931–38	1.33
1938	99.9		
1945	—	(7) 1938–54	—
1954	112.4		
1961	148.7	(8) 1954–61	4.08

* Data from *LTES*, IX, pp. 164, 190.

a) The index is obtained by dividing the index of prices received by farmers by the index of prices of input of non-agricultural origin. Both are linked indexes with 1934–36=100.

The relative slowness of agriculture in raising productivity, as reflected in the trend of relative prices, is highly relevant to the change in the place of this sector in Japan's position in international trade. Broadly speaking, Japan's experience is reminiscent of European economic development in that, as a trend, farm products shifted from export goods to import goods, and the ratio of import to domestic demand tended to increase as industrialization proceeded. In the light of our phasing, however, the following observation deserves attention. Farm products such as cocoons and tea leaves were the raw materials for production of Japan's major export goods, such as raw silk and tea during Phase I. On the other hand, until about the time of the Russo-Japanese War (1904–05) imported food products were negligible except for sugar; the government's efforts to substitute its import by increasing domestic production were not successful. Undoubtedly, agriculture was the largest net contributor to foreign trade, and this largely characterizes Phase I, although we cannot ignore the fact that raw silk and tea are not really "primary products" and the technical and organizational progress of manufacturing them was important. Second, the pattern of farm product imports is to be noted. Despite the acceleration of output increase in agriculture during 1905–19, Japan became a net importer of farm products since around 1905, and through Phase II, the amount of imports of food, feed and allied goods tended to increase as a trend, the most striking example being the increase in rice imports from Korea and Taiwan where Japanese technology and capital were introduced. Needless to say, further increases in foreign payments were thus saved. The loss of colonies changed drastically Japan's trade channels after World War II. Despite its postwar spurt, Japan's agriculture now cannot catch up with the rapid increase in the demand for food, the diversification of which is remarkable as is described in Kaneda's article in this volume. If industrial materials such as cotton and wool are included, Japan is today one of the largest importers of farm products in the world; there is no reason to doubt that the proportion of farm products to total imports will continue to increase throughout Phase III.

The following points draw special attention in terms of price-cost relationship. Given the limited land resources, a trend of increasing comparative disadvantage in agriculture was unavoidable. Nevertheless, raw silk could continue to be the largest foreign exchange earner, not only during Phase I, but also through Phase II until the end of the twenties when it was dealt a severe blow by the Great Depression. What made it possible for sericulture to expand along with the silk industry throughout this long period? A simple answer would be the sustained progress of technology in sericulture, including the improvement and standardization of the quality of cocoons in combination with a fuller use of the flexible supplies of rural labor. In fact, there is evidence to prove that the speed of technological progress in sericulture was higher and more sustained than in agriculture in general (See Chapter 12). Such a differential in the speed of technological progress in favor of export industries is also seen in manufacturing sectors and this provides an important part of the explanation of rapid export expansion despite Japan's inflationary growth.

I want to relate the problem of food imports, on the other hand, to the pattern of domestic food demand, which is thoroughly analyzed by Kaneda in his article in this volume. He concludes that income elasticity for food remained rather low throughout the entire prewar period and that this contributed to Japan's economic growth by minimizing the requirements for foreign exchange for food imports. This is an important finding although there is still a need to explore further "what were the factors underlying this pattern and why did it happen to change so drastically at the beginning of Phase III?" Approaches toward answering this question would lead to a general analysis of demand-expenditure patterns of personal consumption as well as the high rate of personal savings, in addition to the findings in Noda's paper on farm household savings presented in this volume.

Finally, a brief remark will be in order concerning income formation in agriculture with special reference to labor-productivity. This topic discussions is developed in detail in this volume by several papers, either directly or indirectly. One summary point I would like to make here is its relation to phasing. Simple indicators are wages and partial labor productivity in agriculture in relation to those of manufacturing. The selected years in Table 8 differ slightly from those of the previous tables, but will not cause any great difficulties for the purpose of comparison. Use of such simple indicators require some reservations. In addition to the statistical limitations of the labor input series mentioned previously, conceptual problems are involved in both the wages and the productivity series. Japan's agriculture is characterized largely by the use of self-employed and unpaid family labor in contrast to the situation in manufacturing, a rough representative of the modern sectors. The age and sex composition and educational attainment and the proportion of part-time work—all these differ between agriculture and manufacturing, and may change over time. Besides, wages in agriculture do not move in parallel with farm income per household, which is better represented by the output per worker. All these points are acknowledged here, and yet these indicators taken together, I believe, will serve broadly for our present purpose.

TABLE 8

Differentials of Wages and Labor Productivity
between Agriculture and Manufacturing*

(Unit: %)

	Ratio of agricultural wage to manufacturing wage	Ratio of output per worker (Agriculture/Manufacturing)
1886	69.9	50.0
1898	76.5	43.8
1905	69.5	50.7
1919	73.7	44.8
1931	53.8	25.7
1938	56.7	22.8
1954	37.3	28.1
1961	42.0	19.0 (27.8)[a]
1964	48.6	(23.2)[a]

* Data from Kazushi Ohkawa and Henry Rosovsky, "Postwar Japanese Growth in Historical Perspective," *Economic Growth: The Japanese Experience Since the Meiji Era* (Chicago: Richard D. Irwin Inc., 1968).
a) Taken from a different data source with forestry and fishery included in agriculture.

To summarize the broad pattern shown by the ratio of wages, Phase I reveals no tendency to change, Phase II is marked by a decline and Phase III shows a distinctly rising trend. The ratio of partial labor productivity reveals a similar pattern during Phases I and II although its decline seems to begin from 1905. During 1954–64 we see a tendency opposite that of the wage ratio. In sum, during Phase I the wage rate and productivity increases in both sectors were more or less parallel until around 1905 whereas differentials widened from then through Phase II. We have called this phenomenon the creation of a *differential structure,* which was produced as a combined result of the retarded growth potential in agriculture and the continued vigorous growth of manufacturing (Ohkawa and Rosovsky). In contrast to this, until around the Russo-Japanese War, Phase I is marked by a relatively homogeneous structure which characterizes the initial process of concurrent growth between the traditional and modern sectors. Regarding Phase III amplification is needed from a broader viewpoint.

IV. Characteristics of the Third Phase and Concluding Remarks

The problem of Japanese agriculture in Phase III can best be presented in terms of three major dimensions: changes in relative prices of factors, "induced" technological progress, and institutional barriers. To begin with the first, the increase in the Table 8 wage ratio during 1954–64 is a notable change in the traditional structure of Japan's labor market (which continues up to the present). Agriculture no longer continues to be a source of highly flexible supplies of labor which phenomenon had long characterized Phases I and II with respect to the place of agriculture in the national economy. As is described regarding supply prices of farm workers by both Masui and Minami in their papers in this volume, there is evidence to prove the occurrence of related phenomena in the postwar years such as an upturn of marginal productivity of labor and a change in the farmers' attitude in evaluating the labor input in argiculture. Thus I share Minami's conclusion which places the long-term "turning point" in agriculture as well as the national economy somewhere in Phase III (Ohkawa, 1965).

Second, this basic change influences almost every aspect of farming activities and the way of life in rural communities. Among these, the most relevant here is the type of technological advance. In his paper in this volume, Tsuchiya concluded that the effect of small-scale mechanization can mostly be found in substituting machinery for labor. As we have seen previously, the rate of increase in current inputs of external origin has been greatly accelerated in these years. Thus through increases in both fixed capital investment and use of intermediate goods, Japan's agriculture greatly increased its dependence upon industry a great deal. This implies that the technological advance in agriculture began to be more closely linked to that of industrial sectors. The advance of technical knowledge within agriculture should certainly not be ignored, but the type of technological progress induced by industrial growth is becoming more important. A decline of relative prices of capital goods as well as intermediate goods is of crucial significance in this respect. So far as this aspect is concerned, no serious barriers can be expected for the future of Japanese agricultural development. The real problem for technological progress in agriculture lies in another important aspect of the situation: the possibility of realizing economies of scale.

The impact of the postwar Land Reform is discussed in Kawano's paper included in this volume. It is extremely difficult to single out quantitatively the productivity effect of land reform in general. Japan's case is no exception. Broadly speaking, however, two factors seem to be clear in historical perspective. One is positive in that farming incentives have been encouraged much more than under the prewar absentee landlordism.[10] The other is negative in that the Land Reform established a rigid pattern of traditional small-scale holdings of arable land which is not compatible with the type of recent technological progress. It stands out clearly that diseconomies of small-scale farming are now causing serious bottlenecks in raising the labor productivity of Japanese agriculture. The road toward enlarging the scale of farming is hampered by the present land-tenure system and is aggravated by such factors as a rising trend of land prices and a tremendous increase in the number of part-time farm households. This, among other things, is analyzed by Misawa in his article in this volume. Thus, new devices for realizing the economies of scale may be possible in the future.

In view of broad historical trends, therefore, I am much inclined to emphasize the economic significance of the drastic change in the structural composition of the labor force that already marked the "turning point" of Japan's agricultural development, as has previously been stated, after passing through a long, eventful process in the modern economic growth since the Meiji Restoration in 1868. Looking to the forseeable future, it is expected by demographers that quite a modest rate of growth of the labor force will be the

---

[10] It is a controversial issue when absentee landlordism became dominant in Japan, although there is a general consensus that during Phase I landlords had for the most part been active in promoting the development of agriculture. The wide prevalence of absentee landlordism, on the other hand, must have contributed to the agricultural stagnation during Phase II.

normal situation for the Japanese economy. Phase III will thus be increasingly characterized by an entirely new situation, which favors the conditions for making further technological progress in agriculture in order to catch up with the rate of productivity increase in the non-agricultural sector.

By way of conclusion, I would like to mention the following four particular points which have been discussed in this paper:

1. Japan's long experience of agricultural development can be systematically interpreted by demarcating three growth phases whose characteristics are distinct.

2. In each phase, the agricultural growth pattern, either acceleration or retardation, (with some exceptional short periods) appears to be broadly associated with the pattern of non-agricultural growth. The significance of an intersectoral dependence mechanism is strongly suggested not only for the "concurrent growth" in the first phase but also for the subsequent phases.

3. Despite a growth rate of the non-agricultural sector which was rapid by international standards, Japan's agriculture took almost a century to arrive at a "turning point." During the first and second phases, technologies of the labor-intensive type were of great importance in developing Japan's labor-intensive farming with the size of the agricultural labor force remaining almost unchanged. Mechanization is a recent phenomenon which has only begun to take place during the third phase.

4. There are still points missing which would establish these findings more firmly. Supplementary research works are needed both in the historical and statistical fields. This is particularly urgent for earlier years. Such studies would increase our knowledge enough to provide a solid basis for applying more rigorous methods to this difficult but challenging subject.

REFERENCES

Hayami, Yujiro, "Demand for Fertilizer in the Course of Japanese Agricultural Development," *Journal of Farm Economics*, XLVI, No. 4 (November, 1964).

——, "The Non-agricultural Basis for Agricultural Productivity Increase" (in Japanese), presented to Zushi Conference, January, 1967 (Proceedings is forthcoming).

Hayami, Yujiro and Yamada, Saburo, "Technological Progress in Agriculture," *Economic Growth: The Japanese Experience Since the Meiji Era,* L. Klein and Kazushi Ohkawa, eds., Chicago: Richard, D. Irwin Inc., 1968.

Nakamura, James I. *Agricultural Production and the Economic Development of Japan, 1873–1922.* Princeton: Princeton University Press, 1966.

Ohkawa, K., Shinohara, M., Umemura, M., Ito, M., Noda, T. *The Growth Rate of the Japanese Economy since 1878.* Tokyo: Kinokuniya, 1957.

Ohkawa, K., Ishiwata, S., Yamada, S., Ishi, H., *Capital Stock (Shihon Sutokku), Estimates of Long-Term Economic Statistics of Japan Since 1868,* III, Tokyo: Toyo Keizai Shimposha, 1966.

Ohkawa, Kazushi, "Concurrent Growth of Agriculture and Industry: A Study of the Japanese Case," *International Explorations of Agricultural Economics,* R. N. Dixey, ed., Ames, Iowa: 1964.

——, "Agriculture and Turning-Points in Economic Growth," *The Developing Economies,* III, (December, 1965).

Ohkawa, Kazushi and Rosovsky, Henry, "A Century of Japanese Economic Growth," *The State and Economic Enterprise in Japan,* W. W. Lockwood ed., Princeton: Princeton University Press, 1965.

——, "Postwar Japanese Growth in Historical Perspective," *Economic Growth: The Japanese Experience Since the Meiji Era,* L. R. Klein and K. Ohkawa eds., Chicago: Richard D. Irwin, Inc., 1968.

Umemura, M., Yamada, S., Hayami, Y., Takamatsu, N., and Kumazaki, M. *Agriculture and Forestry (Noringyo), Estimates of Long-Term Economic Statistics of Japan Since 1868,* IX, K. Ohkawa, M. Shinohara and M. Umemura, eds., Tokyo: Toyo Keizai Shimposha, 1966.

CHAPTER 2

THE FINANCING OF JAPANESE ECONOMIC DEVELOPMENT†

GUSTAV RANIS

An economy which is able to achieve only subsistence levels of income by means of a full and optimum utilization of its resources is in serious difficulties. Unless it can count on extensive credit from abroad, it may be properly identified as "doomed" rather than "underdeveloped." Domestic capital formation must carry the heaviest burden in any developmental effort and there is very little which can be squeezed out at near-subsistence levels of income and consumption. Happily, most of the world's low income areas are not "doomed" in this sense. Reserves of productivity usually do exist somewhere in the underdeveloped economy; the prime problem of development is to gather them in and utilize them efficiently. It is the purpose of this paper to demonstrate the existence and successful utilization of such reserves in the Japanese economy during the nineteenth century "break-out" phase of her development. We intend to analyze the use of fiscal and monetary policies in the effort to preserve a maximum pool of savings at each subsequent higher level of income, either by a direct siphoning off into government coffers or, through interference with the distribution of income, by channelling it into other "dependable" hands.[1]

I

"Taking up the slack" in any economy means making potential increments of productivity socially available, largely by means of reshuffling resources with a minimum need for additional investment. In the case of Japan, "slack" was in evidence mainly in the form of excess labor on the land and reserves of productivity in the land.

---

† Reproduced here, with slight revisions, from *The Economic History Review*, XI, No. 3 (1959).

[1] For a general treatment of Japanese economic growth see Allen (1946) and Lockwood (1954).

The ability to withdraw labor hours from one sector of the economy and apply them elsewhere without suffering a loss of output in the former represents perhaps the purest form of such "slack." This represents the employment of the "disguised rural underemployed," the squatting uncles and cousins who have become proverbial in the literature. The Japanese rural working population fell from 14.74 million in 1878–82 to 14.19 million in 1928–32, an absolute decline of 3.7 per cent during a period when total population was increasing at a rate of more than 1 per cent annually. This transfer, moreover, is understated since the shift of marginal working hours from agricultural to non-agricultural pursuits in the absence of any physical relocation is unaccounted for.

TABLE 1

Changes in Agricultural Productivity

Year	Agricultural output[a] 5 Yr. average (constant mil. yen)	Agricultural[b] working population 5 Yr. average (million)	Productivity of the agricultural working population 5 Yr. average (constant yen)
1878–1882	904	14.74[c]	61.3
1883–1887	1,032	14.08[c]	69.7
1888–1892	1,196	14.75[c]	81.1
1893–1897	1,308	14.58[c]	89.7
1898–1902	1,558	14.41[c]	108.1
1903–1907	1,628	14.36	113.4
1908–1912	1,875	14.32	130.9
1913–1917	1,966	14.31	137.3
1918–1922	2,189	14.24	153.7
1923–1927	2,057	14.10	145.9
1928–1932	2,287	14.19	161.2
1933–1937	2,534	14.41	175.9

a) Agricultural output from Tsutomu Noda, "Nōgyō to Keizai," *Agricultural Economics* (August, 1953), p. 48 and from working papers of the Economic Research Institute at Hitotsubashi University.

b) From Kenzo Hemmi, "Wagakuni Nōgyō Wa Jinkōzu o Ketteisuru Shojōken (Number of People in Agricultural and Forestry Occupation)," Agricultural Research Institute, Ministry of Agriculture and Forestry (June, 1954).

c) Estimated by simple projection between the years for which figures were available, i.e. 1872, 1884, 1886, and 1903. Since changes in magnitude were not significant throughout this period, a possible error could affect our calculations only slightly.

A second and closely related form of reserve productive capacity becomes evident when we consider reorganization and the limited addition of capital in the agricultural sector. This, in Japan, includes the adoption of a wide variety of new techniques, improved crop selection, breeding and rotation, winter draining permitting the double-cropping of rice and barley, the more intelligent and intensive use of fertilizer. The unit size under cultivation did not change; nevertheless, yields per acre as well as per man increased substantially. A small investment in the improvement of simple tools and techniques led to a large increase in productive capacity. Every investment which breaks through a bottleneck and results in higher levels of income should not, of course, be considered in the same vein; the only pragmatically useful distinguishing feature of this process of "slack" recovery is the extremely high marginal productivity of the first and insignificant injection of capital.[2] Over the same 1878–82 to 1928–32 time span, agricultural output increased by more than 153 per cent (see Table 1), raising the productivity of those remaining on the land by 163 per cent.

It should be clear from our figures that the bulk of this increase in agricultural productivity occurred during the last twenty years of the nineteenth century; the rural working population declined by 2.1 per cent, output increased by 72.3 per cent and agricultural labor productivity by 73.3 per cent.[3] This is also the period, as seen in Table 2, for which the introduction of public capital into agriculture was at a much lower level than in later years; smaller returns in labor productivity concurrent with a larger investment effort leads us to conclude that the considerable reserves of productivity in the Japanese economy were running out after the turn of the century.

The successful gathering in of existing reserves of productivity does not, of course, guarantee that anything but fuller stomachs, or

---

[2] Conceptually, this may differ from "slack" in the puristic sense, but, in a loose sense, some small investment will always be associated with taking it up.

[3] In the twenty years after 1900 productivity increased by only 42.2 per cent. Johnston (1951), pp. 499–500, obtains increases in productivity somewhat higher than mine for most periods. His overestimation seems to be due partly to his use of working population estimates which have since been revised, but largely due to his use of gross production figures for Japan's six major crops rather than net production figures for Japan's total agricultural output.

TABLE 2
Government Subsidies

(Unit: 1,000 Current Yen)

Year	Agriculture and forestry			Industry			Commerce (incl. exp., Imp., transp.)			General			Total	
	Cur.[a]	Real[b]	Per cent of total	Cur.[a]	Real[b]	Per cent of total	Cur.[a]	Real[b]	Per cent of total	Cur.[a]	Real[b]	Per cent of total	Cur.[a]	Real[b]
1880	—	—	—	410	830	20.4	255	515	12.6	1,348	2,723	66.9	2,013	4,067
1882	2	4	—	796	1,595	34.0	125	250	5.3	1,422	2,850	60.7	2,345	4,699
1890	—	—	—	2,328	5,734	58.7	131	323	3.3	1,500	3,695	38.0	3,959	9,751
1895	—	—	—	2,910	7,098	46.4	1,375	3,354	22.0	1,976	4,820	31.6	6,261	15,271
1900	358	644	1.5	12,018	21,615	52.0	6,636	11,935	28.7	4,131	7,428	17.8	23,143	41,624
1905	228	355	1.1	11,588	18,050	55.2	5,929	9,235	28.2	3,242	5,050	15.5	20,987	32,690
1910	328	494	.8	15,322	23,075	38.0	12,472	18,783	30.9	12,213	18,393	30.3	40,335	60,746
1915	2,083	2,950	4.7	15,920	22,550	35.7	12,296	17,416	27.6	14,215	20,135	31.9	44,514	63,051
1920	551	291	.6	19,376	10,230	19.6	32,409	17,111	32.8	46,560	24,583	47.0	18,896	52,215
1925	6,865	4,661	4.3	71,198	48,335	44.4	23,077	15,667	14.5	59,048	40,087	36.8	160,188	108,749
1929	21,421	17,660	10.8	79,868	65,843	40.2	21,645	17,844	10.9	75,571	62,301	38.1	198,515	163,647
1932	28,267	33,061	11.2	43,583	50,974	17.3	27,446	32,101	10.9	152,271	178,095	60.5	251,567	294,231
1935	37,596	36,679	17.8	23,151	22,586	10.9	20,778	20,271	9.9	129,469	126,311	61.4	210,994	205,847
1938	78,167	57,140	20.0	42,066	30,750	10.8	159,665	116,714	40.9	110,780	80,980	28.3	390,678	285,584

a) *Nihon Keizai no Kōzō Bunseki (Analysis of Japanese Economic Structure)*, Ichiro Nakayama, ed. (Tokyo: Toyo Keizai), 1954, Chapter IX, Part 2.

b) Using Ohkawa's general price deflator, 1928–32=100, developed at the Hitotsubashi Economic Research Institute.

more of them, will result. In a low-income economy there invariably exist powerful pressures for consuming the gains which can be made to accrue. To withstand the extremes of such pressures—even more than the need to enhance people's willingness and ability to work— is a central problem of economic growth. If "slack," which constitutes, so to speak, a once-and-for-all bargain, is dissipated, development becomes once again extremely painful or impossible. Pressures against the investible surplus of an economy at each and every stage of development derive from population growth and increases of per capita consumption. It is the purpose of the following section to review the means by which such pressures were contained and high savings propensities achieved.

II

Japan experienced a substantial increase in numbers: from 34 million in 1870 to 44 million in 1900 and 64 million in 1930.[4] There, as elsewhere, increased economic activity was associated with increased numbers. History shows this to be inevitable. A developing economy must either be able to accommodate such increase, or cease growing.

Accepting the inevitability of devoting a share of the potential savings fund to the feeding of additional mouths, the economy must marshal its forces to resist the influences tending to increase per capita consumption. It is, of course, neither possible nor desirable to keep the door against increased consumption levels hermetically shut;[5] nevertheless, it is the size of the attainable margin above the maintenance of an existing capital stock and a growing popula-

---

[4] During the preceding Tokugawa period a classic Malthusian situation obtained: population increases were reported after good harvests with subsequent floods, famines and disease (positive checks) and widespread abortion and infanticide (vices) bringing numbers back to their original level.

[5] There are temporal limits, even in an absolute dictatorship, beyond which people who are experiencing change on all sides will refuse to accept static consumption levels plus promises for the future. Moreover, it may be wise for reasons of incentives to let the population have an early, if small, sample of the fruits of development. Lastly, if the population is in a physically undernourished state, permitting small increases in per capita consumption may raise labor productivity more than devoting the equivalent resources to the purchase of physical capital goods.

tion which makes the difference between successful and unsuccessful attempts at development.

An economy's siphonable savings are composed of the voluntary and involuntary contributions of its people; an economy breaking away from low levels of income and consumption must rely heavily on maintaining a high marginal propensity to save out of new and higher levels of income. In Japan, a severely regressive tax structure, coupled with favorable savings propensities among the upper income groups, served to siphon off, for purposes of development, much of the increment in income accruing during the "breakout" period. Dissipation of resources in consumption or non-productive investment was minimized.

The Land Tax

The peasant traditionally has carried the heaviest burdens in Japanese society. Before 1868 he supported the feudal ruling classes in the court cities; after the Restoration he became the prime source of developmental capital. Good returns to be obtained from the soil—through his labor—were gathered up by means of high rents and the tax on land.[6]

Table 3 indicates that the land tax alone provided more than 70 per cent of central government revenues during the first decades after the Restoration; local governments, for which no revenue breakdown was available, acquired a similarly large proportion of their income from the land. Taxing away the agricultural *produit net* represented the dominant source of government revenue, at least until the turn of the century when the agricultural "slack" was be-

---

[6] The Land Tax Reform of 1873 brought a change from payments in kind to payments in money and from tax burdens as a percentage of gross receipts fluctuating with the harvest to tax burdens as a percentage of an assessed fixed value independent of harvest conditions. The latter value was arrived at as follows: for each 20–30 villages of about equal observed fertility, a "typical village" was selected as a yardstick. The gross yield of a "typical" piece of land in this village was determined by using the average yearly raw yield during the past five years, multipied by the average yearly price. 65 per cent of this gross yield was subtracted for cost of seeds, fertilizer, previous land taxes, etc.; the residual net yield (implicit wages not deducted) was subsequently capitalized at 6 per cent. Similar pieces of land in this as well as other villages were then valued in relation to it and an annual tax of 3 per cent (later 2½ per cent) levied on this base.

TABLE 3

Composition of Central Government Tax Take[a]

(Unit: Current Million Yen)

Year	Land tax	Per cent of total	Excise taxes[b]	Per cent of total	Sub-total (land tax and excises)	Per cent of total	Income tax	Per cent of total	Business taxes[c]	Per cent of total	Customs duties	Per cent of total	Miscellaneous	Per cent of total	Total
1870	11.3	73.9	—	—	11.3	73.9	—	—	—	—	1.1	7.1	2.9	18.9	15.3
1880	42.3	72.9	5.8	10.0	48.1	82.9	—	—	—	—	2.6	4.5	7.3	12.6	58.0
1890	40.1	51.7	16.9	21.8	57.0	73.5	1.1	1.4	.3	.4	4.4	5.7	14.8	19.1	77.6
1900	46.7	24.6	54.4	28.6	101.1	53.2	6.4	3.4	7.3	3.8	17.0	8.9	58.2	30.6	190.1
1910	76.3	15.9	89.6	18.7	165.9	34.6	31.7	6.6	32.5	6.8	39.9	8.3	208.9	43.6	478.9
1920	73.9	6.2	375.4	31.6	449.3	37.8	190.3	16.0	116.7	9.8	69.4	5.8	361.4	30.5	1187.1
1930	68.0	4.8	529.0	37.4	597.0	42.2	200.6	14.2	112.1	7.9	105.4	7.4	401.2	28.4	1416.3

a) Japan, Department of Finance, *Financial and Economic Annual of Japan.*

b) Including tax on sake, tobacco, sugar, soya, textile fabrics, as well as profits from camphor, salt and tobacco monopolies (where applicable).

c) Including business tax, succession tax, on bonuses, capital interest tax, business profits tax, war profits tax, and special profits tax (where applicable).

coming exhausted and increasing returns in secondary production provided an alternative tax base.

The effects of the land tax on incentives and income distribution in agriculture are of prime importance. The initial burden of the 1873 levy was not appreciably different from that imposed during the preceding Tokugawa period. But the resulting pressures were different and gave rise to a seemingly contradictory economic behavior pattern: increased productivity and a reduction of the real tax burden, accompanied by increases in tenancy.[7] The real burden on the individual cultivator of a lump sum tax liability was substantially reduced over time, not only by the increases in agricultural productivity cited above but also by secular increases in the price of rice.[8] In fact, as we shall see, this lower real tax burden benefited only the larger landowners while small cultivators found themselves

TABLE 4

Tenancy in Japanese Agriculture

Year	Percentage of total cultivated land under tenancy
1883[a]	37.0
1887[a]	39.3
1892[a]	40.0
1914[b]	45.5
1921[b]	46.3
1925[c]	45.8
1930[c]	47.7

Sources:
a) Norman (1940), p. 148.
b) Tohata (1953), p. 25.
c) *Norinsho Ruinen Tokeihyo (Statistics of the Ministry of Agriculture and Forestry)* (Tokyo: 1955), p. 10.

---

[7] I am indebted to Professor K. Ohkawa for a helpful discussion of this problem.

[8] An extreme case is illustrated here:

Land Tax Liability	Average Price of Rice	Real Burden of Tax
1877	39.5 mill. yen	5.58 yen per koku	100 (1877=100)
1881	43.3 mill. yen	11.15 yen per koku	55

Compiled from mimeographed materials at the Nōgyo Sōgō Kenkyūjo (National Research Institute of Agriculture), Ministry of Agriculture and Forestry, Tokyo.

under increasing pressures to sell out.[9] The result, as seen in Table 4, was a persistent increase in the proportion of cultivated land under tenancy.

The apparent contradiction here can be cleared up by emphasizing the severe cyclical price fluctuations to which the small peasant-owner fell victim. Unlike the large landlord, he was not in a position to choose his time of tax payment and was forced to dump large amounts of produce on a market over which the former had considerable control. Regardless of volume, the value of the produce marketed could easily fall below the average assumed as a tax base by the original valuation procedure. The only alternative might well be to go into debt[10] and, since the only credit available, short term and expensive was offered by the same landlord in his role of usurer, the end result was clear. The reduced real burden of the land tax benefited only a limited group.

Agricultural rents, of course, were paid in kind and tied to current levels of production. There was no *a priori* necessity for the tenant to derive any benefits from the secular change in prices and productivity. Table 5 permits us to conclude, however, that the burden of rents as a percentage of net output declined somewhat, especially in later years. Widening lags between increasing production and rents helped to strengthen incentives among tenant-tillers. However, the landlord clearly stood to gain the most from the exploitation of agricultural reserves of productivity. Receiving rising direct or rental incomes while paying taxes increasing in smaller proportion, this group was in a position to lay claim to most of the surplus which did not land in government coffers.

The Japanese landlord of the Meiji era presents a sharp contrast to Ricardo's wastrel type. From the outset he devoted himself to improvements, promoted societies for the discussion of agricultural techniques, introduced winter drainage and helped sponsor the growth of superior rice strains. The topographical dictates of Japan-

---

[9] See Norman (1940), pp. 144–9.

[10] Even if we abstract from the manipulation of local markets by the large landlord, it is unlikely that the small proprietor, living near subsistence levels, will be sufficiently sophisticated to build up an anticyclical cache at the conclusion of a good harvest.

TABLE 5
Relative Shares in Agriculture[a]

5A		Percentage of total product		
	Year	Landowner	State	Tenants
	1868[b]	18	50	32
	1873[c]	34	34	32
	1874–76[c]	55	13	32
	1877[c]	50	18	32
	1878[b]	56.5	11.5	32

5B	Rent as a per cent of net agr. output [d]	Tax burden as a per cent of net agr. output [e]	Tenant's share as a per cent of net agr. output
Year			
1878–82	60.4	16.9	22.7
1888–92	56.0	15.5	28.5
1898–1902	50.7	12.1	37.2
1908–1912	55.1	12.5	32.4
1918–22	59.1	9.2	31.7
1928–32	57.9	9.7	32.4

a) Table 5A gives shares of gross rather than net output. The figures are, nevertheless, useful for the purpose of comparison with the results of Table 5B.
b) Kimura (1956), p. 22.
c) Tsuchiya and Okazaki (1937), p. 68.
d) Rent figures from unpublished, mimeographed form of Tohata and Ohkawa (1956)
e) See Table 6, below.

ese rice culture (except possibly in the northern island of Hokkaido), as well as the high level of rents, contributed to the preservation of the small unit of cultivation and the avoidance of "capitalistic" forms of agricultural management. There is no evidence of any sizeable diversion of the landlords' respectable surpluses to high living or speculation. A large share of these surpluses as well as of the Land Tax proceeds was invested outside of the primary sector. In terms of making funds available for an overall development program, the residual rent, the interest on the rural debt, as well as the Land Tax proper must be included.

Other Fiscal Measures

The fiscal system as a whole—rather than single effective levies such as the Land Tax—must, of course, bear the burden of preserving a maximum proportion of the increased real output accruing as the result of developmental activity. Japanese taxes were heavy in an absolute and severely regressive in a relative sense. The total direct tax revenue allocatable to agriculture and non-agriculture as a percentage of the net income in each sector is presented in Table 6.[11] The heavy burden on agriculture becomes even more evident when we recall (see Table 2) that government subsidies in this sector represented only a very small proportion of the total during the nineteenth century. Even in subsequent decades, when non-agricultural income was growing at a faster rate and had reached higher absolute levels, the tax burden on agriculture remained relatively more severe. The absolute burden on the economy as a whole was, however, considerably reduced at the conclusion of the nineteenth-century "take-off" period.

Regressiveness in the tax structure cut across sectoral lines. The dependability of profit receivers in the burgeoning secondary sector left fiscal policy here essentially free to disregard the dangers of potential luxury spending, speculation, or non-productive investment, and to concentrate on containing the broad base of consumption. Following Engel's Law, excise taxes on food and clothing are likely to be most effective in this effort in the low-income area. Moreover, as such an economy grows, the pressure for consuming the increments in income which accrue in the course of development are bound to change direction. An awareness of the specificity of demand at one time and of such shifts over time is essential if the tax structure is to be flexible enough to trap a good share of the increases in per capita income not voluntarily freed for investment.[12]

Excise taxes held a place of prominence, second only to that of the Land Tax, in the Japanese fiscal system. The levy on *sake* alone amounted to about 20 per cent[13] of total tax revenue around the turn of the century. Selective excises on soya, sugar, textiles, and government monopoly profits in tobacco, camphor and salt—really

---

[11] Thanks are due here to Mr. Tsunematsu of the Agricultural Research Institute of the Ministry of Agriculture and Forestry.

[12] Indicative of the helping hand of price inelasticities in preventing shifting is the fact that *sake* (rice wine) production both in the year previous to which a levy on it was first installed (1897) and in the year previous to which the rates were further increased (1899) did not noticeably decline in spite of the price increases. See Matsukata (1900), p. 156.

[13] See Table 3, p. 41.

TABLE 6
Allocation of Direct Tax Burden

Year (Annual average)	Direct tax allocatable to agriculture[a] (cur. mil. yen)	Net income of agriculture[b] (cur. mil. yen)	Tax burden on agriculture (per cent)	Direct tax allocatable to non-agriculture[a] (cur. mil. yen)	Net income of non-agriculture[b] (cur. mil. yen)	Tax burden on non-agriculture (per cent)
1878–1882	63.6	376	16.9	6.3	283	2.2
1884–1887	63.6	287	22.1	9.5	313	3.0
1888–1892	58.5	377	15.5	9.8	420	2.3
1894–1897	65.6	531	12.4	13.2	660	2.0
1898–1902	99.1	816	12.1	35.4	1,106	3.2
1903–1907	113.6	1,015	11.2	79.3	1,467	5.4
1908–1912	153.4	1,222	12.6	132.2	2,077	6.4
1913–1917	167.7	1,422	11.8	145.4	3,216	4.5
1918–1922	295.7	3,205	9.2	431.1	7,967	5.4
1923–1927	304.2	2,892	10.5	506.2	9,706	5.2
1928–1932	205.5	2,117	9.7	421.3	9,723	4.3
1933–1937	197.3	2,539	7.8	559.2	13,159	4.2

a) Tax figures are from an unpublished manuscript by Mr. Seiji Tsunematsu of the Agricultural Research Institute of the Japanese Department of Agriculture and Forestry. They were published later in Tohata and Ohkawa (1956).
b) Income figures from the worksheets of the Economic Research Institute at Hitotsubashi University.

only another form of indirect taxation—constituted the rest. Changes over time in the array of consumer goods subject to tax (e.g., from soya to tobacco) and in the schedule of rates (e.g., selective increases in 1875 and 1882) are evidence that the revenue system was kept flexible in order to block effectively consumption in the course of a shifting pattern of demand.[14]

Government policy called for heavy taxes on both peasant and consumer and a lighter burden for the landlord and industrial-merchant classes. The income tax did not appear until 1887 and then at the low flat rate of 3 per cent. Table 3 shows that proceeds from this source were negligible before 1900; the definition of the tax base, moreover, rendering all interest on government and other savings bonds, all life insurance premia and 40 per cent of all dividend receipts deductible, transformed it into a severely regressive levy.

A so-called business tax, equivalent to a proportional corporate income tax, went into effect only in 1896. It was levied on commercial and industrial enterprises, proportional to a formula using the amount of capital involved, the rental value of the plant and the number of employees.[15] The highest rates (5–6 per cent on the rental value of the premises) were reserved for such luxuries as restaurants and hotels. Transportation and engineering enterprises, on the other hand, enjoyed rates of from 0.1 to 1 per cent. Progressive levies, i.e. the Capital Interest Tax and the Business Profits Tax were not enacted until 1926.[16] Even more significant are vaguely defined exemptions granted to "the iron foundry business" and areas "producing certain important goods."[17] Needless to add, benefits which could not be bestowed in the law itself could be granted in its administration.

Incentives for reinvestment and the accumulation of productive

---

[14] There is ample proof that the Japanese realized the full potentialities of a selective tax structure. The tax on the manufacture of cloth, for example, carried exemptions for materials whose immediate or ultimate destination was in the export market.

[15] One popular formula: 40 per cent of the rental value of the plant as a base, plus one yen additional per employee.

[16] The temporary World War I War Profits Tax is the exception.

[17] Japan, Department of Finance (1926), p. 30.

wealth were further strengthened by the absence of inheritance and real estate taxes before 1905, and the prevalence of very low rates thereafter. In combination with the predominance of primogeniture in the Japanese family such policies guaranteed the transfer of industrial fortunes virtually intact from generation to generation. Negative taxes or subsidies could, of course, supplement tax exemptions where necessary.[18] On the expenditure side also, as we have seen, industry and commerce were favored at the expense of agriculture and the workshops.[19]

The strongly oligopolistic trend in Japanese industry leading to the establishment of conglomerate enterprises reaching into every area of industrial activity made its own contribution to this redistribution of the income shares. The *zaibatsu* and *zaibatsu*-linked enterprises served, in a sense, as an arm of the national treasury; concessions exacted from the small producer in sub-contracted domestic industry can be viewed as a fiscal levy; monopoly prices on the consumer side can be viewed as an indirect tax. In a situation where it is assured that profits will not lie idle or, more importantly, be misused, the old question as to whether a competitive or monopolistic market configuration is better suited to growth seems to resolve itself.

All efforts were directed at siphoning off increments in income which had accrued to undependable would-be consumers, while preferential treatment was accorded those with whom only the ability, never the willingness, to reinvest was at issue. A blatantly regressive tax-expenditure structure is favorable to development

---

[18] Especially in areas where the need for additional protection was felt, since the Unequal Treaty System deprived Japan of the tariff as a tool for development. The shipping trade, for example, was almost wholly dominated by the American Pacific Mail Company from the early Meiji days. The Mitsubishi Steamship Company was encouraged by the government, guaranteed against losses until the American company could be brought to its knees, and received an 8 per cent yearly dividend thereafter.

[19] Subsidies were, moreover, employed as a fine instrument for channelling investment. To relieve the balance of payments pressure, for example, ocean-going navigation, preferably in Japanese-built bottoms, was encouraged. A subsidy of 1.2 yen per ton was offered for ships in excess of 1000 tons. If the engines were a Japanese product as well, an additional payment of 5 yen per unit of horsepower was allowed for.

only if the potential investing classes are naturally disposed in that direction, or are subject to the discipline of an intervening state.

The largest contribution of the landlord-industrialist group came through the direct reinvestment of profits; moreover, this group subscribed to a large share of the banking capital and was instrumental in the flotation of the domestic debt. The fact that they abstained from diverting resources to non-developmental purposes is evidence of a degree of cooperation—or discipline—which makes it difficult to ascertain where the public sector ended and the private began.[20]

During the very first years of the Meiji Restoration, admittedly, the strictly voluntary basis of this upper class "dependability" was open to some doubts. A few days after the new government took office, for example, a notice went out to well-to-do merchants and landowners all over Japan reminding them that "we are constrained to secure revenue" and that "as your firm has been in the financial service of the Imperial Court from the olden time, you are ordered to be in the service of the Revenue Office hereafter."[21] On occasion, representatives of leading houses were assembled and directed to prepare a roster of wealthy local citizens; the latter would then be summoned to the Imperial Palace and told in no uncertain terms that their help was required;[22] it was not easy to refuse compliance.[23] Clearly, such procedures can hardly be dignified as loans; they are, rather, a form of expropriatory tax and were discontinued after the extreme pressures of 1868–69 had passed. The government subsequently extended the promise that all such *goyokin,* or "domestic loans," would become redeemable through the use of land tax proceeds; and in fact, 90 per cent were ultimately repaid.

---

[20] For a detailed discussion, see Ranis (1955).

[21] See Honjō (1933), p. 18.

[22] In February 1868, for example, 650 citizens of Osaka were thus summoned and instructed. This is hardly surprising as Norman (Norman, 1940, p. 49) reports that 70 per cent of the private capital at the time of the Restoration was distributed among the merchants of Osaka.

[23] The Mitsui family, for instance, soon to become the new government's sole fiscal agent, was ordered to turn in 50,000 ryo (an old unit valued at two yen) in 1868. There was immediate agreement to pay 20,000 ryo and the promise of an additional 10,000 in the following year. The government, however, insisted on full and immediate payment and the Mitsui were forced to liquidate assets in order to comply.

The lion's share of voluntary savings was of the "retained" rather than the "transferred" variety. In agriculture some direct accumulation took place in the form of agricultural improvements—by the deployment of an additional fraction of a peasant's time to road construction or fence mending. In small-scale domestic industry a similar expansion or improvement of the workshop during spare hours helped mobilize reserve productive capacity directly.[24] And such contributions are as significant as those flowing from the cumulative reinvestment of profits in the large industrial enterprises.

Landowners and industrialists provided the bulk of "transferred" voluntary savings. They subscribed to a major portion of the banking capital, and there is evidence that a limited amount of government debt found a market outside of the banking system. Some loans floated during the nineteenth century were partly subscribed to by "individuals" and "companies" in what appears to be a normal savings operation. But the public market remained very narrow; 12.47 million of the 12.50 million yen New Loan of 1878, for example, was placed with the Mitsui family.[25] The private equity market was also narrowly based. Most industry employed the closed corporate system, controlled by either the *zaibatsu*, the government, or some form of coalition of the two. Attempts at broadening participation were by no means lacking. The government issued pamphlets explaining the joint stock company structure to the public, established advisory "commercial bureaus," clearing houses on the London model and a Tokyo Stock Exchange in 1878. To the present day, however, there has been little evidence of a widespread willingness or ability to adopt the more advanced financial techniques of this type.

---

[24] The extent of such savings is, of course, not statistically verifiable and undoubtedly an equivalent amount of "transferred" savings would have greater developmental value since it can be precisely channelled. An equivalent amount would, however, not be available.

[25] The small saver was offered a special inducement, a promise that he would receive the full amount of his intended subscription and at the issue price. In view of the claims of oversubscription and the consequent placing of portions of most flotations at premium prices, this offer amounted to a clear incentive. See Matsukata (1900), p. 80.

Surprising, however, is the fact that the lower income groups, dis-criminated against by heavy taxes and an imperfect credit market, nevertheless managed to increase their rate of voluntary savings. The relative success of institutional patterns of savings, in spite of high taxes and moderate inflation, attest to proverbial Japanese thriftiness. Moral suasion from the top of the hierarchical structure was effectively employed in the effort to strengthen such tendencies. Imperial edicts had a considerable impact after the so-called Resto-ration of the Emperor to secular power. "Let us avoid all luxuries," to quote a typical one, "so that we can keep up with the world; truly the development of our national productive strength has its roots in reverent obedience. . . . May you, our people, take these, our wishes, to heart."[26]

Savings banks, of which some 460 were in operation by the end of the nineteenth century, became the most popular vehicle in the effort to strengthen such habits among the lower income groups.[27] The Japanese evidenced a definite affinity for an institutionalized, regulated savings mechanism, as characterized also by the postal savings system,[28] mutual aid associations and cooperative societies. In terms of real magnitudes, however, total voluntary savings, by direct investment on the farm and in the household, and by indirect investment through financial intermediaries, were small compared with the reinvestment of business surpluses, and the use of tax-financed public funds.

Inflation-Forced Savings

It would seem ideal to be able to plan development as follows: initially exploit available reserves with a minimum of investment; tax these funds away and employ them to clear bottlenecks in other sectors, with resulting secondary increases in income; a suitable tax structure can then be expected to yield the capital needed for

---

[26] Quoted from Kraus (1939), p. 47 (translation mine).

[27] "Industry and thrift are the two chief factors in the production of national wealth, and the Savings Banks have for their aim the encouragement of the spirit of thrift." (Sale, 1911, p. 505).

[28] Postal savings, inaugurated in 1874, saw deposits grow from 28.3 million yen in 1897 to 92.9 million yen in 1908. What is more interesting is the relatively broad base of depositors whose number increased from 1.3 to 8 million over the same period. See Wilenkin (1908), p. 97.

further expansion. Unfortunately, this is an unrealistic pattern. Development does not proceed by neat stages; long gestation-period investments in social overhead and capital goods industries are usually required even in the early days of a logically consistent developmental effort. As a result, voluntary plus taxation-forced savings may prove inadequate in terms of the anticipated addition to the capital stock, and the *ex post* savings-investment equality is re-established through inflation.

In spite of the very favorable propensities and policies described above, Japan was forced to resort to credit creation in order to accommodate the total projected investment activity in the course of development. The amount of overall net credit creation[29] is difficult to establish. Agriculture and small-scale industry were faced with a highly centralized money market and did not receive substantial amounts of long-term credit. The considerable overlap between *zaibatsu* enterprises and the banking system makes it impossible to obtain meaningful estimates of business debt. The government itself, initially handicapped by the absence of a dependable market for its bonds, resorted to deficit financing on a considerable scale.

Japan's national debt is presented in Table 7; on the average, it amounted to nearly 30 per cent of the national income during the nineteenth century. A variety of guises for outright credit creation was employed. Old Tokugawa feudal debts were funded by means of a 23 million yen bond issue; in 1876 samurai pension claims were commuted into instruments of credit. In neither case was there an exchange for previously existing purchasing power. The entire domestic debt outstanding in 1878 was credit-financed. The 12½ million yen Public Works Loan of that year, however, initiated efforts to place a portion of the debt with the public. A precise breakdown is not available; but a closer examination of the 1883 twenty million yen Nakasendo Railway Loan,[30] for instance, yields the interesting fact that it was "over-subscribed" to the extent of 18 million yen; "individuals" applied for 30 per cent, "banks and companies" for 68 per cent of the total. Since profit receivers participated as "in-

---

[29] It is understood that net credit creation by the private sector may be offset by the public sector and that government deficits may merely serve to mobilize hoards of an equivalent amount.

dividuals" and ploughed back their profits as "companies," we can assume that banks accounted for the lion's share of the latter. Prob-

TABLE 7

Outstanding National Debt of Japan

(Unit: Million Yen)

Year	Domestic	Per cent of total	Foreign	Per cent of total	Total
1877	213	94	13	6	226
1897	399	100	0	0	399
1907	1,088	48	1,165	52	2,254
1914	991	40	514	60	2,506
1924	3,356	69	1,506	31	4,863
1930	4,476	75	1,479	25	5,955

Source: From Yasuzo Horie, "Japan's Balance of International Payments in the Early Meiji Period," *Kyoto University Economic Review* (April, 1954).

ably 50 per cent of the national debt incurred during the nineteenth century resulted in the creation of new purchasing power.

It should not be surprising that all available indices record price increases for these decades; what is surprising is that these increases were not more substantial. Tsuru's figures show an increase in the wholesale price level of 138 per cent from 1868 to 1900, an increase in the cost of living of 148 per cent from 1873 to the turn of the century.[31] Yamada obtains a 77 per cent advance in wholesale prices from 1875 to 1900[32] and Ohkawa's widely-quoted index shows a similar, more modest increase.[33] A moderate amount of inflation may, of course, serve a useful purpose in "shaking up" an economy, loosening old moorings and providing fresh incentives. In Japan, credit creation resulted simply in moderate price increases and additional forced savings without culminating in spiralling transfers of resources from savings and production to speculation and hoarding.[34]

Except for the years preceding the Satsuma Rebellion, the banking

---

[30] Japan, Department of Finance.
[31] Tsuru (1940).
[32] Yamada (1951), p. 57.
[33] From working papers at the Hitotsubashi University, Tokyo, Japan.
[34] Attempts to develop beyond one's means need not, of course, result in

system exercised restraint and made a significant contribution to stability. The Bank of Japan assumed all power of note issue in 1882 and succeeded in recalling the bulk of earlier wildcat issues. Selective credit controls were used to ensure the deployment of credit to bottleneck areas where it might do the most good. The extent of specialization within the powerful quasi-official banking institutions may be cited here. The Yokohama Species Bank (1880) was set up to serve the foreign trade sector; the Hypothec Bank (1896)—working through prefectural Agricultural and Industrial Banks—to make long-term loans on the security of immovable property to agriculture and small-scale industry (See Chapter 6); the Industrial Bank of Japan (1900) to service the needs of manufacturing establishments. Most of the "private" banks were in the hands of the *zaibatsu* whose close links with the government have been alluded to above. Firm control over the alternative sources of finance by the government and "dependable" groups outside the government assured the effectiveness of credit rationing in realizing any established hierarchy of investment priorities.

Nevertheless, the basic explanation for the avoidance of cumulative inflation must be sought in the fact that Japan was able to put such a large share of her program on a pay-as-you-go basis. If the excess of purchasing power over real resources at any one period of time can be contained, primary pressures are reduced; and if there are favorable anticipations based on confidence and culturally-conditioned obedience—as well as an absence of union pressures and escalator clauses—the impact of such pressures as do result is minimized. Small capital expenditure called forth increases in output sufficiently quickly to absorb unavoidable pressures for increased consumption, and sufficiently large to free resources for an overall development effort. The major responsibility for enabling Japan to avoid the hard choice between stability and development must be assigned to the fiscal policies she pursued.

---

domestic inflation, if the foreign balance can serve to cushion the effects of the extra demand created. Nineteenth-century Japan was, however, neither willing nor able to make extensive use of other people's savings to supplement her own. Prior to the adoption of the Gold Standard in 1899 only two long-term loans totalling less than 17 million yen were floated abroad. The bulk of the inflationary pressure remained at home.

REFERENCES
Allen, George C. *A Short Economic History of Modern Japan, 1867–1937*. 1946.

Honjo, Eijiro, "Goyokin and Meiji Restoration," *Kyoto University Economic Review* (July, 1933).

Japan, Dept. of Finance. *The History of the National Debt,* Tokyo: The Government Press, 1893.

———. *Financial and Economic Annual of Japan* Tokyo: 1926.

Johnston, Bruce F., "Agricultural Productivity and Economic Development," *Journal of Political Economy* (December, 1951).

Kimura, Motokazu, "Fiscal Policy and Industrialization in Japan, 1868–1889," *Annals of the Hitotsubashi Academy* (October, 1956).

Kraus, J. B., "Wirtshaftsgesinnuning und voelkisch-politische Grund-bedingungen als Voraussetzungen des Japanischen Industrialisierungsprozesses," *Weltwirtschaftliches Archiv* (1939).

Lockwood, W. W. *The Economic Development of Japan, Growth and Structural Change 1868–1938*. Princeton: Princeton University Press, 1954.

Matsukata, Masayoshi. *Report on the Post-Bellum Financial Administration in Japan*. Tokyo: The Government Press, 1900.

Norman, E. Herbert. *Japan's Emergence as a Modern State*. New York: Institute of Pacific Relations Inquiry Series, 1940.

Ranis, Gustav, "The Community-Centered Entrepreneur in Japan," *Explorations in Entrepreneurial History* (December, 1955).

Sale, C. V., "Some Statistics of Japan," *Journal of the Royal Statistical Society* (April, 1911).

Tohata, S. *Nihon Nōgyō no Tenkai Katei (The Process of Development of Japanese Agriculture)*. Tokyo: Iwanami, 1953.

Tohata, S. and Ohkawa, K. eds., *Nihon Keizai to Nōgyō (Japanese Economy and Agriculture),* Tokyo: Iwanami, 1956.

Tsuchiya, T. and Okazaki, S. *Nihon Shihonshugi Hatattsushi Gaisetsu (Outline History of the Development of Japanese Capitalism),* Tokyo: 1937.

Tsuru, Shigeto, "The Development of Capitalism and Business Cycles in Japan, 1868–1899," unpublished doctoral thesis, Harvard University: 1940. (The revised version was later published in S. Tsuru's *Essays on Japanese Economy,* Tokyo: Kinokuniya, 1958.)

Wilenkin, G. *The Political and Economic Organization of Modern Japan.* Tokyo: 1908.

Yamada, Yūzō. *Comprehensive Survey of National Income in Japan (Nihon Kokumin Shotoku Shiryo),* Tokyo: Toyo Keizai Shimpo-sha, 1957.

CHAPTER 3

THE JAPANESE "MODEL" OF AGRICULTURAL DEVELOPMENT: ITS RELEVANCE TO DEVELOPING NATIONS[†]

BRUCE F. JOHNSTON

I. Introduction

A considerable consensus seems to have emerged concerning the strategic role of agricultural development in the economic growth of Japan. Three features of agriculture's role have been specially emphasized. First is the fact that agricultural output has been increased with remarkably small demands on the critically scarce resources of capital and foreign exchange. This was possible because of increases in the productivity of the existing on-farm resources of labor and land; and it was done within the framework of the existing small-scale agriculture. Secondly, agricultural and industrial development went forward together in a process of "concurrent" growth. Expansion of the non-agricultural sectors has, of course, proceeded a good deal more rapidly than agriculture so that the overwhelmingly agrarian character of the economy has been transformed. But throughout the period of modern economic growth the interactions between agriculture and the rest of the economy associated with this structural transformation have had profound implications for growth in both sectors. Thirdly, the gains in agricultural productivity were of strategic importance in making possible the increase in savings and investment that were a necessary condition for industrial expansion.

Although there is considerable agreement concerning agriculture's role in Japan's economic development, the agreement is by no

† This chapter is a revised and condensed version of "Agriculture and Economic Development: The Relevance of the Japanese Experience," published in *Food Research Institute Studies*, VI, No. 3 (1966), pp. 251–312. The permission of the Food Research Institute to reproduce portions of that article is gratefully acknowledged.

means complete. According to Nakamura's proposed revision of the official production estimates, which is discussed in detail by Hayami and Yamada in Chapter 4, increase in output in the decades between 1880 and 1920 barely kept pace with the growth of population. This implies a coefficient of income elasticity close to zero which seems highly improbable. But whether "impressive" or not, the rate of expansion of farm output was "sufficient." Apart from the rice riots of 1918, there seems to be no evidence that food shortages hampered industrial expansion. It is significant, however, that until the post-World War II period the income elasticity of demand for food in Japan was surprisingly low relative to the prevailing level of income. As Kaneda points out in Chapter 16, food consumption patterns changed very slowly, and it has only been since the 1950's that there has been a rapid shift away from the cheap starchy staple foods towards meat, dairy products, and other more expensive sources of food calories. Hence, the resource requirements to satisfy the increase in demand associated with population growth and rising per capita incomes were minimized. Although food imports from the Japanese colonies of Taiwan and Korea became important in the 1920's and 1930's, this did not pose a foreign exchange problem. And the large expansion of exports of tea and more especially of silk were highly significant sources of the foreign exchange required for the increased imports essential to industrial growth.

The dissent expressed by Oshima relates to the policies of the Meiji period which, in his view, made the tax burden on Japanese farmers unnecessarily heavy (Oshima, 1965). He concedes that it was necessary to rely on agriculture for a major part of the total tax revenue and requirements for capital formation, but he believes that the government's spending should have been at a lower level. In particular, he argues that it would have been better if military expenditures had been on a smaller scale and if the government had pursued a goal of 50 per cent coverage rather than universal primary education so that the fiscal requirements for educational expansion would have been consistent with a lighter agricultural tax burden.

Despite the vigor of their criticisms, the dissenting views put forth by Nakamura and Oshima do not really challenge the importance of the three features of agriculture's role that were emphasized above. Nor is there room to doubt that agriculture's positive role in facilitating economic growth in Japan was dependent on the fact that the Meiji leaders were able to choose and successfully implement an efficient strategy for agricultural development.

The success of Japan's agricultural development was the result of impressive foresight. Decisions of a long-term nature made early in the Meiji period led to the creation of the agricultural colleges, research stations, and other institutions needed to realize the potential inherent in Japan's rural economy for inexpensive gains in productivity and expanded farm output. Strengthening of education at various levels was important for its influence on those who were to enter farming but also because of the value of the training received by rural youth who were to move into jobs in industry, commerce, and government. Significantly, many of the agricultural scientists and other professionals serving agriculture came from farm households and were able to begin their climb up the educational ladder in a rural schoolhouse. The elementary, technical, and middle schools, which were rapidly expanding their enrollment, served not only to impart technical knowledge but also to strengthen the decision-making capabilities of individual farmers and to enhance their receptiveness to innovations and their ability to recognize development opportunities. Particularly noteworthy was the emphasis given in Meiji Japan to practical and technical training. The preamble to the Education Code of 1872, adopted only four years after the Meiji Restoration, expresses this viewpoint in a manner that seems to anticipate the recent discussions of investment in human resources: "Every man only after learning diligently according to his capacity will be able to increase his property and prosper in his business. Hence knowledge may be regarded as the capital for raising one's self; who then can do without learning?" (Kikuchi, p. 68).

The social and institutional reforms instituted during the first half dozen years of the Meiji period gave a strong impetus to the development of agriculture by striking down restrictions on the sale and cropping of land, on the choice of occupation, and other feudal restraints. In particular, the removal of the Tokugawa restrictions on the movement of goods and people and the creation of a unified nation and national economy accelerated the spread of knowledge and of improved varieties. Recent contributions by Hayami, Sawada, and other Japanese scholars have led to fuller appreciation of the importance of the innovational activity of individual farmers and of their vigorous response to economic opportunities and pressures (Hayami, 1965; Sawada, 1964). Both the central and prefectural governments, however, played an important role in facilitating this diffusion of knowledge of improved practices. Local meetings were held to promote the exchange of promising varieties and techniques and "agricultural improvement societies" were organized in a number of prefectures. In 1880 the Ministry of Agriculture and Commerce instructed all prefectural governments to encourage the establishment of such societies, and a year later 110 leading farmers were invited to Tokyo to consider measures for improving the nation's agriculture. Some of these farmers were appointed as instructors at the newly established Komaba Agricultural College and others were employed as "itinerant instructors" to tour the country and meet with groups of farmers and demonstrate improved farming techniques.

An attempt to introduce "Western" methods of large-scale farming in the 1870's had been a failure. Thereafter efforts were concentrated on increasing the efficiency of the prevailing system of small-scale farming.[1] The so-called "Meiji technology" that was evolved has been aptly described as a "combination of indigenous know-how and very selective borrowing from the West" (Ogura, p. 625). Intimate knowledge of the best of traditional farming methods was thus the starting point for agricultural research and extension activities. Procedures were devised to insure adaptation of improved varieties to varying local conditions. Considerable attention was also given to the analysis and mapping of soil types and to the preparation of instructions for the rational use of fertilizers on different crops and under various soil and climatic conditions.

It is apparent that political leaders and government officials at all

---

[1] In Section III it is emphasized that contemporary developing countries face a basic issue of agricultural development strategy that closely parallels the choice that was made in Meiji Japan between the introduction of "Western" methods of large-scale farming and a strategy of raising the productivity of the existing small-scale farming-system.

levels regarded agricultural improvement as a matter of great importance and gave significant support to the work of agricultural research and extension personnel. Prefectural governors as well as village leaders promoted and took part in country fairs and agricultural meetings. Prizes and subsidies were awarded to encourage improved farming practices and new farm enterprises such as sericulture. The net effect of these activities was to give recognition to the importance of agriculture and to foster attitudes favorable to agricultural progress.

It is also noteworthy that in the Meiji period landlords generally lived in the countryside and frequently took an active part in promoting the adoption of improved practices and in organizing and often financing the extension of irrigation facilities or improved layout of farm units. Since land taxes were revised only rarely and landlords commonly received approximately half of the rice crop as rent (although lesser percentages for other crops), they had a strong incentive to promote measures that would raise productivity and output. For owner-cultivators and tenants as well, economic incentives and pressures were of great importance.

Although the government of Meiji Japan played a crucial role, it limited its activity to certain strategic measures that helped to create a favorable environment. It helped to generate and disseminate promising innovations in agriculture, particularly yield-increasing innovations based on varietal improvement and increasingly heavy use of fertilizers, and the government's "model factories" pioneered new industrial activities. But economic advance on a broad front depended on the decisions and energy of a great many enterpreneurs, including some five million farm operators, responding to market-determined prices.[2]

Before turning to an examination of the relevance of Japan's experience to contemporary underdeveloped countries, a disclaimer is in order. Japan's own experience strongly supports Gerschenkron's criticism of the concept of specific "prerequisites" to modern

---

[2] It is tempting to speculate that because of the "unequal treaties" that restricted her ability to impose protective tariffs, Japan may have been spared the serious distortion of cost-price relationships that seems to have had adverse effects on growth in a number of developing countries in recent years (Mckinnon, 1966).

economic growth. It also illustrates the importance of "processes of substitution" for what appear to have been "prerequisites" in previous historical experience. The influence of Japan's Confucian tradition and various other socio-cultural factors were, in this sense, a substitution for—a "functional equivalent" of—the role of the "Protestant Ethic" in western Europe as stressed by Weber and Tawney. Each country that responds to the challenge of modern economic growth is, of course, unique in important respects, and the actors on stage at this moment in history must confront "the creative task of finding their own answers and shaping their own future" (Gerschenkron, p. 6). The Japanese experience certainly suggests factors that are potentially of great importance. Some features of the "Japanese model" are clearly relevant in the current context, but it is also important to identify areas in which the need for "processes of substitution" is likely to be especially great.

II. Agricultural Development and the Process of Structural Transformation

In a comparative study of Japan and western Europe, David Landes notes that in western Europe, unlike Japan, agriculture was probably not a net source of capital for industrial expansion. His terse conclusion is: "In short, the land gave men and nourishment to the burgeoning industrial society. Need one ask for more?" (Landes, p. 171).

Japan's experience and the nature of the problems faced by a late-developing country in mobilizing capital for industrialization, suggest an affirmative answer. Certainly there is no doubt that the agricultural sector must provide a substantial part of the increased tax revenue that is required for the expansion of education, research, and other developmental services, and of the capital needed to strengthen the economic infrastructure. And the evidence reviewed by Ranis in Chapter 2 makes it clear that at least in the earlier phase of Japan's modern economic growth, the agricultural sector made a significant net contribution to the capital requirements of the non-farm sectors.

There are, moreover, general considerations which suggest strongly that late-developing countries are obliged to use devices for mobilizing capital for industry that were not resorted to in countries that developed at an earlier stage. Gerschenkron has noted that for countries which developed early "the more gradual character of the industrialization process and the more considerable accumulation of capital, first from earnings in trade and modernized agriculture and later from industry itself, obviated the pressure for developing any special institutional devices for provision of long-term capital to industry" (Gerschenkron, p. 14). He suggests, however, that in countries characterized by a greater degree of "relative backwardness" the scarcity of capital and entrepreneurial talent gave rise to a need for special institutional arrangements to mobilize capital. In France and Germany industrial investment banks were such an innovation. In nineteenth century Russia, where the resistances to industrialization were more formidable, "supply of capital for the needs of industrialization required the compulsory machinery of the government, which through its taxation policies, succeeded in directing incomes from consumption to investment" (Gerschenkron, p. 20). Policies which have the effect of increasing the savings rate by channeling an increased share of GNP into investment rather than consumption will almost inevitably draw a greater volume of resources from agriculture than is returned to the sector in the form of reverse transfers such as research and extension services, input subsidies, or investments in infrastructure for agriculture. In considering the impact of agrarian change in Japan's modern economic growth, Thomas C. Smith states the problem in terms that have wide applicability:

> Even though a government is strong and has the will to modernize, it must still find the means to invest on a grand scale in schools, factories, roads, harbors, railways, and so on, or its ambitions will come to nothing. If funds cannot be had from foreign sources, they must be taken from the domestic economy—which in most cases means from agriculture: thus the ability to modernize comes to depend largely on the productivity of agriculture and the willingness of the peasantry to part with current income for distant and half-understood goals (Smith, 1959, pp. 210–11).

The fundamental importance of the process of structural transformation is brought out clearly by the sharp contrast between Japan's experience following the Meiji Restoration and Java's experience in the late nineteenth and early twentieth centuries. In both countries, small-scale peasant agriculture based on production of paddy rice made a considerable technical advance during this period. But in Japan, unlike Java, the traditional labor-intensive, small-scale farming system "came to be complementarily related to an expanding manufacturing system in indigenous hands . . ." (Geertz, p. 135). And, as Geertz rightly concludes, it was "the dynamic interaction between the two sectors which kept Japan moving and ultimately pushed her over the hump to sustained growth" (Geertz, p. 141).

Three aspects of the interaction associated with "concurrent" growth of agriculture and the non-farm sectors had a particularly important impact on Japan's agricultural development: (1) the expansion of the market for cash sales of agricultural products as a growing percentage of the population came to depend on purchased food; (2) the enlarged use of purchased inputs by farmers, that reflected the availability of new and improved inputs (such as fertilizers, improved plows, foot-pedal threshers, insecticides, and eventually small tractors), as well as the enlarged money income that made such purchases possible;[3] and (3) the growth of non-farm employment opportunities that was sufficient to absorb the natural increase in the labor force and has recently made possible a reduction in the absolute size of the farm labor force.

The burden placed on Japan's farmers by the policy of concurrent

---

[3] Folke Dovring's study of the increase of "aggregated labor productivity" in United States agriculture throws new light on the extent to which increases in agricultural productivity are dependent upon the concurrent growth of agriculture and other industries. It is common knowledge that the tremendous increases in the productivity of farm labor in the United States have been associated with a great increase in the use of purchased inputs and the substitution of capital for labor as the size of the farm labor force has declined at an increasing rate. Dovring's analysis demonstrates that the decline in the direct (on-farm) agricultural labor force from over 10 million in the 1920's to 4 million in 1960 was associated with only a slight increase in the indirect (off-farm) labor used for agricultural production, from 1.5 million man years or somewhat more in 1920 to about 2 million in 1960. Thus "the greater efficiency of industrially produced and scientifically based means of production" have clearly been dominant factors in the increase of agricultural productivity (Dovring, 1967, pp. 20, 22).

growth may have been excessive; but it can be said that "the willingness of the peasantry to part with current income for distant and half-understood goals" has paid dividends. In contrast, "horizontal" or "static" expansion and some technical advance in agriculture in Java have supported a sixfold increase in population between 1850 and 1961 but very little structural transformation has taken place. In fact, the share of agriculture in the total labor force declined only a fraction of a per cent between 1930 and 1961—from 73.9 to 73.3 per cent (Jones, 1966). Thus Geertz concludes, "the real tragedy of colonial history in Java after 1830 is not that the peasantry suffered. It suffered much worse elsewhere, and, if one surveys the miseries of the submerged classes of the nineteenth century generally, it may even seem to have gotten off relatively lightly. The tragedy is that it suffered for nothing" (Geertz, p. 143).

The problems faced by contemporary underdeveloped countries differ in many ways from those that confronted Japan. It is useful to consider explicitly how the relevance of the Japanese experience is affected by four differences that stand out as being especially significant. The most fundamental difference is the much higher rates of growth of total population and labor force that characterize today's less-developed countries. A second difference is associated with the pressures, both economic and non-economic, that give rise to a rather capital-intensive pattern of investment in spite of the scarcity of capital and relative abundance of labor. The third difference to be noted is the possibility of supplementing domestic resources by foreign aid; and a final contrast relates to the current climate of opinion and other factors that make it difficult to tax agriculture, especially via a land tax.

Population growth and the arithmetic of structural transformation Rates of population growth in the underdeveloped countries at the present time—typically 2 or 3 per cent per annum—are very much higher than the growth rates that characterized the "population explosion" in western Europe and Japan as they experienced their "demographic transition." One obvious and important implication of these high growth rates is that with even a modest rate of increase in per capita incomes, the growth of demand for food is very rapid.

Another implication of the "awesome power of compound interest" merits much greater attention than it has received to date. The rate of structural transformation as reflected in changes in the occupational composition of a country's labor force will inevitably be slow in countries in which the bulk of the labor force is still in agri-

FIGURE 1a

Hypothetical Growth Paths for Total, Farm, and Non-farm Labor Force
Over 50-year Period in Earlyphasia and Middlephasia
(Initial labor force = 10 million)

Assumption: Moderate Growth of Total Labor Force: 1%

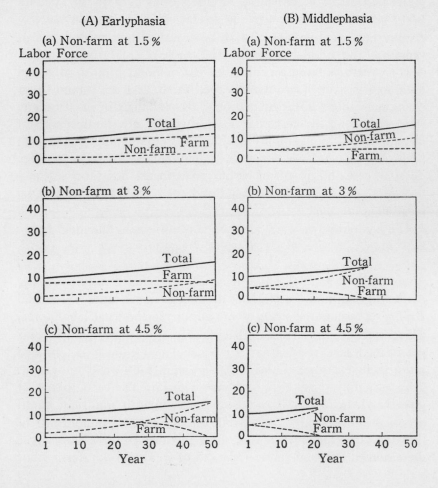

culture and where total population and labor force are growing at 2 or 3 per cent annually.

The growth paths in Figure 1a compare the changes in total, farm, and non-farm labor force in two hypothetical countries over a 50-year period on the basis of alternative assumptions with respect to the rates of growth of the total labor force and non-farm employment. Projections for both countries were made starting with a total labor force of 10 million; but for Earlyphasia it was assumed that the initial farm labor force accounted for 80 per cent of the total, whereas in Middlephasia the labor force is divided equally between agriculture and non-agriculture. Figure 1a is based on the assumption that the total labor force is growing at a "moderate" rate of 1.0 per cent per year; Figure 1b assumes a "very rapid" rate of growth of the total labor force of 3.0 per cent. (Ignoring the lag of, say, 15 years between a change in rate of population growth and a change in rate of growth of labor force, and abstracting from changes in labor force participation rates or changes in age structure, these assumed rates of change in labor force imply identical rates of change in total population.) Then for each assumption the growth path of the farm labor force was computed on the basis of three different rates of growth of employment in the non-farm sector— "moderate," "rapid," and "very rapid" defined as 1.5, 3.0, and 4.5 per cent respectively.

The computations were made by iteration, using the identity

$$P'_A \equiv \frac{P_T}{P_A} P'_T - \frac{P_N}{P_A} P'_N$$

where P'_A, P'_T, and P'_N are the annual percentage rates of change in the agricultural, total, and non-agricultural labor force and P_A/P_T represents the share of agriculture in the total labor force. This procedure thus assumes that the size of the farm labor force is determined as a residual on the basis of exogenously determined rates of change in the total labor force and in non-farm employment. This assumption is fairly reasonable during the early phase of growth when an economy is still predominantly agrarian, but it becomes increasingly implausible as the relative importance of the non-farm sector increases. (For certain sets of assumptions, the assumed constant rates of growth of total and non-farm labor

FIGURE 1b
Hypothetical Growth Paths (Cont'd.)
Assumption: Very Rapid Growth of Total Labor Force: 3%

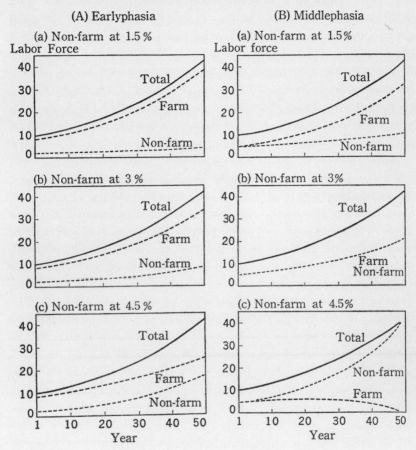

(A) Earlyphasia

(a) Non-farm at 1.5%

(b) Non-farm at 3%

(c) Non-farm at 4.5%

(B) Middlephasia

(a) Non-farm at 1.5%

(b) Non-farm at 3%

(c) Non-farm at 4.5%

force lead to the absurd result that the non-farm labor force exceeds the total and the farm labor force becomes negative.)

For the non-farm population of a country to increase more rapidly than its total population, leading to a decline in the share of agriculture in the total population and labor force, implies an increase in output per farm worker (or increasing food imports). But when the farm labor force continues to bulk large in the total, the "required" rate of increase in farm productivity is fairly slow; so the assumption that the change in the size of the farm labor force is determined essentially as a residual seems plausible for a country at an early phase of development. Although agriculture is the "self-employment sector" par excellence, a part of the residual labor force will be found in urban areas eking out an existence in family workshops, the "service sector," or as casual laborers. In many countries, especially in Africa and Latin America, this problem of a "floating population" or unemployed "school-leavers" queuing up for the limited number of jobs that become available is aggravated by the "excessive" wage differentials characteristic of jobs in "modern" sectors in which government and expatriate firms bulk large.

The hypothetical projections shown in Figures 1a and 1b are obviously not to be taken too seriously. It is indeed to be hoped that careful projections of this nature for individual countries will add fuel to policies and programs that will insure that birthrates will soon begin to fall and with sufficient speed so that rapid growth of their labor force will be a problem of 25 or 30 years rather than a half century or more. The contrast between the "moderate" and "very rapid" assumptions with respect to the rate of increase of total labor force and between the Earlyphasia and Middlephasia situations do, however, point up some significant problems. Comparisons of the hypothetical projections for the rapid growth situation with the historical changes in Japan's labor force summarized in Figure 2 underscores the fact that considerably more than 70 years would have been required for Japan to reach the turning point when its farm labor force began to register an appreciable decline in absolute size if its total population and labor force had been growing at 2 or 3 per cent annually instead of about 1 per cent. It is apparent from Table 1 that the virtual constancy of the farm labor force in Japan between the 1880's and 1940 was a result of reductions in the coefficient of differential growth—the difference between the growth rate of the non-farm and total labor force—which offset the effect of the declining weight of agriculture in the total labor force. The absolute size of the farm labor force would have declined rapidly in the 1920's and 1930's if the coefficient of differential growth had remained at a level as high as the 1.6 to 2.6 per cent figures that prevailed during the 1880–1920 period. But, the reduced rate of increase in non-farm employment after 1920 meant that the change in the structural situation which favored substantial reduction in the absolute size of the farm labor force was offset by the decline in the coefficient of differential growth to less than 1 per cent. It has only been in the past decade that Japan has begun to experience a substantial reduction in the absolute size of its farm labor force, the current annual rate of decrease being close to 4 per cent.

FIGURE 2
Japan: Growth of Total, Farm, and
Non-farm Labor Force, 1883-1964*

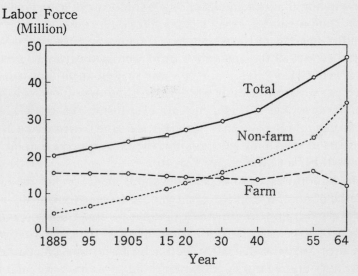

* Data from Table 1. Figures plotted for 1885, 1895, 1905, and 1915 are mid-points of five-year averages. Lines are interpolations from labor force estimates for years shown.

Industrial investment, capital intensity, and the growth of non-farm employment

Although industrial expansion may be limited by various factors, including failure of food supplies to keep pace with the increase in demand on the part of a growing non-farm population, the rate of industrial investment and the average level of capital intensity are likely to be the critical factors determining the growth of employment in the non-farm sectors.

Gerschenkron notes that late-developing countries have usually given a relatively high priority to heavy industry and have tended to adopt the latest technology from more advanced countries. Hence industrial expansion in late-developing countries has been associated with a much more capital-intensive pattern of investment than would be indicated by the relative availability and opportunity cost of capital and labor (Gerschenkron, pp. 9–11). Whereas Gerschenkron seems to regard this as a rational response to the situation that they confront, Ranis and Fei argue that this tendency of underdeveloped countries to emphasize capital-intensive investment is a phenomenon that can and should be avoided or at least minimized. Their comparison of Japan's experience and recent developments in India suggests a marked contrast. In Japan, at least until World War I, growth of the non-agricultural sectors was characterized by a low capital-labor ratio, and the rate of growth of industrial employment was considerably more rapid than the rate of increase in capital stock. But in India, investment during the years 1949–60 was so capital-intensive that the industrial labor force seems to have increased at something less than half the rate of increase in the capital stock (Fei and Ranis, pp. 125–46).

The importance of this issue of capital intensity and the rate of increase of non-farm employment is pointed up emphatically by the effect of rapid rates of growth of population and labor force on the process of structural transformation. Clearly, the issue is especially critical in countries that resemble Earlyphasia. In such countries— where agriculture initially accounts for 80 per cent of the total labor force—the farm labor force will still account for 59 per cent of the total and will be growing at 2.0 per cent per annum after 50 years if the rate of growth of the total labor force is 3.0 per cent even on the highly optimistic assumption that non-farm employment will grow at 4.5 per cent annually.

Taiwan appears to be the only country in which non-farm employment has increased at a rate appreciably above 4 per cent and that was influenced by special circumstances. In Mexico the increase in the non-farm labor force between 1950 and 1960 was nearly 4.0 per cent, but the total labor force was growing at 3.1 per cent so the coefficient of differential growth was only .9 per cent

TABLE 1

Japan: Growth of Total and Non-agricultural Labor Force and
Coefficients of Differential Growth, 1883–1964

(1,000 persons except as indicated)

Period	Agriculture as per cent of total labor force	Total labor force (1)	Agricultural labor force (2)	Non-agricultural labor force		Annual percentage rate of increase (compound) from preceding period			Coefficient of differential growth Col. (6)-(5)
				Total (3)	Manufacturing (4)	Total (5)	Total non-agriculture (6)	Manufacturing (7)	
1883–87	76.2	20,360	15,511	4,849	1,524	...	...	...	...
1893–97	69.2	22,258	15,397	6,861	2,393	.90	3.53	4.48	2.63
1903–07	62.6	24,252	15,184	9,068	3,263	.86	2.83	3.28	1.97
1913–17	56.3	25,967	14,613	11,354	4,131	.68	2.28	2.39	1.60
1920	52.4	27,263	14,287	12,976	4,357	...	...	...	...
1930	47.7	29,619	14,131	15,488	4,891	.83	1.78	1.16	.95
1940	42.3	32,478	13,842	18,636	7,160	.93	1.87	3.88	.94
1955	38.9	41,190	16,040	25,150	7,560	...	...	...	...
1964	25.6	46,730	11,970	34,760	11,370	1.41	3.66	4.65	2.25

Reproduced from Johnston (1966), Appendix II, where the statistical sources and qualifications are discussed in detail.

compared to Japan's maximum rates of 2.6 and 2.3 per cent during the first and last periods shown in Table 1.

Highly pertinent to an understanding of Japan's experience is the fact that a two-sector model does not really do justice to Japan's pattern of development because the non-agricultural sector has itself had a dual structure.[4] Thus, Ohkawa makes a distinction between a "modern sector," characterized by large enterprises, relatively high capital-labor ratios, and comparatively high wage rates, and a "semi-modern sector," made up of numerous small-scale units, using relatively small amounts of capital, and paying wages only a little above the average incomes of the farm population (Ohkawa, p. 483). Moreover, many of these small units are family enterprises, and to some extent they represent a "self-employment sector."

Okita has pointed out that as late as 1956 nearly half of the manufacturing labor force in Japan was working in small enterprises with less than 30 employees. He notes that there are wide differences between the large and small firms in capital intensity and wage levels, and emphasizes that most of the labor force must of necessity be absorbed in medium and small enterprises because of the limited increase in employment associated with the establishment of large-scale, capital-intensive firms. It is his view that this "double structure of the economy is a difficulty that underdeveloped countries have to face on the way to industrialization." If attention is paid only to the creation of capital-intensive industries, a wide gap is likely to be created between the great majority of the labor force and the employees of modern, large-scale factories who become "an aristocracy of labor" (Okita, p. 382 et passim).

---

[4] Inukai and Tussing's account of Japan's first "development plan" makes it clear that this dual pattern of industrial development was no mere accident. The detailed policies enunciated in an 1884 report, *Recommendation for Industrialization (Kōgyō Iken)*, emphasized the mobilization of labor and entrepreneurial skills on a broad front in small-scale enterprises which constituted a "quasi-agricultural sector"—sericulture, *sake* brewing, tea, leather, weaving, spinning, wood products, etc. Major emphasis was given to the improvement of productive techniques in traditional indigenous industries in the belief that with adequate guidance and technical assistance these small and scattered activities would foster overall economic development (Inukai and Tussing, 1965).

Japan's own experience following World War I suggests some of the reasons why the labor absorption problems facing contemporary developing countries are more difficult than those that prevailed during the Meiji era. The slowing down of the rate of growth of non-farm employment in Japan during the 1920's and early 1930's was the result of increasing emphasis on capital-intensive investment by the large-scale modern sector together with circumstances that discouraged the expansion of smaller firms in the semi-modern sector. It has been argued elsewhere that the consequent slowing down of the process of structural transformation had serious political as well as economic consequences, and that the slow rate of labor absorption in the manufacturing sector, as compared to the 1880–1920 period, was influenced strongly by inappropriate economic policies (Johnston, 1962, pp. 241–47). To some extent, however, the greater emphasis on capital-intensive investment in the 1920–32 period was undoubtedly dictated by the changing structure of Japanese industry and the need to carry through "rationalization" policies to make the country's exports more competitive in world markets, although the latter problem was certainly aggravated by the maintenance of an overvalued exchange rate due to the stubborn determination of Japan's financial authorities to return to the gold standard at prewar parity. During the 1955–64 period the rate of increase of non-farm employment has been much more rapid than in the 1920's and early 1930's, but this has been associated with a rate of increase of GNP of 10 per cent and an incredibly high proportion of investment, averaging 34 per cent for the period 1955–63 (Japan Bureau of Statistics, p. 415). It is noteworthy that the rate of increase in non-farm and manufacturing employment between 1883–87 and 1893–97 was nearly as rapid as during this recent period in spite of the fact that the rate of growth of GNP was less than a third as high.

Japan's experience seems to underscore the importance of pursuing what Lewis has termed a "secondary strategy" of industrial development. The "basic development strategy" will normally aim at encouraging industries such as power generation, steel, and petrochemicals in which the technical superiority of the latest processes is decisive. Apart from certain operations such as materials handling, it is uneconomic to use labor-intensive technologies despite enormous differences in relative factor prices. For other lines of production, however, factor proportions are more flexible, and it is advantageous to encourage considerable decentralization of industrial development and rapid growth of small- and medium-sized, labor-intensive enterprises in order to promote fuller utilization of manpower and more rapid overall growth (J.P. Lewis, Chapters 3 and 7).

A further advantage of such a dual pattern of industrial development is that it opens up possibilities of tapping sources of capital and entrepreneurial talent that the modern, large-scale sector is not capable of mobilizing. As the more progressive and successful farmers in a developing country raise their productivity and incomes, they acquire, in aggregate, a considerable capacity to invest in non-farm enterprises as well as in agriculture. The extent to which such potential savings are translated into productive investments depends a great deal on the sort of investment opportunities that are perceived by individuals who have the capacity to save if the inducement is sufficiently attractive. Thus, the parallel development of small-scale, rural-based industries is in considerable measure complementary to the development of the large-scale, modern sector. Nevertheless, a certain amount of competition for scarce resources between the large-scale, modern sector and the development of small-scale industries is inevitable. And there is often a danger that the growth of the rural-based industries will be straitjacketed by exchange controls, licensing requirements, or similar restrictions.

To cite an important recent example, it appears that the rapid expansion of private tubewells in West Pakistan would not have been possible except for the happy though unforeseen circumstance that liberalization of foreign exchange regulations took place at an opportune moment so that small rural workshops were able to obtain the imported raw materials required to produce the simple pumps and motors that were required (Falcon and Gotsch, 1966; Falcon, 1967). These small-scale, rural-based industries were not only important in providing increased non-farm employment but also made available essential farm inputs at much lower capital cost and smaller foreign exchange content than would have been the case if major reliance had been placed, as was originally contemplated, on large-scale, public tubewell projects utilizing larger and more sophisticated pumps and motors.

The nature of the strategy pursued for developing the agricultural sector will have a strong influence on the success of efforts to encourage a dual pattern of industrial development. With the increasing commercialization of agriculture as structural transformation proceeds, a developing country's farm sector will make increasing use of purchased inputs. To the extent that this demand is directed toward relatively simple and inexpensive implements that are within the technical capabilities of small-scale, decentralized industries, the growing market for farm requisites can provide a strong stimulus to industrial expansion. A more capital-intensive agricultural expansion path not only requires scarce capital and foreign exchange that are urgently needed for industrial development but also means that the growing commercialization of agriculture does not lead to the sort of dynamic interaction between agricultural expansion and development of rural-based industries that can lead to more rapid growth of non-farm employment opportunities, more rapid creation of a labor force with industrial skills, and more rapid growth of national product.

Availability of foreign aid

The availability of foreign economic assistance at the present time is another important contrast with the Japanese experience. During the early Meiji period even commercial credits from abroad were of very limited importance, and the climate of opinion that has given rise to substantial foreign aid programs had obviously not emerged. One is tempted to generalize, however, that contemporary developing countries face an offsetting disadvantage in the fairly bleak prospects for enlarging their foreign exchange earnings through expanding exports of primary commodities. (For a good, brief discussion of the factors that seem likely to limit the growth of world demand for imports of tropical products, see Goreux.)

The rapid decline in mortality rates in the less-developed countries since World War II is itself an eloquent testimony to the potential effectiveness of technical assistance programs that can hasten the spread of modern technologies. It is now painfully obvious, however, that gains on the economic front are not so easily won because of both economic and non-economic factors that limit progress. But most basic is the fact that the volume of foreign economic aid that is likely to become available is small in relation to the magnitude of the capital requirements for development; and the current leveling off in the volume of foreign assistance being made available by the industrialized nations would seem to reinforce such an assessment.

For certain countries, even including a large country like Pakistan, foreign aid has accounted for a substantial fraction of net investment in recent years and has made an important contribution in facilitating an increase in the country's rate of growth and an associated increase in the marginal saving rate (Chenery and Strout, pp. 691–95). Aid is, of course, particularly important when it helps a country to achieve a higher rate of increase in domestic output that leads in turn to continuing increases in domestic saving and investment and thus facilitates the mobilization of increasingly large quantities of domestic resources for growth. Clearly, foreign aid cannot be a substitute for domestic policies and efforts aimed at efficient use of the domestic resources—both physical and human—essential for future growth.

Providing economic and technical assistance that is really relevant and useful is a good deal more difficult than was commonly supposed when Point IV and related programs were launched. Foreign economic aid is in fact a mixed blessing for receiving countries. Some of the disadvantages of aid programs have received considerable attention, notably those associated with "tied" aid and the administrative problems that arise because of the diverse policies and requirements of various donor countries. Most important of all, of course, even "soft loans" pose a difficult repayment problem when they are of substantial magnitude, and a large and increasing fraction of economic assistance is in the form of loans.

Of considerable importance in its effects on agricultural development strategy is the tendency for aid programs to bias investment toward excessive reliance on imported capital equipment. This is in part a consequence of the fact that at times development programs are shaped more by the export interests of a donor country than by the development needs of the receiving country. In his study of aid programs in Uganda, Clark notes that under certain circumstances a country's development plan "becomes skewed to meet the demands, not of a realistic appraisal of the country's economic requirements, but of the conditions laid down for the loans under negotiation. Capital intensive projects have therefore been pushed forward and equipment has been purchased ahead of building up the capacity, the organization and the technique to use it effectively" (Clark, p. 88). And still more important insofar as agriculture is concerned, before the country's structural transformation has reached the point that makes it profitable to invest in labor-saving mechanization. Thus scarce funds and trained personnel are diverted from programs to raise the productivity of the country's abundant resources of labor and land and used for projects of low social marginal productivity. Another risk associated with aid programs is that foreign "experts" with insufficient understanding of the economic and other constraints that prevail are sometimes prone to encourage the allocation of scarce resources for projects that are desirable but which are luxuries, given the harsh realities that should govern priorities in a low-income country. Ghulam Mohammad of the Pakistan Institute of Development Economics has attacked proposals for a costly flood-control program in East Pakistan on the grounds that priority should be given to expanding farm output by irrigation schemes such as low-lift pumps and tubewells that can be executed in a large part of East Pakistan without providing major flood protection works. Although he recognizes that flood protection works will eventually be needed and will make a valuable contribution to the country's welfare, at this stage of the country's development, production should be increased by measures that have much more favorable benefit-cost ratios (Ghulam Mohammad, 1966).

Factors influencing agricultural taxation

It is commonly asserted that because of the political realities and welfare concepts which now prevail, the agricultural sector in underdeveloped countries cannot be expected to make a significant contribution to financing development through private savings and investment or via government taxation. It is a fact that the real burden of agricultural land taxes has been greatly reduced in many of the underdeveloped countries as a result of failure to adjust tax rates in accordance with the rise in price levels since World War II.

Historical factors, including the tendency to associate oppressive land taxes with colonial rule, have contributed to the current reluctance to tax the agricultural sector. Administrative problems in countries where no cadastral surveys have been carried out are another obstacle, and even more difficult problems arise in countries where shifting cultivation and "communal" forms of land tenure prevail.

The limited contribution of agricultural land taxes to government revenue and to raising the level of savings and investment in today's underdeveloped countries stands in sharp contrast to the situation in Meiji Japan. Agriculture's share of government tax revenue was on the order of 85 per cent during the years 1888–92 and still accounted for some 40 per cent in 1918–22. And taxes were important in financing investment as well as current services; government investment represented about 30 per cent of gross domestic fixed capital formation for the period 1887–1936.[5] The government's outlays to extend and improve the rail network, to establish "model" factories, and to subsidize the fledgling merchant marine and the shipbuilding industry were particularly significant.

The inter-sectoral flow of private savings and investment is more difficult to measure, but it is well-known that a sizable fraction of the increased profits of landlords was invested in industrial enterprises, frequently in establishing the small-scale factories that were a conspicuous feature of rural Japan (Smith, 1956). Clear evidence of a net outflow of private funds from agriculture is also provided by studies which show that the deposits of farmers in cooperative banks and other financial institutions were in aggregate much larger than the sums borrowed by farmers (Kato, pp. 8–11).

It cannot be denied that mobilization of capital in the Meiji period was made somewhat easier by the timing of Japan's development. Conditions that might have led to rapid and substantial increases in consumption levels were not present in force; and the continuing strength of tradition and the degree of isolation from outside

---

[5] This figure, which excludes military investment, is given by Landes (p. 100). It is based on Rosovsky (1961), but with a rough adjustment intended to correct the exclusion of agriculture from Rosovsky's estimates.

influence combined to slow or even to postpone "the revolution of rising expectations." Similarly, the "demonstration effect" associated with the development of modern communication techniques and mass media that permit a remote villager to become conscious of the affluence of far away countries as well as the relative affluence of his own urban centers was not adding fuel to popular demands to raise consumption levels as fast or faster than the growth of national product. Dore has suggested that the Meiji government's efforts to act as a damper on social and political change had significant favorable effects on economic development: "The authoritarian exploitation of tradition postponed the establishment of liberal democracy until industrialization and the development of education had sufficiently transformed the social base to give democratic institutions a good chance of stability" (Dore, p. 241). Dore goes on to suggest that because of the welfare-state ideals which have since emerged, an underdeveloped country is "forced to accept responsibilities toward its citizens which, however admirable in themselves, divert into consumption resources needed for economic development" (Dore, p. 242).

Although revenue from land taxes has generally not been of much importance in contemporary underdeveloped countries, the farm sector in a number of these countries has been heavily taxed by explicit or de facto taxes on exports and also by tariff protection and various non-tax policies that have the effect of taxing the agricultural sector. In countries such as Ghana, Nigeria, and Uganda where a substantial part of the increase in proceeds from agricultural exports that resulted from the postwar rise in commodity prices was siphoned off by marketing boards or by export taxes, agriculture has made a major contribution toward financing investment in infrastructure and industrial expansion. Much more widespread have been the efforts by less-developed countries to protect domestic industries by import duties, licensing systems for imports, and currency restrictions or multiple exchange rates. These have had the effect of turning the terms of trade against agriculture, and their quantitative importance as a "tax" on agriculture can be considerable.[6]

---

[6] By the interesting device of computing "implicit exchange rates," S. R.

From an economic point of view these devices for taxing agriculture have significant drawbacks.[7] In the present situation of stable or declining agricultural export prices, marketing board surpluses or export taxes are much less promising as a source of funds to finance development programs than in a period of rising world prices when they represent a tax on "windfall" profits. Moreover, since these taxes fall on marketed output, and are often very heavy, they are likely to have important disincentive effects and lead to distortions in resource allocation, notably in discriminating against crops that earn foreign exchange that is badly needed.

In Nigeria marketing board surpluses were a major source of government "tax" revenue between 1947 and 1954; in the latter year these trading surpluses acually exceeded the total tax revenue of all levels of government. Between 1955 and 1962 the marketing board surpluses brought in only about one-fifth as much revenue as in the previous period and accounted for a relatively small fraction of total revenue as the importance of revenue from import duties and the proceeds from domestic excise taxes had increased considerably (Hinrichs, pp. 35–36).

There would seem to be an acute need in most developing countries for a tax structure that will yield increasing revenue from agriculture as its taxable capacity rises with the increase in cash income that results from growth of domestic markets for purchased agricultural products. Where institution of a land tax is particularly difficult, it may be advisable to place considerable reliance on a graduated "personal tax" assessed and collected locally to defray

---

Lewis has shown that the agricultural sector in Pakistan has been taxed very heavily because of the terms of trade effect of quota and tariff restrictions. He estimates that during 1954/55, when particularly tight quantitative controls on imports were imposed following a trade crisis, Pakistan's farmers received only about Rs. 3.25 per dollar's worth of agricultural products that they sold but paid around Rs. 9.50 per dollar's worth of manufactured products that they bought. Agriculture's terms of trade have subsequently become more favorable as "the disequilibrium of Partition and its aftermath" has been eliminated, but even in the mid-1960's the farm sector received only about Rs. 5.00 for agricultural products worth one dollar but paid Rs. 8.00 for manufactured goods worth one dollar (S. R. Lewis, 1966).

[7] S. R. Lewis provides an excellent analysis of the advantages and disadvantages of various tax and non-tax devices in a paper on "Agricultural Taxation in a Developing Economy" (S. R. Lewis, 1967).

the cost of education and other public services at that level (Due, 1963; U. K. Hicks, 1961). At present these local services are often heavily dependent on grants from the central government, and decentralized administration of land taxes or personal taxes is desirable not only to reduce the huge burden of the central government but also because, as W. A. Lewis has argued, "teaching the people to pay taxes for the services they want is the chief fiscal problem of underdeveloped countries" (W. A. Lewis, p. 129). Japan clearly enjoyed special advantages in the extent to which the Meiji leaders were able to mobilize support, including tax support, for national goals. But even so, prefectural and local authorities were required to raise revenue locally for many public services, including the universal primary education that was made compulsory as a matter of national policy.

The major differences between the conditions faced by Japan and those faced by the contemporary underdeveloped countries accentuate the importance of the problem of "how to extract from the product of agriculture a surplus for the financing of capital formation necessary for industrial growth without at the same time blighting the growth of agriculture" (Kuznets, p. 115). For some countries the problem is primarily one of failing to recognize the importance of developing a tax structure that insures that agriculture makes a contribution to total revenue commensurate with its importance in the economy. Elsewhere there is a need to reform the structure of tax and non-tax devices which add up to a total "tax" burden on agriculture that is sometimes excessive and often inefficient because of its adverse effects on production incentives and resource allocation.

More directly relevant to the present paper is the fact that the type of strategy adopted for achieving an expansion of agricultural output has an important impact on this problem of agricultural taxation. The increase in the taxable capacity and savings potential of the agricultural sector in Japan was large relative to the increase in gross farm income because the expansion of output resulted in such large measure from increasing the productivity of the farm-supplied inputs of land and labor. By the same token rapid industrial expansion was facilitated because the demands of the agricultural sector for the scarce resources of loanable funds and foreign exchange were held to a minimum.

A key issue that has been raised is whether a similar option exists for the contemporary less-developed countries. Ruttan, for example, has argued that the investment requirements for agricultural expansion are so large that, in contrast to the Japanese experience, it is likely that the agricultural sector may require a net flow of capital from the industrial sector (Ruttan, p. 22).

There is no doubt that the developing nations face a formidable challenge in the need to satisfy simultaneously the resource requirements for agricultural expansion and for industrialization—but the fact of rapid population growth accentuates not only the problems of food supply but also those related to achieving the structural transformation that is a necessary condition for sustained economic growth. It is argued shortly that there is currently a very large potential for raising the productivity of the relatively abundant farm-supplied resources. Hence, the needed expansion of farm output can be achieved by measures that yield large returns relative to their cost. Thus Ruttan's gloomy conclusion does not appear to be warranted. If—and the proviso is obviously an important one—an efficient strategy of agricultural development is pursued, the savings potential and taxable capacity of the farm sector can be increased significantly as output is expanded to satisfy the requirements of a developing economy.[8]

Two other interactions between agricultural development strategy and overall economic growth may also be of importance. The broad thrust approach to agricultural development as pursued in Japan would seem to offer a more propitious environment for bringing about changes in knowledge and attitudes with respect to birth control than a pattern of agricultural development that concentrates progress within a small sub-sector of large-scale, capital-intensive agriculture. In addition, a situation in which rising productivity and incomes are achieved by a large majority of the farm population, and in which a part of the increase in cash income is subject to land or personal taxes that do *not* allow exemptions or deductions for dependent children, could have an appreciable impact on the motivations that are a crucial element in the success of family planning.

III. The Choice of Strategy for Agricultural Development

Generalizations with respect to the choice of an efficient strategy for agricultural development are obviously hazardous because of the great variation among countries lumped together as "underdeveloped." This difficulty stems in part from the extreme diversity characteristic of agricultural production, conditioned as it is by particular combinations of climate, soil, and topography, to say nothing of differences in the educational levels and attitudes of the farm population and in the existing institutions that impede or foster agricultural progress. It is equally important to take account of significant differences in the economic milieu—the degree of structural transformation that has taken place, a country's economic size and the bearing that has on its potential for expanding export earnings as compared to domestic sales, the abundance or scarcity of land relative to the size of the farm population, and other factors.

Although it is clearly essential to frame strategies for agricultural

---

[8] Shigeru Ishikawa, like Ruttan, has expressed the view that in contemporary developing countries the agricultural sector is likely to require a net inflow of capital because of the heavy investment requirements for irrigation, flood control, and drainage. His conclusion, however, seems to be influenced considerably by certain characteristics of the structural model that he uses. The hypothetical solutions that he calculates on the basis of alternative values for some of the key parameters in his model leads him to the view that a net outflow of resources from the agricultural sector would be possible only under very special conditions. Cownie's review article demonstrates that his model is biased in that direction because he assumed, for example, that certain critical parameters such as the capital-output ratio and the average product per farm labor unit, remain fixed (Cownie). An important lesson of the Japanese experience, however, is that input-output relationships can be made substantially more favorable through accelerated technological progress and emphasis on new inputs complementary to the relatively abundant on-farm (internal) resources. Ishikawa clearly recognizes that the magnitude of agriculture's requirements for the critically scarce resources will depend a good deal on the type of strategy that is pursued. His excellent discussion of the choice between major and minor water control facilities reflects this viewpoint in the emphasis that he gives to the "investment-inducement effect" of central government subsidies or low-interest loans for small-scale local projects since this approach facilitates the mobilization of local funds and labor because these projects will be of direct benefit to the farmers of the locality (Ishikawa, 1967, pp. 137–53).

development in terms of the unique characteristics of the farm economy of a particular country—and of the various farming regions within a country—this does not mean that each developing country must approach the task of formulating agricultural development policies on a purely ad hoc basis. That would be a counsel of despair because of the complexity of the process. Choice of measures to foster development of agriculture is not merely a matter of choosing among known, existing alternatives. A critical dimension of an efficient strategy of agricultural development is to generate new production possibilities characterized by much more favorable input-output relationships than those obtainable with existing technologies. In Schultz's terminology, expansion of agricultural output "depends predominantly upon the availability and price of modern (non-traditional) agricultural factors" (Schultz, p. 145). But the crucial questions are: *which* "modern agricultural factors" and *what type of strategy* will be most efficient in promoting the development and widespread adoption of appropriate innovations?

Most developing countries face a basic issue of agricultural development strategy that can be crudely defined as a choice between the "Japanese model" and the "Mexican model." Brief reference will be made to the "Stalinist model" and the "Israeli model," but the fundamental choices can be illuminated best by focusing on the contrasts between the Japanese and Mexican models.

Japan and Mexico represent success stories in their respective categories. Both categories include failures as well because the success of efforts to foster agricultural development is by no means assured by the enunciation of appropriate policies. The final outcome depends at least as much upon implementation—upon hard work and vigorous response to economic opportunities on the part of individual farm operators and upon purposeful government action to create and strengthen institutions required to develop and support the use of productive technologies.

In essence the contrast between the Japanese and Mexican approaches to agricultural development lies in the fact that the increase in farm output and productivity in Japan resulted from the widespread adoption of improved techniques by the great majority of the nation's farmers whereas in Mexico a major part of the impressive increases in agricultural output in the postwar period have been the result of extremely large increases in production by a very small number of large-scale, highly commercial farm operators.

In Japan, although there were naturally individual differences in skill, energy, and receptiveness to new opportunities, the bulk of the nation's farmers were involved in the increases in agricultural productivity associated with use of improved varieties, fertilizers and other current inputs, and improved but simple implements such as the short-soled plow, the rotary weeder, and the foot-pedal thresher. But until the 1950's when reliance on purchased inputs began to rise sharply, Japan's farmers continued to rely predominantly on the farm-supplied resources of labor and land, and apart from substantially increased purchases of fertilizer, their reliance on capital inputs remained very limited. The great bulk of the nation's farmers participated in the considerable increase in Japan's total farm output and the somewhat more rapid increase in the marketable surplus.

To a remarkable degree growth of farm output in Mexico has been concentrated in the semi-arid regions in the north where large-scale commercial operators rapidly expanded production of cotton and wheat as major irrigation projects made possible expansion of the cultivated area (W. W. Hicks, 1965). These enterprises were both technically progressive and highly mechanized. The average yield of wheat increased from about 1,000 kilograms per hectare in the early 1950's to over 2,500 kilograms in 1964. Owing to somewhat special circumstances, these large operators were able to obtain ample credit, much of it from large cotton merchandizing firms in the United States. Particularly for cotton production, the technology was largely transferred from the southwestern United States where cotton was being grown under similar ecological conditions. These heavy investments in rather capital-intensive farm enterprises were profitable in part because credit was obtainable on favorable terms, but more basically because the market outlets were available for a rapid expansion of output. In the case of cotton, the export market was especially attractive during the 1950's because of the "umbrella effect" of the United States price support program. Presumably, acreage quotas on cotton in the United States sharpened the interest of the large American merchandizing firms in assisting Mexican producers to expand their output and exports. For wheat, there was a potential for rapid expansion of domestic sales because of the scope that existed for import substitution, together with a fairly rapid increase of total consumption.

This brief account obviously fails to do justice to the complex reality of agricultural development in Mexico. Moreover, Mexico does not contrast as sharply with the Japanese strategy of agricultural development as many other Latin-American countries because of the considerable emphasis in Mexico on agricultural research and rural education. These efforts have contributed to economic progress among some of the small-scale farmers and provide the potential for a considerably greater impact in the near future. Even this sketchy statement should also note that the Mexican land reform had a profound, though largely indirect, impact on development. Although the feudal haciendas were broken up, the actual implementation of the reform permitted large holdings to continue to exist—but on sufferance. Landholding ceased to be important as a source of political power or prestige; it became highly important as a business enterprise for profit-maximizing entrepreneurs able and willing to exploit the economic opportunities that emerged. On the other hand, the difficulty of obtaining credit and a host of other factors contributed to the lack of progress among farmers of the ejidal sector. Although the ejidatarios were supposed to have been the beneficiaries of the land reform, the major benefit seems to have been in its contribution to general economic growth. "Land reform," Flores argues, "gave Mexico a government with a new concern for the people and the nation"; it destroyed the caste system, increased mobility, instilled the idea of progress and personal ambition, and helped create a climate favorable to road building, irrigation programs, and industrialization (Flores, p. 7).

Although it was the large-scale, commercial units of northern Mexico that accounted for the bulk of the increase in farm output, the small-scale farmers of the South Pacific region have also achieved impressive increases in farm output during the past three decades as Reynolds has emphasized in his excellent analysis. The fivefold increase in output between 1929 and 1959 was associated with a doubling of the region's farm labor force and close to a threefold increase in cultivated area. Expansion of cash crops—coffee, cotton, bananas, and cocoa—accounted for much of the growth of output which seems to have had many of the characteristics of the sort of "export explosion" that has been discussed by Myint. Moreover, this expansion in the South Pacific region was achieved by a capital-saving, labor-intensive process; the measurable capital stock actually in creased *less* than output so that the capital-output ratio fell from .3 to .2. A good deal of capital formation in the establishment of tree crops and other types of non-monetary investment is, of course, excluded from the capital stock estimates. The slightly more rapid growth of output in the North Pacific region was associated with a twelvefold increase in capital stock, and the capital-output ratio rose over the 30-year period from .9 to 2.5 (Reynolds).

It is always hazardous to challenge success, and in any event it would seem that the Mexican approach was well-suited to exploiting the opportunities that existed for rapid and profitable expansion of cotton and wheat. It has meant, however, that the bulk of the nation's farmers have been largely bypassed by recent progress, and the Mexican economy is now sharply divided between a relatively affluent sector engaged either in modern industry or the commercial sub-sector of agriculture and a large backwater still eking out an existence in semi-subsistence agriculture. Yet the process of structural transformation has already progressed far enough in Mexico so that in perhaps another twenty or thirty years a large proportion of the small-scale ejidal or private operators will be able to find employment in the modern, high-wage sector of the economy if non-farm employment continues its rapid growth and the rate of increase of population and labor force begins to taper off.

Japan's approach, demonstrating as it does the potential that exists for increasing farm output within the framework of a small-scale, labor-intensive agriculture by the development and widespread adoption of yield-increasing innovations, appears to have great advantages for developing countries with the economic structure characterized by Earlyphasia. The implications of rapid growth of population and labor force examined in Section II point up the fact that the farm labor force will grow in absolute size for some decades and will have low opportunity cost because of the slow increase in non-farm job opportunities. Moreover, the formidable task of transforming the productive structure of an underdeveloped economy under such conditions underscores the importance of increasing farm output by means that make minimal demands on the critically scarce resources of capital and foreign exchange that are indispensable for expansion of the non-farm sectors.

Although the broad strategy pursued in Japan seems to have considerable relevance to many contemporary underdeveloped countries, it certainly does not follow that the techniques that were used to increase farm productivity and output in Japan can merely be copied. In fact, one of the principal lessons to be derived from the Japanese experience is the importance of progressively modifying existing farming systems rather than attempting the wholesale substitution of "modern" for "traditional" agriculture. The specific elements incorporated in programs of agricultural development need to be based on a thorough understanding of a country's existing farming systems and diagnosis of the bottlenecks and potentials for increasing output and productivity that are important in the specific context of its major farming regions. Nevertheless, the nature of the interrelationships between agricultural development and the process of structural transformation that characterize countries of the Early-phasia variety define a subset of possibilities that merit particular attention. On the positive side, this means that it is enormously important to create the conditions necessary for expanding farm output mainly by making available new inputs such as improved varieties, fertilizers, and other biological-chemical forms of capital, improved implements useful for breaking seasonal bottlenecks, and improved technical knowledge inasmuch as these are *complementary* to the farm-supplied resources of labor and land. Fertilizers and other biological-chemical forms of capital also have the important advantage of being highly divisible and therefore neutral to scale and readily incorporated into a system of small-scale farming. Moreover, problems of providing credit are eased because these inputs give a quick payoff. On the negative side, there is a strong presumption against achieving increases in farm output and productivity by relying heavily on the use of the scarce resources of capital and foreign exchange to purchase labor-saving equipment that is mainly a substitution for the resources of low opportunity cost.

Neglect of positive measures to achieve increases in farm output and productivity at low cost and choice of an unduly capital-intensive approach in contemporary underdeveloped countries has been due to various causes. In a number of South American countries it appears to have been largely the result of circumstances that create a discrepancy between the private and social productivity of investment in labor-saving equipment. Where the agricultural sector is characterized by a "dual-size structure," the large landowners often have fairly easy access to capital and technical knowledge and make their investment decisions on the basis of prices that overvalue labor and undervalue land in relation to their opportunity cost. Exchange rates are often below their equilibrium level, and foreign exchange limitations that might curb imports of farm machinery are (temporarily) overcome by loans from countries supplying the machinery. Since large-scale farmers satisfy the bulk of the commercial demand for farm products, the cash income of smallholders and their capacity to make use of purchased inputs is severely limited. Moreover, the "knowledge inputs" required for higher productivity are grossly deficient because a "socio-politically dominant landlord class will rarely be willing to tax itself in order to support such public services as education and agricultural extension" (Nicholls, p. 17).

In many newly independent countries the neglect of measures to enhance the productivity of the farm-supplied resources of labor and land has been a result of policies aimed at creating a "modern" agriculture which is equated with mechanization. The urban-oriented leaders often lack confidence in the possibility of increasing the efficiency of the existing small-scale farm units and even have a tendency to turn their backs on traditional agriculture as something "primitive." In some countries, notably Nigeria, these attempts have made the local leaders receptive to the "Israeli model" as represented by the Moshav type of organization. This has led to an emphasis on government-financed settlement schemes which have absorbed a very large fraction of the financial resources and skilled personnel available. Because of the high cost per settler these schemes have affected only a minute fraction of the nation's farmers, and returns have by and large been unimpressive. Most important, the opportunity cost in terms of the adverse effect on research, extension, and other supporting services has been extremely high (Eicher, 1966).

The tendency of economic planners to be preoccupied with the evaluation of specific "projects" also tends to encourage an unduly capital-intensive approach. Expansion of foreign aid programs for agriculture by organizations such as the World Bank may accentuate this tendency if emphasis is given to loans for individual production units rather than grants to promote expanded output by farmers in a district or region through construction of roads, irrigation facilities, plants for agricultural processing or production of farm inputs, or by making funds available to a local credit agency for loans to small- and medium-size farm units. Loans by an organization like the World Bank for narrowly defined production projects tend to be biased toward a relatively small number of large-scale units which are identifiable as "bankable." This may result in isolated islands of success but is unlikely to represent an efficient strategy for agricultural development. Emphasis on relatively large units is also likely to be based on an *a priori* notion concerning the "economic size" of a farm unit rather than considering the efficient allocation of scarce resources for developing the agricultural *sector*. In particular, there is often insufficient recognition of the fact that the average farm size, or, more precisely, the number of farm workers per cultivated acre, can only be varied within fairly narrow limits. For the reasons considered earlier, in countries of the Earlyphasia variety the farm labor force is large and, for several decades or more will continue to grow nearly as fast as the total labor force. Except where scope exists for substantial expansion of export production, the size of the domestic market will tend to set a limit on the total cultivated area. Thus there is restricted scope for adjusting the relationship between the total cultivated area and the total labor force; and creation of any considerable number of large-scale, capital-intensive units will mean increased overcrowding among the bulk of the nation's farmers and make it more difficult for them to expand their cash income and use of purchased inputs.

Pursuit of what Eckstein has called the "Stalinist model"[9] also encourages preoccupation with large-scale units that are capital-intensive in a very unbalanced way. This reflects in part the tradition in Marxist thought of glorifying bigness and exaggerating the economies of scale in agriculture. The forced consolidation of farmers into collectives in the Soviet Union was also motivated in part by concern about the political power of an independent farm population, but above all the collectivization drive seems to have been motivated by a desire to maximize extraction of food supplies for the non-farm population. The essence of the "Stalinist model" is that an overriding priority is given to the goal of industrialization. So far as agriculture is concerned much more emphasis is given to squeezing agriculture harder than to increasing total farm output. Although extravagant claims were made about the virtues of deep plowing, the real importance of mechanization in the Soviet Union was related to other factors: first, it offset the loss of draft power resulting from the slaughter of livestock by peasants resisting the forced collectivization of Soviet agriculture; second, it facilitated increased production through acreage expansion; and third and most important, the Machine Tractor Stations provided an effective means of siphoning off a large fraction of current output to meet the food needs of the non-farm population so that the farm population, rather than the industrial labor force, became the residual claimants for available food supplies.

It is important to recognize that the appeal of the "Stalinist model" is strengthened when countries rely on alternative methods[10]

---

[9] Tang (1967), presents a highly interesting analysis of the application of the "Stalinist model" to agriculture in Communist China and the USSR.

[10] On the basis of his study of agriculture in the Soviet Union and in Eastern Europe, Karcz has reached the conclusion that command farming is the logical consequence of policies of surplus collection based on coercion and that "the environment of command farming is basically hostile to introduction of new technology and to the dissemination and acceptance of information on new techniques." Hence, the potential that exists for increasing factor productivity in agriculture is not exploited efficiently, relatively little use is made of new inputs such as better seeds, and their impact is reduced by the failure to supply complementary factors (Karcz, 1967b, p. 35). On the basis of his comprehensive analysis of the circumstances leading up to the Soviet regime's decision to rely on coercion, Karcz concludes that the decision was based on erroneous information concerning the nature of the grain procurement problem and a series of inappropriate policy decisions. If it had not been for inept price and fiscal policies and an untimely reorganization of the grain procure-

that prove to be inefficient. Japan's experience demonstrates conclusively that small independent farm units have a distinct advantage because of the scope that exists for increasing productivity of the existing farm-supplied resources which means that the resource requirements for expanded agricultural output can be minimized. But that potential can be exploited only if an efficient strategy of agricultural development is pursued. Agriculture's role in Japan's economic development also points up the need for mechanisms that insure a high marginal rate of saving and investment. Undue solicitude for the short-term welfare of the farm population is apt to be self-defeating if rural tax programs do not help to insure that the agricultural sector makes a significant contribution to the development requirements for capital and tax revenue.

Application of the "Japanese model" in contemporary countries has also been restricted by lack of knowledge with respect to technical innovations capable of achieving increased output at low cost. Japan seems to have been unusual in the extent to which there was a backlog of promising innovations available. Wide diffusion of improved varieties and techniques developed by progressive farmers during the Tokugawa period accounted for much of the increase in output and productivity during the early part of the Meiji period.

Although the backlog of locally developed knowledge is more limited than in Meiji Japan, contemporary underdeveloped countries have the opportunity to exploit a much greater accumulated backlog of scientific knowledge and research techniques that can be transferred at relatively small cost. Thus, the international transfer of technical innovations provides a potential for enormously favorable benefit/cost ratios. But this potential obviously cannot be exploited at zero cost, and research budgets in many underdeveloped countries have been close to zero, at least in comparison with the sums devoted to agricultural research in economically advanced countries. Inasmuch as most of today's underdeveloped countries are located in the tropics or subtropics whereas the in-

---

ment apparatus, the crisis of 1927/28 could have been prevented and "it would have been possible to avoid catastrophic decline in livestock herds, the necessity of devoting huge amounts of scarce capital to the task of merely replacing the loss of draught power, and the tying up of much scarce administrative talent in the apparatus of control and compulsion" (Karcz, 1967a, pp. 429–30).

dustrialized countries are in temperate regions, the possibilities for *direct* borrowing are distinctly limited. Nevertheless, there is no longer room to doubt that there is a tremendous potential for increased output and productivity in the tropics and subtropics, provided that agricultural research programs are strengthened and focused on a set of priority programs determined in accordance with an efficient strategy of agricultural development.

Until recently the strongest evidence with respect to the potential for highly profitable yield-increasing innovations applicable to the tropical and subtropical regions related to export crops. Striking increases in yields of cocoa, coffee, oil palm, and other export crops can be obtained with relatively modest increases in production costs. In view of the very limited allocation of resources for research relating to food crop production it is not surprising that the progress in evolving valuable innovations applicable to those crops has been much more limited. But for the three food crops that have received considerable attention in recent years—maize, rice, and wheat—the prospects range from good to spectacular. These highly significant developments have been reviewed in an earlier paper (Johnston, 1966, pp. 292–93), and subsequent developments provide further evidence of the profound impact that high-yielding varieties and chemical fertilizers will have in increasing output of those major crops.[11]

---

[11] The Mexican dwarf varieties of wheat are having an impact on wheat production in West Pakistan and in the Indian Punjab that can only be described as spectacular. In spite of one of the worst droughts on record, in 1966/67, Pakistani farmers planted 250,000 acres of the Mexican wheat which had only been introduced two years earlier. With the increased availability of seed resulting from the great increase in area this year, it is estimated that 4 to 5 million acres—about half the total irrigated area in West Pakistan—will be planted to the Mexican varieties in 1967/68. The use of fertilizers, which was negligible just a few years ago, rose from 70,000 tons of N and P_2O_5 in 1966/67 to about 150,000 tons in 1967/68, and is likely to be at least 260,000 tons in 1968/69 (Ghulam, personal communication, May 9, 1967). In Kenya, the rapid adoption by smallholders of hybrid and synthetic varieties of maize, together with fertilizers and a complement of improved practices, has had a similarly dramatic impact on production of the country's major crop. It appears that the high-yielding varieties developed by the International Rice Research Institute will have a similarly dramatic impact in the areas where growing conditions are well suited to the new rice varieties such as IR-8 and IR-5.

In some countries realization of these potentials will require heavy investment in irrigation and drainage works. It has been suggested that the type of facilities required to serve the broad river valleys and plains of Southeast Asia will give rise to investment requirements that will be much larger and more capital-intensive than in Japan and Taiwan where short river valleys and narrow coastal plains could be served by locally organized, small-scale, and labor-intensive irrigation and drainage works (Hsieh and Ruttan, 1967). In an efficient strategy for agricultural development, outlays to improve and extend water control should obviously be associated with the introduction of improved varieties, fertilizers, and associated practices in order to fully exploit the potential for greatly increased yields. Under those conditions investments in extending irrigation facilities can be phased over a considerable period of time, and therefore the annual interest and amortization costs need not be large relative to the associated increases in output even though the individual projects are large.

IV. Conclusion

The thesis of the present paper can be summarized very briefly. Japan's experience with respect to agriculture's role in economic development emphasizes the importance of the opportunity which contemporary underdeveloped countries have to exploit the potential that exists for drastically raising crop yields at relatively low cost in terms of the scarce resources of capital and foreign exchange. In the light of the formidable task that these countries face in transforming the structure of their economies, it would appear to be of the greatest importance for them to seize this opportunity and, further, to ensure that suitable fiscal and related measures are taken so that a sizable fraction of the increment in net farm incomes is channeled into investments that promote the process of structural transformation. Although much more is required to achieve success in such an effort, this would seem to be a necessary condition. Needless to say, it is important to avoid stifling the incentives that are essential for agricultural progress, and considerations of equity dictate that the already low levels of living of traditional farmers should not be further depressed. But, as is suggested by Geertz's analysis of the effects of abortive development on the peasant population of Java, it is equally important that "they should not suffer for nothing."

Success in Japan was dependent not only on appropriate policy decisions but also on their effective implementation, including an energetic response on the part of the mass of the nation's farmers. The question arises whether there was something unique about the ability of officials and entrepreneurs in Japan to pursue a goal with determination or in the capacity for hard work that was characteristic of Japanese farmers. In their interesting analysis of Taiwan's experience, which in important respects parallels that of Japan, Hsieh and Lee assert that "the main secret of Taiwan's development" was "her ability to meet the organizational requirements" (Hsieh and Lee, 1966, pp. 103, 105).[12] They even suggest that this aspect of Taiwan's experience is "unique" and may not be transferable to other countries. But is not the real point that there are organizational requirements that must be fulfilled, institutional and other obstacles that must be overcome, not that these are capacities possessed only by the Taiwanese, the Japanese, or certain other population groups.

The means whereby the requirements will be met and the obstacles overcome will no doubt have important "unique" features in every situation. The expansion and strengthening of education is likely to be a powerful influence in most countries given the commitment to that goal in so many of the developing nations. Moreover, the availability and adoption of more productive technologies and the presence of more and more examples of individuals who have seized new economic opportunities and profited thereby is a powerful yeast that is at work in many countries of Asia, Africa, and Latin America. The earlier view that peasant farmers respond perversely or not at all to economic incentives has now been pretty well discredited. Evidence accumulates that a goodly number of the unique

---

[12] Their discussion is strongly influenced by Brewster's brilliant analysis of the way in which traditional social structures and their associated attitudes can impede growth (Brewster, 1967). My earlier paper also utilizes Brewster's analysis in considering at some length the reasons why the Meiji leaders were able to make and implement policy decisions which appear to have been so appropriate and why the response on the part of the mass of the people was so energetic (Johnston, 1966, pp. 254–65, 300).

population groups around the world share a pervasive human tendency to seize economic opportunities—and to create and staff the various organizations essential for the development and widespread application of more productive technologies.

This is not to deny that it is a difficult, time-consuming task to "break the cake of custom," to create an institutional environment that fosters rather than impedes growth. Nor is it to deny that there are significant differences among social groups—especially at a given point in time—in their receptiveness to change and readiness to not only accept but devise innovations. The fundamental point is that there are cogent reasons that suggest that this type of approach is feasible and advantageous and which therefore justify the effort to create the conditions, institutional as well as technological, that are needed to expand farm output mainly by raising the productivity of the farm-supplied resources of labor and land.

For reasons suggested earlier, it may seem tempting to ignore the mass of the rural population and concentrate resources in an effort to develop a really modern sub-sector of large-scale, capital-intensive units in the expectation that in due course the families thus bypassed will be absorbed with the growth of output and employment in industry and large commercial farm enterprises. The analysis of "population growth and the arithmetic of structural transformation" in Section II suggests, however, that this is simply not a realistic expectation for most of the contemporary underdeveloped countries. As was emphasized in Section II, the farm labor force in Japan did not increase during the Meiji period because of the fairly moderate rate of growth of the total population and labor force associated with rapid growth of non-farm employment. But when population and labor force are growing at 2 or 3 per cent annually and agriculture still accounts for 70 to 80 per cent of the total labor force, the transformation of the structure of an economy is bound to be a slow and difficult process.

Under such conditions the prospect is that the farm labor force will double or triple over the next fifty years, and much more than a half century will elapse before the turning point is reached when the farm population begins to decline in absolute numbers. Hence the need for the underdeveloped countries to devise and implement measures that will bring about a lowering of birthrates—and within societies that are still predominantly agrarian. Not the least of the advantages of a strategy of agricultural development that involves the bulk of the farm population is the likelihood, as suggested earlier, that this will provide a relatively propitious environment for fostering the changes necessary to the spread of family planning.

Finally, there are persuasive considerations which suggest that the long-term goal of economic growth, as well as the welfare of the bulk of the population who will unavoidably remain in agriculture for some decades at least, will be far better served if agricultural development strategy is directed at raising the productivity of the existing small-scale, labor-intensive agriculture. The potential that exists for increasing productivity through yield-increasing innovations with fairly small investments in fertilizers and other complementary inputs means that labor-substituting investment can be deferred until the non-farm population that depends on purchased food becomes fairly large relative to the farm labor force. This also means that a higher proportion of the scarce resources of capital and foreign exchange can be allocated to the expansion of output and employment in the non-farm sectors. This type of strategy for agricultural development appears to have a further advantage because it encourages the growth of a decentralized, labor-using, capital-saving industrial sub-sector capable of making a highly significant contribution to increasing incomes and facilitating productivity increases in agriculture by providing plows, pumps, carts, and a host of other inputs that become important as the need and ability of farmers to rely on purchased inputs increases.

REFERENCES

Brewster, J. M., "Traditional Social Structures as Barriers to Change," *Agricultural Development and Economic Growth,* H. M. Southworth and B. F. Johnston, eds., Ithaca: 1967.

Chenery, H. B. and Strout, A. M., "Foreign Assistance and Economic Development," *The American Economic Review* (September, 1966).

Clark, Ralph. *Aid in Uganda—Programmes and Policies.* Overseas Development Institute, London: 1966.

Cownie, John, "Economic Development in Asian Perspective: A Review Article," *The Developing Economies* (June, 1968).

Dore, R. P., "Latin America and Japan Compared," *Continuity and Change in Latin America,* J. J. Johnson, ed., Stanford: 1964.

Dovring, Folke. *Productivity of Labor in Agricultural Production.* University of Illinois College of Agriculture Agricultural Experiment Station Bulletin 726, Urbana: 1967.

Due, J. F. *Taxation and Economic Development in Tropical Africa.* Cambridge: 1963.

Eicher, C. K., "Transforming Traditional Agriculture in Southern Nigeria: The Contemporary Experience," Paper presented at the 9th Annual Meeting of the African Studies Association, Bloomington, Indiana: October, 1966.

Falcon, W. P., "Agricultural and Industrial Interrelationships in West Pakistan," *Journal of Farm Economics* (December, 1967).

Falcon, W. P. and Gotsch, C. H. *Agricultural Development in Pakistan: Past Programs and Future Prospects.* Harvard University, Center for International Affairs: unpublished data, 1966.

Fei, J. C. H. and Ranis. *Development of the Labor Surplus Economy: Theory and Policy.* Illinois: 1964.

Flores, Edmundo. *Land Reform and the Alliance for Progress.* Princeton University, Center for International Studies, Memorandum No. 26, May, 1963.

Geertz, Clifford. *Agricultural Involution: The Process of Ecological Change in Indonesia.* Berkeley: 1963.

Gerschenkron, Alexander. *Economic Backwardness in Historical Perspective.* New York: 1965.

Goreux, Louis Marie, "Prospects for LDC's Agricultural Trade," Paper presented at the Conference on the Role of Agriculture in Economic Development, Princeton: December 1967 (proceedings forthcoming).

Ghulam, Mohammad, "Development of Irrigated Agriculture in East Pakistan: Some Basic Considerations," *Pakistan Development Review* (Autumn, 1966).

Hayami, Yujiro, "A Critical Note on Professor Tang's Model of Japanese Agricultural Development," *Kikan Riron Keizaigaku,* 15, No. 3 (1965).

Hicks, Ursula K. *Development from Below.* London: 1961.

Hicks, W. W. *The Agricultural Development of Mexico, 1940–1960, with Special Emphasis on Cotton and Wheat Production in Northern Mexico.* unpublished Ph.D. thesis, Stanford University, California: 1965.

Hinrichs, H. H. *Mobilizing Government Revenues for Development in Nigeria.* (unpublished data, 1966).

Hsieh, S. C. and Lee, T. H. *Agricultural Development and Its Contributions to Economic Growth in Taiwan.* Joint Commission on Rural Reconstruction, Economic Digest Series No. 17, Taipei: 1966.

Hsieh, S. C. and Ruttan, V. W., "Environmental, Technological, and Institutional Factors in the Growth of Rice Production: Philippines, Thailand, and Taiwan," *Food Research Institute Studies,* VII, No. 3 (1967).

Inukai, Ichirou and Tussing, A. R. *Kōgyō Iken: Japan's Ten Year Plan, 1884.* University of Alaska, mimeo., n.d., a revised version of a paperp resented by Professor Inukai at the Colloquium of the Center for Japanese and Korean Studies of the University of California, Berkeley, December 13, 1965.

Ishikawa, Shigeru. *Economic Development in Asian Perspective.* Tokyo: 1967.

Japan Bureau of Statistics, Office of the Prime Minister. *Statistical Handbook of Japan 1965.* Tokyo: 1965.

Johnston, B. F., "Agricultural Development and Economic Transformation: A Comparative Study of the Japanese Experience," *Food Research Institute Studies,* III, No. 3 (1962).

——, "Agriculture and Economic Development: The Relevance of the Japanese Experience," *Food Research Institute Studies,* VI, No. 3 (1966).

Jones, G. W., "The Growth and Changing Structure of the Indonesian Labour Force, 1930–81," *Bull. Indonesian, Econ. Studies,* No. 4 (June, 1966); data reproduced in D. H. Penny, "Indonesia's Agricultural Economy," May 1968 (chapter for inclusion in *Agricultural Development in Asia,* R. H. Shand, ed., forthcoming).

Karcz, J. F., "Thoughts on the Grain Problem," *Soviet Studies* (April, 1967a).

——, "Comparative Study of Transformation of Agriculture in Centrally Planned Economies: The Soviet Union, Eastern Europe and Mainland China." Paper presented at the Universities-National Bureau Committee for Economic Research Conference on the Role of Agriculture in Economic Development, Princeton: December 1–2, 1967b.

Kato, Yuzuru, "Mechanisms for the Outflow of Funds from Agriculture into Industry in Japan," *Rural Economic Problems* (December, 1966).

Kikuchi, Baron. *Japanese Education.* London: 1909.

Kuznets, Simon, "Economic Growth and the Contribution of Agriculture: Notes on Measurement," *Agriculture in Economic Development,* C. K. Eicher and L. W. Witt, eds., New York: 1964.

Landes, D. S., "Japan and Europe: Contrasts in Industrialization," *The State and Economic Enterprise in Japan,* W. W. Lockwood, ed., Princeton: 1965.

Lewis, J. P. *Quiet Crisis in India.* New York: 1964.

Lewis, S. R., "Implicit Exchange Rates, Relative Prices, and the Efficiency of Industrial Growth in Pakistan," Preliminary version of Chapter VI of a monograph on *Economic Policy and Industrial Growth in Pakistan,* Center for Development Economics, Williams College, Williamstown, Massachusetts: August, 1966.

——, "Agricultural Taxation in a Developing Economy," *Agricultural Development and Economic Growth,* H. M. Southworth and B. F. Johnston, eds., Ithaca: 1967.

Lewis, W. A. *Development Planning.* New York:1966.

McKinnon, R. I., "Intermediate Products, Differential Tariffs, and a Generalization of Lerner's Symmetry Theorem," *Quarterly Journal of Economics* (November, 1966).

Myint, Hla. *The Economics of Developing Countries.* London: Hutchinson University Library, 1965.

Nicholls, W. H., "An 'Agricultural Surplus' as a Factor in Economic Development," *Journal of Political Economy* (February, 1963).

Ogura, Takekazu, ed. *Agricultural Development in Modern Japan.* Tokyo: 1963

Ohkawa, Kazushi, "Agriculture and Turning Points in Economic Growth," *The Developing Economies,* III (December, 1965), pp. 471–86.

Okita, Saburo, "Choice of Techniques: Japan's Experience and Its Implication," *Economic Development with Special Reference to East Asia,* Kenneth Berrill, ed., New York: 1964.

Oshima, H. T., "Meiji Fiscal Policy and Agricultural Progress," W. W. Lockwood, ed., *The State and Economic Enterprise in Japan.* Princeton: 1965.

Reynolds, C. W., "Agrarian Revolution in Mexico: A History of Agricultural Production and Productivity, 1900–1960," *The Structure and Growth of the Mexican Economy: 1900–1960,* Chapter 3 (forthcoming).

Rosovsky, Henry. *Capital Formation in Japan, 1868–1940.* New York: 1961.

Ruttan, V. W., "Considerations in the Design of a Strategy for Increasing Rice Production in South East Asia," Paper prepared for presentation at the Pacific Science Congress Session on Modernization of Rural Areas, Tokyo: August, 1966.

Sawada, Shujiro, "Review of Johnston (1962)," *Rural Economic Problems,* (November, 1964.)

Schultz, T. W. *Transforming Traditional Agriculture.* New Haven: Yale University Press. 1964.

Smith, T. C. *The Agrarian Origins of Modern Japan.* Stanford: 1959.

——, "Landlords and Rural Capitalists in the Modernization of Japan," *Journal of Economic History* (June, 1956).

Tang, A. M., "Agriculture in the Industrialization of Communist China and the USSR," *Journal of Farm Economics* (December, 1967).

PART II

CHAPTER 4

AGRICULTURAL PRODUCTIVITY AT THE BEGINNING OF INDUSTRIALIZATION[†]

Yūjirō Hayami and Saburō Yamada

Industrialization and modern economic growth are basically conditioned by the level of agricultural productivity inherited from the pre-modern period. On the basis of the growth experiences of Western nations, especially England, an agricultural revolution and a subsequent rise in agricultural productivity are often considered prerequisites for take-off or the initial spurt of industrialization.[1] This hypothesis is called the "prerequisite thesis."

According to a well-established thesis postulated primarily on official government statistics, the economic growth of Japan is unique in that the rapid growth of agricultural productivity from a level prevalent in monsoon Asia occurred not before, but side by side with, industrialization.[2] The concurrent growth in agriculture and industry has been considered to suggest a model applicable to the development of Asian countries today. In the model the rapid rise in agricultural productivity within the framework of a traditional peasant agriculture performs a crucial role in generating agricultural surpluses during the process of industrialization. We will refer to this model as the "concurrent growth thesis."

The validity of the concurrent growth thesis largely depends on the reliability of the government statistics. It is well-known, however, that the statistics of the early period of economic development, as

---

[†] We wish to gratefully acknowledge suggestions received from Professors B. F. Johnston, R. Komiya, S. Kuznets, K. Ohkawa, J. Tsukui and M. Takeuchi.
[1] For example, see Rostow, p. 24.
[2] For statements of this thesis see Ohkawa (1964) and Ohkawa and Rosovsky (1960).

well as those of today's underdeveloped countries, are of limited reliability. The general tendency is to underestimate output in the early stage of economic development due to incomplete coverage. Moreover, in the initial stage, the Japanese government started to collect statistics for the assessment of taxation (Kojima, 1958). It is natural to infer that there existed a tendency to underestimate agricultural production due to the farmers' efforts to conceal or under-report output. On these grounds James Nakamura, not without reason, challenged the concurrent growth thesis in his *Agricultural Production and the Economic Development of Japan, 1873–1922* (hereafter referred to as *Nakamura-A*). He has insisted that the official statistics underestimate agricultural production for the early period of Meiji by 30 to 50 per cent and the growth rates of output and productivity derived from the government statistics are over-estimated by several orders of magnitude. Thus, he postulated an alternative hypothesis that, by the beginning of industrialization, agricultural productivity in Japan had reached a level considerably higher than that in today's Asian countries and that the creation of the institutions to exploit the already existing surpluses and/or the dispossession of the unproductive feudal ruling class made it possible to extract funds for industrialization. For Nakamura, a sufficiently high level of agricultural productivity capable of generating agricultural surpluses was a prerequisite for industrial development in Japan, too. In this regard Japan was no exception to the Rostovian generalization, based on the experience of Western countries, in following a determined order or sequence of industrial development.

In judging which of these two theses, i.e. the prerequisite or the concurrent growth thesis, is more suitable, we are faced with essentially an empirical, not a logical, problem. We are fortunate that for this task we now have the new estimates of historical statistics for agriculture and forestry which have recently been compiled in the ninth volume of the *Long-Term Economic Statistics* (*LTES,* IX). It is the aim of this essay to clarify the issues in conflict on the basis of the *LTES,* IX data which will in turn require that the reliability of the *LTES,* IX estimates themselves be deliberately tested. First, we shall compare our new estimates with the previous estimates in order to give quantitative perspective to the problem. Second, the reliability of the rice yield data we used will be evaluated for its consistency. Third, the plausibility of the *LTES,* IX and the Nakamura series will be compared using an analysis of food consumption data. Finally, the implication of our findings for the general development model will be discussed.

I. *Initial Levels and Growth Processes*

What was the agricultural productivity in Japan at the beginning of industrialization as compared with the level prevailing in monsoon Asia today? Taking the rice yields per unit of area planted as the best available indicator of agricultural productivity for Asian countries, we see that even the government figures, the lowest among the three types of estimates in Table 1, indicate that the level of rice yield per hectare in Meiji Japan was high in comparison with that of Asian countries today. Considering the most unfavorable man-land ratio, however, the level of labor productivity of Meiji Japan would rank among the lower levels of Asian countries. The *LTES,* IX estimates, some 9 per cent higher than the official statistics, place Japan close to the level of Korea and Taiwan, implying that labor productivity in Meiji Japan would have been about the average of today's Asian countries.[3] These estimates, however, are entirely different from Nakamura's figures.[4] According to his data, by the beginning of modern economic growth, the productivity of rice cul-

---

[3] Rice yield per hectare planted may not be an appropriate measure to compare land productivities between Japan and Taiwan. Taiwan's land productivity is higher than the rice yield per hectare planted indicates because double cropping of rice is a common practice in most areas in Taiwan. More appropriate measures would be the aggregate of summer crop (rice) and winter crops (wheat, barley, rape seeds, etc.) for Japan and the aggregate of double rice crops for Taiwan per unit of paddy land area. Since such measures are not easily available, we were obliged to use the rice yield per hectare as the measure for comparison.

[4] Nakamura presumed three alternative linear growth paths in the national average of per-*tan* rice yields from 1874–77 to 1918–22: (1) a high growth path from 1.5 *koku* to 2.0 *koku,* (2) a medium growth path from 1.6 *koku* to 1.95 *koku* and (3) a low growth path from 1.7 *koku* to 1.9 *koku.* Corresponding to those are the three different series of total agricultural production. Henceforth in this paper when we refer to Nakamura's figures, unless otherwise noted, they are the one based on his medium growth path of rice yield from 1.60 *koku* to 1.95 *koku.* This is just for expository purposes and our conclusion will be largely unaltered if one considers his alternative series.

TABLE 1

Comparison of Rice Yields and Man-Land Ratios between
Japan and Other Countries in Monsoon Asia*

	Rice yields per unit of area planted		Arable land area[b] per farm worker (ha./worker)
	Paddy[a] (ton/ha.)	Brown rice *(koku/tan)*	
Japan, 1878–1882			
Official	2.36	1.20	—
LTES	2.53	1.29	0.326
Nakamura	3.22	1.64	0.334
Japan, 1918–1922			
LTES=Official	3.79	1.93	0.433
Nakamura	3.83	1.95	0.435[c]
Monsoon Asia, 1953–62			
Philippines	1.17	—	1.31 (1961)
India	1.36	—	1.28 (1960)
Thailand	1.38	—	0.77 (1960)
Pakistan	1.44	—	1.72 (1961)
Burma	1.49	—	1.74 (1959)
Ceylon	1.57	—	0.91 (1954)
Indonesia	1.74	—	0.75 (1954)
Malaya	2.24	—	1.76 (1958)
Korea	2.75	—	0.45(1961)
Taiwan	2.93	—	0.45 (1960)
Japan	4.73	—	0.43 (1960)

* Official rice yields per unit of area planted, from the Ministry of Agriculture and Forestry, *Historical Statistics of the Ministry of Agriculture and Forestry (Norinsho Ruinen Tokeihyo)* (1955), pp. 24–25.
LTES rice yield figures from *LTES*, IX, p. 37.
Nakamura rice yields data from *Nakamura-A*, p. 92.
Monsoon Asia rice yield data from FAO, *World Rice Economy in Figures 1909–1963* (1965), pp. 17–18, 23–24.
    LTES arable land area data from *LTES*, IX, pp. 216–217.
Nakamura arable land area data from *Nakamura-A*, pp. 43, 48.
Monsoon Asia arable land data from FAO, *Production Yearbook* (1961–1965), p. 3–9; except in case of Thailand for which data is from the Ministry of Agriculture, *Agricultural Statistics of Thailand* (1960), p. 154.
    The number of farm workers data for Japan for 1878–1882 and 1918–1922 from *LTES*, IX, pp. 226–227.
Monsoon Asia data for the number of farm workers from I.L.O., *Yearbook of Labor Statistics* (1965), pp. 40–225, except for Burma and Taiwan for which the data are taken from Chujiro Ozaki, "Economic Growth and Agriculture" (Ajia ni okeru Keizaiseicho to Nogyo), *Ajia Keizai*, VI (Nov. 1966), pp. 52–63.
a) Japan's figures for 1878–1882 and 1898–1921 were obtained by multiplying the rice yields per *tan* in terms of brown rice by 1.964, which is based on the following conversion factors:
    1 metric ton of paddy is equal to 0.77 tons of brown rice
    1 *koku* of brown rice is equal to 0.15 metric tons
    1 *tan* is equal to 0.099174 hectare.
b) Figures in parentheses specify the years in which land area was measured.
c) The sum of corrected are planted to paddy rice and corrected area of dry land crop fields.a

ture in Japan had nearly surpassed that of present day levels in other Asian countries.

Corresponding to such different estimates of the initial level, we have different views of agricultural growth. In Table 2 the growth rates of agricultural production and productivities are compared for the period 1878–1882 to 1918–1922. We will tentatively identify the first two decades as the period of take-off or initial spurt of industrialization in which light industries such as cotton spinning and silk reeling were established. By 1920, the end of the second two-decade period, Japan had established herself as an industrial nation with half of her labor force engaged outside of agriculture and with about 70 per cent of national income generated in the non-farm sector. It was during those four decades that agriculture continued to be a net supplier of capital to industry.[5]

There exist great differences between the growth rates in Ohkawa's *GRJE* which are primarily based on the official statistics and those of *Nakamura-A* which completely deny the reliability of the official statistics. For the initial phase of the industrial spurt, in terms of gross output, the rates of growth in production and labor productivity in *GRJE* are as much as triple those in Nakamura, and land productivity rates are seven times as great. It is interesting to note that the *LTES,* IX estimates for the growth rate of output lie just in between those of *GRJE* and *Nakamura-A* for the initial phase.[6]

If we accept Nakamura's figures, we must be aware of the profound difference in the implications of *Nakamura-A* and *GRJE* estimates. If we accept Nakamura's conjecture that the initial level of rice yield was 3.2 tons per hectare of paddy, and if we also accept

---

[5] Since the 1920's, the net flow of capital seems to have been reversed, i.e. from industry to agriculture. See Ohkawa and Rosovsky (1960).

[6] All figures shown in Table 2 should be judged with allowance for sizable margins of error. In addition to measurement errors we cannot escape from the index number problem. In *LTES,* IX we have constructed 10 indices of gross agricultural production and 6 indices of value added in agriculture with different formulas and weights. It was found that, with few exceptions, growth rates calculated from those indices are within the range of 10 to 20 per cent of medium figures. Henceforth in this paper we will resort to the indices (those specified at the notes in Table 2) which give medium rates of growth. In our discussion, however, allowances of 10–20 per cent must always be kept in mind.

his assertion that such a high level is required as a prerequisite for industrialization, Asian countries today would have little chance for take-off. On the contrary, if we accept *GRJE*'s position, even the nations with the lowest agricultural productivity would have a good chance to attain rapid industrialization.

TABLE 2

Annual Compound Rates of Growth in Output, Inputs and Productivities*

		1878–1882 to 1898–1902	1898–1902 to 1918–1922	1878–1882 to 1918–1922
Agriculture production				
LTES	Gross[a]	1.8	2.1	2.0
	Net[b]	2.0	1.8	1.9
GRJE	Gross	2.8	2.1	2.4
	Net	2.7	1.6	2.2
Nakamura Gross		0.9	1.2	1.0
Farm labor (no. of workers)		−0.2	−0.1	−0.1
Arable land area		0.6	0.6	0.6
Man-land ratio (land/worker)		0.8	0.6	0.7
Labor productivity				
LTES	Gross	2.0	2.2	2.1
	Net	2.2	1.9	1.9
GRJE	Gross	3.0	2.2	2.5
	Net	2.5	1.7	2.3
Nakamura Gross		1.1	1.3	1.1
Land productivity				
LTES	Gross	1.2	1.5	1.4
	Net	1.4	1.2	1.3
GRJE	Gross	2.2	1.5	1.8
	Net	2.1	1.0	1.7
Nakamura Gross		0.3	0.6	0.4

* *LTES* agricultural production data from *LTES*, IX.
Gross agricultural production data from *LTES*, IX, Series 10 in Table 35, pp. 225–233.
Net production data from *LTES*, IX, Series 6 in Table 13, pp. 182.
GRJE production data from *GRJE*.
Gross production figures from *GRJE*, pp. 58, 130.
Net production data from *GRJE*, pp. 72–73, 130.
Nakamura agricultural production figures from *Nakamura-A*, p. 115.
Farm labor data from *LTES*, IX, Series 4 in Table 37, pp. 226–227.
Arable land area data from *LTES*, IX, Series 14 in Table 32, pp. 216–217.
a) Gross refers to gross agricultural production.
b) Net refers to value added in agriculture.

The point in conflict must be clarified by a detailed critique of the materials on which the various estimates were based.[7] But even at the outset it would seem unlikely, as Nakamura contends, that Japan, during her feudal era, could have attained a level of productivity that Korea and Taiwan, under similar climatic conditions and techniques of rice cultivation (transplanted systematically from Japan during the 1920's and 1930's of this century), have not attained to this day. It is hard to believe that the land productivity of the pre-modern Japanese agriculture which relied on *karishiki* (cut wild grasses) and human excrement as the primary source of plant nutrients could surpass that of present-day Korea and Taiwan whose commercial fertilizer input levels are now close to those of present-day Japan.[8]

On the other hand, the *GRJE* growth rates, 2.8 per cent per annum in output and 3.0 per cent in labor productivity, seem too high for the initial spurt of industrialization. Data for European countries for the comparable periods, though extremely vulnerable, suggest that the *GRJE* growth rates are unmatched in Europe. Gross farm output and output per male worker in France increased respectively by 1.3 and 1.0 per cent per annum from 1825–34 to 1855–64, the period of take off for the French economy (Toutain, pp. 126–127, 207). Agricultural production rose by 1.7 per cent and output per worker by 1.6 per cent per annum in Sweden from 1861–65 to 1891–95 (Clark, p. 268). In Germany agricultural production increased by 1.9 per cent and output per worker by 1.3 per cent per annum for 1816–61 (Hoffman, p. 103). The growth rate of agricul-

---

[7] We made a complete critique of the materials on which *Nakamura-A* was based, including those of rice yield levels in the premodern period (Hayami, 1968).

[8] Quantities of three basic plant nutrients contained in commercial fertilizers consumed per hectare of arable land in Japan, Korea and Taiwan were (in kilograms):

	N	P_2O_5	K_2O
Japan (1878–82)	5	4	4
Japan (1953–62)	102	60	71
Korea (,,)	75	24	3
Taiwan (,,)	112	35	28

Data are from *LTES,* IX for 1878–82 and FAO, *Production Yearbook* for 1953–62 (fertilizer consumed are ten-year averages, and land areas are those of 1960 for Japan and Taiwan and of 1961 for Korea).

tural output seems much higher in Russia with crop production (including all grains) in the fifty provinces of European Russia increasing from 1885–95 to 1905–14 by 2.3 per cent per annum (Goldsmith, pp. 369–386). But, since the rual population in Russia increased from 81.6 million in 1897 to 102.7 million in 1916 (Timoshenko, p. 26), the annual growth rate in labor productivity could well be less than 2 per cent. Compared with the above European levels, it would be natural to ask how Japanese agriculture, without drastic changes in the man-land ratio, could have attained such dramatic rises in output and productivity as those suggested in *GRJE*.

The picture which emerges from the *LTES*, IX estimates is the following: what Japan inherited from the pre-modern period as initial conditions in agriculture in terms of today's Asian levels was a high land productivity, an unfavorable man-land ratio and an average labor productivity. From this starting point Japanese agriculture grew at a high, but not exceptionally high, rate for the initial phase of modern economic growth which permitted the generation of agricultural surpluses to finance industrialization. The *LTES*, IX estimates thus provide evidence basically in support of the concurrent growth thesis, but do deny the uniqueness of the speed of the growth of Japanese agriculture as suggested by the *GRJE* figures. On this point we concur with the view in *Nakamura-A*.

The conclusion suggested by the *LTES*, IX data may seem reasonable but, of course, the real test is the reliability of these estimates which we will attempt to test in the following sections. Since the *LTES*, IX series are obvious improvements on the *GRJE*'s estimates relying largely on the same data while correcting obvious defects and enlarging the coverage, comparison will be made primarily with *Nakamura-A*.[9]

II. Consistency Test of Rice Yield Series

In this section we will test the reliability of the *LTES*, IX series

---

[9] In this paper we do not go into a detailed discussion on why the revisions of *GRJE* such as embodied in *LTES*, IX were made because this has already been done in *LTES*, IX. See especially pp. 4–14 and pp. 31–51 of the volume. English readers may refer to pp. 130–135 of the English summary.

of per-hectare rice yields in terms of their consistency with the relevant series of inputs. It is generally agreed that three kinds of improvements underlie the increases in rice yields in Japan: (1) improvements in seeds, (2) increased application of fertilizer and (3) land improvement including better irrigation and drainage facilities. The former two factors were together the key to the growth in rice yields at the stage of Japanese agricultural development with which we are concerned.[10] If changes in the rice yield in a series are consistently explained by the movements in seed improvements and fertilizer inputs, the plausibility of the estimates will be considerably greater.

We already have estimates of fertilizer inputs (Hayami, 1963). Here we will construct an index of improvement in rice seeds. As presented in Appendix A-I, we have estimated areas planted in major improved varieties of rice (pp. 130-31).[11] On the basis of data collected from the reports of experiment stations we have specified in Appendix A-II (pp. 132-33) certain standard levels of per-*tan* yields for respective varieties which we assume constant for the whole period. Those standard levels are averaged by using the planted areas in respective periods in Appendix A-I as weights. The resultant figures for national average yields at the experiment station levels are what we will call the index of rice seed improvements. We have constructed the index only for 1893–1937. Before that we have little information on the varieties planted, and no meaningful results could be expected by extending the index construction.[12]

---

[10] We share the view of Ishikawa that by the beginning of modern economic growth Japan had completed the transition from the stage in which irrigation is the leading input to the stage in which fertilizer in combination with seed improvements constitute the leading input (Ishikawa).

[11] We have grouped the varieties other than the major improved varieties together under the label "traditional varieties." However, all of those "traditional" varieties are not necessarily traditional. Some improved varieties are included in the "traditional varities" because they did not spread widely and, hence, did not obtain nationwide recognition. The later the period, the more will be the percentage of such local improved varieties in the "traditional varities." Therefore, the constancy of the standard level of the yield of the "traditional varieties" in the following analysis is an unrealistic assumption, though we have to make it due to data limitations.

[12] We cannot expect any useful information to be procured by extending the series over the years in which the weight of the "traditional varieties" dominates.

The rice seed improvement index and the series of fertilizer inputs per unit of arable land area are compared with the rice yield series in Table 3. In order to check the consistency of the *LTES*, IX series of rice yields, *Y*, with the seed improvement index, *X*, and the fertilizer inputs, *Z*, we estimated the log-linear regressions of *Y* on *X* and *Z*. This was done for two *Z*-series: one for commercial fertilizer, Z_1, and the other for total fertilizer, Z_2 (aggregate of commercial fertilizers and self-supplied fertilizers such as manure, green manure, composts and night soil). Theoretically, the latter is the more appropriate series for the regression, but the reliability of data is decisively higher in the former.

TABLE 3

Rice Yields per *Tan*, Seed Improvement Index and Fertilizer
Input per *Tan*, Five-Year Averages, 1893–1937*

LTES=Government Series of rice yields (*koku/tan*) Y	Seed improvement index[a] X	Fertilizer input per *tan* 1934–36 constant *yen*[b]	
		Commercial Z_1	Total Z_2
1893–1897[c]	1.43	2.59	6.1	46.5
98–1902[c]	1.52	2.61	7.4	48.2
1903– 07	1.63	2.68	10.3	51.4
08– 12	1.73	2.70	17.7	58.3
13– 17	1.84	2.72	21.9	63.1
18– 22	1.93	2.73	29.6	69.0
23– 27	1.88	2.72	36.6	76.8
28– 32	1.91	2.72	44.4	87.1
33– 37	2.01	2.76	48.0	97.6

 *   Rice yield data from the Ministry of Agriculture and Forestry, *Historical Statistics of the Ministry of Agriculture and Forestry (Norinsho Ruinen Tokeihyo)* (1955), pp. 24–25.

   Fertilizer input data from Yujiro Hayami, "Measurement of Fertilizer Input (Hiryo Tokaryo no Suitei)," *Nogyo Sogo Kenkyu*, XVII (1963), pp. 247–260.

a) Seed improvement index is constructed by the authors in the way explained in the text of the paper.

b) Current price series deflated by the price indices.

c) In order to adjust for the extraordinarily bad crop in 1897, the 1897 yield was replaced by the average of 1895, 1896, 1898 and 1899.

In order to assert that our yield series are consistent, the regression coefficients of *X* and *Z* must be estimated positive and significantly different from zero at standard significance levels. Also, the suitability of the fit of the equation must be great without much serial correlation in the residuals. We have one more condition for the consistency check: the coefficient of Z must be significantly smaller than 1, which implies a decreasing return to fertilizer input. It is generally known that the dramatic rise in fertilizer input accompanied the decline in marginal physical productivity, especially after the 1920's, in spite of the efforts made in seed improvements to overcome the trend toward decreasing returns.[13] The results of the regression estimates are shown on Figure 1 which compares the original observations with the values expected from the regressions. All the conditions for the consistency of the rice yield series are beautifully met. It is especially encouraging to see that the kink in the rice yields at around 1920 is explained well by the regressions.

The above analysis confirms the consistency of the $LTES=$government series of rice yields per *tan* back to 1893–97.[14] This does not necessarily disprove the adequacy of Nakamura's estimates, however. What he did actually was only to ascertain the levels of per-*tan* rice yields for 1874–77 and 1918–22 (their medium levels are 1.6 *koku* and 1.95 *koku*, respectively). He did not make any assertion on the path between the 1874–77 level to the 1918–22 level, though he used linear interpolation for illustrative purposes. It is possible, at least theoretically, for Nakamura to presume an equally consistent series connecting the two base periods, though it would be next to impossible to construct such a series from any convincing evidence. What we can say from our analysis is that the $LTES=$ government series extending back to 1893–97 have a greater likelihood because they are consistent as they stand.

Accepting the $LTES=$government series which extend back to 1893–97 on the basis of the consistency test, we will proceed to evaluate the rice yield levels at the beginning of industrialization. We have the Z_1 series back to 1878 and the Z_2 series to 1883. We may extrapolate Z_2 to 1878 by the exponential trend from 1883–87 to 1893–97. Far more risky is the extrapolation of the X-series. We have tried two kinds of extrapolation of X: one uses the growth rate from 1893–97 to 1898–1902 (quinquennial rate of 0.77 per cent) and

---

[13] See as evidence Hayami (1967), p. 29.
[14] It is only before 1890 that the government statistics of per-*tan* rice yields are corrected for *LTES*, IX.

the other uses the one from 1893–97 to 1903–07 (quinquennial rate of 1.72 per cent).[15] Yields expected from the regressions with those

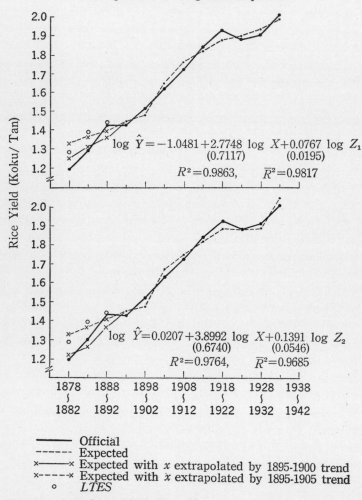

FIGURE 1

Comparison of Rice Yields: Official, *LTES* and Expected from Regression Equations

$$\log \hat{Y} = -1.0481 + 2.7748 \log X + 0.0767 \log Z_1$$
$$(0.7117) \qquad (0.0195)$$
$$R^2 = 0.9863, \qquad \bar{R}^2 = 0.9817$$

$$\log \hat{Y} = 0.0207 + 3.8992 \log X + 0.1391 \log Z_2$$
$$(0.6740) \qquad (0.0546)$$
$$R^2 = 0.9764, \qquad \bar{R}^2 = 0.9685$$

Rice Yield (Koku/Tan)

——— Official
----- Expected
×———× Expected with x extrapolated by 1895-1900 trend
×----× Expected with x extrapolated by 1895-1905 trend
  ○   *LTES*

* Data from Table 3 and *LTES*, IX, p. 37.

[15] Regression estimates of the quinquennial growth rate on the observations from 1893–97 to 1918–22 is 1.13 per cent. Values of X and Y extrapolated by this rate fall within the boundaries formed by the two kinds of extrapolation.

extrapolated, dependent variables are plotted on Figure 1. The *LTES*, IX yields are within the boundaries formed by the yields expected from the regressions while the government statistics are out of the boundaries for the initial period. This may be taken as evidence for the adequacy of the *LTES*, IX correction of the government statistics.

III. Check on Calorie Consumption

In this section the reliability of the *LTES*, IX production statistics will be tested against an analysis of food consumption. National aggregate food consumption may be calculated roughly as food production plus imports minus exports. The international trade statistics are known to be highly reliable; therefore, if the series of aggregate food consumption thus calculated are adequate, the production statistics can be considered adequate.

The adequacy of food consumption levels can be best discussed in terms of calories. In fact, Nakamura used as evidence the estimates of calorie intake by Nakayama which were based on government production statistics (Nakayama, 1958). Nakayama's estimates for the calorie intake of earlier periods are clearly below subsistence as shown in Table 4. Even assuming a 10 per cent greater amount was supplied from sources omitted in Nakayama's estimates such as fish and sugar, the intake of 1351 calories per day per capita is inadequate.

We have used the *LTES*, IX production statistics instead of the government's in the estimation of calorie consumption. Our estimation largely follows Nakayama's procedures,[16] and our results are compared with his in Table 4; 1668 calories per day per capita for 1874–77 seems too low. We are inclined to admit there exists underestimation in the *LTES*, IX production statistics for that quinquennum. But, the level for the next quinquennum 1878–82, 1795 calories, is comparable with the estimate of 1730 calories for the Philippines or 1850 calories for India during 1954–56 given by the FAO's Food Balance Sheets. The reasonableness of our estimates of calorie consumption levels should be evaluated in economic as well as physiological terms.

---

[16] See Appendix B, p. 134.

TABLE 4

Estimates of Calorie Intake per Day per Capita, Five-Year Averages, 1874–1927*

Period	Nakayama estimates			Hayami-Yamada estimates[a]				
	Staple foods[b]	Livestock products	Total	Staple foods[b]	Livestock products	Others[c]	Total	Per consumption unit[a]
1874–1877	—	—	—	1571	2	94	1,668	2,138
78– 82	1,349	2	1,351	1,669	3	123	1,795	2,319
83– 87	1,520	3	1,523	1,732	5	144	1,880	2,435
88– 92	1,830	3	1,833	1,861	7	165	2,033	2,623
93– 97	1,876	7	1,883	1,873	9	178	2,060	2,658
98–1902	1,941	7	1,948	1,907	11	188	2,105	2,727
1903– 07	2,006	8	2,014	1,975	12	185	2,172	2,836
08– 12	2,119	9	2,128	2,021	14	190	2,225	2,897
13– 17	2,084	10	2,094	2,031	16	216	2,263	2,954
18– 22	2,189	12	2,201	2,087	20	269	2,375	3,092
23– 27	2,031	15	2,046	1,987	25	308	2,320	3,021

* Data for Nakayama estimates from Seiki Nakayama, "Long-term Trend of Food Consumption in Japan, 1878–1955 (Shoku-ryo Shohi no Choki Henka ni tsuite)," *Nogyo Sogo Kenkyu*, XII (1958), pp. 13–38.
a) Hayami-Yamada estimates have been constructed as explained in Appendix B, p. 134.
b) Grains, potatoes, and pulses.
c) Marine products, sugar, vegetables and fruits.
d) Total calorie consumption divided by the total population in terms of consumption units (equal to male aged 20–29 years).

First, the estimates will be evaluated in economic terms. The criterion for evaluation should be the magnitude of income elasticity for calorie consumption. A problem in the estimation of income elasticity is that the *GRJE* national income series is now being completely revised.[17] Therefore, at this stage we have no alternative but to use our own tentative estimates of national income given in Appendix C (p. 135).

The income elasticities we estimated on the quinquennial observations from 1878–82 to 1823–27 are presented in Table 5.[18] We made two kinds of estimation: one based on simple per capita calorie consumption figures and another on calorie consumptions per consumption unit (equivalent to a male of 20–29 years old). How adequate are our calorie intake figures in terms of the estimated income elasticities? International comparison reveals that no other country except Greece with a per capita national income of less than 300 U.S. dollars has an income elasticity of calorie consumption in 1950–58 lower than that of Japan of 1878–1927. Since any possible underestimation of agricultural production was largely eliminated by 1920, the internationally low income elasticities of calorie consumption suggest there exists little possibility of underestimation in our estimates of calorie consumption and, hence, in the *LTES*, IX production statistics we used for the earlier periods.

It might be that the estimates of income elasticities based on quinquennial data over a half century are not comparable with those based on eight years' annual observations. International cross-section analysis which similarly estimates the long-run equilibrium relation over a wider income range incorporating the changes in consumption patterns that accompany economic development might provide coefficients for a more appropriate comparison. In Figure 2, FAO's data on per capita calorie consumption in 1957–59 are

---

[17] Forthcoming in *LTES*, I.

[18] $\log C_1 = 2.972 + 0.183 \log I, \quad r^2 = 0.918$
$\phantom{\log C_1 = {}} (0.038)\ (0.019)$

$\log C_2 = 3.071 + 0.190 \log I, \quad r^2 = 0.923$
$\phantom{\log C_2 = {}} (0.038)\ (0.019)$

where C_1 is simple per capita calorie intake, C_2 is per consumption unit calorie intake and I is national income per capita in 1934–36 *yen*.

TABLE 5

International Comparison of Income Elasticities for Calorie Consumption*

	Income elasticity	Per capita national income (1958 US Dollars)
Japan, 1878–82 to 1923–27		
Simple per capita	0.18	122 (218)[a]
Per consumption unit	0.19	
Time series, 1950–1958		
India	0.64	69[b]
Taiwan	0.33	90[b]
Philippines	0.44	113[b]
Ceylon	0.49	116[b]
Brazil	0.29	126[b]
Turkey	0.18	245[b]
Portugal	0.21	248[b]
Greece	0.12	287[b]
Mexico	0.30	317[b]
Spain	0.23	331[b]
Japan	0.20	370[b]
International cross-sections		
Hayami-Yamada		
all countries	0.16	650[b]
less than NI $300	0.20	173[b]
Jureen[c]	0.12	125
Ohkawa[d]	0.11	420

* The coefficient of income elasticity estimate for Japan, 1878–1882 to 1923–1927 based on the information collected by the authors. Time Series 1950–1958 data from FAO, *Agricultural Commodities Projection for 1970* (1962), *Annex on Methods*, A 14–15.

Hayami-Yamada international cross-sections estimates based on data collected by the authors.

Jureen international cross-section estimate from Lars Jureen, "Long-term Trends in Food Consumption: A Multi-Country Study," *Econometrica*, XXIV (Jan. 1956), pp. 1–21.

Ohkawa's international cross section estimate from K. Ohkawa, "Conditions of Economic Progress in Agriculture (Nogyo Sinpo no Shojoken)," *Nogyo Sogo Kenkyu*, II (Oct. 1948), pp. 103–137.

Per capita national income estimate for Japan, 1878–1882 to 1923–1927 based on the national income data as collected by the authors (See Appendix C to this paper) and Population data from the Bank of Japan, *Hundred Year Statistics of the Japanese Economy (Honpo Shuyo Keizai Tokei)* (1966), pp. 12–13.

Time series, 1950–1958 estimate of per capita income based on the national income data in U.N., *Yearbook of National Accounts Statistics* (1963), pp. 3–297; and Population data from U.N., *Demographic Yearbook* (1962), pp. 130–141.

a) Figures in parentheses indicate the average of 1923–1927, while figures not in parentheses indicate the average of 1878–1927.

b) National incomes in 1958 were converted into U.S. dollars with the help of purchasing parity rates and then divided by the mid-year population to obtain · per capita income.

c) Inserted $r=100$ U.S. dollars in 1949 prices ($=125$ dollars in 1958 prices) into $E(r)=13/(r+13)$

d) 245 International Units of Colin Clark$=420$ U.S. dollars in 1958 prices.

plotted against 1958 per capita national income by country. In spite of the wide range of income, the log-linear equation seems to be an adequate representation of the relation. Income elasticities estimated on the cross-country data,[19] especially the one for nations with per capita incomes of less than 300 US dollars, are quite compatible

FIGURE 2
International Comparison of Calorie
Consumption Per Capita per Day in
Relation to National Income Per Capita

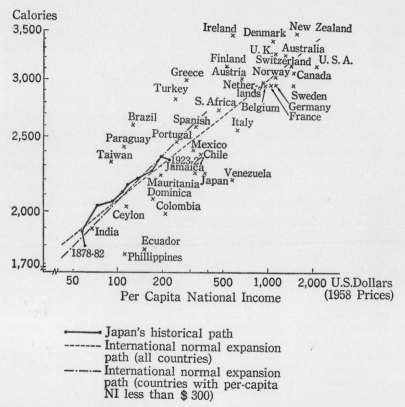

———— Japan's historical path
------- International normal expansion
path (all countries)
—·—·— International normal expansion
path (countries with per-capita
NI less than $ 300)

---

[19] For all 37 countries:

$$\log C = 3.001 + 0.158 \log I, \qquad r^2 = 0.637$$

and for 13 countries of which national income per capita is less than 300 U.S. dollars:

$$\log C = 2.917 + 0.198 \log I, \qquad r^2 = 0.257$$

where C is per capita calorie intake and I is national income per capita.

with the estimates for 1878–1927 of Japan. It is rather surprising to see how well Japan's historical income-consumption expansion path fits the normal international expansion paths.

Some of the previous studies of calorie consumption on the basis of international cross-section data may be noted. If we insert the average per capita income for 1878–1937 into Jureen's estimate of income elasticity in Tornquist form (Jureen, 1956), we obtain an income elasticity of 0.12.[20] Of course, it is dangerous to make inferences about this level of income of Jureen's equation which was estimated from the data of high income countries in Europe. An income elasticity of 0.11 can be derived from Ohakwa's study on food consumption and calorie cost which was based on Colin Clark's income data for around 1930 (Ohkawa, 1948).[21] This figure, too, does not contradict the coefficients estimated for Japan of 1878–1927 when we take into account the differences in income levels.

At the most conservative estimate, the income elasticity of calorie consumption for the level of income which prevailed in Japan for the period concerned could not be lower than 0. 1 on the basis of all international evidence. If we take Nakamura's word that under-reporting prevailed in field crops at a degree similar to that of rice, the calorie supply from staple food products must be raised by about 25 per cent over our estimates for the initial period.[22] This would make the average calorie consumption per day per capita 2270 for the decade 1878–87. Considering the arable land area in *Nakamura-A* is about 2 per cent larger than in *LTES,* IX for that

---

[20] Average national income per capita in Japan for 1878–1927 was 105 yen in 1934–36 prices, equivalent to 122 U.S. dollars in 1958 prices. Since the consumer price index in the U.S. as computed by the Bureau of Labor Statistics rose by 21.3 per cent from 1949 to 1958, we may consider 122 U.S. dollars in 1958 are about equivalent to 100 dollars in 1949 for which Jureen's income data were prepared. By substituting 100 dollars for r in Jureen's estimate of income elasticity (Jureen, 1956):

$$E\ (r) = \frac{13}{r+13} \text{ , we obtain } E\ (r) = 0.12 \cdot$$

[21] The average national income of the 28 countries for which Ohkawa's analysis was conducted was 245 in terms of Colin Clark's International Unit, i.e ., par to a 1929 U.S. dollars. From 1929 to 1958 the consumer price index of BLS rose by 68.5 percent; we may consider 245 IU's are about equivalent to 420 U.S. dollars in 1958 prices.

[22] See *Nakamura-A,* p. 92–95.

decade,[23] Nakamura's agricultural production statistics would give per capita calorie consumption for 1878–87 equal to or even larger than 2290, the average of the fifteen years from 1913 to 1927. In other words the conjecture of Nakamura on agricultural production and productivity in the early Meiji period presumes the income elasticity of calorie consumption was zero in Japan at a level of income of less than 200 U.S. dollars at 1958 prices.[24] All available international comparative evidence contradicts such a presumption.

We will now turn to an evaluation of our calorie consumption data from the standpoint of human physiology. Western scholars seem to feel the level of 1800 calories per day per capita is "threateningly low" or "semi-starving."[25] Calorie requirements are, however, dependent on body size; therefore our estimates of calorie consumption for early periods must be checked with the data on the body sizes of Japanese people. Information on the long-term changes in body size are obtained from two sources: one is the records of physical examinations at conscription by the Ministry of the Army and the other is the records on the body sizes of grade-school children by the Ministry of Education. As shown in Table 6, steady

---

[23] The arable land area for 1878–87 calculated as the sum of the corrected area planted to paddy (*Nakamura-A*, p. 43) and the corrected national upland field area (*Nakamura-A*, p. 48) is 4.91 million cho, some 1.8 per cent larger than then 4.82 million *cho* in *LTES*.

[24] By inflating Nakamura's agricultural production index in *Nakamura-A*, p. 114 by the *LTES*, IX agricultural price index, we would obtain the value of agricultural production in current prices which is consistent with Nakamura's assertion. Compared with the *LTES*, IX estimates, the gross value of agricultural production, thus calculated, is about 30 per cent larger and the value added 60 per cent larger for 1878–87. By substituting this figure for the *LTES*, IX estimate of value added in agriculture in Appendix C, the national income for the period will be raised by 30 per cent. The average national income calculated in this way for 1878–1927 is, however, 131 dollars in 1958 prices, only 7.4 per cent larger than 122 dollars, our tentative estimate in Appendix A. Also, even admitting that the national income tentatively calculated for the early periods follows Nakamura's assertion, national income would have almost tripled during 1878–1927. It must be noted that in the estimation of national income in Appendix C, we used Shionoya's estimates of value produced in manufacturing industries which make the value added in manufacturing almost 70 per cent larger than those obtained from the index of Nagoya Commercial College for 1878–87.

[25] For instance, see Farnsworth (1958).

TABLE 6
Changes in Body Sizes*

	Army conscription[a] height	Grade-school children					
		8 years		10 years		12 years	
		Height	Weight	Height	Weight	Height	Weight
	cm	cm	kg	cm	kg	cm	kg
1883–1892(A)	156.5[b]	—	—	—	—	—	—
1898–1907(B)	157.4	110.9[c]	19.2[c]	120.1[c]	22.9[c]	128.5[c]	27.0[c]
1913–1922	158.6	111.6[d]	19.3[d]	120.9[d]	23.2[d]	129.6[d]	27.5[d]
1928–1937(C)	160.1	113.6	19.9	123.1	24.0	131.8	28.6
	%	%		%		%	
(C−A)/A ×100	2.3	—	—	—	—	—	—
(C−B)/B ×100	1.7	2.4	3.6	2.5	4.8	2.6	5.9

* Data from Mataji Umemura and Ryoshin Minami, *Population and Labor Force, LTES*, II (forthcoming).
a) At 20 years of age.
b) Average for 1884–88 and 1891–92.
c) Averages for 1900, 1902, 1904 and 1906–07.
d) Averages for 1914–16, 1919–20 and 1922.

growth in height and weight are evident over the period concerned. Needless to say such growth in stature should have required a larger amount of calories. On the basis of this evidence alone, Nakamura's presumption of constancy in calorie consumption seems to be unfounded.

In 1941 the Ministry of Welfare published a report on food requirements in Japan in which it is estimated that the standard calorie requirement for 21–30 year old male performing medium labor is 2500 calories (Committee on Resource Survey, p. 103). Basic calorie requirements are known to be proportional to the surface area of body. The relation between body surface area, A, weight, W, and height, H, estimated by Dr. Takahira as

$$A = 72.46 W^{0.425} H^{0.725}$$

was used in that report (Committee on Resource Survey, p. 26). The above equation implies that 1 per cent increases in weight and height are associated respectively with increases of 0.425 and 0.725 per cent in basic calorie requirements. Now, judging from Table 6 we may rather conservatively assume the average height and weight of Japanese increased by 2.5 and 5 per cent respectively from 1880 to 1940. Hence, average calorie requirements for a 21–30 year old male in the period around 1880 should have been 4 per cent less than 2500, that is, 2400. Our estimate of calorie consumption per consumption unit (equivalent to a 20–29 year old male) for 1878–82 is only 3 per cent less than 2400, which is within the allowance for errors. On this account we may say that our estimates of calorie intake were neither "threateningly low" nor "semi-starving."

IV. Conclusion

On the basis of the evidence provided from the preceding analysis we may take the *LTES*, IX series of agricultural production and productivities as largely reliable which would further imply that the picture of agricultural development drawn from the *LTES*, IX data could also be taken as reliable. To reiterate, Japanese agriculture, given the initial conditions in terms of today's Asian countries, a high land productivity, an unfavorable man-land ratio and about average labor productivity, achieved rapid growth concurrently with the initial spurt of industrialization. The tempo of growth is, however, not so fast as was indicated by the *GRJE* series. It now appears that the growth rates of agricultural production and productivities in the take-off period were relatively high but not exceptionally high compared with Japan's Western counterparts. Thus, the Japanese experience was not unique in this respect.

To offer a generalization based on evidence that is not yet complete, Japan's experience was only a specific case of the general pattern common to relative latecomers to industrialization. We recall the famous thesis of Gerschenkron that backward countries who do not possess certain "prerequisites" for industrialization can find their substitutes (Gerschenkron, pp. 31–51). At the beginning of industrialization Japan did not possess a sufficiently high level of agricultural productivity, but she found a substitute not recognized by Gerschenkron, namely the concurrent growth of agricultural productivity with industrialization.[26] The general pattern manifested in the faster growth of Japanese agriculture might be "the later the start the faster the growth." It seems that the useful lessons, if any, to be derived from the study of the Japanese growth experience may be found by seeking the generally applicable patterns in Japan's seemingly unique growth process.

REFERENCES

Clark, Colin. *The Conditions of Economic Progress*. 3rd ed., New York:Macmillan, 1957.

Committee on Resource Survey, Board of Science and Technology, Ministry of Welfare. *1959 Revision on the Requirements of Japanese for Nutrition (1959 Kaitei Nihonjin no Eiyō Shoyōryō ni tsuite)*. 1959.

Farnsworth, Helen, "The Role of Wheat in Improving Nutritional Status and Labor Productivity in Lesser Developed Countries," *International Wheat Surplus Utilization Conference Proceedings*, Dept. of Economics, South Dakota State College: 1958, pp. 52–65.

Gerschenkron, Alexander. *Economic Backwardness in Historical Perspective*. Cambridge: Harvard University Press, 1962.

Goldsmith, R. W., "The Economics of Tsarist Russia 1860–1913," *Econ. Develop. and Cult. Change*, IX (Apr. 1961), pp. 369–386.

---

[26] How this was made possible would be the most fascinating topic in the analysis of the Japanese growth experience. We are in a position to stress the existence of backlog or potential of technology accumulated in the feudal period and its realization with the Meiji Reforms. See Hayami and Yamada (1968).

Hayami, Yujiro, "Measurement of Fertilizer Input (Hiryō Tōkaryō no Suitei),"
Nōgyō Sōgō Kenkyū, XVII (Jan. 1963), pp. 247–260.
——, "Structural Changes in Fertilizer Demand and the Two Phases of
Agricultural Development (Hiryō Jūyo Kōzō no Henka to Nōgyō Hatten
no Nikyokumen)," *Econ. Studies Quarterly,* XVII (March, 1967).
——, "On the Japanese Experience of Agricultural Growth," *Rural Economic
Problems,* IV, No. 2 (May, 1968), pp. 79–88.
Hayami, Yujiro and Yamada, Saburo, "Technological Progress in Agriculture,"
Economic Growth—The Japanese Experience since the Meiji Era, L. Klein
and K. Ohkawa, eds. Chicago: Richard D. Irwin, 1968, pp. 135–161.
Hoffman, W. G., "The Take-off in Germany," *The Economics of Take-off into
Sustained Growth,* W. W. Rostow, ed., New York: Macmillan, 1963, pp.
95–118.
Ishikawa, Shigeru. *Conditions for Agricultural Development in Developing Asian
Countries, CTES, No. 42.* Tokyo: Committee for Translation of Japanese
Economic Studies, The International House of Japan.
Jureen, Lars, "Long-term Trends in Food Consumption: A Multi-country
Study," *Econometrica,* XXIV (Jan. 1956), pp. 1–21.
Kojima, Toshihiro, "On the Statistical Survey of Agriculture in Meiji Era
(Meiji Nōgyō Tōkei no Mondai Ishiki)," *Nōgyō Sōgō Kenkyū,* XII (Oct.
1958), pp. 77–100.
Nakamura, James, I. *Agricultural Production and the Economic Development
of Japan, 1873–1922.* Princeton: Princeton University Press, 1966.
Nakayama, Seiki, "Long-run Trend of Food Consumption in Japan, 1878–1955
(Shokuryō Shōhi Suijun no Chōki Henka ni tsuite)," *Nōgyō Sōgō Kenkyū,*
XII (Oct. 1958), pp. 13–38.
Ohkawa, Kazushi, "Conditions of Economic Progress in Agriculture (Nōgyō
Shinpo no Shojōken)," *Nōgyō Sōgō Kenkyū,* II (Oct. 1948), pp. 103–137.
——, "Concurrent Growth of Agriculture and Industry: A Study of the
Japanese Case," *International Explorations of Agricultural Econhmics,*
D. N. Dixey, ed., Ames, Iowa: Iowa State University Press, 1964, pp. 201–
212.
——, Shinohara, M., Umemura, M., Ito, M., Noda, T. *The Growth Rate of the
Japanese Economy Since 1878.* Tokyo: Kinokuniya, 1957.
——, Shinohara, Miyohei and Umemura, Mataji, eds. *Estimates of Long-Term
Economic Statistics of Japan Since 1868.* 13 Volumes, Tokyo: Toyo Keizai
Shinposha.
—— and Rosovsky, Henry, "The Role of Agriculture in Modern Economic
Development," *Econ. Develop. and Cult. Change,* IX (Oct. 1960), pp. 43–
67.
Rostow, W. W. *The Stages of Economic Growth.* Cambridge: Cambridge Univ.
Press, 1960.
Timoshenko, Vladimir, P. *Agricultural Russia and the Wheat Problem.* Stanford:
Food Research Institute, 1932.
Toutain, J. C. *Le Produit de l'agriculture francaise de 1700 à 1958: II, La
croissance.* Paris: L'institut de Science Economique Appliquee, 1961.

APPENDIX A: Data for the Construction of Seed Improvement Index.

1. Eastern prefectures: Aomori, Iwate, Miyagi, Akita, Yamagata, Fukushima, Ibaragi, Tochigi, Gunma, Chiba, Saitama, Tokyo, Kanagawa, Niigata, Nagano, Yamanashi, Shizuoka, Aichi.

   Western prefectures: Toyama, Ishikawa, Fukui, Gifu, Mie, Shiga, Kyoto, Osaka, Hyogo, Nara, Wakayama, Tottori, Shimane, Okayama, Hiroshima, Yamaguchi, Tokushima, Kagawa, Ehime, Kochi, Fukuoka, Saga, Nagasaki, Kumamoto, Oita, Miyazaki, Kagoshima.

2. Areas planted in individual varieties in the original data are grouped into the specified varieties by prefectures which are in turn aggregated into Eastern and Western Regions.

3. Areas planted in respective varieties are assumed to increase linearly from the years of their selection to 1907 by prefectures.

4. Rōnō varieties are the improved varieties selected by the Rōnō (veteran farmers) (See Hayami and Yamada, 1968). The Rōnō varieties in the following tables include those which were improved by experiment stations after selection by farmers.

5. Traditional varieties include improved varieties which can not be specified here.

6. 1 koku = 150 kilograms (husked, brown rice)
   1 cho = 10 *tan* = 0.99174 hectare

Sources:

Ministry of Agriculture and Forestry. *Suitōhinshu no Hensen to Ikuseihinshu no Tokusei Narabini Fukyūjōkyo no Gaiyō (Summary Report on Changes in Rice Varieties and the Characteristics and Diffusions of Improved Varieties)*. 1953.

———. *Suitōhinshubetsu Sakuzuke Menseki Chōsasho . . . 1951 . . . (Survey Report on Area planted in Respective Rice Varieties in 1951)*. 1952.

———. *Ine Mugi Hinshu no Tokuseihyō (Tables of Characteristics of Rice, Wheat, Barley and Naked Barley)*. 1955.

——. *Suirikuto Mugirui Shōreihinshu Tokuseihyō* (*Tables of Characteristics of Selected Rice, Wheat, Barley and Naked Barley*). 1964.

——. *Suitō oyobi Rikutō Koshu Yōkō* (*Report on Rice Cultivation*). 1936.

Nōgyō Hattatsushi Chōsakai, Meijiikōni okeru Suitōhinshu no Hensen (*Changes in Rice Varieties since the Meiji Era*). 1955.

Appendix: TABLE A-1-1

Areas Planted in Rice by Varieties: Eastern Prefectures

(Unit: 1,000 chō)

	1875	1880	1885	1890	1895	1900	1907	1910	1919	1928	1932	1936	1939	1946	1951	1956	1963
Rōnō varieties																	
Aikoku					4	23	143	142	176	253	249	221	197	97	149		
Asahi									1	38	73	95	111	152	123	17	
Kameno-o							17	52	133	121	70	21	12	6	3		
Omachi							1	3									
Shinriki					2	27	80	82	110	63	34	28	22	7			
Others																	
Bōzu					3	22	67	66	61	131	203	209	148	28	31		
Gin-bōzu										35	72	92	81	29	37		
Ishiziro					1	5	15	17	25	15	12	3	2	17	14		
Oba							4	4	5	4	3						
Takenari			1	3	7	19	37	29	5								
Experiment station Varieties																	
Prewar selection																	
Norin numbers											11	73	179	370	383	276	55
Rikuu-132											121	212	210	62	63	19	
Others											5	15	55	54	47	222	64
Postwar selection																	
Norin numbers														18	157	462	470
Others															28	217	274
Major improved																	
Varieties total			1	3	17	96	364	395	516	660	853	969	1,017	840	1,035	1,213	1,133
Traditional varieties	1,150	1,187	1,192	1,228	1,224	1,152	922	923	858	826	696	558	436	547	451	389	556
Total	1,150	1,187	1,193	1,231	1,241	1,248	1,286	1,318	1,374	1,486	1,549	1,527	1,453	1,387	1,486	1,602	1,689

Appendix: TABLE A-I-2

Areas Planted in Rice by Varieties: Western Prefectures

(Unit: 1,000 chō)

	1875	1880	1885	1890	1895	1900	1907	1910	1919	1928	1932	1936	1939	1946	1951	1956	1963
Rōnō varieties																	
Aikoku									21	54	86	86	79	38	62		
Asahi									12	81	296	435	481	285	296	40	
Omachi	1	3	5	7	12	41	122	113	96	40	28	17	9		3		
Shinriki	1	1	10	28	72	211	440	441	500	318	171	68	49	28	30		
Others																	
Gin-Bōzu									6	28	62	80	57	29	23		
Ishiziro			1	4	7	14	25	19	13	15	16	14	15	10			
Kameji								3	21	26	37	29	24	7	9		
Oba					2	18	45	51	52	29	22	5	2				
Takenari					1	3	14	7	8								
Experiment station																	
Varieties																	
Prewar selection																	
Nōrin number												42	79	330	394	320	125
Rikuu-132													1	1	8		
Others														5	46	321	142
Postwar selection																	
Nōrin number														1	104	338	475
Others															14	144	176
Major improved Varieties total	1	4	16	39	94	287	646	634	729	591	718	776	796	734	989	1163	918
Traditional varieties	1,338	1,378	1,364	1,442	1,390	1,213	888	918	836	953	824	734	679	598	426	320	552
Total	1,339	1,382	1,380	1,481	1,484	1,500	1,534	1,552	1,565	1,544	1,542	1,510	1,475	1,332	1,415	1,483	1,470

Appendix: TABLE A-II-1

Rice Yields per *Tan* by Varieties in Experiments: Eastern Prefectures   (Unit: *koku*)

	Number of experiments	Parameters			Standard levels	Remarks on the standard levels[a]
		Arith. mean	Median	Upper quartile		
Rōnō Varieties						
Aikoku	43	2.83	2.8	3.0	3.0	Upper quartile
Asahi	17	2.71	2.7	2.8	2.7	Median
Kameno-o	16	2.82	2.8	3.1	2.8	Median
Omachi	—	—	—	—	2.9	Same as western prefectures
Shinriki	37	3.04	3.0	3.5	3.0	Median
Others						
Bozu	16	2.54	2.6	2.9	2.6	Median
Gin-bōzu	11	2.75	2.8	3.0	2.8	Median
Ishiziro	4	2.79	2.7	2.7	2.7	Median
Oba	—	—	—	—	2.7	Same as Ishiziro
Takenari	—	—	—	—	2.8	Same as Gin-bōzu
Experiment station Varieties						
Prewar selection						
Norin number	81	2.71	2.7	3.0	3.0	Upper quartile
Rikuu–132	13	3.00	2.9	3.3	2.9	Median
Others	13	2.80	2.8	2.9	2.9	Upper quartile
Postwar selection						
Nōrin number	60	2.91	2.9	3.2	3.2	Upper quartile
Others	14	3.15	3.2	3.2	3.2	Upper quartile
Traditional varieties	71	2.28	2.4	2.6	2.4	Median

a) Upper quartiles of the experiment yields are adopted in the case of varieties which were tested in many prefectures widely over the nation.

Appendex: TABLE A-II-2

Rice yields per *Tan* by Varieties in Experiments: Western Prefectures   (Unit: *koku*)

	Number of experiments	Parameters			Standard levels	Remarks on the standard levels[a]
		Arith. mean	Median	Upper quartile		
Rono varieties						
Aikoku	26	2.90	2.9	3.1	2.9	Median
Asahi	70	2.92	2.9	3.1	3.1	Upper quartile
Omachi	19	2.97	2.9	3.2	2.9	Median
Shinriki	31	3.17	3.1	3.5	3.1	Median
Others						
Gin-bozu	11	2.93	2.9	3.2	2.9	Median
Ishiziro	—	—	—	—	2.7	Same as eastern prefectures
Kameji	9	2.93	2.9	3.0	2.9	Median
Oba	2	3.08	3.1	—	3.1	Median
Takenari	—	—	—	—	2.8	Same as eastern prefectures
Experiment station						
Varieties						
Prewar selection						
Norin numbers	101	2.72	2.8	3.0	3.0	Upper quartile
Rikuu-132	—	—	—	—	2.9	Same as eastern prefectures
Others	19	2.84	2.8	3.1	3.1	Upper quartile
Postwar selection						
Norin numbers	81	2.87	3.0	3.2	3.2	Upper quartile
Others	7	2.99	3.0	3.2	3.2	Upper quartile
Traditional varieties	84	2.73	2.7	3.0	2.7	Median

a) See footnote at Table A-II-1.

APPENDIX B: Estimation of Calorie Consumption.

Since we expect to publish later the detailed estimation procedures and the sources of data, we will only describe here the principles of estimation.

1. It was designed to cover 100 per cent of food items. Coverage of area was mainland Japan including Okinawa (excluding the oversea's territories of the old Japan Empire).

2. By items we deduced from production (a) net exports (exports minus imports), (b) seeds, (c) industrial uses and (d) produce in storage and in the marketing process. Quantities by items thus obtained were aggregated in terms of calories contained. Calories contained in concentrate feeds were estimated independently from the series of livestock numbers and were deducted as aggregates.

3. Aggregations were made in the forms of materials for foods, but not in the forms of processed foods.

4. Consumption-unit populations were obtained by summing up men and women of different ages with the following weights:

Ages	Male	Female
0–4	0.40	0.40
5–9	0.67	0.63
10–14	0.82	0.77
15–19	0.98	0.84
20–29	1.00	0.84
30–49	0.96	0.76
50–59	0.91	0.72
60–	0.84	0.68

APPENDIX C: Tentative Estimates of National Income and NDP at Market Prices.

	Industrial origin of net domestic product (Current prices: Mil. yen)				Total NDP (1934–36 prices: Million yen) V	Per-capita NDP (1934–36 prices: yen) VI	National income (1934–36 prices: US dollars) VII
	Primary I	Secondary II	Tertiary III	Total IV			
1878–1882	375	116	160	651	1,876	52	60
83– 87	297	111	179	587	1,881	50	58
88– 92	372	169	229	770	2,429	62	72
93– 97	527	293	352	1,172	3,274	79	92
98–1902	824	501	604	1,929	4,070	92	107
1903– 07	1,046	675	899	2,620	4,704	101	117
08– 12	1,335	857	1,310	3,502	5,808	117	136
13– 17	1,601	1,592	1,851	5,044	7,596	143	166
18– 22	3,479	3,793	5,047	12,319	9,382	168	195
23– 27	3,701	3,712	6,861	14,274	11,125	188	218
28– 32	2,490	3,717	6,876	13,083	12,520	196	227
33– 37	2,970	5,420	8,744	17,134	16,815	245	284
38– 40	5,413	12,511	14,462	32,386	21,548	302	350

I.   Value added in agriculture (*LTES*, IX, p. 182), forestry (*LTES*, IX, pp. 232–3) and in fishery (*GRJE*, pp. 72–3).
II. Manufacturing: Gross production in Yuichi, Shionoya, *Nihon no Kogyo Seisan Shisū*, Addition to Shinohara, Miyohei, *Sangyo Kozoron* (Tokyo: Chikuma, 1966), multiplied by value added ratios calculated from *GRJE*, pp. 79–80. Mining: *GRJE*, pp. 79–80.
III. NDP at factor cost were taken from *GRJE* for 1923–1940, and were obtained for 1878–1922 by following the procedures adopted in *GRJE*, pp. 100–106 with NDP in the goods-producing industries estimated as I and II. NDP at factor cost were converted to NDP at market prices by the coefficients used in K. Ohkawa, and K. Akasaka, Rockefeller Project, Mimeographed Report D11, Institute of Economic Research, Hitotsubashi Univ., 1961.
V.   IV deflated by general price index in *LTES*, II.
VI. V divided by population in *LTES*, II.
VII. National income accounts (revised) of Economic Planning Agency provide for 1958 per-capita NDP at market prices in 1934–36 prices 319 yen and per-capita national income 289 yen which are equivalent to 370 U.S. dollars by the purchasing parity rate in 1958 in *The Yearbook of National Accounts Statistics*. 370 dollars were multiplied by the index of per-capita NDP in VI with 314 yen in 1958=1.00.

CHAPTER 5

TECHNOLOGICAL CHANGE IN JAPANESE AGRICULTURE: A LONG-TERM ANALYSIS[†]

SHŪJIRŌ SAWADA

Introduction

The object of this paper is to undertake the controversial subject of measuring the effects of technological change in Japanese agriculture since the Meiji Era. This paper does not offer a new technique of measurement, but attempts to measure the effects of technological change with the "residual" model first, and a CES type of function next. I feel it is necessary to offer a few words of explanation as to why I take up these two models for the present purpose and to refer briefly to past studies made in this field.

We have only a small number of studies on technological change in Japanese agriculture which cover a long period. They have mostly been carried out along the following two lines: (1) to measure the effects of technological change on saving inputs per unit of output as Schultz successfully did with respect to American agriculture (Schultz, 1953) and (2) to measure them by the production function approach in a broad sense. In the first group, we find Shishido, who analyzed prewar agriculture and presented comparisons with the American experience (Shishido, 1956); Yamada, who analyzed the whole period before and after the war, estimating again the fixed capital inputs (Yamada, 1953); and Umemura et al., who recently

[†] I owe much to Mrs. T. Seki, Messrs. M. Hayashi and T. Kawaguchi for the laborious caluculations undertaken for this paper. Special gratitude is due Professor K. L. Robinson for his helpful comments on an early draft, and Professor V. Ruttan for his valuable comments at the Tokyo Symposium. My greatest debt is due Professor Ohkawa for his helpful comments in the preparation of the final version. I also benefited very much from comments and suggestions by Professors T. Watanabe, K. Tsuchiya, Y. Hayami and Dr. S. Ishiwata.

completed a thorough analysis, examining closely all data available
(*LTES*, IX). Those who belong to the second group are also few.
The production function approach in analyzing Japanese agriculture was pioneered by Kamiya (Kamiya, 1941) and Ohkawa
(Ohkawa, 1945). Since the war, Tsuchiya (Tsuchiya, 1955) and
many others have done a considerable amount of work. But most
of them adopted cross-section analysis instead of time-series analysis and consequently, they were less concerned with technological
change per se. Research on the effects of technological change in
terms of non-conventional inputs has only just begun. If the studies
on the "residual" model, which resemble the method of Solow
(Solow, 1956) are included in this category, the group would include
the following studies. I once measured the effects of technological
change in prewar agriculture on a model simpler than Solow's
(Sawada, 1959). Tsuchiya measured the effects of technological
change in rice culture as "residuals" over the period from 1922 to
1963, utilizing a series of production functions obtained from cross-
section data (Tsuchiya, 1966). After estimating that part of the increase in output "unexplained" by the increase in conventional inputs in prewar agriculture, Tang tried to explain it in terms of
government outlays for rural education and for agricultural research, development and extension, assuming a specific scheme of
lag distribution (Tang, 1963). Hayami criticized Tang's paper
(Hayami, 1965) and starting from that criticism, he and Yamada
analyzed the process of technological change by distinguishing the
effects of the inherited technical potential and its diffusion throughout the country (Hayami-Yamada, 1967). Hayami analyzed also
the fertilizer demand in prewar agriculture and explained its large
increase by technological advances in both agriculture and the fertilizer industry (Hayami, 1967). Recently, he and Yamada tried to
explain the increase of rice yield by fertilizer inputs and the adoption
of improved varieties (See Chapter 4, this volume).

What I attempt first in this paper is to measure the effects of technological change by a "residual" model. This is to measure the
effects of technological change as a "residual," the amount of output obtained by subtracting from the current output the amount
expected from current inputs under the former level of technology,

using the ratios of relative shares as production elasticities. Solow worked out such a model early in 1956. I use it in spite of later advances in analytical methods, including the subsequent contribution by Solow himself, for the following reasons. First, as mentioned above, the model has hardly been used for the measurement of the effects of technological change in Japanese agriculture, although it seems appropriate as one of the initial steps for research in this field. Because the estimates of annual capital inputs covering a period of almost 100 years were completed recently, as well as revised estimates of land and labor inputs (Umemura et al.), we can proceed with such an analysis more easily. More important, I still believe that the "residual" does not necessarily represent a "measure of ignorance," but is rather a positive measure of the effects of technological changes since it is measured as a kind of surplus, i.e., the amount of output noi distributed to factors according to the former level of their marginal productivities. Such surplus forms a source of profit which will generally disappear in the course of time because of the dissemination of the new technology which, in turn, results in the change in the marginal productivities of factors throughout the economy.

The models of this type measure the effects of technological change as a whole. To discern the qualitative aspects of technological change, we should use some other models which distinguish the effects of technological change such as the change in efficiency of each factor of production and in the substitution or complementary relation between different factors, and the effects of various non-conventional factors. Here, I use a CES type of function, in which the variables denoting factor-inputs each has an "augmenting" coefficient. One could assume some other type of function, for instance, a function of the Cobb-Douglas type associated with adequate shift variables, but here the elasticity of substitution between factors, denoted by σ, is always unity. However, σ itself may change with technological change. For instance, changes in the relative amount of resources in the agricultural sector caused by the increasing demand for resources in the non-agricultural sectors seem to be instrumental in altering technology and consequently σ. Thus, a CES type of function, where σ can take values other than unity will be better for a long-term analysis of Japanese agriculture. But here, we are faced with at least two difficulties. First, although the magnitude of σ depends on the technology adopted and accordingly changes over time, the CES type of function assumes the constancy of σ, though it is neither unity, as in the Cobb-Douglas case, nor zero, as in the Leontief case. Accordingly, it would seem that the CES type of function would not be adequate in measuring the effects of technological change with respect to σ. But according to our empirical work, there seem to exist certain "technological epochs," each extending over many years and having different, but reasonably constant, σ. If we can discern such epochs and estimate respective CES functions, each with a specific σ, the change in σ and therefore effects of technological changes on σ will be determined. The method used by Brown is most precise in determining these technological epochs (Brown, 1964). Here, dividing the whole period into three parts, i.e., (I) Pre-World War I; (II) Interwar; (III) Post-World War II, and assuming that the overall economic situation differed in each period, I try to gauge σ and other coefficients relating to technological change. The division of the period should be examined for its validity by the results of the measurement. Second, the CES type of production function originated as having two factors, labor and capital. But for agriculture, particularly in countries where capital is still scarce and land plays a large role, some production functions composed of at least three factors, i.e., land, labor and capital, are desirable. Uzawa has developed the n-factor case from the original two-factor CES function (Uzawa, 1962). But as the restrictions for the n-factor case are severe, I use the original form, limiting the factors to only land and labor. Therefore, the effects of technological change embodied in capital inputs will be included in the effects of technological change which appear in either the land or labor, or both inputs. Even such an analysis as this will produce most of the essential features of the problem because the two factors still play major roles in the agriculture of Japan.

I. Measurement by the "Residual" Model
Model and Assumptions

Let the production function F be

$$V = F(L, T, K_1, K_2, t), \tag{1}$$

where V is value added, L is labor, T is land, K_1 is capital stock, K_2 is current inputs, and t is time.

Differentiate (1) with respect to t and divide the resulting derivatives by V, assuming that F is homogeneous of degree one.

Then,

$$\frac{\dot{V}}{V} = \frac{\dot{F}}{F} + \alpha\frac{\dot{L}}{L} + \beta\frac{\dot{T}}{T} + \gamma_1\frac{\dot{K_1}}{K_1} + \gamma_2\frac{\dot{K_2}}{K_2}, \tag{2}$$

where α, β, γ_1, and γ_2 are relative shares in V to L, T, K_1, and K_2, respectively, and $\dot{V}$, $\dot{F}$, $\dot{L}$, $\dot{T}$, $\dot{K_1}$, and $\dot{K_2}$ are derivatives with respect to time.

If V, L, T, K_1, K_2, α, β, γ_1, and γ_2 are given in time series, one can get $\dot{F}/F$ as a residual, and may call it "the rate of technological change" in a broad sense.[1] However, some comments will be needed on γ_2. As mentioned above, K_2 denotes current inputs. It may seem strange to set a share to current inputs, taking V as value added. But in agriculture, even current inputs take time, although comparatively little, for the products to mature as is the case with capital stock. A share is assigned to each input after maturity. Although each current input differs in the period of maturity, one year has been assigned to each input as the time required to reach maturity.

It should be noted that the neutrality of technological change is not necessarily assumed here. Solow, assuming neutral technological change, started with a production function, $V = A(t)F(L,K)$, where $A(t)$ is the multiplicative factor, and obtained an equation similar to (2) with $\dot{A}/A$ instead of $\dot{F}/F$. Most writers refer to Solow's model as assuming neutral technological change. But it should be remembered that Solow offered a production function like (1) first, derived an equation corresponding to (2) and maintained that $\dot{F}/F$ or $\dot{A}/A$ would be estimated "depending on where these relative shifts appeared to be neutral or not" (Solow, 1956).

---

[1] It includes climatic influences. But taking several year averages of annual output over the country, we will considerably lessen the climatic effects that appear in the results, except for extraordinarily good or bad harvests throughout the country.

Definitions, Estimating Procedures and Source of Data

Output and Input Notations and Definitions are as follows:

V: Value added in agriculture estimated by constant prices, 1934–36,

L: Number of gainful workers in agriculture, male and female,

T: Area of paddy and upland fields,

K_1: Gross capital stock, excluding buildings and structures, estimated by constant prices, 1934–36,

K_2: Fertilizer and other current inputs estimated by farm-prices, 1934–1936.

Here, α, β, γ_1, and γ_2 were estimated as follows: For the prewar period,

$$\alpha = 1 - (\beta + \gamma_1 + \gamma_2),$$

$$\beta = \frac{R_1 T_1 + R_2 T_2}{V_n},$$

where R_1 is rent rate of paddy, nominal, R_2 is rent rate of upland field, nominal, T_1 is area of paddy, T_2 is area of upland fields, and V_n is value added in agriculture, nominal.

$$\gamma_1 = K_{1n} \cdot \frac{R}{V_n},$$

where K_{1n}: gross capital stock, nominal value,

$$R = \frac{R_1}{P_{T_1}},$$

where P_{T_1} is price of paddy, nominal, and

$$\gamma_2 = K_2 \cdot \frac{R}{V_n},$$

where K_2 is fertilizer and other current inputs, nominal value.

For the postwar period, α was estimated in the same way as the prewar period. But, β, γ_1, and γ_2 were estimated as follows:

$$\beta = (P_{T_1} \cdot r \cdot T_1 + P_{T_2} \cdot r \cdot T_2) / V_n,$$

where r is official rate of interest on long term deposits in agricultural co-ops.

$$\gamma_1 = K_{1n} \cdot \frac{r}{V_n}$$

and

$$\gamma_2 = K_{2n} \cdot \frac{r}{V_n}.$$

All data for the measurement were derived from *LTES*, IX.

Results of the Measurement

For the prewar period, five-year averages were used for the measurement of $\dot{F}/F$ every five years, and one-year rates were calculated from the results. For the postwar period, three-year moving averages were used to obtain the rate of $\dot{F}/F$ for every year. For the period before 1953, however, the prices of land seem to have been under severe restriction as a result of the land reform. Hence, postwar measurements were made only for the period after 1954. The results are shown in Table 1.

II. Measurement by a CES Function
The Model and Assumptions

To analyze some qualitative aspects of the effects of technological change, I assume a different function,

$$V = F\,[E_L(t)L,\ E_T(t)T,\ E_{K_1}(t)K_1,\ E_{K_2}(t)K_2] \tag{3}$$

where E_i $(i=L,\ T,\ K_1,\ K_2)$ is efficiency of L, T, K_1, and K_2, respectively Here E_i denotes the "augmenting" effect, and is a function of time.

Differentiate (3) with respect to t and divide the resulting derivatives by V, assuming that F is homogeneous of degree one with respect to L, T, K_1, and K_2, each carrying its efficiency term. Then

$$\frac{\dot{V}}{V} = \alpha\left(\frac{\dot{L}}{L}+\frac{\dot{E}_L}{E_L}\right)+\beta\left(\frac{\dot{T}}{T}+\frac{\dot{E}_T}{E_T}\right)+\gamma_1\left(\frac{\dot{K}_1}{K_1}+\frac{\dot{E}_{K_1}}{E_{K_1}}\right)+\gamma_2\left(\frac{\dot{K}_2}{K_2}+\frac{\dot{E}_{K_2}}{E_{K_2}}\right) \tag{4}$$

From (2) and (4),

$$\frac{\dot{F}}{F} = \alpha\frac{\dot{E}_L}{E_L}+\beta\frac{\dot{E}_T}{E_T}+\gamma_1\frac{\dot{E}_{K_1}}{E_{K_1}}+\gamma_2\frac{\dot{E}_{K_2}}{E_{K_2}} \tag{5}$$

Thus, the effects of technological change can be decomposed into four components each expressing a specific factor-augmenting effect.

To measure $\dot{E}_i/E_i$ and σ, the elasticity of substitution between factors, I assume a CES type of function such as (6), limiting factors only to L and T.

$$V = [(E_L L)^{-\rho}+(E_T T)^{-\rho}]^{-\frac{1}{\rho}}, \tag{6}$$

where

TABLE 1

Period	$\dfrac{\dot{V}}{V}$	$\dfrac{\dot{L}}{L}$	$\dfrac{\dot{T}}{T}$	$\dfrac{\dot{K}_1}{K_1}$	$\dfrac{\dot{K}_2}{K_2}$	α	β	γ_1	γ_2	$\dfrac{\dot{F}}{F}$ Five-year rate	$\dfrac{\dot{F}}{F}$ One-year rate %	R (Prewar) r (Postwar) %
1883–87	0.099	−0.012	0.020	0.057	0.067	0.189	0.640	0.139	0.030	0.080	1.5	10.1
88–92	0.018	−0.006	0.021	0.088	0.083	0.064	0.791	0.116	0.028	0.068	1.3	9.2
93–97	0.129	0.000	0.030	0.060	0.058	0.135	0.725	0.113	0.026	0.101	1.9	6.1
98–02	0.091	−0.008	0.021	0.089	0.207	0.283	0.595	0.098	0.022	0.069	1.3	8.5
1903–07	0.097	−0.004	0.047	0.136	0.121	0.344	0.532	0.099	0.024	0.058	1.1	9.1
08–12	0.127	−0.004	0.036	0.079	0.121	0.400	0.460	0.072	0.017	0.102	1.9	6.7
13–17	0.044	0.000	0.033	0.056	0.128	0.456	0.459	0.067	0.016	0.024	0.4	6.3
18–22	−0.014	0.000	−0.009	0.054	0.113	0.445	0.450	0.085	0.019	−0.016	−0.3	7.0
23–27	0.056	−0.001	0.007	0.080	0.073	0.483	0.428	0.072	0.015	0.048	0.9	6.4
28–32	0.050	−0.012	0.021	0.045	0.110	0.509	0.416	0.061	0.013	0.045	0.8	4.7
33–37												
1953–55	0.095	−0.009	0.006	0.057	0.060	0.643	0.253	0.075	0.029		9.4	6.1
54–56	0.082	−0.012	0.006	0.055	0.074	0.601	0.299	0.072	0.028		8.3	6.1
55–57	−0.004	−0.030	0.004	0.054	0.053	0.575	0.327	0.070	0.028		0.8	6.1
56–58	0.037	−0.027	0.003	0.057	0.084	0.524	0.371	0.075	0.030		4.4	6.1
57–59	0.019	−0.031	0.001	0.074	0.095	0.503	0.390	0.076	0.031		2.7	6.1
58–60	0.006	−0.024	0.001	0.086	0.088	0.480	0.406	0.080	0.034		0.9	6.1
59–61	0.002	−0.028	0.000	0.101	0.058	0.468	0.409	0.087	0.036		0.5	5.9
60–62	−0.018	−0.035	0.000	—	—	0.491	0.380	0.092	0.037			
61–63			0.000									

$$\rho = \frac{1-\sigma}{\sigma} \geq -1$$

and where σ is elasticity of substitution between L and T.

Equation (6) contains only two factors, L and T. Accordingly, the effect of the changes in capital-inputs and their efficiency is included in those of either L or T, or both.

Estimating Procedures and Sources of Data

If we differentiate (6) with respect to L, we have:

$$\frac{\partial V}{\partial L} = E_L{}^{-\rho}\left(\frac{V}{L}\right)^{1+\rho}. \tag{7}$$

From (7),

$$\frac{\frac{\partial V}{\partial L}L}{V} = \alpha = E_L{}^{-\rho}\left(\frac{V}{L}\right)^{\rho} = w^{1-\sigma}E_L{}^{\sigma-1}, \tag{8}$$

where $w(=\partial V/\partial L)$ is wage rate.

If E_L grows through time at an exponential rate λ_L, the equation (8) leads immediately to an expression in natural logarithms, (9), from which σ and λ_L will be estimated by the least square method applied to the time series data of α and w for each epoch (Arrow et al.; David and Klundert).

$$\alpha = w^{1-\sigma}E_L(O)\exp[\lambda_L(\sigma-1)t],$$
$$\ln \alpha = \ln E_L(O) + (1-\sigma)\ln w + \lambda_L(\sigma-1)t. \tag{9}$$

Then, $\dot{E}_T/E_T$ will be given by

$$\frac{\dot{V}}{V} = \alpha\left(\frac{\dot{L}}{L} + \frac{\dot{E}_L}{E_L}\right) + \beta\left(\frac{\dot{T}}{T} + \frac{\dot{E}_T}{E_T}\right), \tag{10}$$

and $\dot{F}/F$ will be given by

$$\frac{\dot{F}}{F} = \alpha\frac{\dot{E}_L}{E_L} + \beta\frac{\dot{E}_T}{E_T}. \tag{11}$$

Some further comments are needed on the foregoing equations. First, in (8), w used in the measurement is the daily wage rate while L is enumerated in man-years. From (8), letting n be the number of working days a year:

$$\frac{wnL}{V} = \alpha = (nw)^{1-\sigma}E_L{}^{\sigma-1} = w^{1-\sigma}\left(\frac{E_L}{n}\right)^{\sigma-1}.$$

Thus, our λ_L indicates the exponential growth rate of E_L/n. If n be constant, λ_L will also express the exponential growth rate of E_L. The time series data of n are not known yet, and the following measurement assumes its constancy. But in reality, n must have decreased over a long period of time. If so, the real λ_L must have been smaller than the measured λ_L.

Second, one of the controversial questions is whether or not $\partial V/\partial L$ is equal to w (more precisely nw). However, one can assume $\partial V/\partial L = mw$, where m is constant and > 0. Then,

$$\alpha = \frac{wL}{V} = \frac{\dfrac{\partial V}{\partial L} \dfrac{L}{m}}{V},$$

then,

$$\alpha = \left(\frac{w}{n}\right)^{1-\sigma} E_L{}^{\sigma-1} = w^{1-\sigma}(mE_L)^{\sigma-1}.$$

Thus, λ_L expresses the exponential growth rate of E_L, since m is constant.

Third, concerning relative shares, α and β, used here, β was estimated first as mentioned above, and α was estimated by $\alpha = 1 - \beta$. Accordingly, α contains γ_1 and γ_2. However, as γ_1 and γ_2 are rather small relative to α and β, the measurement using such gross value of α will still provide some information on the real $\dot{E}_L/E_L$ and σ.

All data are the same as those used for the measurement by the "residual" model. However, three-year averages of data were used for the prewar period.

Results of the Measurement

The structural equations are as follows:

Period   I: $\ln \alpha = -0.87842 + 0.64094 \ln w + 0.04701\, t$
$\qquad\qquad\qquad (0.63167) \qquad\quad (0.02809)$
$\qquad\quad R^2 = 0.74, \qquad D.W. = 1.22$

Period   II: $\ln \alpha = -0.59553 + 0.09636 \ln w + 0.01220\, t$
$\qquad\qquad\qquad (0.08370) \qquad\quad (0.00590)$
$\qquad\quad R^2 = 0.66, \qquad D.W. = 2.67$

Period III: $\ln \alpha = -0.16898 + 0.60263 \ln w - 0.06006\, t$
$\qquad\qquad\qquad (0.82170) \qquad\quad (0.04053)$
$\qquad\quad R^2 = 0.80, \qquad D.W. = 0.95$

The estimates of σ, $\dot{E}_L/E_L$ and $\dot{E}_T/E_T$ are given in Table 2.

TABLE 2

period	σ	$\dfrac{\dot{E}_L}{E_L}$	$\dfrac{\dot{E}_T}{E_T}$	$\dfrac{\dot{F}}{F}$
		(One-year rate)		
I	0.268	−0.025	0.057	0.025
II	0.903	−0.044	0.071	0.009
III	0.397	0.097	−0.052	0.041

III. Summary of Statistical Findings
Measurement by the "Residual" Model

For the prewar period, the rates of $\dot{F}/F$, the residual, were all over 1.0 per cent before around 1920 and, those in the period after around 1920 were obviously lower than those in the former period. For the whole prewar period, the rates of $\dot{L}/L$, were minus or zero, and decreased almost consistently in their minus value over time except during the last period. On the other hand, $\dot{T}/T$, the rate of hange in land, and $\dot{K_1}/K_1$, that of capital stock, increased gradually until the period from 1903–07 to 1908–12 and decreased thereafter. It should be noted further that α, the relative share of labor, increased and β, the relative share of land, decreased consistently for he whole period, with the increase in α being particularly marked. As for γ_1, the relative share of capital stock, and γ_2, that of current inputs, the former decreased substantially, while the latter was kept almost constant. The decrease in γ_1 comes from the decrease in K_1 and R.

For the postwar period, the rates of $\dot{F}/F$ in the early years were as large as 8.3–9.4 per cent, but decreased year by year to the level of 0.4 per cent. $\dot{F}/F$ often exceeded $\dot{V}/V$, the rate of increase in output. Such results may seem strange, but when factor-inputs, such as L in this case, decrease substantially in combination with an increase in V as in this period, the $\dot{F}/F$ measured by keeping the level of factorinputs constant, appears to be quite large and sometimes exceeds $\dot{V}/V$ The rates of $\dot{L}/L$ were negative, as in most of the prewar period, but were quite large in their negative values particularly after around 1957. The rates of $\dot{T}/T$ were slightly positive, but decreased in value over time, showing no recent increase at all. $\dot{K_1}/K_1$ increased markedly, while $\dot{K_2}/K_2$, the rate of change in current input, remained almost constant. It should be noted that while α decreased gradually, γ_1 and γ_2 were increasing gradually contrary to the tendency that appeared in the prewar period. The value of β remained almost constant.

The estimation of β between 1883 and 1902 should be further improved. As the rental data were available only sporadically for that period, some figures were interpolated by the least square method. However, that procedure seems to have estimated β rather high and hence α low.

Measurement by the CES Function

In the structural equations, the standard errors of the coefficients of ln w are still large, although those of the coefficients of t are relatively small. For Period III, a serial correlation may exist. Moreover, the correlation coefficient between ln w and t, though not shown above, is rather high for this period. Accordingly, the value of σ and the various growth rates estimated may contain unknown biases. I tried to change the division of the period in many ways to get better structural equations, for the postwar period was too short to be analyzed by subdivisions.

Although the statistical rigor of the present approach leaves much to be desired, the reader will be interested in the following findings:
(1) In Period I, $\dot{F}/F$ was as large as 2.5 per cent a year, almost 2.5 times larger than the figure for Period II. This was due mainly to the large value of $\dot{E}_T/E_T$ and β. The value of β is closely related to the value of α, because γ_1 and γ_2 are rather small.
(2) In Period I, σ, the elasticity of substitution, was as small as 0.268, but increased substantially to 0.903 in Period II. The rate of technological change expressed in $\dot{F}/F$ was small at 0.9 per cent a year in Period II, comparing with the 2.5 per cent of the preceding period. Thus, the technological change in Period II seems to have occurred mainly on the side relating to σ.
(3) In Period III, something new seems to have appeared. $\dot{E}_L/E_L$ be-

came positive for the first time and had a substantial value. On the other hand, $\dot{E}_T/E_T$ had a negative value. $\dot{F}/F$ reached its highest value.

IV. Implications

Some implications of the statistical findings can be suggested here, although rigorous confirmation will require considerably more research.

1. According to the results obtained by both "residual" and CES models, it is evident that $\dot{F}/F$, the rates of technological change, in Period II were low relative to those in Period I. Agriculture was said to have developed at a rate almost equal to that of the non-agricultural industries in Period I and did not become the depressed sector until Period II. The measurement confirms the validity of such a hypothesis.

If changes in technology were closely related to factor-inputs, particularly those of capital goods, the downward tendency in $\dot{F}/F$ as shown above should be considered in reference to the changes in such factor-inputs. As shown in Table 1, $\dot{K}_1/K_1$, the rate of capital stock increase, became relatively small in Period II. Among the items included in K_1 which increased the productivity in the prewar agriculture, we should take notice of farm implements. Farm machinery appeared in large quantities only after the war. In Period I, several kinds of useful implements such as short-soled plows, rotary weeders, and foot pedal rotary threshers appeared and were diffused rapidly. They played a large role in raising the agricultural productivity accompanied by land improvements, new varieties of seeds, and the increasing use of fertilizer, which not only saved labor, but also raised yields. Even foot pedal rotary threshers enabled farmers to prepare for second crops to get larger yields, thus avoiding any diversion of their efforts during the busiest season. Although we cannot statistically confirm this, such implements were already widely used by Period II. Some improvements in them were carried out in this period, but the adoption of new kinds of implements, and their rapid diffusion took place mostly in Period I. Motorization of farm implements, particularly in pumping water for irrigation and drainage and in rotary threshers, began in Period II, but such improvements were still limited to only a few districts. This observation seems to be consistent with the present findings that $\dot{K_1}/K_1$ increased towards the end of Period I and decreased thereafter; and accordingly, $\dot{F}/F$ remained high in Period I and low in Period II.

One of the main reasons for the retardation of $\dot{K_1}/K_1$ in PeriodII could be the retardation of the rate of decrease in labor during the same period. By the end of the period, when the war economy set in, labor began to decrease considerably, but $\dot{K_1}/K_1$ did not recover, probably because of the war-induced scarcity of various kinds of materials.

2. In Period II, the technological change expressed in terms of $\dot{F}/F$ was small, but a substantial change in the elasticity of substitution between labor and land (σ) can be seen. In this period, there was a surplus of labor in the agricultural sector. The number of those gainfully employed in agriculture actually increased by 2.2 per cent between 1923–27 and 1933–37, in contrast to the 1.5 per cent decline in the preceding decade. The main objective of the farming improvements of that period was to absorb labor gainfully into agriculture. But the land area was limited, and the main task was, naturally, to avoid or delay the tendency of diminishing returns to labor.[2] This seems to have been responsible for the increase of σ as seen above. In reality, farmers diversified and intensified their farming with second crops, raising of livestock and poultry and the processing of farm products. The slogan "farming with livestock" (*Yūchiku-Nōgyō*) became one of the catch phrases of that period. However, it should be noticed that most of the concentrates for feed were imported and not produced from the land of this country. Another phrase which became popular was "Plow deep and manure enough" (*Shinkō-tahi*), which was to encourage increased yields. "Produce manure in larger quantities" became almost a philosophy of good farming. But grass land was very scarce, and grass and leaves for making manure had to be obtained mostly from common moun-

---

[2] Otsuki has emphasized the necessity of increasing the intensity of farming in Japan in order to avoid the tendency toward diminishing returns to labor and to compete with foreign agriculture through trade (Otsuki, 1961).

tains which were generally sterile and located a distance from their farms. Statistics show, however, that the rice yield per *tan* increased only slightly in this period. Even the *Shinkō-tahi* seems to have resulted only in a small increase of yield in return for much labor. Deep plowing was hardly attained with the Japanese plow, although it had been improved in many ways. New varieties of rice such as *Asahi* and others were introduced because of their better response to fertilizer. However, the combination of new varieties and much fertilizer, which was said to be a breakthrough from the traditional farming, seems to have achieved little in this period. Thus, in this period, σ increased, but F/F, relating more or less to the average productivity of factors, hardly increased. In other words, technological change in Period II was qualitatively, but not quantitatively, related to σ.

3. Through both Period I and II the rates of $\dot{E}_T/E_T$ were positive and those of $\dot{E}_L/E_L$ negative, although their values for both periods were slightly different from each other. The two-factor model where α contains γ_2 and γ_1 in this case leaves some ambiguous points concerning the real value of $\dot{E}_L/E_L$ which appears negative here. But throughout the whole prewar period, particularly in Period II, technological change seems to have taken place with noticeable emphasis on raising E_T at the cost of a low E_L. Although land improvement was carried on throughout the whole period, at first it was aimed at making horse-plowing easier by adjusting the partition of land. However, it soon became a means for better irrigation and drainage. New varieties of rice, particularly those responding better to fertilizers, were used widely, and the use of fertilizer such as soybean cake and later inorganic chemicals began to be used widely (Otsuki, 1961; Hayami, 1964). Commercial fertilizer saved labor while supplying the same amount of nutritive elements more efficiently than manure. But the use of commercial fertilizer was mainly to raise yields, and not necessarily to substitute for manure (Hayami, 1964). In fact, manure was used in an increasing amount along with the increasing use of fertilizer. Other practices, such as the regular planting of rice seedlings, the laborious ridding of moth and eggs of rice-borers and careful paddy weeding, were also to raise the yield of rice at the cost of much labor. Some farm imple-

ments, which were adopted and diffused rapidly, saved in particular the most toilsome parts of labor and eased the burden during the busiest season. But as in the case of fertilizer, their main target was to increase yields, including those of second crops, as stated above. Such are the implications of the values of $\dot{E}_T/E_T$ and $\dot{E}_L/E_L$, as measured above, and these trends may well be said to be the essence of the Meiji farming method (*Meiji-Nōhō*). These trends continued not only through the latter half of the Meiji Period, but for a long time thereafter in an undiluted form.

4. In Period III, the rates of $\dot{F}/F$ reached unprecedentedly high values. Particularly remarkable are the values of the early years which reached a high 9.4 or 8.3 per cent per year (Table 1). It should be noted that the food control carried out during and after the war was revised considerably in 1955 so that farmers would offer to sell rice to the government prior to the harvest on their own volition, whereas previously they had to sell according to pre-harvest assignments of quotas by the government. Because of the possibility of an underestimation of harvests during the period of severe food controls, the growth rate for those years might be exaggerated. Accordingly, the high rate, 9.4 per cent for 1953–55 to 1954–56, might be an overestimate. But the rates in the fifties can well be said to be quite high in contrast to those in the prewar periods. However, it should also be remarked that by the end of the fifties and the beginning of the sixties the rates had decreased to almost the prewar level.

$\dot{E}_L/E_L$ became positive for the first time, and reached a substantial value. On the other hand, $\dot{E}_T/E_T$ became negative. This is surely because of the recent trend towards increasing mechanization. The number of power-tillers amounted to nearly 2.2 million in 1965, while it was 88,840 in 1955 and only 88 in 1931. Such speedy mechanization was the result of an increasing exodus of population from villages to urban areas, and the increase of part-time farmers. That E_T did not increase stemmed from the characteristics of mechanization in Japan. The size of the farm in Japan is still very small and is kept from growing by various restrictions, including the complicated irrigation system and the land law. Before the war, farmers mechanized only the threshing and hulling processes to some extent and irrigation in some regions was also mechanized. It was a true sign of progress that field works were mechanized after the war. Thus, the power-tiller became the postwar star of mechanization. But it had to be a type that was suitable for use on a small farm. More so because the fields belonging to a farm were fragmented into several, or sometimes more than ten, groups of field-lots each having a different shape and elevation. The most popular type of power-tiller was one which could break soil with tines fixed to a wheel; it could not till deeply, and sometimes tilled even shallower that the old Japanese plows did. Nevertheless, the work could be done very fast, and it seems that the main role of power-tillers has been to save labor, and had nothing to do with increasing yields (See Chapter 6, this volume). For increasing yield, most essential were new varieties, the application of a large amount of fertilizer and agricultural chemicals and timely irrigation. It should be noted that these were rather traditional means of increasing yields. In Saga Prefecture, for instance, the rice yield per tan recently set a new record. Although this seems to have been accomplished by mobilizing a good combination of all such techniques, the limit seems to have been reached in the yield increase which can be attained from the traditional means. On the other hand, the cultivation of second crops, of which wheat was most important, decreased remarkably owing to the mounting import of grains. The planted area of wheat and barley on both paddy and upland fields was only 809 thousand hectares in 1965, compared with 1.8 million hectares in 1950. Furthermore, the number of cows, hogs, and chickens increased impressively. The increase in the number of cows offset the decrease of draft-cattle, but they were maintained largely with imported feed as was the case in the beginning of livestock rearing in Period II. These were, I think, the main reasons for the increase of $\dot{E}_L/E_L$ and the decrease of $\dot{E}_T/E_T$. Although the value of σ decreased slightly, this might be due to mechanization which always tends toward production methods where factor proportions are more or less fixed.

Taking the above into account, the fundamentals of technological changes in Period III do not seem to have changed so much. However, perhaps we can look forward to some real departures from the traditional features of Japanese agriculture which may come from the further industrialization of the Japanese economy.

REFERENCES

Arrow, K. J., Chenery, H. B., Minhas, B. S. and Solow, R. M., "Capital-Labor Substitution and Economic Efficiency," *Review of Economics and Statistics,* XLIII, No. 3, (Aug. 1961).

Brown, M. *On the Theory and Measurement of Technological Change.* 1964.

David, P. A. and van de Klundert, T., "Biased Efficiency Growth and Capital-Labor Substitution in the U.S., 1899–1960," *American Economic Review,* LV (No. 3, 1965).

Hayami, Y., "A Critical Note on Professor Tang's Model of Japanese Agricultural Development," *Kikan Riron Keizaigaku,* XV, No. 3 (1965).

——, "Demand for Fertilizer in the Course of Japanese Agricultural Development," *Journal of Farm Economics,* XLVI, No. 4 (Nov. 1964).

——, "Innovation in the Fertilizer Industry and Agricultural Development: The Japanese Experience," *Journal of Farm Economics,* IL, No. 2 (May, 1967).

—— and Yamada, S., "Technological Progress in Agriculture," *Economic Growth, The Japanese Experience since the Meiji Era,* L. Klein and K. Ohkawa eds., Chicago: Richard D. Irwin, 1968, pp. 135–61.

Kamiya, K., "On Productivity of Agricultural Labor (Nogyo-Rodo no Seisansei ni tsuite)," *Journal of Rural Economics (Nogyo Keizai Kenkyu),* VXII, No. 3 (Sept. 1941).

Nerlove, M., "Notes on Recent Empirical Studies of the CES and Related Production Function," *Technical Report,* No. 13 (July, 1965).

Ohkawa, K. *Theory and Measurement of Food Economy (Shokuryo-Keizai no Riron to Keisoku).* Tokyo: 1945.

Otsuki, M. *Labour Productivity and Employment in Japanese Agriculture.* Bul., No. 4, National Research Institute of Agriculture, Tokyo: 1961.

Sawada, S., "Innovation in Japanese Agriculture, 1880–1935," *The State and Economic Enterprise in Japan,* W. Lockwood., ed., 1965.

——, "Technological Progress in Agriculture and Employment (Nogyo-Gijutsu-Shinpo to Koyokoka)," *Over-occupation and Japanese Agriculture (Kajoshugyo to Nippon-Nogyo),* K. Ohkawa, ed., Tokyo: 1959.

Schultz, T. W. *The Economic Organization of Agriculture.* 1953, Chap. VII.

Shishido, H., "Development and Stagnation in Agricultural Productivity (Nogyo-Seisansei no Hatten to Donka)," *Japanese Economy and Agriculture (Nippon no Keisai to Nogyo),* I, S. Tobata and K. Ohkawa, eds., Tokyo: 1956.

Solow, R. M., "Technical Change and the Aggregate Production Function," *Review of Economics and Statistics,* XXIX (Aug. 1956).

Tang, A. M., "Research and Education in Japanese Agricultural Development, 1880–1938," *Economics Studies Quarterly (Kikan Rironkeizaigaku),* XIII, Nos. 2, 3. (Feb., May, 1963).

Tsuchiya, K., "Rate of Technological Progress in Japanese Agriculture, 1922–1963 (Nippon-Nogyo no Gijutsu Shinporitsu, 1922–1963)," *Journal of Rural Economics (Nogyo Keizai Kenkyu)*, XXXVIII, No. 2 (Sept. 1966).

Tsuchiya, K., "Study of Agricultural Production Function (Nogyo ni okeru Seisankansu no Kenkyu)," *Quarterly Journal of Agricultural Economy (Nogyo Sogo Kenkyu)*, IX, No. 1 (Jan. 1955).

Umemura, M., Yamada, S., Hayami, Y., Takamatsu, N., and Kumazaki, M., *Agriculture and Forestry (Noringyo), Estimates of Long-Term Economic Statistics of Japan Since 1868 (Chokikeizaitokei)*, IX, K. Ohkawa, M. Shinohara, and M, Umemura, eds., Tokyo: Toyo Keizai Shimposha, 1966.

Uzawa, H., "Production Function with Constant Elasticities of Substitution," *Review of Economics and Statistics*, XXIX, (Oct. 1962).

Yamada, S., "Long-Term Change in Agricultural Output and Input (Nogyo ni okeru Tonyu-Sanshutsu no Choki-Hendo)," *Analysis of the Growth of Japanese Agriculture (Nippon Nogyo no Seicho-Bunseki)*, K. Ohkawa, ed.,

CHAPTER 6

ECONOMICS OF MECHANIZATION IN SMALL-SCALE AGRICULTURE†

KEIZŌ TSUCHIYA

I. Introduction

In this paper it will be our objective to study the economics of mechanization in small-scale farming in Japan, the most crucial elements of which can be seen in Tables 1 and 2. Table 1 shows the trend of increase of major types of farm equipment. In 1931 there were only about 100 power tillers; in 1937 there were approximately 1,000, but with rapid expansion, the number rose to 89,000 in 1955 and by 1965 there were some 2,500,000 power tillers in Japanese farms. The increase in other types of machinery has also been striking. Table 2 shows the total value of the main items of farm machinery produced between 1961 and 1965 in Japan. As exports of farm machinery are still very limited in comparison with total production, the major portion is distributed for domestic use. Inasmuch as power tillers constitute 56 per cent of the total farm machinery produced, it can be said that the mechanization of Japanese agriculture has been mainly represented by power tillers.

We must mention, however, that the process of mechanization of Japanese agriculture is different from that of Western countries. First, the mechanization in Western countries was in upland fields, whereas in Japan it was seen mainly in paddy fields. The 1964 survey showed that the fraction of area cultivated by mechanical power was 78.6 and 29.0 per cent in paddy and in upland fields, respectively (Ministry of Agriculture and Forestry, 1965). Secondly, mechanization in the Western countries has applied to the whole range of field

† I am indebted to T. Kawaguchi, M. Shintani, for assistance received with regard to some of the computations. I am grateful to K. Ohkawa, S. Sawada, C. Nakajima, O. Tanaka, H. Ichiko, T. Yori, Y. Maruyama, Y. Hayami and G. S. Tolley for their comments on an earlier draft of this paper.

155

TABLE 1

Major Equipment on Farms*

(Unit: 1,000)

Year	Power threshers	Hullers	Power tillers	Spraying machines	Conventional tractors
1927	30	39	—	—	—
1931	56	77	0.1	—	—
1933	67	95	0.1	0.4	—
1935	92	105	0.2	1	—
1937	129	108	1	2	—
1939	211	133	3	5	—
1942	357	180	7	—	—
1945	352	177	—	—	—
1947	444	199	8	7	—
1949	764	348	10	11	—
1951	972	—	16	20	—
1953	1,269	540	35	44	—
1955	2,038	690	89	87	—
1957	2,283	—	227	155	—
1959	2,459	800	514	305	—
1961	2,703	—	1,020	361	7
1962	2,832	—	1,414	436	11
1963	2,982	—	1,812	565	—
1964	3,085	827	2,183	704	24.8
1965	3,048	—	2,490	851	17.7

* Data from *Farm Machinery Yearbook* (*Nōgyō Kikai Nenkan*) (1967).

TABLE 2

Production of Farm Machinery between 1961 and
1965 by Types of Farm Machinery*

	Value in million yen	Percentage
Power tillers	208,745	56.6
Power threshers	45,099	12.2
Hullers	14,664	4.0
Spraying machines	24,550	6.7
Others	75,669	20.5
Total	368,725	100.0

* Data from the Ministry of Agriculture and Forestry, *A Report on the Mechanization of Japanese Agriculture* (*Nōgyō Kankei Shiryō*) (1966).

operations, but in Japan this has not been the case. Power tillers, the main machinery in Japanese agriculture, have not been utilized throughout the processes of cultivation, but have been restricted to such processes as tillage, breaking of clods, levelling, and puddling. Rice transplanting and rice harvesting have not been mechanized so that a great deal of labor is still required for these processes. Thirdly, the mechanization in Western countries increased the yield of farm products. However, the results of research done by agricultural experimental stations of prefectural governments in Japan show that the introduction of power tillers did not increase the yield of farm products such as rice and wheat (Ministry of Agriculture and Forestry, 1960). Fourthly, Table 3 shows that the estimated horsepower of draft animals has decreased rapidly since 1955 because of the introduction of power machinery which shows that the power tiller has been substituted for animal power. But when we compare columns (A) and (B) in Table 3, we see that the horsepower increase in farm machinery is faster than the horsepower decrease in draft animals. Therefore we are led to infer that the introduction of the power tiller has saved more man hours than that it has replaced animal power.

Because the process of mechanizing Japanese agriculture was different from that of Western countries, many Japanese authors have emphasized the peculiar behavior of the Japanese farm family which, they thought, must be different from that of industrial enterprises.[1] Kayo has summarized these non-rational factors in the following five categories (Kayo, 1963): (1) Over-investment—even if the efficiency of investment in power tillers was low and the increase in yields was not predicted, power tillers were still, in many cases, purchased, thus giving rise to over-investment. This over-investment stems from the fact that the enterprise and household are not separated in Japanese agriculture, but combined as one economic unit. It is argued that power tillers were introduced as durable consumers' goods, rather than producers' goods, as were electric washing machines, without giving consideration to economic ac-

---

[1] The development of the machinery industry has of course contributed much to promoting farm mechanization. In this paper, however, attention will not be devoted to this aspect; instead we concentrate primarily on the demand side for farm machines.

TABLE 3

Estimated Horsepower of Draft Animals and Farm Machinery*

(Unit: 1,000)

Year	Draft animals (A)		Power machinery			Total horse-power
	Number of animals	Estimated horsepower of animals	Number of motors	Number of gasoline engines	(B) Estimated horsepower of machinery	
1907	2,163	1,277	—	—	1	1,278
1912	1,334	1,334	—	—	5	1,339
1919	2,266	1,320	1	2	4	1,324
1935	2,416	1,403	425	96	1,019	2,422
1949	2,503	1,400	444	316	1,129	2,529
1955	3,575	1,880	956	1,134	4,127	6,007
1960	3,013	1,573	1,124	1,698	6,338	7,911
1964	2,604	1,341	1,366	1,903	7,295	8,636

* Data for 1907–1949 from the Ministry of Agriculture and Forestry, *The Mechanization in Japanese Agriculture (Nihon Nōgyō no Kikaika)* (1963). Data for 1955–1964 from the author's estimates.

counts of production. (2) Demonstration effect—Misawa and Kato discussed capital formation in Japanese agriculture after World War II from the point of view of the demonstration effect and have pointed out that farm machinery was not utilized fully (Misawa and Kato, 1959). Because the concept of the demonstration effect as developed by Duesenberry was mainly concerned with consumers' goods, it implies, they argue, that power tillers were not introduced as producers' goods, but as consumers' goods. (3) The demand of young farm successors—after World War II, most of the second or third sons of farmers moved to the cities in order to find jobs, and even the intended heir has often tended to move to the city during the past several years. Farm mechanization was viewed as being necessary to induce them to stay on farms because young people want very much to have machines (Wataya, 1959). (4) The increase in leisure time—the labor saved through mechanization is not utilized in intensifying farming, or facilitating part-time working to increase income, but in increasing leisure. It is this desire to increase leisure that has promoted mechanization. (5) Physical stamina —before World War II, the training of children for endurance in hard labor began from the age of 12 years, the graduation age of primary school, but, after World War II, the change in the family system and the spread of higher education made it difficult to train people to endure hard labor. This has served to enhance mechanization.

Additional factors are cited in an interesting study on the introduction of power-tillers by Matsuzawa (1958). He has offered the following four reasons for farm mechanization: (1) The decline in the marginal valuation of money because of the increase in part-time income and the penetration of a money economy, (2) the decline in the price of power-tillers, (3) the increase in the amount of work per man made possible with the advent of the power tiller giving rise to the psychological factor of keeping up with one's neighbors, and (4) the difficulty in employing hired labor. As can easily be seen this study likewise does not deal with the introduction of power tillers as a product of the rational behavior of entrepreneurs.

However the price of power tillers remains fairly expensive, and

TABLE 4
Reasons for the Introduction of Power Tillers*

Farm size (ha)	Reduction of labor	Part-time	Other
0.3–0.5	58	10	28
0.5–1.0	73	11	15
1.0–1.5	85	6	10
1.5–2.0	92	2	6
2.0 over	90	2	9
Total	84	6	10

* Data from the Machinery Association (Kikai Shinko Kyokai), *A Study of the Effects of the Introduction of Power-Tillers in Agriculture (Dōryoku Kōunki Dōnyu Kōka ni Kansuru Kenkyū)* (1963, 1964).

according to the Survey Report "Price and Wage Rates in Farm Villages," the price of a power tiller in 1964 amounted to approximately ¥190,000 (excluding attachments). This was very high compared with the farm household income of ¥670,000 and farm income of ¥320,000 of the same year. Furthermore, if a farmer wanted to buy a power tiller, he had to take the entire responsibility for payment. The Machinery Association (Kikai Shinko Kyokai) made a survey of 2061 farms in which power tillers were introduced. According to this survey, 84 per cent of the farms surveyed explained that the decrease in labor force was the main reason for this introduction of power tillers (Table 4). Very few respondents cited the demonstration effect or other non-economic reasons. This raises doubts concerning the non-economic explanation of the mechanization of Japanese agriculture. Rather, it would have been more appropriate to discuss this mechanization from the viewpoint of economic factors. In what follows this paper will attempt to present a case for the economic rationality approach.

II. Derivation of Models

As can be seen in the regional distribution of Table 5, the widest application of power tillers is found in the northeastern districts of Japan (Tohoku and Hokuriku) where rice production is dominant: 44 power tillers per 100 farms, whereas in the remote districts, e.g., Kyushu, only 17 power tillers per 100 farms are used.[2] As the distribution of power tillers and causes of mechanization differ between regions, separate models are needed for each region. In this

TABLE 5

Number of Power Tillers Per 100 Farms and the Percentage of Total
Farm Land Tilled by Power Tillers by Regions*

Districts	Number		Percentage	
	1960	1965	1960	1965
National Average[a]	8.6	38.2	34.6	59.7
Industrial districts				
Districts surrounding big industries	9.6	38.0	25.5	59.5
Suburb district of local industries	6.6	39.7	28.3	58.6
Agricultural districts				
Districts with high rice production	12.1	44.0	50.1	75.3
Districts producing commercial agricultural products	9.1	40.6	28.8	50.7
Districts producing rice crop in general level	7.5	36.7	31.7	62.2
Districts producing crops excluding rice	6.6	38.6	29.0	57.4
Remote districts	2.1	17.3	14.8	35.5

* Data from the Ministry of Agriculture and Forestry, *Analysis of Regional Farming (Chiiki Nōgyō no Bunseki)* (1965).

a)   Excludes Hokkaidō.

paper, the economics of mechanization in small-scale farming in
Japan will be discussed by concentrating our attention on the Tohoku district where the largest spread of power tillers is observed.
The Tohoku district is a single crop area, and the construction of a
model for this district is easier because rice yields per *tan* have not
increased substantially (see Table 6), thereby eliminating the need to
treat technological progress. As mentioned previously, prefectural
experimental stations report that there is no increase in the yield of
rice resulting from the use of power tillers. As is shown in Table 6,
for the period between 1957 and 1964 no increase in rice yields was
observed following the introduction of power tillers in the Tohoku
district. Other inputs such as new varieties, agricultural chemicals
are more relevant to the yield performance. In this paper, therefore,
we can safely ignore the yield effect of power cultivation.

---

[2] The fact that the greatest spread of power tillers occurred in the districts
where rice production is dominant could be attributed to land schemes. See
Tsuchiya (1964).

TABLE 6

Yield of Rice Per *Tan* in the Tohoku District*

(Unit: Kg)

Year	Average	0.3–0.5^{ha}	0.5–1.0^{ha}	1.0–1.5^{ha}	1.5–2.0^{ha}	2.0^{ha} & over
1957	451	471	433	450	439	473
1958	442	431	421	431	434	471
1959	464	451	450	458	456	487
1960	488	486	473	486	491	499
1961	482	462	474	489	482	492
1962	486	481	484	488	482	489
1963	475	480	472	469	484	482
1964	475	468	461	467	481	485

  * Data from the Ministry of Agriculture and Forestry, *The Cost Survey of Rice Production (Kome Seisanhi)* (Annual editions, 1957 through 1964).

In our analysis we have assumed the following conditions: a) perfect competition in the labor and farm machinery markets, b) a constant acreage of farm land cultivated by the farmer himself, and c) farm costs being equal to labor and machinery costs.

Nakajima and Tanaka have developed the theory of utility maximization as the behavioristic principle of small-scale farming. Our model here is suggested by their works,[3] and the behavioristic principle of the farm household is adopted to maximize the utility function.

$$U = U(A, M) \qquad (1)$$

subject to the isoquant equation:

$$\bar{y}(b) = f(a, k) \qquad (2)$$

and the money equation:

$$M = P_y \bar{y} + W(A - a) + P_k(\bar{K} - k), \qquad (3)$$

where

$\bar{y}$:   real net farm product,

a: labor input in owned farm,

k: utilization hours of power machinery in owned farm,

$\bar{b}$:   farm land,

M: money income (farm household income),

---

[3] For further information, see the papers by C. Nakajima in Ohkawa and Kawano, eds. (1958) and *The Study of Agriculture and Forestry* (1966) and also a paper by Tanaka (1967). This model was originally suggested by T. Yori of Kyoto University.

W: wage rate of hired worker,

P_y: price of y,

A: family labor input in farm and non-farm sector,

K: total utilization hours of owned power machinery, and

P_k: hourly rent for power tillers.

If $A<a$, labor is hired from another farm but if $A>a$, labor is sold to another farm. If $A<a$, $W(A-a)$ would be negative and would imply a wage payment. Similarly, if $\bar{K}<k$, $P_k(\bar{K}-k)$ would be negative and would imply a payment of rent. If $\bar{K}>k$, $P_k(\bar{K}-k)$ would be positive and would mean a receipt of rent.

The equilibrium conditions will be as follows:

$$\frac{\partial f / \partial a}{\partial f / \partial k} = \frac{W}{P_k}, \tag{4}$$

$$W = \frac{-U_A}{U_M}. \tag{5}$$

If we take equations (2), (3), (4) and (5) simultaneously, a, A, k and M are obtained by taking W, P_k, $\bar{K}$ and $\bar{y}$ as parameters. Here, attention should be paid to the fact that at first $\bar{y}$ is determined by $\bar{b}$, and then a and k are determined by equations (2) and (4). Then, A and M are determined by (3) and (5).

Equation (4) is synonymous with the enterprise behavior which minimizes the production cost in order to produce a given output. Namely, if we minimize cost function,

$$C = Wa + P_k k \tag{6}$$

subject to equation (2), the equilibrium condition becomes

$$\frac{\partial f / \partial a}{\partial f / \partial k} = \frac{W}{P_k}. \tag{4'}$$

Equation (4) and equation (4') are exactly the same, and the equilibrium values of a and k are solved by considering equations (2) and (4) simultaneously. A and M are determined by maximizing the utility function subject to equation (3), substituting equilibrium values of a and k.

Now, as a means of summarizing the model mentioned above, we note that in the models where the markets for labor and machinery are perfectly competitive, the farm household minimizes the cost of production in the same way as other industrial enterprises (profit maximization of farm sector). Furthermore, the farm household maximizes the utility function based on the laborer's household. This model should be tested by the following model structure:

The isoquant equation is assumed as

$$\bar{y} = va^\alpha k^\beta, \tag{7}$$

and the cost equation is

$$C = Wa + P_k k, \tag{8}$$

where

$\bar{y}$:   real net farm products,

a: hours of labor input in owned farm,

k: utilization hours of power machinery in owned farm,

α, β, v: parameter to be estimated,

C: cost,

W: wage rate of hired worker, and

P_k: hourly rent for power farm machinery.

If $\bar{y}$, W, P_k are taken as parameters, the equilibrium condition becomes

$$\begin{pmatrix} \log a \\ \log k \end{pmatrix} = \begin{pmatrix} -1 & 1 \\ \alpha & \beta \end{pmatrix}^{-1} \begin{pmatrix} \log W - \log P_k + \log \beta - \log \alpha \\ \log y - \log v \end{pmatrix}. \tag{9}$$

III. Empirical Estimation of the Models

The equations described above were fitted to the data obtained from the *Survey of Farm Household Economy* for the Tohoku district. These data such as $\bar{y}$, a, k and W were obtained from the records of the survey and were classified according to the operating acreage spread over the eight years from 1957 to 1964 (see Appendix). We might note here that the number surveyed in Tohoku was 694 and that the accuracy of the survey was very high. The reason for using 1957 as the base year was that a big revision of the survey method was carried out in that year. The change in the survey method raises difficulties in establishing continuity of the data for the years before and after 1957.

However, difficult problems arose in the estimation of the hourly rent for tilling by power tillers which we have estimated as follows. The rent of power tillers per 10 acres or 1 *tan* is obtained from the

Survey of Farm Household Economy (see Appendix Table A-2, p. 169). The capacity of a power-tiller is estimated as one hour per 10 acres.[4] Therefore, the hourly rent for tilling has been estimated as the rent per 10 acres.

Regression Results

At first, the function

$$k = v'a^{\alpha'}\bar{y}^{\beta'}u' \tag{10}$$

instead of

$$\bar{y} = va^{\alpha}k^{\beta}u \tag{7}$$

is used to estimate parameters. This is because $\bar{y}$ is almost constant, as shown in Table A.1, and in equation (2), $\bar{y}$ is considered as a parameter. Here we consider a parameter to be a predetermined variable so that $\bar{y}$ will not involve any disturbance, and thus the disturbance is included only in k where u and u' are random disturbances. The statistical results of the function (10) are tabulated in Table 7 and Table 8 with Table 8 being derived from Table 7; detailed tables are shown in the Appendix.

TABLE 7

Regression Results:
$$k_t = v'a_t^{\alpha'}\,\bar{y}_t^{\beta'} \tag{10}$$

Farm size	v'	α'	β'	R^2	d
0.3–0.5ha	9.0763 (2.5243)	−2.9297 (0.5397)	6.0836 (1.6338)	0.8688	1.3383
0.5–1.0	3.5783 (1.0139)	−1.9601 (0.3606)	2.3133 (1.0741)	0.8615	1.9139
1.0–1.5	2.9200 (0.7196)	−1.4751 (0.5615)	1.1124 (1.4057)	0.7255	1.2318
1.5–2.0	3.1468 (0.9958)	−1.4072 (0.6083)	2.1917 (1.6912)	0.8057	1.2006
2.0 over	2.3031 (0.3532)	−0.8564 (0.1895)	1.4970 (0.5564)	0.8130	2.0799

a) The figures in parentheses denote the standard error in the estimated values.
b) R denotes the coefficient of multiple correlation.
c) d is a statistical quantity which shows verifications using the Durbin and Watson serial correlation.

[4] According to the records of a national test, a middle size power tiller (3–6. hp.) takes from 65 minutes to 95 minutes to till 10 acres of land. Also, according to the *Journal of Mechanized Agriculture (Kikaika Nogyyo)*, in June, 1959, the time required for cultivating 10 acres was from 55 to 60 minutes for power-tillers over 7 hp. Therefore, it is estimated that it takes about 1 hour for 10 acres to be tilled.

TABLE 8

Regression Results*

$$y_t = v a_t{}^\alpha k_t{}^\beta \tag{7}$$

Farm size	v	α	β
0.3–0.5ha	0.224930	0.481571	0.164378
0.5–1.0	0.212920	0.847337	0.432288
1.0–1.5	0.072440	1.326090	0.898990
1.5–2.0	0.237930	0.642084	0.456269
2.0 over	0.214710	0.572090	0.667985

*This Table is derived from Table 7.

Optimum values

The solutions of equation (9) are tabulated in Table 9 and Table 10. The upper rows in Tables 9 and 10 show actual values, and the lower rows show optimum values. The difference between actual values and optimum values in Tables 9 and 10 are small as shown in Fig. 1. Therefore, this model is, I believe, appropriate for explaining the actual behavioristic principle of farm households. Kudo's explanation (Kudo, 1962) also supports our results. He pointed out that "such rational behavior is seen because power tillers are so expensive. Farmers have to buy power tillers with their own funds. Because a special credit-financing system for farmers has not yet been developed, they are forced to calculate the economic feasibility of buying machines on their own account."

TABLE 9

Comparison of Actual and Optimum Hours of Utilization of Power Farm Machinery by Farm Size

(Unit: 10 hours)

	0.3–0.5ha	0.5–1.0ha	1.0–1.5ha	1.5–2.0ha	2.0ha over
Actual hours	32	66	145	210	349
Optimum hours	25	66	137	184	356

TABLE 10

Comparison of Actual and Optimum Hours of Farm Labor by Farm Size

(Unit: 10 hours)

	0.3–0.5ha	0.5–1.0ha	1.0–1.5ha	1.5–2.0ha	2.0ha over
Actual hours	157	303	447	543	692
Optimum hours	163	295	456	583	667

FIGURE 1
Isoquant Curve and Cost Curve*

(Unit: 100 hours)

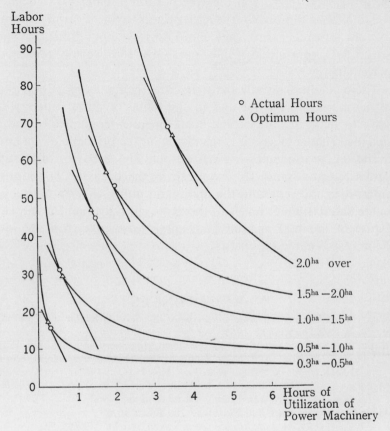

Labor
Hours

o Actual Hours
△ Optimum Hours

2.0^{ha} over

1.5^{ha} —2.0^{ha}

1.0^{ha} —1.5^{ha}

0.5^{ha} —1.0^{ha}

0.3^{ha} —0.5^{ha}

Hours of
Utilization of
Power Machinery

IV. Conclusion

The recent mechanization of Japanese agriculture has been carried out through the introduction of power tillers. As the price of
power tillers is very high relative to farm income, the mechanization of Japanese agriculture has been treated from the standpoint of
non-economic reasons such as the demonstration effect. However,
my opinion concerning mechanization differs from that of the non-
economic interpretations mentioned above. Rather, it is my view
that mechanization has resulted from the structural change which

has occurred in the labor market. The Japanese economy has undergone a high rate of growth since 1955; consequently, the industrial sector has absorbed a considerable portion of laborers, thus giving rise to a labor shortage in the agricultural sector. If farmers wanted to work for other farms, they could do so without difficulty. There are always opportunities, either part-time labor work or renting out power tillers.

These conditions show that very near perfect competition exists in the markets for labor and in the rental of power tillers which serve to make Japanese agriculture operate economically and rationally. That is to say, it is operating on the principle of cost minimization for producing a given output. This behavior of the agricultural sector is exactly the same as the behavior of industrial enterprises and results in the maximum utility of farm households in the districts under review. I therefore conclude that the mechanization of Japanese agriculture is quite reasonable from the viewpoint of economic rationality.

REFERENCES

Kayo, N., ed. *Problems of Mechanization of Japanese Agriculture (Nihon Nogyo no Kikaika no Kadai).* 1963.

Kudo, Z., "An Economic Study of the Farm Machinery on a Japanese Family Farm," *Bulletin of Tohoku National Agricultural Experiment Station (Tohoku Nogyo Shinkenjo Hokoku),* No. 25 (Oct. 1962).

Matsuzawa, M., "Mechanization in Family Farm," *A Study of Agricultural Economics (Nogyo Keieikeizaigaku no Kenkyu),* 1958.

Ministry of Agriculture and Forestry. *The Effect of the Introduction of Power Tillers (Doryoku Kounki nikansuru Shiken Seiseki).* 1960.

Misawa, T. and Kato, Y., "Capital Formation in Japanese Agriculture after World War II," *Journal of Rural Economics (Nogyo Keizai Kenkyu),* XXIX, No. 4 (Dec. 1959).

Nakajima, C., "An Equilibrium Theory of Farm Household," *Survey of Contemporary Agricultural Economics (Gendai Nogyo Bunseki no Tenbo),* K. Ohkawa and S. Kawano, eds., 1958.

Nakajima, C., "The Utility Function of Farm Households," *The Study of Agriculture and Forestry (Noringyo Mondai Kenkyu),* II, No. 1 (1966).

Tanaka, O. *Agricultural Equilibrium Analysis (Nogyo no Kinko Busseki).* 1967.

Tsuchiya, K., "Land Improvement Schemes and Innovations in Agricultural Technology," *Rural Economic Problems,* I, No. 1 (May, 1964).

Wataya, T., "Change of Family System and Farm Management," *Journal of Agriculture and Economics (Nogyo to Keizai)* (Aug. 1959).

APPENDIX

Appendix: TABLE A-1
Real Net Farm Product*

(Unit: 1,000)

Year	0.3–0.5^{ha}	0.5–1.0^{ha}	Farm size 1.0–1.5^{ha}	1.5–2.0^{ha}	2.0^{ha} & over
1957	231	423	716	919	1,465
1958	216	432	652	937	1,440
1959	216	451	694	959	1,494
1960	243	470	750	986	1,584
1961	246	471	721	989	1,569
1962	233	469	756	1029	1,522
1963	218	441	745	1025	1,439
1964	209	417	709	945	1,384
Average	226	446	717	973	1,487

* Data from the Ministry of Agriculture and Forestry, *Report on the Survey of Farm Household Economy (Nōka Keizai Chōsa Hōkoku)*, (Annual editions, 1957–1964).

a) The figures of real net farm product were obtained after deflating by the price of rice.

Appendix: TABLE A-2
Rent for Tilling Per 10 Areas by Power Tiller

(Unit: Yen)

Year	1957	1958	1959	1960	1961	1962	1963	1964	Average
Rent	707.3	915.9	847.4	848.9	840.5	1,115.5	1,200.0	1,180.0	956.0

* Data from the Ministry of Agriculture and Forestry, *Report on the Survey of Farm Household Economy (Nōka Keizai Chōsa Hōkoku)* (Annual editions, 1957–1964).

Appendix: TABLE A-3
Wage Rate of Hired Worker (Male) Per Day*

(Unit: Yen)

Year	0.3ha–0.5	0.5–1.0ha	Farm size 1.0–1.5ha	1.5–2.0ha	2.0ha & over
1957	276	279	297	276	300
1958	296	292	278	308	302
1959	335	324	312	311	314
1960	329	369	319	326	328
1961	420	403	405	365	400
1962	448	470	478	518	524
1963	611	578	596	594	616
1964	668	551	692	690	718
Average	423	422	422	424	438

* Data from the Ministry of Agriculture and Forestry, *Survey of Prices and Wage Rates in Farm Villages (Bukka Chingin Chōsa Hōkokusho)* (Annual editions, 1957–1964).

Appendix: TABLE A-4
A Comparison of Actual and Optimum Hours of Labor and Utilization
of Power Machinery on a 0.3–0.5ha-Size Farm

(Unit: 10 hours)

Year	Labor Actual hours	Optimum hours	Power farm machinery Actual hours	Optimum hours
1957	175	187	17	18
1958	187	167	10	18
1959	175	161	21	20
1960	175	194	37	23
1961	167	186	41	28
1962	130	168	51	27
1963	132	140	37	31
1964	115	128	44	31
Average	157	163	32	25

Appendix: TABLE A-5

A Comparison of Actual and Optimum Hours of Labor and Utilization of Power Machinery on a 0.5–1.0ha-Size Farm

(Unit: 10 hours)

Year	Labor		Power farm machinery	
	Actual hours	Optimum hours	Actual hours	Optimum hours
1957	342	326	39	48
1958	330	326	48	50
1959	336	326	52	56
1960	332	321	61	63
1961	328	312	72	67
1962	260	295	83	75
1963	245	262	87	81
1964	251	240	92	85
Average	303	295	66	66

Appendix: TABLE A-6

A Comparison of Actual and Optimum Hours of Labor and Utilization of Power Machinery on a 1.0–1.5ha-Size Farm

(Unit: 10 hours)

Year	Labor		Power farm machinery	
	Actual hours	Optimum hours	Actual hours	Optimum hours
1957	497	525	94	110
1958	493	517	109	102
1959	503	507	119	113
1960	482	521	154	118
1961	442	465	166	134
1962	394	444	161	151
1963	378	403	184	171
1964	388	371	178	182
Average	447	456	145	137

Appendix: TABLE A-7
A Comparison of Actual and Optimum Hours of Labor and Utilization
of Power Machinery on a 1.5–2.0ʰᵃ-Size Farm

(Unit: 10 hours)

Year	Labor		Power farm machinery	
	Actual hours	Optimum hours	Actual hours	Optimum hours
1957	614	660	124	135
1958	592	642	162	147
1959	601	653	194	151
1960	578	653	209	159
1961	538	629	219	170
1962	474	563	244	214
1963	467	530	274	234
1964	479	463	253	237
Average	543	583	210	184

Appendix: TABLE A-8
A Comparison of Actual and Optimum Hours of Labor and Utilization
of Power Machinery on a 2.0ʰᵃ & Over-Size Farm

(Unit: 10 hours)

Year	Labor		Power farm machinery	
	Actual hours	Optimum hours	Actual hours	Optimum hours
1957	799	808	275	296
1958	782	794	305	293
1959	752	801	338	311
1960	742	820	368	329
1961	693	731	385	357
1962	612	617	364	395
1963	587	540	392	407
1964	567	482	372	423
Average	692	667	349	356

PART III

CHAPTER 7

AGRICULTURE AND LABOR SUPPLY IN THE MEIJI ERA[†]

MATAJI UMEMURA

Introduction

According to S. Kuznets' illuminating international comparison of the long-run rates of economic growth of nations (Kuznets, 1956), the most rapidly growing nations in the world have been the United States, Canada, Sweden, and Japan in terms of national product, and Sweden and Japan in terms of per capita national product. Thus, in the past several years, many attempts have been made to investigate the process by which the Japanese economy has been able to sustain such a high rate of growth. Among them, Ohkawa's study of the changes in the pattern of the Japanese economic growth is most helpful (Ohkawa, 1965). The main findings of his study, which employs a two-sector approach and concentrates mainly on the pattern of economic growth in the non-agricultural sector, can be summarized as follows: as far as the non-agricultural sector is concerned in the first period which ends about 1905, the rate of growth of the labor force was definitely higher than that of productivity per worker, while in the second period, 1905–40, the relationship was completely reversed. Thus, the changes in the rates of growth of both labor supply and productivity per worker played important roles at different times in changing the pattern of economic growth in the non-agricultural sector. On the basis of this and other evidence, Ohkawa, in my opinion, rightly concludes that the labor-growth pattern dominated the first period, while the productivity-growth pattern characterized the second period.

The purpose of this paper will be to make clear the process through which the labor-growth pattern appeared in the Meiji era

---

[†] Reproduced here, with slight revisions, from *The Developing Economies*, III, No. 3 (Sept., 1965).

and to evaluate the contributions of agriculture to that process through an analysis of the structure of the labor market in the Meiji period. In Section I, we will deal with the growth of population as the basic determinant in the increase of labor supply. In Sections II and III, we will discuss the outflow of the labor force from agriculture and its quantitative importance in the expansion of employment in the non-agricultural industries. In these sections, the structural characteristics of the labor market in the Meiji era will be pointed out and the importance of the expansion of side-businesses in the peasant household economy will be emphasized.

I. The Growth of Population

The amount of labor available for the production of goods and services is determined by a large variety of demographic, economic, and social factors, the most important of which are those associated with the size of the population. Long-term trends in fertility, mortality, and migration determine the size and structure of the population and set the upper limits of the labor force. Therefore, it is reasonable to deal first with the growth of population as the basic determinant of the labor supply.

The biggest event characterizing the beginning of modern demographic history of the presently economically well-developed countries is the so-called "Vital Revolution."[1] After a long demographic history of repeated alternations of growth and decline in population, the history of which may be conceived of as the real background of the Malthusian population theory, the size of the population in many European countries began to grow steadily as economic development proceeded.[2] Compared with the gloomy stories of mass death caused by the successive occurrence of famines and epidemics of the earlier periods, this change in the population trends appears to be so impressive and so progressive that it has been celebrated as the Vital Revolution. In Japan too, a similar picture of demographic evolution can be found in the Meiji era.

Before entering into a discussion of our main topic of demograph-

---

[1] For a general discussion of this see Helleiner (1957).

[2] For a more detailed treatment, the reader is referred to United Nations (1953), Chap. 2.

ic evolution in the Meiji era, however, we will attempt to give a rough sketch of demographic trends in the Tokugawa period.[3] Since the beginning of the 17th century when the Tokugawa government was firmly established and people began to enjoy a peaceful life following protracted periods of war, surveys of population and agricultural land had been made on a local basis by many of the individual feudal lords *(daimyo)*, chiefly for purposes of tax collection. Furthermore, fortunately for present-day scholars, the unique religious registration system adopted by the Tokugawa government made available, as a by-product, a voluminous annual which was, in fact, a "who's who" of the entire population in all towns and villages throughout the country. Unfortunately, however, the results of these population surveys were not tabulated in the form of nationwide population statistics until 1721 when the 8th Shogun Yoshimune requested all the feudal lords to report the number of civil inhabitants under their control. This action was taken in order to facilitate the inauguration of his policy of reform undertaken during the Kyoho period *(Kyoho Kaikaku)*. In 1726, Yoshimune ordered that every six years regular population reports should be made on a nationwide scale. The records of this nationwide population survey, which are now available, are presented in Tables 1 and 2. Unfortunately, the population statistics suffer much from the lack of uniformity of the feudal lords' reports concerning population less than 15 years old and some inevitable incompleteness of population registration. For example, Kanazawa Han did not report those less than 15 years old, and Wakayama Han did not include any of the population less than 7 years old in its report. It is believed, however, that the reporting practices maintained by the individual lords did not change throughout the entire period thanks to their conservative, unreceptive-to-change attitudes. Therefore, the demographic trends observed from Tables 1 and 2 can be considered to approximate the real ones although the absolute size of population cannot be taken as reliable.

The demographic trends of the 18th century and the first half of the 19th century, observable from Tables 1 and 2, can be summarized as follows:

---

[3] For the details of the discussion which follows, see Umemura (1965a).

TABLE 1
The Japanese Civil Population, 1721–1846*

(Unit: 1,000)

Year	Number of population				Average annual rate of change (%)	Female/Male (%)
	Male	Female	Total	Index		
1721			26,065	100.0		
1726			26,549	101.9	0.37	
1732	14,407	12,515	26,922	103.3	0.23	86.9
1744			26,153	100.3	−0.24	
1750	13,819	12,099	25,918	99.4	−0.15	87.6
1756	13,833	12,229	26,071	100.1	0.09	88.4
1762	13,785	12,136	25,921	99.5	−0.09	88.0
1768			26,252	100.7	0.21	
1774			25,990	99.7	−0.17	
1780			26,011	99.8	0.01	
1786	13,231	11,856	25,086	96.2	−0.59	89.6
1792			24,891	95.5	−0.13	
1798	13,361	12,111	25,471	97.7	0.39	90.6
1804	13,427	12,195	25,622	98.3	0.10	90.8
1822	13,894	12,708	26,602	102.1	0.21	91.4
1828	14,161	13,040	27,201	104.4	0.38	92.1
1834	14,053	13,010	27,064	103.8	−0.08	92.6
1846	13,854	13,054	26,908	103.2	−0.05	94.2

* Data from N. Sekiyama, *Structure of Japanese Population in the Modern Era (Kinsei Nihon no Jinkō Kōzō)* (Tokyo, 1958), pp. 123, 267.

(1) The size of the civil population was decreasing in the 18th century, but began to increase in the first half of the 19th century although the observed trends were not very clear.[4] It is important to note that the gradually accelerating upward population trend in the second half of the 19th century, i.e., the Meiji era discussed below, was led by a slightly increasing population trend in the first half of the same century. This leads us to emphasize here the continuity of the demographic trend.

(2) Significant decreases of population were recorded in the 1730's, 1780's and 1830's when the three biggest famines in the Tokugawa era occurred. The losses of population due to famine and accom-

---

[4] According to fragmentary population statistics in some regions and other evidence, it is estimated that in the 17th century the Japanese civil population showed an increasing trend.

TABLE 2
The Japanese Civil Population by District, 1721–1846*

(Unit: 1,000)

Year	Kinki	Tokai	Kanto	Tohoku	Tosan
1721	4,670	2,320	5,123	2,840	1,598
1750	4,448	2,373	5,043	2,630	1,603
1756	4,564	2,341	4,974	2,644	1,642
1786	4,420	2,307	4,375	2,368	1,633
1798	4,366	2,328	4,350	2,442	1,695
1804	4,336	2,340	4,295	2,473	1,694
1822	4,484	2,499	4,242	2,559	1,758
1828	4,531	2,476	4,343	2,626	1,889
1834	4,470	2,474	4,171	2,632	1,827
1846	4,366	2,482	4,438	2,520	1,774
	Hokuriku	Sanin	Sanyo	Shikoku	Kyushu
1721	2,155	703	2,023	1,523	3,074
1750	2,160	739	2,037	1,562	3,165
1756	2,212	768	2,073	1,607	3,213
1786	2,108	787	2,139	1,661	3,226
1798	2,269	834	2,214	1,702	3,237
1804	2,307	844	2,223	1,760	3,299
1822	2,511	895	2,351	1,863	3,396
1828	2,598	913	2,425	1,896	3,442
1834	2,640	933	2,464	1,932	3,449
1846	2,534	877	2,433	1,943	3,468

* Data from N. Sekiyama, *op. cit.*, 1958, pp. 140–141.

panying epidemics were very severe in the eastern part of Japan which is characterized as marginal land for rice growing.[5] Much crop damage due to cold weather or drought continued even through the Meiji era, but the large-scale effects on the human population did not recur following the disaster of the 1830's. This may be attributed to the more efficient administration of the modern government and the improvement of transportation facilities.[6]

[5] In the medieval period, most of the recorded famines came from drought and occurred in the western part of Japan. The recorded shift of severe famine region from the western part of Japan to the eastern part is supposed to be mainly due to both the eastward movement of population and improvements in the irrigation facilities in the western region.

[6] The Finnish experience in the end of the 17th century makes the point clear. See Jutikkala.

(3) Throughout the entire period under discussion, the female population was, to a significant extent, less than the male population although we cannot dismiss the possibility that undercounting might occur more often in the case of females than males. However, there are reasons to believe that the abnormal sex composition of population suggested by the data did, in fact, occur. It is highly probable that the weakest segment of the population would suffer most from the practices of abortion and infanticide which prevailed during that period. It is also inferred that the abnormal sex composition of the population might limit the population's growth potential by preventing marriage. The deficiency in the number of females gradually disappeared as conditions favorable to population increase were created by the turn of the century.

(4) The civil population declined in the Tohoku, Kanto, and Kinai districts, but increased in other districts. This observed regional difference in population trends can be considered as a reliable index showing regional differences in economic development. As a test of this hypothesis, the regional rate of change of the civil population during the period of 1721–1834 is correlated with the corresponding rate of change for the standard taxable output of a community assigned by the lords' officers. Fig. 1 shows a significant positive correlation among regions except for the Kanto and Tohoku districts where repeated mass damage to the population was severe.

Having briefly outlined the general picture of demographic trends in the later Tokugawa period, we will turn our attention to the main issue of the demographic evolution in the Meiji era. According to the unpublished estimates of Miss K. Akasaka[7] based on the available sources of vital and migration statistics, the Japanese population (excluding foreigners) increased by about 63 per cent from 34.4 million in 1873 to 55.9 million in 1920 when the first modern population census was taken. We might also note here that these figures are close to the official estimates of the Cabinet Bureau of Statistics (C.B.S.). In spite of the great effort made by Akasaka and the C.B.S., the population figures for the early Meiji period seem to

---

[7] Akasaka's estimates of the Japanese population will be published in a volume of the *Estimates of Long-Term Economic Statistics of Japan since 1868 (Choki Keizai Tokei)*.

FIGURE 1
Correlation of Rates of Change
Between Kokudaka[a] and Population*

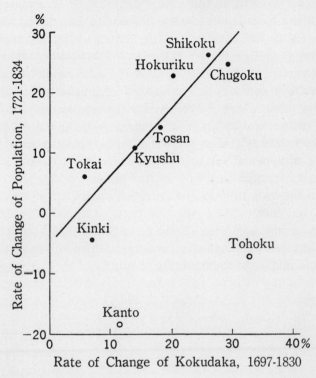

* Population data from Table 2.
Kokudaka from T. Kikuchi, *Reclamation of Arable Land (Shinden Kaihatsu)* (Tokyo, 1958), I, p. 137.
a) Kokudaka corresponds to the standard taxable output of a community. If Kanto and Tohoku are excluded from comparison, the following numerical relationship is obtained:
$Y = 1.1355\ X - 5.21$ $r^2 = 0.8542$,
where X and Y represent rates of change of Kokudaka and of population respectively.

suffer from a possible incompleteness in population registration and from a conceivable undercounting of births and deaths which still remain unadjusted in both series. Therefore, it may be said that the growth rate of the population thus far derived is somewhat overstated by both the Akasaka and the C.B.S. series.

According to the generally accepted doctrine of demographic

transitions, the growth of population in the early phase of demographic evolution comes from the widening difference between a sustained high birth rate and a steadily declining death rate.[8] In the course of the recent controversy concerning English demographic history in the 18th century, however, this traditional theory has been strongly challenged by Habakkuk (Habakkuk, 1953, 1958), Karuse (Karuse, 1958, 1959), and others. The Scandinavian experience in the 18th century, as reported by Gille, seems to be favorable to the new theory (Gille, 1949). As for the Japanese case in the second half of the 19th century, Fig. 2 clearly shows that the rising birth rate plays a definite role in preparing for population growth in the Meiji era, although the magnitude of the rise of the birth rate may be somewhat exaggerated by the possible incompleteness of registration in the early period. The observed rise of the death rate may be explained partly by the incomplete registration of deaths in the early period and partly by the increasing baby population whose death rate is naturally high. We may remark here that the role played by international migration is quite minor.

FIGURE 2
Crude Birth and Death Rates, 1873-1920*

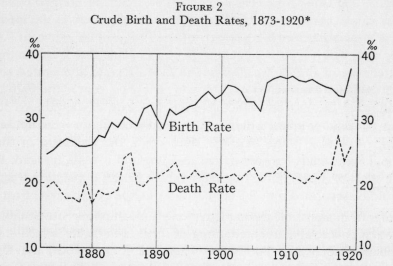

*   Data from K. Akasaka's unpublished estimates.

---

[8] For example, see Notestein (1950).

It is generally believed that this population increase was very influential in accumulating a large reservoir of labor which was subsequently siphoned off to meet the rapidly expanding employment opportunities which were created during the course of industrialization.

If the surprisingly rapid expansion of the Japanese economy during the Meiji era could be explained mostly by the reserve army of labor supply thus far accumulated, we might expect the rate of growth of the population to have been much higher in Japan than in any other country which had already been industrialized. But we will have more to say on this point below.

According to the 18th and 19th century experiences of the present economically well-developed countries, the rate of growth of population in the early periods of economic development was not very great and seldom exceeded 1 per cent per annum. This was also true in Japan, and this aspect of the picture is quite different from that of the recent experience of developing countries which are now experiencing spurts of population growth. A comparison of the rate of population growth between Japan and Britain is given in Fig. 3, and similar patterns of population trends in the two countries can be easily identified. The annual rate of growth of the Japanese population in the latter part of the 19th century averaged 0.8 per cent, which is almost equal to that of England and Wales in the latter part of the 18th century. The Japanese rate accelerated remarkably until it reached its peak rate of 1.42 per cent in the 1920's. Following this period of acceleration, the rate has continued to show a trend of gradual decrease, with only the minor interruption which followed World War II. Here again, the similarity of the population trends between Japan and England is quite marked. If the effect of international migration on the British population trend could be separated out, the similarity would be even clearer. From these observations, we may conclude that the course of demographic evolution in Japan has corresponded with that of Britain with a time lag of a little more than a century. Therefore, as far as the rate of growth of the population is concerned, Japan possessed no special advantages for accumulating a reserve army of labor.

FIGURE 3
Annual Compound Rate of Growth of Total
Population, Japan and Britain*

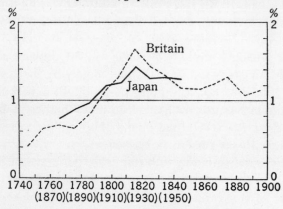

* Data for Japan from K. Akasaka's unpublished estimates.
Data for Britain from G. T. Griffith, *Population Problems of the Age of Malthus* (London, 1926), p. 18; *Royal Commission on the Distribution of Industrial Population-Report*, Cmd. 6135 (Jan. 1940), p. 138; and ILO, *Year Book of Labor Statistics*.
a) Data before 1801 is for England and Wales, while data since 1801 is for Great Britain. Years indicated in parentheses are for Japan.

II. Inter-Industrial Movement of the Labor Force

It is a well-recognized fact that the outflow of the labor force from agriculture provides a big source of labor for the rapidly expanding non-agricultural industries. Marxian economists have traditionally regarded the function of enclosure in providing labor in the Industrial Revolution as crucial, and have rejected the alternative view that the appearance of the reserve army of labor was merely a product of growing population.[9] Recently, however, J. D. Chambers attempted to test the Marxian abstract formula of an institutional creation of the reserve army by fitting it to the local facts in Nottinghamshire, and made a great contribution to correcting the biased view of enclosure's role (Chambers, 1953).

As seen in Table 3, the rate of increase of total employment in Japan has remained almost constant at a rate of some 1 per cent per annum throughout the whole period of modern economic growth.

---

[9] See, for example, Dobb, Chap. 6.

In Britain, it was a little higher than 1 per cent per annum in the latter 19th century and dropped to a level of about 0.5 per cent after World War I. Due to the lack of relevant data, we cannot deal with the British experience in the Industrial Revolution although rough estimates will be presented later. To be noted here is the fact that the rate of increase of total employment appears to be a little higher in Britain than in Japan.

TABLE 3

Annual Compound Rate of Growth of Employment
by Sector: Japan and Great Britain*   (Unit: %)

Period	All industries		Non-agriculture		Agriculture	
	Great Britain	Japan	Great Britain	Japan	Great Britain	Japan
1851–61	1.38		1.59		−0.42	
1861–71	1.08		1.53		−1.15	
1871–81	0.95	0.84[a]	1.27	4.67[a]	−1.07	−0.02[a]
1881–91	1.38	1.01	1.64	4.15	−0.69	0.01
1891–1901	1.06	0.81	1.23	3.10	−0.56	−0.30
1901–11	1.18	0.94	1.25	2.56	0.41	−0.06
1911–21	0.54	0.98	0.62	2.27	−0.47	−0.06
1921–31	0.84	0.80	0.99	1.67	−1.24	−0.05
1931–41	0.36	0.90	0.40	1.82	−0.36	−0.15
1941–51		1.08		0.53		1.76

* Data for Japan from M. Umemura, *Wages, Employment and Agriculture (Chingin, Koyō, Nōgyō)* (Tokyo, 1961), p. 117.
Data for Great Britain from F. D. W. Taylor, "Numbers in Agriculture," *Farm Economist*, VIII, No. 4 (1955).
a) For the period 1875–1880.

Regarding the long-term trend of agricultural employment, we have a sharp contrast between the two countries as shown below. In Great Britain, according to the studies of Chambers (Chambers, 1953) and Saville (Saville, 1957), agricultural employment did not decrease under the influence of the enclosure movement during the Industrial Revolution, but on the contrary, it increased through the adoption of labor intensive farming, namely the introduction of root crops into the traditional rotation system and an increased number of livestock. Agricultural employment did not begin to decline until after the middle of the 19th century. In Germany, France, Italy, and other countries in continental Europe, the agricultural work force increased from about 1880 until around 1920 when its peak level was finally attained. Thus, the absolute decline in the number of the agricultural work force in many European countries is a relatively recent phenomenon which began only in the 1920's. In contrast to this, the long-run trend of the number of persons engaged in agriculture in Japan remained almost constant with a slight tendency to decrease throughout the entire period before World War II. It is one of the most distinctive features of the Japanese economy that employment in agriculture never did increase during the early stages of economic development. Various factors are believed to have been influential in keeping the agricultural work force stable. Among them, the limited supply of virgin land suitable for cultivation, little progress in livestock production, and the creation of job opportunities for the growing rural population by the rapid expansion of traditional small-scale manufacturing and commerce in the rural districts were most important in checking a possible increase in the agricultural work force.

Since the motive power driving an economy into sustained growth lies in the non-agricultural industries, especially mining and manufacturing, the changes of employment in these sectors are crucial for economic development. In Britain, the rate of increase of employment in the non-agricultural industries seems to have been almost entirely governed by the growth of the labor supply as a whole and seems not to have been influenced to any sizable extent by the changes in agricultural employment. On the contrary, the rate of increase of employment in the non-agricultural sector in Japan appeared to be quite independent of the growth rate of the labor supply as a whole. In spite of the fact that the total labor supply continued to grow at a constant rate of 1 per cent per annum, non-agricultural employment grew at a rate of more than 4 per cent per year both in the 1870's and 1880's, though the rate of growth gradually declined year by year. A similar pattern in the increase of non-agricultural employment can also be observed in the United States although the mechanism by which it was realized, namely, waves of immigration from Europe, was quite different. But in Japan there was no such immigration, and the main spring of the labor supply for the rapid expansion of the non-agricultural work force had to be sought in the internal migration of the labor force from the agricultural sector.

An estimate of the inter-industrial movement of the labor force from agriculture in the Meiji era is given in Table 4 in successive quinquennial averages. It was about 170,000–180,000 per year, showing a slight tendency to increase over time. M. Namiki's estimates (Namiki, 1957), based on different sources, which put the figure at 180,000–210,000, almost coincides with ours. The contribution rate, which is defined as the proportion of the outflow of the labor force from agriculture to the increase of the non-agricultural employment, was some 85 per cent in the early Meiji era and was still a little more than 70 per cent at the end of the Meiji period.

TABLE 4

The Inter-Industrial Movement of the Labor Force, 1875–1915*

(Unit: 1,000)

Period	Outflow of the agricultural working force per annum	annual increase in employment in non-agricultural industries	Contribution rate (%)	Outflow rate (%)
1875–1880	146	159	91.8	0.99
1880–1885	165	192	85.9	1.12
1885–1890	171	199	85.9	1.16
1890–1895	178	204	87.3	1.21
1895–1900	174	213	81.7	1.19
1900–1905	178	228	78.1	1.24
1905–1910	172	228	75.4	1.20
1910–1915	166	229	72.5	1.16

* Data from M. Umemura, *Wages, Employment and Agriculture (Chingin Koyō, Nōgyō)* (Tokyo, 1961), p. 159.

The following numerical example will illustrate the role of the inter-industrial movement of the labor force in satisfying the rapid expansion of labor supply in the non-agricultural sector. For the sake of simplicity, we will assume an economy consisting of two sectors, namely agriculture and manufacturing (hereafter cited as the A and M sectors, respectively) and the same rate of growth of labor supply, n, in both sectors. Then, n_a and n_m are the rates of increase of employment in the A and M sectors respectively; p_a and p_m are the proportions of employment in the A and M sectors to the total employment at the beginning of the period. Using the above notation, the following relationship is derived:

$$n_m = 1/p_m(n - p_a n_a), \quad \text{where } p_m + p_a = 1.$$

From this it is apparent that, in the case of given magnitude of n and n_a, the lower the numerical value of p_m, the higher the numerical value of n_m, and vice versa. For example, where $n = 1\%$, $n_a = 0\%$, and $p_m = 20\%$, n_m will be 5 per cent, and where $n = 2\%$, $n_a = 0\%$, and $p_m = 80\%$, n_m will be 2.5 per cent. The difference between n_m and n, 4% and 0.5% respectively, represents the magnitude of inter-industrial migration of the labor force from A to M expressed as its proportion to the size of employment in M at the beginning of the period. Then, by dividing the difference between n_m and n by n_m, the contribution rate defined above is derived, namely 80% and 20% respectively in the above example. On the other hand, the difference between n and n_a, 1% and 2% respectively, also represents the magnitude of the outflow of the labor force from agriculture, being expressed as its proportion to the initial size of employment in A which is called the outflow rate. The argument above clearly suggests that the rapid increase in the non-agricultural work force in the Meiji era can be attributed mainly to the inter-industrial migration of workers from agriculture, which corresponded to only a small portion of the total agricultural work force. The large observed differences in n_m between Japan and Britain can be easily explained by the large difference in the proportion of agricultural employment given as an initial condition between the two countries.

The above conclusion is reinforced by a further examination of the labor supply during the course of the Industrial Revolution in England. Due to the lack of relevant data at hand, we are obliged to speculate on an approximate numerical relationship among the values of n, n_a, n_m, p_a and p_m in the latter 18th century in England and Wales. Based on Griffith's estimates of the growth rate of the total population as shown in Fig. 1, the maximum value of n can be assumed to be 1 per cent per annum. According to Chambers, n_a is assumed to be positive but nearly equal to zero, and, based on Phyllis Deane's estimates (Deane and Cole, p. 142) for 1801, p_a is assumed to have a value of about 35 per cent. Consequently, on the basis of these assumptions, we obtain $p_m = 65$ per cent. Then, putting these figures together into the above identity, we get 1.5 per cent as a possible maximum value of n_m. Now, it becomes clear that the value of n_m realized in the Meiji era was really two or three times as high as that of England and Wales in the latter 18th century.

In Japan, since the number of the agricultural work force (which occupied the dominant part of the total labor force) was almost constant at the level of some 14 million throughout the period in spite of a relatively moderate growth in total population, the supply of labor in the non-agricultural industries was able to grow at a rate of more than 3 or even 4 per cent per annum. Furthermore, since the outflow of the labor force from agriculture was limited to the incremental part of the agricultural population, little reorganization of agricultural production was needed, and this in turn assisted the smooth process of the inter-industrial movement of the labor force. In Britain, however, the proportion of the agricultural work force to the total labor force had already fallen substantially before the time of the Industrial and Vital Revolutions in the mid-18th century, and consequently there remained little room for the full operation of the mechanism which contributed very much to creating the condition of an abundant labor supply in Japan.

From the large differences observed in both the initial conditions underlying subsequent economic development and the rate of population growth, three different cases of economic development can be discerned: (1) In Britain the process of economic growth was restrained somewhat by the relatively limited supply of labor; (2) In Japan it was facilitated by the reserve army of labor; and (3) In the present developing countries in which the traditional agriculture still dominates, but in which population grows quite rapidly, there is a shortage of food instead of labor. Thus, the comparison seems to suggest that the Japanese experience in the Meiji era is the typical case of economic development with unlimited supplies of labor.[10] This aspect of the problem will be discussed in greater detail in the following section.

III. Channels of Labor Movement

The migratory movement of the labor force from agriculture has

---

[10] For a description of this pattern of development, see Lewis.

two distinct channels, one of which comes from the relative expansion of side-businesses in the peasant household economy whereas the other comes from the direct outflow of members of peasant families who go to factories or shops and become wage-earners. Reallocation of the labor force through the first channel is usually free from most of the frictions caused by a large variety of social, psychological, and moral factors, while reallocation through the second channel is generally accompanied by an interregional movement of labor and consequently suffers from the regional immobility of labor.

Turning our attention to expansion via side-business, Table 5 illustrates one aspect of the employment structure in the early Meiji era and its subsequent changes up to 1920. On two points, limitations of the data are so severe that we must be careful in drawing any conclusions. First, the data available are limited to only two prefectures in the eastern part of Japan, namely Yamanashi and Yamagata Prefectures, and the nationwide picture may differ from that observed from the table. Second, the data for Yamanashi Prefecture refer to an inflationary period, while that for Yamagata Prefecture refer to a recovery phase of the business cycle. Therefore, the observed differences between the two prefectures may reflect merely a difference in the level of economic activity in the two periods associated with cyclical fluctuations. In spite of these shortcomings of the data, they will still give us some idea of the employment structure in the early stage of economic development.

In the early Meiji period one third of all the gainfully occupied persons in the two prefectures had side-jobs. This situation did not change greatly until 1920. To be noted here is the difference observed between sectors of the economy. In 1879 in Yamanashi Prefecture the proportion of workers having side-jobs was 33 per cent in sector A consisting of agriculture, forestry, and fisheries, and 37 per cent in sector M—composed of mining, construction, manufactures, transportation, and communications; however, the workers of the service industries sector S, were already engaged in fairly specialized occupations. However, as time went on, the proportion having side-jobs in sector M, especially that of females, fell and in sector A has risen remarkably both for males and females. Unfortunately, such data are not available for Yamagata Prefecture.

TABLE 5

Structure of Employment: Yamanashi and Yamagata Prefectures*

(Unit: %)

		Total	A Sector[a]	M Sector[b]	S Sector[c]
Proportion of workers with side-occupations classified by main occupation:					
	Male	31.8	35.6	5.2	9.7
1879, Yamanashi	Female	33.4	29.8	47.4	10.5
	Total	32.5	33.1	37.1	9.9
	Male	54.5	73.7	22.3	22.0
1920, Yamanashi	Female	37.5	51.2	17.9	8.1
	Total	46.8	63.3	20.0	17.0
	Male	30.5	49.5	11.6	13.9
1920, Nationwide	Female	27.7	40.0	7.6	6.7
	Total	29.4	45.3	10.5	11.3
Ratio of side-occupation workers to main-occupation workers in each sector indicated:					
	Male	31.8	14.8	162.2	121.1
1879, Yamanashi	Female	33.4	17.4	87.4	17.7
	Total	32.5	15.9	107.1	100.0
	Male	54.5	69.0	31.9	25.7
1920, Yamanashi	Female	37.5	55.3	7.7	12.5
	Total	46.8	62.3	19.2	20.9
	Male	30.0	26.5	39.4	32.4
1887, Yamagata	Female	20.1	18.9	39.9	9.7
	Total	24.9	22.9	39.6	23.1
	Male	32.9	41.5	16.5	22.0
1920, Yamagata	Female	38.8	42.2	52.2	13.6
	Total	35.4	41.8	28.9	18.5
	Male	30.6	40.9	22.1	19.1
1920, Nationwide	Female	28.0	31.9	28.3	7.6
	Total	29.6	37.0	26.3	11.3

* Data for Yamanashi Prefecture from *Population Census of Kai District (Kai no Kuni Genzai Jinbetsu Sirabe)*, Tokyo, 1882; and *Report on 1920 Population Census of Japan*. For detailed discussions, see Tussing's research which appears in Chapter 8 of this volume.
Data for Yamagata Prefecture from *Occupation Statistics of Yamagata Prefecture (Yamagata Ken no Shokugyō Tōkei Sho)*, 1890; and *Report on 1920 Population Census of Japan*.
a) A Sector includes Agriculture, Forestry and Fishery.
b) M Sector includes Mining, Construction, Manufacture, Transportation and Communications.
c) S Sector includes Commerce, Finance, Public Services and other Services.

In the same table gainfully occupied persons having side-jobs are reclassified by their side occupations and their proportions to the corresponding main-job workers are computed. The proportions thus computed could be understood as a rough index of the relative importance of the labor input performed by the side-job workers in the three sectors of the economy, though possible differences in man-hours per gainfully occupied person between the main-job and the side-job workers cannot be neglected. In 1879 in Yamanashi Prefecture the proportions were very high both in sectors *M* and *S,* but low in sector *A,* with these differences being much more distinctive for male workers than for female workers. This suggests that in the early Meiji period the national economy still remained at a primitive stage of development, the specialization of economic activity had not yet proceeded within the traditional framework of the peasant economy, and a large part of economic activity both in sectors *M* and *S,* which should be the engine of economic development in ᵗhe subsequent period, consisted only of subsidiary businesses operated mainly by some of the peasant family members. However, as time passed, the division of labor, celebrated as the main spring of economic progress by Adam Smith in his *Wealth of Nations,* was gradually promoted. Until 1920 the proportions of the number of side-job workers to those of main-job workers dropped remarkably in both the *M* and *S* sectors, while in the *A* sector the proportion rose sharply, and a part of economic activity, formerly performed as a main-job occupation, now became a subsidiary occupation performed by a part of the gainfully employed workers in other sectors. These characteristics are not as distinct in the case of Yamagata Prefecture as in the case of Yamanashi Prefecture. Although the reason for this is not clear, it may be attributed partly to regional differences in the employment structure and also explained in part by the fact that the relative importance of side-jobs in Yamagata Prefecture might have been much reduced by the Matsukata depression while that in Yamanashi Prefecture was not affected by the depression. However, much more evidence must be gathered before arriving at any definite conclusion.

The most important implications of our findings may be summarized as follows: In the early Meiji period there was no appreciable progress in the specialization of occupations, and most of the various types of economic activity in the nation as a whole (which might be classified into agriculture, manufacturing or commerce by a simple application of the modern technique of industrial classification) were usually managed as a branch of a single, unique production-and-consumption unit, the peasant household economy. Therefore, if production in the side-business sector of the peasant household economy, say, silk reeling or weaving, was gradually expanded relative to agricultural production, a reallocation of the given re-sources, namely labor and capital, between sectors would naturally follow. This process provided the inter-sectoral movement of the work force and of savings which were almost free from the friction caused by various non-economic factors. In this case, the only ex-pected obstacle to be overcome would be how to prepare additional finance for the investment required to expand silk reeling or weaving production. However, under the prevailing putting-out system in the rural districts, the purchase of raw materials, i.e., cocoons or yarn, the biggest items of business expenditure, was usually financed in some form or another by clothiers or merchants. Furthermore, thanks to the still low level of prevailing technique, a set of machines and tools, the only items in which producers under the putting-out system actually invested, were not extremely expensive compared with the producers' saving potential and sometimes even could be rented from clothiers or merchants.[11]

Although our conclusions depend entirely upon our observations concerning the changes of the employment structure in only two prefectures and although regional differences in various aspects of rural economic life in the early Meiji era are supposed to be rather great, these observations can be taken to represent in some sense, a typical picture of the rural economy which prevailed throughout Japan during the early Meiji period. And it must be emphasized that the channels through which the agricultural work force was transferred to the non-agricultural industries were also effective for

---

[11] For example, according to H. Hayashi's study of the cotton weaving industry in Bisai district in the northern part of Aichi Prefecture, a (Takahata) traditional wooden weaving machine cost about five or six yen about 1900. See Hayashi.

promoting the outflow of savings originating in agriculture to the non-agricultural side-job sector.

Now we want to turn our attention to the second channel of labor movement where the picture is quite different from that described above. Here skilled and unskilled laborers should be treated separately since the labor market situation of each is believed to be very different. Treating the skilled laborer first, we see that factory owners were obliged to train raw recruits into skilled workers in the factory. This was the case because the establishment of the modern factory system of production in the Meiji era was not made possible through any self-generated technical ability, but through government-sponsored transplants of techniques from developed Western countries and because there were remarkable differences in the levels of the foreign techniques as compared to those that prevailed in Japan. Under these conditions, a shortage of skilled laborers was inevitable since the supply of skilled workers depends entirely upon past employment and training. Consequently, a high rate of turnover and an increase in wages for the skilled laborers were quite natural.[12]

In contrast to the fact that the shortage of skilled labor was of historical origin, the problems of recruiting unskilled workers, especially female textile workers, occurred because of "geography." The development of the modern factory system of production was necessarily accompanied by a concentration in the location of factories on the one hand, and by a rapidly growing demand for wage laborers on the other. These coincided with a lack of regional mobility of labor and from the 1890's produced episodes of scrambles for laborers.

Turning first to the geographical distribution of factories, we see in K. Yamaguchi's study (Yamaguchi, Chap. 4) that around 1884 about 77 per cent of all the factories, excluding breweries, in 43 prefectures were scattered through the purely rural districts, and the remaining 23 per cent were located in urban and semi-urban districts. The chief factor underlying this pattern of distribution can be considered to be the availability of water power. Also of interest is the fact that the size of the factory, in terms of the number of work-

---

[12] For a more detailed treatment, see T. Watanabe, p. 109.

ers employed, was small, with factories having less than 20 workers accounting for up to 72 per cent of all factories. These two conditions combined made it possible for factory owners to employ their workers from the surrounding neighborhoods of their factories. By 1892, however, the situation had drastically changed with the simultaneous increase of the number of factories, the concentration of factories in urban districts, and the expansion in the size of factories. The proportion of factories located in urban districts increased from 23 per cent to 49 per cent over a span of some 8 years, and the percentage of the number of factories having more than 20 workers reached 50. Because of the rapid progress of industrialization as such, it became almost impossible for factory owners to continue to secure all the needed manpower from nearby villages, and it became necessary to recruit from distant places.

Thus, with rapid industrialization the regional immobility of the sons and daughters of peasant families began to strongly affect the labor market. Because of the keen competition and scramble for laborers between factory owners, labor recruitment practices were becoming so expensive and so disordered[13] that factory owners were forced to come to some agreement over the orderly recruitment of labor, and following the turn of the century,[14] most of the local governments enacted Labor Recruitment Regulation Acts. According to the record of a silk reeling company in the Suwa district of Nagano Prefecture, the proportions of recruitment costs to wage and salary payments ranged from 3 to 22 per cent during the three decades from 1900. When industry was prosperous the proportion of recruitment costs increased, and when trade was slack the proportion decreased (Dai Nihon Sanshi Kai, pp. 1347–48).

From this evidence, it is clear that in the early stages of economic development the inter-sectoral movement of the agricultural working force through this channel was very difficult. Though it cannot be denied that this difficulty was one of the largest obstacles in the steady advance of industrialization, we must also be careful not to exaggerate this aspect of the problem. The quantitative importance

---

[13] For a more detailed treatment, see Fujibayashi, pp. 137–176.

[14] Labor Recruitment Regulation Acts were enacted by local governments in 30 prefectures out of 47, see S. Watanabe, pp. 168–173.

of the labor movement through this second channel surely increased throughout the Meiji period, but at the same time it was not as large as that through the first channel, though we have no creditable statistical evidence on this point. It must be also noted here that the labor shortage in some local labor markets which stemmed from an insufficient mobility of labor in spite of a plentiful aggregate supply of labor was entirely different from the usual meaning of labor shortage when the supply of labor falls short of the demand for labor at the prevailing wage rate. In the former case a revision of the wage rate may not be effective in increasing the supply of labor, and recruitment activities must be stimulated; in the latter case, the opposite is the policy that should be followed. This picture of the labor market in the Meiji era, that is to say, the coexistence of an unlimited supply of labor and of regional labor shortages in some centers of industrial production may appear somewhat paradoxical, but it is real. In general, at the beginning of industrialization one of the basic requirements for capitalistic development is a smooth route for the transfer of the labor force from the shiny green villages to the gloomy factories or the dark underground mines.

REFERENCES

Chambers, J. D., "Enclosure and Labour Supply in the Industrial Revolution," *Economic History Review* (April, 1953).

Dai Nihon Sanshi Kai Shinano Shikai. *History of the Silk Industry in Shinano District (Shinano Sanshigyo Shi)*, II. 1937.

Deane, P. and Cole, W. A. *British Economic Growth 1688–1959*. London: Cambridge University Press, 1962.

Dobb, M. *Studies in the Development of Capitalism*. London: Routledge & Kegan Paul, 1946.

Fujibayashi, K., "Labor Turnover in the Japanese Cotton Spinning Industry, 1887–1897 (Meiji 20 Nendai ni okeru Waga Bosekigyo Rodosha no Ido Gensho ni tsuite)," *Labor Problems in the Early Meiji Era (Meiji Zenki no Rodo Mondai)*, Meiji Shiryo Kenkyu Renrakukai, Tokyo: Ochanomizu Shobo, 1960.

Gille, H., "The Demographic History of the Northern European Countries in the Eighteenth Century," *Population Studies* (June, 1949).

Griffith, G. T. *Population Problems of the Age of Malthus*. London: Cambridge University Press, 1936.

Habakkuk, H. J., "English Population in the Eighteenth Century," *Economic History Review*, 2nd series, VI, No. 2 (1953).

——, "Economic History of Modern Britain," *Journal of Economic History*, XVIII, No. 4 (1958).

Hayashi, H., "Contract Workers in the Bisai District during Latter Meiji (Bisai ni okeru Meiji Koki no Kogyo Rodo)," *Contract Workers during the Breakdown of Feudal Society (Hoken Shakai Kaitaiki no Koyo Rodo)*, T. Ichikawa et al., eds., Tokyo: Aoki Shoten, 1961.

Helleiner, K. F., "The Vital Revolution Reconsidered," *Canadian Journal of Economics and Political Science* (Feb. 1957).

Jutikkala, E., "The Great Finnish Famine in 1696–97," *Scandinavian Economic History Review*, III, No. 1 (1955).

Krause, J. T., "Changes in English Fertility and Mortality, 1781–1850," *Economic History Review*, 2nd series, XI, No. 1 (1958).

——, "Some Neglected Factors in the English Industrial Revolution," *Journal of Economic History*, XIX, No. 4 (1959).

Kuznets, S., "Quantitative Aspects of the Economic Growth of Nations: Levels and Variability of Rates of Growth," *Economic Development and Cultural Change*, V, No. 1 (Oct. 1956).

Lewis, W. A., "Economic Development with Unlimited Supplies of Labour," *Manchester School of Economic and Social Studies* (May, 1954).

Namiki, M., "Migratory Movements of the Rural Population (Noson Jinko no Ido)," *Rural Population (Noson no Jinko)*, S. Nojiri, ed., Tokyo: Chuokeizaisha, 1957.

Notestein, F. W., "The Population of the World in the Year 2000," *Journal of the American Statistical Association* (Sept. 1950).

Ohkawa, K., "The Pattern of Japanese Long-Term Economic Growth," *Asian Studies in Income and Wealth*, International Association for Research in Income and Wealth, V. K. Rao and K. Ohkawa, eds., Asia Publishing House, 1965.

Saville, J. *Rural Depopulation in England and Wales, 1851–1957*. London: Routledge & Kegan Paul, 1957.

Sekiyama, N. *Structure of the Japanese Population in the Modern Era (Kinsei Nihon no Jinko Kozo)*. Tokyo: 1958.

Umemura, M. *Wages, Employment and Agriculture (Chingin, Kōyō, Nōgyō)*. Tokyo: Taimeido, 1961.

——, "Population Trends and Their Controlling Factors in the Tokugawa Period (Tokugawa Jidai no Jinko Susei to Sono Kisei Yōin)," *Keizai Kenkyu*, XVI, No. 2 (April, 1965).

——, "Agriculture and Labor Supply in Japan in the Meiji Era," *The Developing Economies*, III, No. 3 (Sept. 1965).

United Nations. *The Determinants and Consequences of Population Trends*. New York: 1953.

Watanabe, S. *Rural Population in Japan (Nihon Noson Jinko Ron)*. Tokyo: Nankosha, 1938.

Watanabe, T., "The Formation of a Labour Market in Early Meiji (Meiji Zenki no Rodoryoku Shijo Keisei o Megutte)," *Labour Problems in Early Meiji (Meiji Zenki no Rodo Mondai)*, Meiji Shiryo Kenkyu Renrakukai, Tokyo: Ochanomizu Shobo, 1960.

Yamaguchi, K. *An Analysis of Early Meiji Economy (Meiji Zenki Keizai no Bunseki)*. Tokyo: Tokyo Daigaku Shuppankai, 1956.

CHAPTER 8

THE LABOR FORCE IN MEIJI ECONOMIC GROWTH: A QUANTITATIVE STUDY OF YAMANASHI PREFECTURE[†]

ARLON R. TUSSING

I

Economic development and "modernization" have certain universal consequences for the structure and organization of the labor force. The history of each advanced country shows a shift of population out of agriculture and the replacement of family enterprise and particularistic employment relationships by large enterprises and wage labor. But the pace and completeness of these inevitable changes have varied widely among different countries.

To take one example, Umemura has pointed out that in each of the classic Western instances of industrialization, the first phase of modern economic growth was accompanied by an absolute increase in the agricultural population and labor force, and that absolute declines in most cases came relatively late in the process of modernization. In the United Kingdom, the decline probably set in very early in the nineteenth century, but in the United States, France, Germany, and Italy, the agricultural population continued to increase well into the twentieth century. Japan is the apparent major exception, and despite substantial differences among the estimates of the agricultural labor force by various scholars, there is a consensus that it exhibited no sustained rise (Umemura, 1961). In another direction, Rosovsky and Ohkawa have emphasized the important role played very late in Japanese economic development by "indigenous" manufactures and productive organization (Rosovsky and Ohkawa, pp. 476–501). Abegglen and others have described the pre-capitalist aspects of the employment relationship which

[†] Reproduced here, with slight revisions, from *The Journal of Economic History,* No. 1 (March, 1966).

persist even (especially?) in large-scale enterprise in modern Japan (Abegglen, 1958).

Quantitative measures of changes of these kinds during the Meiji era would be very useful in understanding the peculiarities of Japanese economic growth. Unfortunately, the most important record of the shifts in the composition of the labor force—the occupational tables of a modern population census—begins for Japan only in 1920, after the foundations of a modern industrial society had been completed.

This paper summarizes some of the results of a study of the labor force in one prefecture for which a comprehensive population census exists for the early Meiji era (Bureau of Statistics, *Census*).[1] Yamanashi Prefecture, extending north from Mount Fuji, was chosen for a pilot census conducted as of the end of 1879. The prefecture is even today almost totally rural, but economically it was one of the most developed areas in Meiji Japan, including some of the most important centers of sericulture, silk reeling, and silk textiles. In addition to the early population census, we have virtually complete factory statistics for the prefecture in the Yamanashi Prefecture Statistical Yearbook *(Yamanashi Ken Tōkeisho)*, beginning in 1883.

II

The pattern of economic activity in Yamanashi Prefecture was highly specialized, but such specialization was not atypical even in pre-industrial Japan. In almost every region the vast majority of the labor force seems to have been engaged in agriculture, specifically in cereal cultivation, as a primary occupation. A large number of manufactures and trades were ubiquitous, either because they could be carried on practically only at the site of consumption or because the raw materials were ubiquitous and the work could be carried on anywhere. Examples of the first kind of "residentiary" activities are construction and retail trade; examples of the latter are *sake* brewing and the fabrication of straw products. These activities

---

[1] I am indebted to the Ford Foundation Foreign Area Fellowship Program for a grant under which part of the research reported in this paper was conducted in 1960–62, and to Mataji Umemura for calling my attention to the 1879 census of Yamanashi Prefecture.

were carried on in Yamanashi in proportions similar to those of Japan as a whole.

Another category of products, of both agricultural and manufacturing origin, was produced for a national or overseas market and was more or less concentrated in certain regions and prefectures. This regional specialization had its origin in part in comparative advantages of climate, soil, or proximity to the sea or to urban markets and in part in the monopoly system of the feudal era. Yamanashi Prefecture had its silkworm products and, to a lesser extent, Japanese-style paper and crystalware. Similarly, indigo production was concentrated in Tokushima Prefecture, edible seaweed in Tokyo and Hiroshima, tea in Kyoto and Shizuoka, ceramics in Gifu, and so forth. Specialization had proceeded far even in the earliest years of the Meiji era. In the 1874 Commodity Output Tables *(Meiji 7-nen Bussanhyō)*, the first comprehensive survey of commodity output for 24 of the 52 products listed, 30 per cent or more of the output was accounted for by only 2 of the 64 prefectures (Yamaguchi).

In Tokugawa times there were some occupations which were particularly urban, either as part of the *bakufu* and *han* administrations or the court or as catering to their personnel. After the opening of the ports, we might add activities catering to foreigners. Apart from these urban specialties, concentrated in the three great cities and a few of the larger castle towns, almost all manufacturing and service activity was carried on in farm households,[2] and almost all agricultural specialties were produced by households which also engaged in cereal cultivation. Since the labor demand in agriculture is highly seasonal, this arrangement was an economical allocation of activity in a population which had to devote a great proportion of its total resources to feeding itself. Viewed in terms of cereal production, the marginal cost of labor in these side occupations was almost nil up to the point at which the entire population could be occupied throughout the year. The existence of underemployment of the available labor time can be seen in the literature of late Tokugawa, in which the traveler was always besieged by porters and

---

[2] "Farm household" *(nōka* or *nōgyō shotai)* is used here as it is in the Japanese data, as a household in which at least one member is engaged in agriculture.

would-be entrepreneurs of all kinds. The clear impression is that there was a great excess in the supply of their services.

The activities in which the greater part of Meiji economic growth took place were largely rural occupations, depending for their labor supply on the slack time of the farm population, at least in the earlier years.[3] Scholars of the period have devoted great attention to the handful of establishments using imported techniques—in shipbuilding, mining, engineering, etc.—but "modern" industries and modern techniques were almost irrelevant to the main thread of economic growth until about the Sino-Japanese war, except as they consumed tax revenues and foreign exchange. The major export items were tea and silkworm products (eggs, cocoons, raw silk, and silk textiles) in varying proportions; and the growth of consumption was overwhelmingly in "indigenous" products, made by traditional techniques. In each case the main reservoir of labor supply was the excess (off-peak) labor time of the farm household.

Rapidly increasing production of agricultural specialties, such as cocoons and tea, fruits and vegetables, each having its peak labor demand at a different time of the year, absorbed much of the slack time of the farm population. In addition, as the demand for non-agricultural goods and services increased, former side occupations became primary occupations, first of individual members of farm households. Later, individuals might become entirely committed to non-agriculture, "going out" *(dekasegi)* to work for long periods of time, and farming might fall from the primary occupation of the household as a whole to the status of a side occupation. None of these patterns was uncommon even in pre-Meiji society; what was rare, however, was the abrupt transition of an entire household out of agriculture. The number of persons whose primary, even exclusive, occupation was in non-agriculture did increase, as did at least the proportion of totally non-agricultural households. But time series which purport to show the occupational or sectoral composition

---

[3] This point is emphasized by Ranis: "Reserves of productivity usually do exist somewhere in the underdeveloped economy. . . . *Taking up the slack* in any economy means making potential increments of productivity socially available. . . . In the case of Japan, *slack* was in evidence mainly in the form of excess labor on the land and in reserves of productivity in the land" (see Chapter 2).

of the labor force in these terms are necessarily very inadequate as indicators of the changing composition of economic activity.

The most significant quantitative studies of Japanese economic development[4] utilize the labor force estimates of Hijikata (1929) and Hemmi (1956), both of whom trace their estimates back from the 1920 census. Hijikata used a variety of measures of economic activity, while Hemmi estimated the agricultural labor force as a function of the so-called farm household in the population registers. In the absence of a previous census to use as a benchmark, their estimates are extremely speculative.

III

For Yamanashi Prefecture, where we have the two censuses, 1879 (Bureau of Statistics, *Census*) and 1920 (Cabinet Bureau of Statistics, *Report*), to use as benchmarks, we used a different technique to estimate labor inputs by sector. We calculated an annual series for the native-born and resident population of the prefecture by using various series from the population registers to link figures from the censuses. The total labor force was estimated by applying to each year's population figures, subdivided by sex and into urban and rural, participation rates derived by interpolating between the two census years.[5]

These population series were used as the basis of estimates of net out-migration in Table 1. Yamanashi Prefecture had a higher rate of natural population increase than the national average during the early Meiji period, but there was no great net outward movement of population until about the time of the Sino-Japanese War. Some out-migration on the part of males was offset by in-migration of females recruited to the silk filatures. About 1894, however, the rapid conversion of silk reeling to steam power reduced labor requirements within the prefecture just as the rapid growth of modern manufacturing was beginning elsewhere in the country. From 1894 forward, Yamanashi has been a net exporter of population.

---

[4] Among these would be included Umemura (1961) and the following works: Ohkawa (1961); Shinohara (1961); Yamada (1957).

[5] The resulting population and labor-force estimates for 1879–1911 are shown in the Appendix Table 1 in Tussing (1966), p. 82.

TABLE 1
Net Out-Migration, Yamanashi Prefecture, 1879–1912*

Years	Net annual out-migration
1879–83	340
1884–88	60
1889–93	380
1894–98	2,520
1899–03	1,680
1904–08	1,520
1909–12	1,880

* Difference between change of native-born population and change of resident population, Tussing (1966), p. 82.

Economic activity in the prefecture, except for agriculture, revolved almost completely around silk products. In 1879 over 95 per cent of the labor force was engaged as a primary occupation or a side occupation either in agriculture or in one or another branch of the silk-products industries; the proportion in 1920 was around 90 per cent. The commencement of massive movement out of this highly specialized area suggests that, despite continued growth of the silk-products industries, they ceased to be the "leading sector" of the Japanese economy about the time of the Sino-Japanese war.

The concept used here to measure labor input, which takes into account both primary and side occupations, is the man-year, full-time equivalent (FTE). Both the 1879 Yamanashi Prefecture census and the 1920 population census show the number of persons engaged in each activity either as a primary occupation or as a secondary occupation. The number of FTE in each year was taken to equal the total labor force, but weights were chosen so that each primary "job" would contribute as much to labor input as two side "jobs." In the case of factory workers, however, where we have the average number of days of employment per year, 300 days were counted as one FTE. The occupational categories of the two censuses were adjusted to make them comparable, and full-time equivalents were calculated for 81 individual classifications.

For each of these classifications, labor-input series were estimated for the years between the censuses with the aid of various indicators of activity from the factory data and other information in the Yamanashi Prefecture Statistical Yearbook *(Yamanashi ken Tōkeisho)*,

TABLE 2

Man Years of Labor Input (Full-Time Equivalent) by Sector, and by
Percentage of Total Labor Force, Yamanashi Prefecture, 1879–1911*

Years	(Five-year averages number of full-time equivalents)				Percentage of labor input		
	Agriculture, Forestry, Fishery	Mining, Manufacturing	Services	Total	Agriculture, Forestry, Fishery	Mining, Manufacturing	Services
1879–82[a]	186,585	31,973	18,798	237,358	78.6	13.5	7.9
1883–87	193,674	31,820	20,715	246,208	78.7	12.9	8.4
1888–92	196,028	38,369	25,105	259,502	75.5	14.8	9.7
1893–97	198,593	41,376	28,178	268,146	74.1	15.4	10.5
1898–02	204,125	43,409	30,132	277,666	73.5	15.6	10.8
1903–07	220,625	42,765	31,894	295,284	74.7	14.5	10.8
1908–11[a]	218,318	50,147	35,614	304,080	71.8	16.5	11.7

* Tussing (1966), pp. 84–5.
a) Less than five years.

the Statistical Tables of Agriculture and Commerce *(Nōshōmu Tōkeihyo),* the Statistical Yearbook of the Empire of Japan *(Nihon Teikoku Tōkei Nenkan),* and elsewhere. Labor input to agriculture was treated as a residual. The series were aggregated sectorally, and are shown by five-year averages in Table 2, and in five-year moving averages in Figures 1 and 2.[6]

FIGURE 1
Labor Input by Sector, Full-Time Equivalents,
Yamanashi Prefecture, 1879-1911
(Five-year moving averages; thousands of man-years, full-time equivalent)

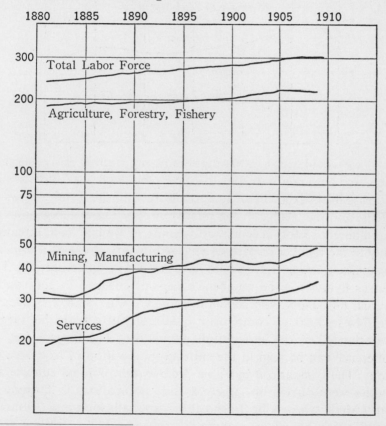

---

[6] A complete description of the techniques used to estimate population, labor force, and FTE by sector can be seen in Chapter III and in the Appendix of my unpublished doctoral dissertation (Tussing, 1965).

FIGURE 2
Proportion of Labor Input by Sector, Full-Time Equivalents,
Yamanashi Prefecture, 1879-1911

(Five-year moving averages)

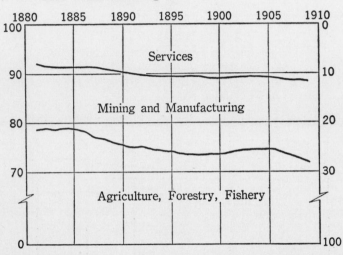

As we would expect, labor input in manufacturing and in services increased both relatively and absolutely, but there was also a steady increase in the labor input to agriculture until the last few years of Meiji; and the change in the relative proportion of labor input to the different sectors is remarkably gentle. If we had paid attention only to the number of persons engaged in agriculture as a primary occupation, however, we would have had a very different result. The census figures for the number of persons engaged in cultivation, animal husbandry, and sericulture in 1879 was 193,872 as against 193,714 in 1920—a comparison quite congruent with the alleged "constancy" of the agricultural population. The reasons for the difference can be seen in the shifting composition of side occupations. The comparison in Table 3 shows that non-agricultural activities were carried on largely as side occupations to farming in early Meiji, whereas by Taisho times, specialization and "commitment" were the rule in manufacturing and services, while a great number of persons engaged in agriculture as a side occupation. Consideration of primary occupations alone would have resulted in a serious underestimation of manufacturing and service activity in the early period, and an under-estimation of farming activity later.

TABLE 3

Sectoral Distribution of Labor Force, Primary and Side Occupations, Yamanashi Prefecture, 1879 and 1920

	1879[a]			1920[a]		
	(1)	(2)	(3)	(1)	(2)	(3)
Agriculture, forestry, fishery	194,164	29,238	13.1	196,259	127,511	39.4
Mining, manufacturing	26,418	21,375	44.7	64,059	14,245	18.2
Services	14,498	15,035	50.9	46,991	11,786	20.1

a) The columns are:
  (1) number of persons engaged as primary occupation;
  (2) number of persons engaged as side occupation;
  (3) side occupations as percentage of total.
Note: Column (2) is the total *number* of side "jobs" in each sector, and includes the side occupations of persons whose primary occupation is in the same sector (e.g., persons who engage in silkworm breeding as a side-occupation to agriculture), so that the sum of (1) and (2) in each sector is greater than the number of *persons* engaged in that sector.

IV

In our study we also attempted to compare the role of "indigenous" and modern industries in the two census years.[7] Here, however, we have confined our attention to primary employment. In 1879, only 445 persons were engaged as a primary occupation in activities which could be regarded as "modern," and another 749

---

[7] Following Rosovsky and Ohkawa (1961), we have considered both the nature of the product or service and the productive organization in classifying activities into traditional (indigenous) or modern components. Our definition of a traditional product is slightly different from theirs; here a traditional item is one which was regularly available before 1859. Some products must be regarded as "hybrids" of traditional and modern—for instance, machine-reeled silk, a "traditional" product manufactured at least partially by modern techniques. Some products, like beef and clocks, were certainly produced in Japan in Tokugawa times but only in minute quantities, and the increase in their production and consumption can hardly be distinguished from that of completely new or foreign products. These cases have been classified here as "ambiguous," along with those services which combine both modern and traditional elements—for instance, the retail sale, in traditional family enter-

in occupations whose place in a traditional-modern classification is ambiguous. Of the persons employed in economic activities of a modern type in 1879, only 23 were engaged in manufacturing. Employment in the "modern sector" grew 20.8 times, from 445 to about 9,260, in the 41 years between the censuses; or six times, from 5,810 to about 35,000,[8] if the "hybrid" case of silk reeling and the ambiguous categories are included. Even in 1920, the bulk was not in manufacturing, but in banking, communications, transport, and such services; only 3,068 persons were engaged primarily in the manufacturing activities we have classified as modern; the ambiguous occupations other than silk reeling accounted for another 753 persons engaged in manufacturing.

Traditional employments outside of agriculture did not fail to flourish. Excluding all ambiguous categories, the increase in non-agricultural traditional employments was almost threefold, from 22,221 to about 65,000. Absolutely, this is more than seven times the increase in the entire modern sector, and more than twice the increase in the modern, "hybrid," and ambiguous categories together. To the extent that this pattern was that of all Japan, it testifies to the enormous vitality of the indigenous sector of the Japanese economy, particularly to the remarkable elasticity of both supply and demand with respect to income of the traditional (pre-Meiji) Japanese manufactures and of traditional productive organization.

V

Silk reeling illustrates the process, described above, of gradual and partial specialization and commitment of the labor force. The industry was the biggest manufacturing activity in Japan from the

---

prises, of modern or imported goods. Moreover, there were "teachers" and "soldiers" in pre-Meiji Japan, but whether this fact justifies regarding a primary school teacher or an army officer as pursuing an "indigenous" calling is a purely arbitrary matter; such occupations too have been classified as "ambiguous" cases. All occupations listed specifically as occurring in companies *(kaisha)* were classified as modern.

[8] The rounded figures for 1920 here and following are a result of the rough division of some of the 244 occupational categories in the 1920 census which clearly lumped together indigenous and modern-type activities. The 744 categories in the 1879 census could be grouped according to the preceding definitions with considerable confidence.

beginning of the Meiji era to its end in terms of the number of establishments, the number of persons engaged, and the value of output. At first, almost all silk was reeled on the primitive, hand-operated *zaguri* apparatus in rural households. By 1911, the industry was dominated by steam-powered factories employing several hundred girls apiece, yet several hundreds of thousands of households in Japan still produced raw silk by the old method. Machine-reeled silk and *zaguri* silk were of different quality, suitable for weaving in different kinds of looms, but there was a close economic connection between the two. The continued existence of the *zaguri* reeling in the face of competition from modern factories indicates that the marginal opportunity cost of domestic female labor was still extremely low; in addition, the household industry was a major element in the labor supply for the factories.

Silk filature was a skilled occupation, requiring dexterity of hand and eye to find the filament ends and feed them into the spinning yarn at the proper time to maintain uniformity. But the basic skill was essentially the same in both the household and the factory operation. Wages remained low in the face of increased labor demand in the factories because there was a virtually unlimited supply of girls who had learned silk reeling literally at their mothers' knees.

Our series for the Meiji era from Yamanashi Prefecture illustrate some of these trends. Table 4 presents our estimates of the relative labor input to household and to factory silk reeling between 1873 and 1911. The increase in labor time used by the silk-reeling factories expanded rather steadily, with one rather severe recession between 1897 and 1901; but the labor input in household production reached a peak only in those years. The fluctuations of the latter were much greater, as we might expect, but household reeling remained an important part of the silk industry throughout the Meiji era.

The course of real wages in silk-reeling factories is further evidence of the elasticity of supply of this kind of labor. Daily wage rates, deflated by a local cost of living index, appear to have risen irregularly between the first years for which we have wage data and the end of the Meiji era, but the hours of labor also increased almost exactly enough to offset this increase. (See Table 5.)

TABLE 4

Labor Input, Full-Time Equivalents, Silk-Reeling Industry: Yamanashi Prefecture, 1873–1911*

(Five-year average)

Year	Silk-reeling factories			Households			Total		
	Male	Female	Total	Male	Female	Total	Male	Female	Total
1873–77	157	970	1,127	32	1,957	1,989	189	2,927	3,116
1878–82	286	1,905	2,191	78	4,298	4,276	364	6,203	6,567
1883–87	510	3,457	3,967	63	2,429	2,492	573	5,886	6,459
1888–92	661	5,375	6,036	129	3,631	3,760	790	9,006	9,796
1893–97	734	6,768	7,502	227	4,739	4,966	961	11,507	12,468
1898–02	603	5,540	6,143	505	7,544	8,049	1,108	13,084	14,192
1903–07	921	8,157	9,078	527	5,393	5,920	1,448	13,550	14,998
1908–11[a]	1,595	12,490	14,085	384	4,816	5,200	1,979	17,306	19,285

* Tussing (1966), pp. 86–87.
a) Less than five years.

TABLE 5

Daily and Hourly Wages of Female Operatives in Silk-Reeling Factories,
Constant (1885–87) Prices: Yamanashi Prefecture, 1885–1911*

(Five-year averages)

| Years | Real daily wage (Sen) | Working days (Hrs.) | Real hourly wage (Sen) | Index (1885 – 7=100) | | |
				Real daily wage	Working day	Real hourly wage
1885–87[a]	11.6	11.5	1.01	100	100	100
1888–92	11.9	11.7	1.01	102	102	100
1893–97	14.1	11.9	1.19	122	103	118
1898–02	12.5	12.0	1.04	108	104	103
1903–07[b]	12.6	12.5	1.01	109	109	100
1908–11[a]	13.0	13.1	1.02	113	114	100

* Wages, Tussing (1966), p. 92; working day, Tussing (1966), pp. 88–89.
a) Less than five years.
b) 1905 data missing.

Our data for Yamanashi Prefecture do not yield usable series on the working day for other industries, but the highly elastic labor supply, expressed in the stability of real wages, was apparently not confined to silk reeling. The next biggest single non-agricultural consumer of labor power in the prefecture was silk-textile weaving. The structure of the industry was similar to that of silk reeling, in that domestic handloom weaving continued to exist side by side with powered factory enterprise. Table 6 presents the movement of real daily wages in Kōfu and in Tanimura (today's Tsuru City), which was the center of the handloom weaving district.

The one "modern" manufacture which was relatively important in the Japanese economy in terms of labor demand and in contribution to total output in the late Meiji period was cotton spinning. The industry was almost unrepresented in Yamanashi, and we will not presume to generalize from the statistics of the two factories which existed in the prefecture during the Meiji era. Yet the conditions of labor supply to the spinning industry were not substantially different from those for the silk-reeling factories, and recruiters for each competed for the same workers. The mass of cotton-spinning employees comprised young girls recruited from farm families for periods of one to three years, and their low wages reflected the low

TABLE 6

Daily Wages of Weavers, Constant (1885–87) Prices: Kōfu and Tanimura, 1883–1911*

Year	Kōfu				Tanimura	
	Real wages (Yen)		Index		Real wages	Index
	(Male)	(Female)	(Male) 1885=100	(Female) 1885–87=100	(Female)	1885–87=100
1883–1887	.178[a]	.188	100	106	105[c]	110
1888–1892	n. a.	n. a.			n. a.	
1894–1897	n. a.	.152		86	.098	103
1898–1902	.170[b]	.136	95	77	.079[d]	83
1903–1907	.183	.171	103	97	.099[e]	104
1908–1911	.170	.158	95	89	.087	91

* Wages, *Yamanashi Prefecture Statistical Yearbook*, corresponding years. Deflators, Kōfu and Tanimura consumer price indexes, Tussing (1966), pp. 90–91.

a) 1885 only.
b) 1899–1902.
c) 1883, 1885–87. (Data for 1888–1893 not used because cited as monthly rates.)
d) 1898–1901.
e) 1904–7

marginal product of (extra) daughters in agriculture.[9] Ōkōchi (Ōkō-chi, 1958) and Sumiya (Sumiya, 1955) have found the supply of female labor to the cotton-spinning industry highly elastic in the late-Meiji-early-Taisho period, despite the often violent competition for trained operatives, and they explain recurring complaints of labor shortages by temporary regional disequilibria caused by lack of information. Umemura (Umemura, 1961) has provided support for this thesis by showing that it was recruiting expenditures, rather than wage rates, which responded most conspicuously to cyclical upswings in labor demand.

Silk reeling, textile weaving, and cotton spinning all had predominantly female work forces, and our wage figures for the first two industries are for female operatives. But real daily wages in the construction trades, which were almost completely male, show a declining tendency until the last years of Meiji, and a similar index of real daily wages for forty-seven manufacturing occupations shows no clear trend (see Tables 7 and 8). All of these occupations were of a "traditional" character, and their existence as rural side occupations is again probably a key to their wage behavior.

TABLE 7

Daily Wages of Construction Workers, Constant (1885–87)
Prices: Yamanashi Prefecture, 1883–1911*

Year	Real daily wage (Yen)	Index (1885 – 7 = 100)
1883–1887	.299	116
1888–1892	.276	106
1893–1897	.277	107
1898–1902	.218	84
1903–1907	.233	90
1908–1911	.318	124

* Wage rates, Yamanashi Prefecture Statistical Yearbook *(Yamanashi Ken Tōkeisho)*; deflator, Kōfu consumer price index, Tussing (1966), pp. 90–91. Daily wages in seven construction trades, Kōfu. Weights by straight-line interpolation between number of persons engaged, 1879 and 1920 censuses.

---

[9] For a classic first-hand account of the labor market in the cotton-spinning industry in the first decades of this century see Hosoi (1925).

TABLE 8

Daily Wages of Workers in Manufacturing, Constant (1885–87) Prices:
Yamanashi Prefecture, 1883–1911

Year	Real daily wage (Yen)	Index (1885 – 7=100)
1883–1887	.189	114
1888–1892	.172	104
1893–1897	.180	108
1898–1902	.160	96
1903–1907	.173	104
1908–1911	.180	108

* Wage rates, Yamanashi Prefecture Statistical Yearbook (*Yamanashi Ken Tōkeisho*): deflator, Kōfu consumer price index, Tussing (1966), pp. 90–91. Daily wages in 47 manufacturing occupations—Kōfu quotations except for factory employment, where prefecture averages were used. Weights by straight-line interpolation between number of persons engaged, 1879 and 1920 censuses.

The failure of manufacturing real wages to rise in the face of rapidly increasing manufacturing employment indicates that the "slack" in the rural labor supply had not yet been taken up. Indeed, the behavior of the purchasing power of yearly contract wages in agriculture suggests that the surplus labor time on the land was increasing.[10] (See Table 9.)

TABLE 9

Wages of Annual Contract Laborers in Agriculture,
Constant (1885–87) Prices: Kōfu, 1885, 1894–1911*

Years	Real annual wage (Yen)		Index (1885=100)	
	Male	Female	Male	Female
1885	22.3	11.6	100	100
1894–97	16.6	10.9	74	94
1898–02	13.6	8.7	61	75
1903–07	14.0	9.0	63	78
1908–11	12.9	8.6	58	74

* Wage rates, Yamanashi Prefecture Statistical Yearbook (*Yamanashi Ken Tōkeisho*), corresponding years; deflator, Tussing (1966), pp. 90–91.

[10] Real daily wage rates for agricultural labor did not fall but moved roughly in the same fashion as daily wage rates in manufacturing. These rates, however, reflect supply and demand conditions at the seasonal peaks and are not an indicator of the year-round marginal productivity of agricultural labor but rather of wages in occupations alternative to agriculture at those times of year in which the labor market was tightest.

In spite of this evidence that the *marginal* product of labor in agriculture was falling, output per capita and output per worker— that is, the *average* product of labor—rose substantially during the Meiji era, as Ohkawa has shown for Japan as a whole. Expansion of the market and improved techniques brought greater economic opportunity, even on the land; but the result was not an increase in the unit price of labor in real terms, because the growth of opportunity was outstripped by the growth of available labor time. Agricultural wage rates, and the wage rates in occupations which drew their workers from the labor reservoir in the countryside, remained extremely low.

While wage *rates* in manufacturing remained stable, wage *earnings* increased prodigiously, both in the aggregate, and per worker. Not only were there more persons engaged in manufacturing occupations, but these occupations took an increasing portion of each worker's potential labor time. In silk reeling, for instance, the average number of days of factory operation approximately doubled between 1883 and 1911, and as a consequence real annual earnings per worker also doubled (see Table 10).

TABLE 10

Days of Operation Per Year and Annual Earnings, Current and Constant (1885–87) Prices: Silk-Reeling Factories, Yamanashi Prefecture, 1883–1911*

| | | Annual earnings | | (Five-year averages) Index (1885 – 7=100) | |
| | | | | Days of | |
Years	Days of factory operation per year	Current prices (Yen)	1885–87 Prices (Yen)	factory operation per year	Real earnings
1883–1887	142.9	16.7[a]	16.9[a]	99	100
1888–1893	157.6	20.7	19.6	109	116
1893–1897	174.8	35.1	24.5	121	145
1897–1902	190.2	48.2	23.8	131	141
1903–1907	214.7	56.4	27.1	148	161
1908–1911[b]	251.2	76.4	33.3	174	198

* Days of operation, Tussing (1966): pp. 88–89; annual earnings, Yamanashi Prefecture Statistical Yearbook (*Yamanashi Ken Tōkeisho*)—see Tussing (1966), p. 92, n.; deflator, Tussing (1966), pp. 90–91.
a) 1885–87.
b) Less than five years.

Japanese wage rates in the Meiji era were a pittance either by Western or by contemporary standards; and the wage rates for female silk-reeling operatives were among the lowest in Japan. In our Yamanashi Prefecture data, we have silk-reeling wage rates both from individual factories and in the form of annual or quarterly wage quotations for predominantly non-factory occupations. Daily wages of female silk-reeling employees were twenty-second out of 30 categories of factory workers in the prefecture in 1906–1911, and their hourly wages were seventeenth out of 20 categories for which the latter measure can be calculated. In the lists of predominantly non-factory occupations in the yearbooks, over the entire period 1883–1911, daily wages of female silk-reeling operatives were fifty-first out of 53 occupational categories in Kōfu, below even agricultural day laborers and exceeding only male and female domestic servants.[11] But by the criteria of Meiji Japan, such wages might provide a handsome income, especially for farm girls whose productivity was close to zero at home except perhaps on the days of peak farm activity. Despite the severe sex differential in wages which was ubiquitous in Japan, female wage earnings in Yamanashi's silk-reeling industry more than kept pace with the average product for all gainfully employed in Japanese agriculture at a time when the latter was rising rapidly. Authorities may not agree whether or not the cultivator reaped much of the benefit of the growth of agricultural output in the Meiji era, but it is clear that a daughter or two in the filatures, or even more, a son in one of the better-paying construction trades, was a tremendous boost to the income of a farm household, and to a poorer tenant family was a fortune. The comparison in Table 11 is especially striking when one reflects that the values in the second column include the share of primary product taken by landlords and the government, as well as by the cultivators.

---

[11] The values ranked in this case were the arithmetic means of the ratios between five-year arithmetic means of daily wages for each occupational category and those of female silk-reeling workers. Not all of the six five-year periods were available for every occupational category, and where values were missing within any one five-year period, the ratio was calculated for the remaining years.

TABLE 11

Average Wage Earnings of Adult Female Workers in Silk-Reeling
Factories, Yamanashi Prefecture: and Income Produced Per
Gainfully Employed in Primary Industry, Japan
(Ohkawa's Estimates)* 1885–1911

Years	Annual earning (Yen) female silk-reeling operatives Yamanashi	Annual income (Yen) produced per worker primary industry, Japan	Ratio
1885–87[a]	16.7	21.3	.78
1888–92	20.7	27.6	.75
1893–97	35.1	35.2	1.00
1898–02	48.2	53.8	.90
1903–07[b]	56.4	70.0	.81
1908–11[a]	76.4	79.5	.96

* Annual earnings, Yamanashi Prefecture Statistical Yearbook (*Yamanashi Ken Tōkeisho)* ; see Tussing (1966), p. 92, n. Income produced, Ohkawa, p. 249.
a) Less than five years.
b) 1905 missing.

Another "indigenous" measure of the level of factory earnings is
its rice equivalent. In Tokugawa Japan, 180.5 liters (one *koku*) of
rice was reckoned as the income necessary adequately to sustain
one person for a year. On this basis, toward the end of the Meiji era
the earnings of one girl in the silk filatures could have supported a
whole family at pre-Meiji standards (see Table 12).

TABLE 12

Annual Wage Earnings of Adult Female Workers in Silk-Reeling
Factories, Yamanashi Prefecture, and Price of Rice, Kōfu,
1885–1911*

Years	Annual earnings female silk-reeling operatives (Yen)	Price of Rice Yen/Koku	Ratio
1885–87	16.7	6.59	2.54
1888–92	20.7	7.44	2.79
1893–97	35.1	10.60	3.31
1898–02	48.2	14.87	3.24
1903–07[a]	56.4	16.68	3.38
1908–11[b]	76.4	17.10	4.46

* Annual earnings, Yamanashi Prefecture Statistical Yearbook (*Yamanashi Ken Tōkeisho)* ; see Tussing (1966), p. 92, footnote. Rice prices, Yamanashi Prefecture Statistical Yearbook, corresponding years, commodity price tables.
a) 1905 missing.
b) Less than five years.

A third view of the magnitude of silk-reeling wages in the perspective of Meiji living standards can be seen in the wage deductions and company expenditures for workers' board. For 1907, the Statistical Yearbook *(Tōkeisho)* shows for each factory, by age and sex, the numbers of workers who receive room and board *(makanai)* at work; the wage rate for those workers who do and who do not take *makanai*; and the total expenditure of the factory in providing for them. From these an average deduction for board and its average cost can be imputed. Apparently, meals were not subsidized, as deductions from wages averaged 8.7 sen per day, and the factory expenditure averaged 8.0 sen per worker per day.[12] In the same year, the mean daily wage for adult female silk-reeling operatives was 27.2 sen. Even if the expenditure for *makanai* were entirely for food, and that of the most meager sort and quantity, a wage which left the worker 70 per cent after her keep could hardly be called one of grinding penury.

VI

It is hazardous to generalize from a few characteristics of one prefecture, but these findings in part have suggested to the author an hypothesis about the character of Meiji economic growth.

The increase in labor productivity in agriculture was apparently adequate to counter diminishing returns and to sustain some increase in the proportion of labor power which could be devoted to non-agricultural pursuits, but this increase was not nearly as remarkable as some authorities have suggested. The intersectoral movement of the labor force was not primarily a shift of population totally out of agriculture, but occurred first as the absorption of the slack time in farm households, especially that of the women, into various side occupations.

The availability of this previously un-utilized labor time, plus the rapid increase in population, was sufficient to assure a virtually "unlimited supply of labor" over the whole period, even in the highly skilled indigenous occupations. The unit price of labor in real terms, whether measured explicitly in wage rates or implicitly in the in-

---

[12] The mean deduction for adult female workers alone was 9.2 sen, but we could not calculate mean expenditures separately by age and sex.

comes of family enterprise, remained low despite unprecedented increases in total income per household, per capita, or per worker. Outside of a few industries, these increases were not realized primarily by improvements in techniques but by the more complete utilization of existing labor time and by its reallocation among primary and side occupations. This reallocation was, of course, facilitated by the growth of population and by the freedom of movement consequent on the Meiji revolution.

In this context, the output of products like raw silk and silk textiles could respond readily to the pull of outside demand, and the income generated by their export had a multiplier impact on the indigenous consumer economy. These latter industries generally had low capital requirements, and the skills required were plentiful because they had been practiced in the pre-modern economy as side occupations.

The dynamic of Meiji economic growth had already been described with remarkable insight in 1863 or 1864 by Yukichi Fukuzawa in a pamphlet polemicizing against the partisans of *jōi*,[13] who asserted that foreign trade was impoverishing the country by driving up the cost of necessities:

"Now, it is commonly said that the people are suffering on account of the rise in commodity prices, but in truth, there has not been an increase in the value of goods, but only a fall in the value of money. The goods which cost 1 *ryō* in the past now cost 3 or 4, but daily wages have risen even more, and the value of the rice allotments of the warrior class *(bushi)* has risen in a similar proportion, so that it can hardly be said that everybody is in distress.

"Since the beginning of foreign trade, the circulation of money has quickened, and there are fewer people in distress than before. There are all kinds of evidence, but we will give one or two examples. When times are bad it is difficult to make a living, and we expect to see many people offering themselves out for work at very low pay, only to get something to eat. But recently the number of laborers has diminished, even to the palanquin carriers on the highways. Doesn't this mean that

---

[13] The slogan of the militant nationalists, "Expel the barbarians."

there are better ways of making a living than going out into service?

"In Oshu, a certain *daimyo* with a rice income of only 100,000 *koku* has been selling silk from his fief and has brought its value up to over 900,000 *ryō* in a year. Estimating 100,000 *koku* to correspond to a population of 100,000, this means about 9 *ryō* per person. One must say that this is really a huge profit! In this fief, people are outdoing one another in working at silk, and do not hire themselves out at all. Family incomes are good enough that everybody is building houses and buying *kimono*. People who in earlier years wanted for salt to put on their adulterated rice *(bakumeshi)*, now eat fish with pure rice, so that the prices of both rice and fish have risen. The farmer who grows the rice and the fisherman who takes the fish, plus the carpenter and the plasterer, become prosperous, and conditions improve throughout the province.

"This situation is not limited to this one fief in Oshu, but is the same throughout Japan. A province which does not produce silk grows cotton, and if an area is not suitable for cotton, it grows oil seeds. Even in the case of rice and barley, which are not produced for foreign demand, domestic demand is fluid throughout the country. All manner of trade is being augmented, so that farmers and merchants both are now extremely busy at their respective callings" (Fukuzawa, p. 17).

Generally, outside of specific modern facilities such as the railroads and perhaps the technical aspects of cotton spinning, the main threads of Meiji economic growth seem not to have constituted an Industrial Revolution, if the latter means mainly urbanization, mechanization, and the appearance of new industries. Rather, there was a vast increase in the scale of an already functioning economic order in response to population increase, the widening of the market, and a permissive political arrangement. The incomes of the common people rose substantially, largely as a result of increased participation by the existing labor force. In plain English, the Japanese did it mostly by working longer and working harder.

REFERENCES
Abegglen, James C. *The Japanese Factory: Aspects of Its Social Organization.* New York: Free Press (Macmillan), 1958.

Bureau of Statistics *(Tōkeiin). Census of Individuals in the Province of Kai (Kai [no] Kuni Meiji 12-nen Jimbetsu [no] Shirabe).* Tokyo: 1882.

Cabinet Bureau of Statistics *(Naikaku Tōkeikyokyu). Report of the 1920 Population Census: Nationwide, Part 8—Occupations (Taishō 9-nen Kokusei Chōsa Hōkoku: Zenkoku no Bu dai 8—Shokugyō).* Tokyo: 1934.

Fukuzawa, Yukichi, "Coming and Going of the Foreigners (Tōjin Ōrai)," *Complete Works of Fukuzawa Yukichi (Fukuzawa Yukichi Zenshū),* I. Tokyo: Iwanami, 1951.

Hemmi, Kenzō, "Constancy of the Agricultural Population (Nōgyō Jinkō no Kōteisei)," and "Estimates of the Employed Population in Agriculture (Nōgyō Yūgyō Jinkō no Suikei)," I, *Japan's Economy and Agriculture (Nihon no Keizai to Nōgyō),* Seiichi Tōbata and Kazushi Ohkawa, eds., Tokyo: Iwanami, 1956.

Hijikata, Shigeyoshi, "The Unemployment Problem Seen Through Changes in the Employed Population by Industry (Shokugyōbetsu Jinkō no Hensen o Tsūjite Mitaru Shitsugyō Mondai)," *Shakai Seisaku Jihō* (Sept. 1929).

Hosoi, Wakizō. *The Sorry History of the Factory Girls (Jokō Aishi).* Tokyo: Iwanami, 1925.

Ohkawa, K., Shinohara, M., Umemura, M., Ito, M., Noda, T. *The Growth Rate of the Japanese Economy Since 1878.* Tokyo: Kinokuniya, 1957.

Ōkōchi, Kazuo. *Labor in Modern Japan.* Tokyo: Science Council of Japan, 1958.

Rosovsky, Henry and Ohkawa, Kazushi, "The Indigenous Components of the Modern Japanese Economy," *Economic Development and Cultural Change,* IX (Apr. 1961), pp. 476–501.

Shinohara, M. *Growth and Cycles in the Japanese Economy (Nihon Keizai no Seichō to Junkan).* Tokyo: Kinokuniya, 1961.

Sumiya, Mikio. *Dissertation on the History of Wage Labor in Japan (Nihon Chin Rōdō Shiron).* Tokyo: Tōdai Gakujutsu Sōsho, 1955.

Tussing, Arlon R., "Employment and Wages in Japanese Economic Development: A Quantitative Study of Yamanashi Prefecture in the Meiji Era" (unpublished Ph.D. thesis, University of Washington, 1965), Ann Arbor: university microfilms.

——, "The Labor Force in Meiji Economic Growth: A Quantitative Study of Yamanashi Prefecture," *Journal of Economic History,* XXVI (March, 1966), pp. 59–92 (reproduced as Chapter 8 in this volume).

Umemura, Mataji. *Wages, Employment, and Agriculture (Chingin, Koyō, Nōgyō).* Tokyo: Taimeidō, 1961.

Yamada, Yūzō. *Comprehensive Survey of National Income Data in Japan (Nihon Kokumin Shotoku Suikei Shiryō).* Tokyo: Tōyō Keizai Shimpōsha, 1957.

Yamaguchi, Kazuo. *An Analysis of Early Meiji Economy (Meiji Zenki Keizai no Bunseki).* Tokyo: Tōkyō Daigaku Shuppankai, 1956.

Yamanashi Prefecture Statistical Yearbook (Yamanashi Ken Tokeisho), annual, from 1883 (Kōfu).

CHAPTER 9

THE SUPPLY PRICE OF LABOR: FARM FAMILY WORKERS†

Yukio Masui

Introduction

The number of farm households and workers in the labor force engaged in farming remained fairly constant at about 5.5 million and about 14 million, respectively, without being affected much by business cycles from the Meiji era up to World War II (Hemmi, p. 126). The stability in the above two numbers is, however, replaced by declining trends in the postwar period. The number of farm households was 6.18 million in 1950 and 5.67 million in 1965; the number of workers engaged in farming was 16.0 million in 1950 and 10.9 million in 1965. The decrease in the number of farm households and labor force engaged in farming is more than simply a restoration of the prewar level from the abnormally high levels which prevailed immediately following the war. The rate of out-migration of the farm labor force tripled in the postwar period while the wage differences not only did not diminish, but even rose.

This paper is an attempt to explain the long-run behavior of the out-migration of the labor force from farms in the light of supply conditions of the farm family workers *in* the non-farm labor market. Here I shall depart from the conventional concept of supply price of labor of farm workers in terms of individual outflow and instead employ the concept of the supply price of labor in the family outflow of farm workers. It is essential to specify the cost of outflow of farm family workers on a family basis and to count it in the supply price of labor. The observed difference in wage earnings between

---

† Although many persons have offered valuable comments on this study, I am most indebted to K. Ohkawa, C. Nakajima, T. W. Schultz, M. Umemura, J. R. Bellerby, and O. Tanaka. Any remaining errors and omissions are, of course, my sole responsibility.

farming and comparable non-farm occupations is accounted for by the cost of outflow of labor on a family basis. The long-term behavior of outmigration of labor from farms is consistent with a prediction based on the wage earnings difference net of the cost of outflow on a family basis.[1] The higher wage difference has been needed to induce farm workers with a higher migration cost to respond to the expanded demand for labor in the non-farm sector in the postwar period.

Prevailing opinion ascribes the chronically low income of farm labor to a disequilibrium in the non-farm labor market with the presumed supply price of labor of the farm family worker being the farm wage. Lewis (Lewis, p. 139ff.) and Ohkawa (Ohkawa, 1955, pp. 117–131) maintain that the labor supply of peasants to non-farm occupations is peculiar and use the farm income per worker for the supply price. Bellerby advocates a "farmer's incentive income" that is measured by net return to farm labor per family worker for the supply price of labor (Bellerby, p. 40). The kind of supply price mentioned above belong to the concept of the supply price of labor in individual outflow. However, it is my contention that this supply price alone may not be the relevant parameter of the labor supply of the farm family in the non-farm labor market. Rather, a more important parameter seems to be the supply price of labor in the family outflow of farm workers at the margin.

I. Estimation of Supply Price

The supply price of labor of farm workers to non-farm occupations may be conceptually defined as the compensation for all the costs (incomes foregone) incurred in moving labor out of farming into comparable non-farm occupations. This cost, I assume, includes the opportunity earnings in farming, the cost of labor outflow on a family basis, the cost of closing out a farm, the cost of leaving the village, the costs of job information, retraining and income foregone during retraining and migration. However, in calculating these

---

[1] Sjaastad's approach to human migration is relevant here. He maintains that wage differences can not be indicative of disequilibrium in the interoccupational labor market unless the cost of human migration is adequately taken into consideration (Sjaastad, pp. 80–94).

costs, the last three will have to be omitted due to the lack of available data. Thus in this paper I shall confine myself to an analysis of the supply of farm workers to non-farm occupations which do not require any significant pretraining.

There are two factors which should be taken into account in the analysis of the supply conditions of farm family labor. First, the outflow of labor from agriculture can involve family migration out of rural areas to urban areas. Second, the farm family consists of a number of income earners including the farm operator as well as other family members. Combining these two factors will lead us to a particular concept of the supply price of farm family labor in family outflow. Wherever a family farm is located in an industrial district, e.g., an urban farm, the farm operator could commute to a non-farm job without migration to the city on a family basis. Here, the conventional concept of the supply price of labor, i.e., individual opportunity earnings in agriculture, may be applied effectively to analyze the labor supply. Again, wherever a family head is the sole income earner of the family, the conventional concept of the supply price of labor may well be applied whether the outflow of labor from the farm involves migration or not.

Suppose, however, that a farm operator shifts to a non-farm occupation in the city from a farm which is located in a remote rural area through migration on a family basis. This will mean that the total family earnings of the operator and the other family workers will be lost. The farm labor income of the other family workers, however, are not necessarily counted in the supply price of labor of the farm operator whenever the other family workers can find non-farm employment opportunities in the city which are as profitable as their opportunity earnings on the farm. For example, the wife and children of the family might be employed in the city as domestic servants or do some kind of take-home work. In the non-farm sector nearly 60 per cent of female factory workers were accounted for by workers of less than 24 years of age in 1920 and 1930 (Kobayashi, 1961, p. 144), which tells us that most job opportunities were limited to single female workers. In contrast to the general conditions in the non-farm labor market, female farm workers, both single and married, formed a substantial part of the total farm labor force. Nearly

45 per cent of total farm workers were accounted for by female workers (the comparable figure is less than 30 per cent for the non-farm sector), and in the prewar period more than 70 per cent of these female workers were 25 years of age or older (Kayō, 1958, p. 157). Thus, the difference between the farm labor earnings of the other farm family workers and their expected wage earnings in the city should be counted in the supply price of labor of the farm operator when treating family outflow. The earnings difference be-tween farm and non-farm works for the other family workers is assigned to *the cost of labor outflow on a family basis*. This cost is largely a result of the low saleability in the non-farm sector of the labor of family workers such as housewives and the aged.[2]

Another cost which will be incurred in migrating out of the farm must be counted in the supply price. It is assumed that farm prop-erty other than farm land would be reduced in value when the farm is closed out since their salvage value may be small. The lost property income, i.e. the interest of farm capital other than farm land, is assigned to *the cost of closing out a farm*.

It is generally accepted that a considerable difference in the retail prices of consumer goods and services is found between cities and rural areas.[3] The higher cost of living in a city is assigned to *the cost of leaving the village*.

Thus we have:

the supply price of labor of a farm operator in family outflow=
    total returns to the farm operator+cost of labor outflow on a family basis+cost of closing out a farm+cost of leaving the village.

According to the accounting system used in farm records, this is assessed as follows:

    Real farm income—real land income—expected non-farm wage

---

[2] In theory, it is expected that earnings of a housewife decrease with an increase in the earnings of the family head. But as far as factory laborers' households are concerned, it is observed that the earnings of the housewife do not decrease, but increase with the earnings of the family head (S.B.P.M.O., 1926, p. 26). It is assumed in this paper that the participation rate of female family members in labor force is not affected by the income of family head.

[3] The cost of living on a farm base was higher in the cities by 22.4 per cent than in rural farm areas (Ohkawa, 1953, pp. 96–99).

earnings of the family workers other than the operator+
imputed house rent.[4]
The word "real" reads "in terms of consumer prices in the city."

The estimate of the supply price of labor is to be related in the
present paper to the marginal farm operator for the purpose of
equilibrium analysis of the inter-sectoral labor allocation between
agriculture and other industries. The supply price of the farm operator in family outflow will be estimated for farms in the 0.5–1.0
hectare class which is assumed to be the lowest supply price for full-
time farm operators. For farms of smaller size, most are classified as
part-time farms on which farm labor income accounts for less than
50 per cent of the total family labor income (S.B.P.M.O.,1929b,
p. 10).

When a farm is located in an industrial district and the farm operator can find a full-time, non-farm job within commuting distance,
the supply price of labor of the farm operator is determined solely
by the opportunity labor income of the farm operator in agriculture.
The costs of labor outflow on a family basis, the cost of closing out
a farm and that of leaving the village, are not incurred in this case
with the cost of commuting usually being paid by the employer in
the form of a commuting allowance.

Thus we have in this case:

the supply price of labor in individual outflow of farm operator
=total returns to farm operator.

The total returns to the operator on a marginal farm may be assessed
by farm wage earnings.

Turning our attention next to the supply price of the expected
successor (the first son), we find two types of outflow: family outflow and individual outflow. The family outflow of the expected
successor implies a future decrease of the farm family. It is equivalent to the family outflow of the operator in the future. (The supply
price of the expected successor, therefore, is the same as that of the

---

[4] The rental of farm houses is not counted in farm income in the usual farm
record, and the salvage price of farm house, as I assume, is exhausted by the
cost of transportation and that of arranging a new residence in the city. For
these reasons, the imputed rental of farm house is counted in the supply price
of labor in family outflow. The rental of owned farm houses may be included in
the cost of leaving the village.

supply price of the operator.) The individual outflow of the expected successor is an outflow to full-time, non-farm work within commuting districts with the other family members being engaged in farming. The supply price is also equivalent to that of the individual outflow of the operator.

While an expected successor is assured of making a living on the inherited farm, the second and the third sons are entitled to no inheritance to secure their livelihood under the traditional family system. The economic opportunities in agriculture open to them are positions as tenant farmers and agricultural laborers. In case they live in a rural farm area and migration on a family basis is needed in order to take a non-farm job in a city, the supply price of labor of these sons is then the sum of expected earnings as a tenant farmer or agricultural laborer, the cost of labor outflow on a family basis and the cost of leaving the village. Based on the evidence that wage earnings of farm laborers were on a par with the labor return of tenant farm operators,[5] opportunity earnings of other sons in agriculture are estimated by farm wage earnings.

Then we have:
the supply price of labor of the other son in the family outflow
=farm wage earnings+the cost of labor outflow on a family
basis+the cost of leaving the village=the supply price of
labor of farm laborers in family outflow.

This supply price will be assessed here as follows:

The supply price of labor of farm laborers in family outflow= real wage earnings of a male farm laborer+(real wage earnings of a female farm laborer—expected non-farm wage earnings of a female laborer in city).

It is assumed that there are two income earners in the family: a male and a female family worker.[6]

---

[5] In 1925 the labor return to tenant farm operators was 33.93 yen per month, and the wage earnings of a farm laborer was 33.85 yen per month with similar conditions being found in other years: 30.39 to 29.15 in 1924; 36.15 to 36.25 in 1927; 26.91 to 26.98 in 1931; 24.31 to 24.64 in 1934; 28.71 to 28.45 in 1938 (in real terms, five year moving averages, yen per month) (M.A.F., *Survey of Farm Household Economy, Yearbook of Agricultural Statistics*).

[6] The number of family workers engaged in farming was 2.1 for farms of less than 1.0 hectare (M.A.F., 1921b).

Whenever the other son lives in industrial districts and can commute to a non-farm job without migration on a family basis, the supply price of labor in the individual outflow is determined by his farm wage earnings.

The supply price of labor of the other son in individual outflow
=the wage earnings of the male agricultural worker.
=the supply price of the farm laborer in individual outflow.
Finally, we will want to discuss here the supply price of labor of the female family worker whose supply price is determined by the opportunity labor income of the female family worker in agriculture. This can be measured by the farm wage earnings of the female laborer, i.e.,

the supply price of labor of a female family worker
=wage earnings of a female farm laborer.

Up to this point we have confined our discussion of the supply conditions of farm family labor[7] to the prewar period. We will want to examine next the changed situation which followed World War II. One of the most striking phenomena of the postwar period has been the remarkable rise in the price of farm land. For example, the real price of paddy fields in 1965 stood at 1.81 times its level in 1955 (N.C.A., pp. 9–10). Under this type of situation we would normally expect substantial capital gains to accrue to land owners from the price rise. However, under the Agricultural Land Act of 1946, the absentee ownership of farm land has been abolished, and hence an owner-operator is forced to give up future capital gains from farm land when he closes out the farm to migrate to a non-farm occupation. Although some farmers re-invest the farm land capital in urban residential land which yields comparable capital gains, this is limited to only a few cases. Thus, in the postwar period, the future capital gains from farm land should be counted in the cost of closing out a farm.

The marginal supply price of farm family labor is estimated empirically for each farm operator, expected successor of the operator,

---

[7] Changes in occupation and migration cause psychic friction and uncertainty in job performance as well as problems of adjustment to human relationships in the new job and community. For these reasons some income incentive may be needed to compensate for the psychic cost. However, the psychic cost is not counted in the supply price of labor due to lack of adequate information.

and farmer's sons other than the expected successor, and female family workers for the two types of outflow, individual and family.[8] It is assumed that the supply price of labor of the farm operator in family outflow is equal to that of the expected successor. Here again we have the assumption of identical supply price of labor, this time between the farm operator, the expected successor and the other sons in case of individual outflow at the margin which is measured by the farm laborer's wage earnings.

Thus we have estimated here the supply price of labor of the farm operator in family outflow P_1, the supply price of labor of male farm laborers in family outflow P_2, the supply price of labor of male farm workers in individual outflow P_3, and the supply price of labor of female farm workers in individual outflow P_4. These estimates are given in Tables 1 and 2; explanations of the method of calculation can be found in the footnotes to the tables.

Allowing for measurement errors and fluctuations in farm income, P_1 is a little higher than P_2 in the prewar period, except for the depression years 1929–1933. The difference between P_1 and P_2 represents the cost of closing out a farm, and it seems reasonable that the cost would not be high for the marginal farm families.[9] During the Depression, farm wage earnings did not follow exactly the declines in farm income. This accounts for the fact that P_2 was higher than P_1 at that time.

P_1 is, on the average, higher than P_3, the supply price of labor in individual outflow, by some 11 yen. The difference essentially represents the cost of labor outflow on a family basis and the cost of leaving the village. In the prewar period half of the difference is accounted for by the cost of labor outflow on a family basis and the remaining half is accounted for by the cost of leaving the village.

In the postwar period, the situation is quite different with P_1 being quite high relative to P_2. P_1 has come to be some three times

---

[8] For similar treatments of farm family workers by age, sex, and status in the family see Namiki (1950), p. 197, Kobayashi (1959), pp. 59–63 and Dipak Mazumdar, pp. 328–340. These works, however, lack adequate explanation of the labor supply behavior of family workers.

[9] In response to Professor Tanaka's comments at the Conference, the source of over-estimation of the P_1 supply price has been essentially eliminated in the present paper.

230 Agriculture and Economic Growth

TABLE 1

Estimated Supply Price of Labor of Farm Family, 1923-1939*

(Unit: Yen)

Year	P_1	P_2	P_3	P_4
1923	44.53	32.53	23.46	14.81
1924	40.72	34.98	24.32	16.49
1925	35.30	38.31	26.26	17.94
1926	42.20	40.21	26.72	19.59
1927	39.81	40.64	27.82	19.09
1928	36.08	41.59	28.59	19.46
1929	34.33	39.53	27.46	18.76
1930	33.79	35.83	24.72	17.89
1931	30.87	31.78	22.39	16.53
1932	31.12	33.36	23.07	16.54
1933	30.68	34.09	25.00	15.99
1934	34.07	34.36	24.64	15.14
1935	36.78	35.84	25.87	16.56
1936	35.84	35.54	24.19	16.36
1937	38.14	37.82	26.56	16.15
1938	41.94	39.65	28.45	15.97
1939	41.41	40.75	30.10	15.18

* Farm income and land rental data from Ministry of Agriculture and Forestry, *Survey of the Farm Household Economy (Nōka Keizai Chōsa)* (1920–1942), hereafter referred to as SFHE..

Coefficient of retail price differences data from Ohkawa, *Estimation of the Level of Living (Seikatsu Suijun no Sokutei)* (Tokyo, 1953), pp. 96–99.

The adjustment of the above coefficient to annual price changes based on data from H. Shishido, Index of Farmer's purchases (Nōka Kōnyuhin Bukka Shisu), in *Japanese Economy and Agriculture (Nihon no Keizai to Nōgyō)*, edited by S. Tobata and K. Ohkawa, I, (Tokyo, 1956).

Wage earnings of the other family members data from Bureau of Statistics, Office of the Prime Minister, *Consumer Price Indices (Shōhisha Bukka Shisū)*, *1920–1942; Survey of Retail Price Control (Kouri Kakaku Tōsei Chōsa Hōkoku)*, *1941–1942;* and finally *Family Income and Expenditure (Kakei Chōsa Hōkoku)*, *1926–1942* (hereafter cited as FIE).

Real wage earnings for female workers data from *Historical Analysis of Wage Structure in Japan (Wagakuni Chingin Kōzō no Shiteki Kōsatsu)*, Shōwa-Dōjinkai, ed. (Tokyo, 1960), p. 463.

Annual number of effective farm work days per male worker data from Ministry of Agriculture and Forestry, *SFHE*.

Farm wage rate data from Ministry of Agriculture and Forestry, *Yearbook of Agricultural Statistics (Nōrinshō Tōkeihyō), 1920–1942*.

a) The figures in the table present five-year moving averages in real terms with 1921–1923 as base year, and are in yen per month.

b) P_1 represents the supply price of labor of a farm operator or expected successor in family outflow, and is *equal to* (farm income of the farms of 0.5–1.0 ha. size *minus* the imputed rental of owned farm land) *multiplied by* coefficient of difference in retail prices between rural and urban areas *minus* the estimated wage earnings of the other family members in non-farm sectors *plus* imputed rental of farm house.

c) P_2 represents the supply price of a male farm laborer in family outflow, and is *equal to* (Farm wage rate of male farm laborer *multiplied* by estimated days of work i.e., 15 days) *plus* farm wage rate of female farm laborer multiplied by estimated days of work, i.e., 12 days *multiplied* by coefficient of difference in retail prices between rural and urban areas *minus* the estimated wage earnings of the other family members in non-farm sectors.

d) P_3 represents the supply price of labor of male farm workers in individual outflow and is *equal to* farm wage rate of male farm laborer *multiplied* by estimated days of work, i.e., 15 days.

e) P_4 represents the supply price of labor of a female farm worker in individual outflow and is *equal to* the farm wage rate of female laborer *multiplied* by estimated days of work, i.e., 12 days.

f) Land rental is assessed by market rate of rent, while house rental is imputed by the rent paid by urban workers.

g) The estimate of wage earnings of other family members represents the average wage earnings of family members other than the family head in a factory laborer's household. The year 1926, when wage was 7.50 yen, is assumed as the benchmark year.

h) Due to non-availability of any series on wage earnings of farm laborers for selected years, the wage earnings are estimated here, with the help of information on daily wage rates.

i) The days of farm work is estimated as 180 days per year for a male worker, while the same is assumed for female worker to be 80 per cent that of the male worker.

j) The farm wage rate includes the value of meals and wages in kind.

higher than P_2 because the cost of closing out a farm has risen substantially due to the capital gains cost. For example, the average value of the farm land in the 0.5−1.0 ha. farm class was 1,442 thousand yen in 1960. With the rate of increase in real land prices being 7.1 per cent a year over the last ten years, the expected future capital gains can be estimated at 8,500 yen a month ($=1,442 \times 0.071 \div 12$). The difference between P_1 and P_2, 12,837 yen in 1960, is accounted for by the expected capital gain of 8,500 yen, the lost property income of the other farm assets of 2,130 yen and the imputed farm house rent of 2,207 yen.

Another striking difference between the prewar and postwar periods is that P_2 is now essentially on a par with P_3. In other words, we can now treat the cost of labor outflow on a family basis as being negligible. This is a reflection of the fact that the non-farm labor market for female workers, especially for the married women in wholesaling, retailing, and manufacturing (Kobayashi, 1961, p. 178), has been expanding very rapidly and wage earnings are considerably improved relative to opportunity earnings in agriculture. According to the Census on Population figures for the non-farm sector, the number of female workers in 1955 (6,028,000) was

TABLE 2

Estimated Supply Price of Labor to Farm Family, 1950–1960*

(Unit: Yen)

Year	P_1	P_2	P_3	P_4
1950	8,313	3,170	3,010	1,836
1951	9,859	3,849	3,617	1,980
1952	11,303	3,742	3,968	2,244
1953	10,812	3,622	4,433	2,520
1954	12,680	4,554	4,951	2,784
1955	17,683	4,886	5,192	2,868
1956	15,532	5,373	5,313	2,976
1957	16,959	6,034	5,589	3,132
1958	16,771	6,197	5,865	3,756
1959	17,771	5,877	6,020	3,456
1960	18,917	6,080	6.211	3,768

* Data concerning retail price differences between farms and cities from Yasu-naga, Takemi, "Comparison of Level of Living between Cities and Rural Villages in Recent Years (Saikin no Toshi to Nōson no Seikatsu Suijun no Taihi)," *Rural Population Problem Research,* No. 2 (Tokyo, 1952).

Data on house rent from Housing Bureau, Ministry of Construction, *Report on the Price of Land and House (Tochi Oyobi Jūtaku Kakaku Kekka Hōkoku) 1959.* Data concerning the market prices of farm land from National Council of Agriculture, *Report on Market Price of Paddy Field and Upland (Denbata Baibai Kakaku ni Kansuru Chōsa Kekka), 1956–1960.*

Wage data for other family members in the non-farm sector from Bureau of Statistics, Office of the Prime Minister, *FIE, 1950–1960;* and *Consumers' Price Indices (Kouri Kakaku Tōkei Chōsa Hōkoku), 1950–1960.*

Farm wage earnings data from Ministry of Agriculture and Forestry, *SFHE 1950–1960;* and *Yearbook of Agricultural Statistics (Nōrinshō Tōkeihyō) 1950–1960.*

a) The figures in Table 2 are expressed in nominal terms, and in yen per month.

b) P_1 refers to the supply price of labor of farm operator of expected successor in family outflow, and is *equal to* (Farm income of the farms of 0.5–1.0 ha. size *minus* imputed rental of farm land) *multiplied* by coefficient of differences in retail prices between rural and urban areas *minus* the estimated wage earnings of the other family members in non-farm sector *plus* imputed rental of farm household *plus* expected future capital gains from farm land.

c) P_2 refers to the supply price of a male farm laborer in family outflow, and is *equal to* (Farm wage rate for male farm worker *multiplied by* the estimated days of work i.e., 15 days *plus* farm wage rate of female farm worker *multiplied by* the estimated days of work i.e., 12 days) *multiplied* by coefficient of difference in retail prices between rural and urban areas *minus* estimated wage earnings of the other family members in non-farm sector.

d) P_3 refers to the supply price of labor of a male farm worker in the individual outflow.

e) P_4 refers to the supply price of labor of a female farm worker in the individual outflow.

f) Land rent is estimated by 6 per cent of interest rate on the land capital.

g) The coefficient of difference in retail price between farms and cities takes 1951 as the base year and 1.072 as base farm coefficient, and is adjusted annually for cities and rural areas.

h) Expected future capital gains from farm land is estimated by the rate of increase in real price of land over the last ten years for each year.

i) Farm wage rate includes value of meals and wages in kind.

1.65 times that of 1930 (3,681,000), while the number of male workers in 1955 (12,331,000) was 1.47 times as much as that of 1930 (8,373,000). Female workers 25 years old or older accounted for 50 per cent of the total female workers in the non-farm sector in 1955 while accounting for only one-third in 1930. At the same time family members other than the family head of a factory laborer's household earned as much income as did female farm workers (S.B.P.M.O., 1956). Thus, this new development in the non-farm labor market for female workers, particularly for the married female worker, has led to a reduction in the cost of moving out on a family basis.

II. Implications of Empirical Data

It has been seen that the supply price of the labor of male farm workers largely depends on the general conditions of the non-farm labor market, i.e., whether there are non-farm job opportunities within commuting distance and whether non-farm job opportunities for family members other than family head are as profitable as those in farming. In the prewar period, there were only limited opportunities for non-farm jobs within commuting distance, and the non-farm jobs that were available to housewives were not as profitable as those in farming. As a result, the supply price of labor of the male farm worker in family outflow differed considerably from the supply price in individual outflow because of the cost of labor outflow on a family basis, the cost of leaving the village, and the cost of closing out a farm.

Comparing the two types of farms, one located within commuting distance and the other beyond, the lowest supply price of male labor is that of individual outflow from farms within commuting districts. Suppose that the non-farm supply curve of labor of young family workers in individual outflow be represented by the curve AB in Fig. 1. It is upward sloping because of the diminishing marginal productivity of labor (=farm wage rate). The feasible range of supply of labor is limited to Ol of farmer's sons, expected successors and other sons within commuting districts. When the supply of labor in individual outflow within commuting distance is exhausted, the supply of labor in the form of family outflow of the other sons outside the commuting districts comes into the picture. It is represented by segment CP_2 in Fig. 1. The supply price of labor in family outflow of the other sons is higher than the supply price of labor in individual outflow by CG, i.e., the cost of labor outflow on a family basis and the cost of leaving the village.

FIGURE 1
Supply Curve of Labor of Farm Family Workers in
Non-Farm Labor Market in the Prewar Years*

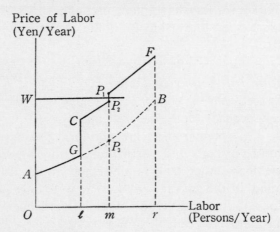

* Based on data in Table 1.

When the supply of labor of the other sons in family outflow, *lm*, is exhausted, the supply of labor in family outflow of the expected successors outside the commuting districts, P_1F comes into the picture. The supply price of labor of the expected successor in family outflow is higher than that of the other sons by the cost of closing out a farm, P_1P_2. Thus, the supply curve of labor of young male farm workers may be formulated as the step function as shown in Fig. 1. The estimates of the supply price of labor of male farm workers in individual outflow correspond to P_3 in Fig. 1. The estimates of the supply price of the other sons in family outflow correspond to P_2 while the estimates of the supply price of the expected successor in family outflow correspond to P_1.[10]

At this point we want to treat the general conditions of the non-farm labor market in order to facilitate a meaningful comparison of the supply price with non-farm wage earnings. In so doing, attention is drawn to the following characteristics of the non-farm labor market:

First, the wage rate is customarily increased in proportion to the years of one's service. For example, wage rates in manufacturing industries in 1940 for employment of 6 months, 5 years, 10 years and 20 years were, in terms of index numbers, 100, 156, 186 and 254, respectively. This situation remains unchanged even now and is referred to as "the escalator structure of wage rate" (Abegglen, pp. 47ff). This escalator structure of the wage rate is associated with "the lifetime commitment system," both having evolved from the paternalistic apprenticeship system which enabled the employer to bind workers of a certain skill to his firm. A labor market of this kind is accessible only to the young, newly entering workers. Aged farm workers, say 40 years old, can hardly enter the labor market for skilled labor. The farm operators who are highly skilled in farming would find no rewards for their acquired farming skills in the non-farm labor market. In addition, to invest in acquiring the new industrial skills is much less attractive to the old male than to the younger male for the simple reason that there are fewer remaining years during which the older man can obtain a return on his investment.

In the context of this paper the escalator structure of wage rates allows us to avoid certain complications in the supply price of labor of young family workers which stem from cost considerations of job training. The wage rate is adjusted for the cost of training at each stage of on-the-job training, and the workers receive wages net of the cost of training.[11]

Second, we must call attention to the fact that there was no program of unemployment insurance during the prewar period. Ob-

---

[10] The reasoning which underlies this statement will be given later when the rate of labor outflow from farms is explained in relation to the non-farm demand conditions for farm workers.

[11] For a relevant study of the cost and returns of job training, see Becker, pp. 9–50.

viously the outflow of labor from agriculture is unfavorably affected by the low level of security in the hired-employment sector. Taking this into account, we can see how the stability of employment on the family farm can outweigh a higher non-farm income during periods of high unemployment.

Finally, we must note that a considerable wage differential exists according to the size of the firm. For example, in 1932 wage earnings in small firms were 30 per cent lower than wages in large firms. This tendency of wage earnings to increase with size of the firm was applicable to all branches of employment in the non-farm sector, and the situation has remained unchanged, even until the present (Umemura, pp. 209ff). It seems that the differential structure of wage earnings reflects the differential quality of labor such as education and skill levels, which exists among firms of different size. Furthermore, even though the beginning wage may be identical, the subsequent improvement will follow different paths, depending on the size of the firm.

In addition to higher wages, workers of the larger firms acquire more specific skills than those of smaller firms. The more specific is the skill, the higher is its reward and the more immobile is the labor. It is also true that the turnover rate of workers is much less for workers of larger firms than those of smaller firms. In 1959 the average duration of a worker's service was 11.5 years in firms employing more than 1,000 persons while only 4.6 years for firms employing 10–99 persons (Ministry of Labor, pp. 458–9). In 1958 more than 70 per cent of the rural farm youth who left the farm after completing 9 years of schooling entered firms employing less than 100 persons (Namiki, 1960, p. 178). Wage earnings in firms employing 50–99 persons was 157,000 yen per year, that is 60 per cent of wage earnings in firms employing 1,000–1,999 persons (Umemura, p. 217).

One of the typical occupations open to the farm operator was that of a day laborer on construction and building projects. Column W_2 of Table 3 shows the wage earnings of such unskilled laborers. The level of the wage earnings here is higher than the supply price of labor in the individual outflow of the operator, but the wage earnings were not sufficiently attractive to induce the family outflow of the operator except during the Depression. During this period the wage earnings of day laborers in construction and building were higher than the supply price of the farm operator, but lack of job opportunities restricted the family outflow of the operator.

A situation similar to the one described above also pertains to the outflow of expected successors. However, in this case a comparable

TABLE 3

Wage Earnings[a] in Non-Farm Sector, 1923–1939*

(Unit: Yen)

Year	$W_1{}^b$	$W_2{}^c$	$W_3{}^d$	$W_4{}^e$
1923	33.30	38.12	31.46	19.12
1924	34.82	38.92	33.55	19.46
1925	36.52	39.20	33.19	19.64
1926	37.71	41.78	38.40	20.35
1927	39.01	41.81	38.68	20.91
1928	41.04	41.55	36.76	21.00
1929	39.85	40.36	39.71	22.30
1930	38.24	41.27	40.99	22.60
1931	38.31	41.13	38.72	23.80
1932	40.20	39.22	38.18	20.86
1933	42.06	37.70	36.86	19.77
1934	47.26	35.08	36.63	17.14
1935	45.64	34.58	36.15	17.24
1936	43.74	33.25	36.56	16.71
1937	41.56	33.03	35.48	16.30
1938	39.31	34.26	33.44	15.90
1939	38.20	35.08	33.30	15.10

* Wage data for laborers employed in manufacturing firms and those employed in agricultural processing industry of *sake* and soy sauce brewing industries from Shōwa-Dōjinkai, editor, *Historical Analysis of Wage Structure in Japan* (Tokyo: 1960), Statistics Table 1, p. 463.

Wage data for male and female day laborers employed in textile industry from the Ministry of Agriculture and Commerce later (Commerce and Industry), *The Reports on Wages by Occupation (Zenkoku Shokugyō-Betsu Chingin),* 1920–1940.

a) The figures in Table 3 are expressed in real terms with 1921–1923 as a base year and in yen per month.

b) W_1 represents wage earnings of laborers in manufacturing firms which employ 4 persons or more.

c) W_2 represents the wage earnings of day laborers.

d) W_3 represents the wage earnings of male artisans in agricultural processing industries of *sake* and soy sauce brewing.

e) W_4 represents the wage earnings of laborers (female) in the textile industry. The available data does not cover all the selected years. For the intervening years, the daily wage rate multiplied by estimated days of work is used.

non-farm occupation might be that of a laborer in manufacturing industry. The wage earnings here were higher than the supply price of labor in the individual outflow of the expected successor, but was not higher than the supply price of family outflow except during the Depression.

We find that in 1931 hired employment declined by 26.5 per cent and half of the employed returned to their farm families (S.B. P.M.O., 1934a, p. 247).

The supply price of labor of the second or third sons, both in family outflow and in individual outflow, was lower than the wage earnings for laborers in manufacturing industry throughout the period.

During 1927–40 the outflow of male family workers was distributed as follows: to manufacturing and construction—44.1 per cent, wholesale and retailing—24.1 per cent, and service industries (including public services)—14.6 per cent (Nojiri, p. 300). In view of the industrial distribution of the outflow of farm workers, the comparison of the supply price with the wage earnings of laborers in manufacturing industry may be the most relevant.

For female family workers it is important to examine the non-farm wages which existed in the textile industry, given that in 1934, 70 per cent of the individual outflow of female family workers went into the textile industry (Nojiri, p. 305). The wage earnings of female laborers in the textile industry was higher than the supply price of the individual outflow of female workers from agriculture throughout the period.

To summarize the above, we can say that the non-farm wage earnings of the relevant occupations provided the necessary incentive to induce the outflow of farm family workers, except in the case of the family outflow of farm operators and expected successors. Umemura estimates the net outflow of the labor force from farms to have been 180–240 thousand persons per year during the period between the two World Wars (Umemura, p. 163). More specifically, the outflow of labor from farms was limited to the full outflow of non-heirs of farm families, i.e., farmer's sons and daughters other than the expected successors, and to the individual outflow of farm operators and expected successors within limited commuting districts (Namiki, 1959, p. 150).

Looking again at Fig. 1, the rate of outflow of farm youth may be represented by $\overline{Om}$ with the relevant supply price of labor of farm youth at the margin being P_2. As indicated earlier, the supply price P_2 seems to be equilibrated with the relevant non-farm wage earnings in normal times (See Tables 1 and 3).

For farm operators, the supply curve of labor in the non-farm labor market may be formulated as the step function $A\ P_3\ P_1\ F$ in Fig. 1, on a scale of the abscissa different from that for farm youth. Here the relevant non-farm wage earnings were less than the supply price in family outflow at the margin, i.e., P_1 in normal times.

For female farm workers the supply curve may be formulated as the curve AB in Fig. 1 on the proper scale of the ordinate and the abscissa. The estimated supply price of female farm workers at the margin, P_4, was lower than the comparable non-farm wage earnings in textile industry. It may reflect the low saleability of labor of older female farm workers in the non-farm labor market and thus oversupply in agriculture.

During the Depression, the non-farm (excess) demand for farm workers declined and thus restricted the job opportunities for workers coming from the farms. When real wage rates occasionally rose due to rigidities in the money wage relative to the general price level in the non-farm sector, job opportunities became further limited. At the same time, the supply price of labor of farm workers was lowered due to declines in farm income as well as an oversupply of labor in agriculture during the Depression. Umemura, (Umemura, p. 159) and Minami (Minami, p. 186) explored the fluctuations in the net outflow of the labor force from farms in relation to business cycles. It is clear from their studies that the rate of the outflow was affected by job opportunities in the non-farm sector. The number of farm households appeared to increase in depression and decrease in prosperity, but over the period of 1920–1940, as a whole, the total number of farm households remained fairly stable. On the other hand, the size of the labor force engaged in farming showed a tendency to decline without being affected by business cycles (See Table 5).

The situation of the non-farm labor market for young male farm workers has changed considerably in the postwar period. Turning to Fig. 2 and the non-farm supply curve of labor of young male workers from farms, we see that the differential supply of labor between individual outflow and family outflow of the sons disappears since the cost of labor outflow on a family basis and the cost of leaving the village are reduced in this period. Estimates of the supply price of labor in individual outflow, P_3, are essentially equal to those of the supply price in family outflow of the other sons, P_2, in Table 2. At the same time, the differential supply of labor between family outflow of the other sons and family outflow of the expected successors is more conspicuous since the cost of closing out a farm is, during this period, augmented by the expected future capital gains from farm land. Segment EC in Fig. 2, represents the cost of closing out a farm, while segment EF refers to the supply curve of labor of the expected successors in family outflow. As a result, the total supply curve of labor of young male workers from farms takes the shape of the step function $A\ C\ E\ F$ shown in Fig. 2.

FIGURE 2
Supply Curve of Labor of Farm Family Workers in Non-farm
Labor Market in the Postwar Years*

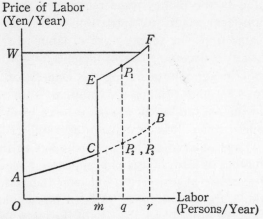

* Based on the data in Table 2.

Suppose that the rising trend in real farm land prices can be brought down by a change in farm price policy or a change in the

Agricultural Land Act which now prohibits the absentee ownership of farm land by outmigrated farmers. The cost of closing out a farm, then, will be lowered by the smaller expected future capital gains from farm land or by retention of the capital gains with the right of absentee ownership of outmigrated farmers in a city. Thus, the total supply curve will begin to approach the AB curve of Fig. 2. In addition, if the capital gains are shared by the other sons[12] under the right of parcenary recognized during the postwar period, then only the expected successor's share of capital gains from farm land, not the total amount of the capital gain, should be counted in the cost of closing out a farm. If this is done, we can expect a lower supply price of labor of the expected successor in family outflow so that P_1 comes closer to P_2.

Non-farm employment opportunities have increased by leaps and bounds in the postwar period. The annual rate of increase in non-farm, hired employment was 900,000 persons for 1950–1960, while only 280,000 for 1920–1940 (Census of Population). The greatest expansion was shown in job opportunities in manufacturing industry, especially in machinery and equipment manufacturing, and in the wholesale and retail trades. In response to the unprecedentedly rapid expansion of non-farm employment, the rate of net out-migration[13] of the labor force from agriculture amounted to 410,000 persons per year, two times the rate of the prewar period. The rate of commuting outflow amounted to 283,000 and a total

---

[12] It is noted that the other sons may avail themselves of the shared capital gains in improving their education so that they can enter into higher paid non-farm occupations. As a matter of fact, the high school enrollment rate is significantly higher for the other sons than for the expected successors. In 1956, 60 per cent of the other sons entered high school after they had finished their compulsory education while 40 per cent of the expected successors did so (Kobayashi, 1961, p. 360).

[13] The out-migration which is defined in official statistics does not correspond exactly to the family outflow used in the terminology of this paper. The official use of "out-going" *(dekasegi)* includes the outflow of farm workers who migrate from farm to non-farm jobs and return to the farm after working for more than one year. Here, this type of outflow is classified as individual outflow with some part of the individual outflow of the farm worker taking this form. Concerning the commuting outflow, the definition used in official statistics can include the family outflow in our terminology, if the family outflow does not involve migration out of rural farm areas.

net outflow of 693,000 persons took place in 1961 (M.A.F., 1962a, p. 22). As mentioned earlier, more than 70 per cent of the outflow was absorbed in the relatively low paid jobs of smaller size firms in the non-farm sector.

In 1961, the outflow of male farm workers was distributed as follows: manufacturing, 48.3 per cent; service industries, 10.8 per cent; and wholesale and retailing, 14.1 per cent. The outflow of

TABLE 4
Wage Earnings^a in Non-Farm Sector 1950–1960*

(Unit: Yen)

Year	$W_5{}^b$	$W_6{}^c$	$W_7{}^d$	$W_8{}^e$
1950	7,463	6,750	9,417	· 3,420
1951	7,885	7,703	10,970	3,794
1952	8,125	8,892	12,740	4,191
1953	8,650	10,264	13,018	4,353
1954	9,174	11,031	13,388	4,786
1955	9,615	11,647	13,787	5,005
1956	9,991	11,709	14,448	5,470
1957	10,172	13,644	15,164	5,521
1958	10,325	13,208	13,989	5,511
		(18,403)	(18,192)	
1959	10,500	13,908	14,569	5,678
		(19,238)	(19,650)	
1960	10,813	15,421	15,384	6,019
		(20,871)	(26,214)	

* Wage data from Ministry of Labor, *Yearbook of Labor Statistics* (1960).

a) The figures in Table 4 are expressed in nominal terms, and in yen per month.

b) W_5 represents the wage earnings of day laborers of contractors.

c) W_6 represents, for the period 1950–56, an average of earnings in manufacturing establishments which employ 50–99 workers. For 1957 an average of wage earnings of male workers in establishments employing 30–99 workers; for 1958–60, average of wage earnings of male workers in establishments employing 10–99 workers; figures in parantheses refer to the wage earnings of male production workers with high school education or better in establishments which employ 100–999 workers.

d) W_7 represents, for the period 1950–56, average of wage earnings of all workers in wholesale and retail firms employing 50–99 workers; for 1957 an average of wage earnings of male workers in establishments which employ 30–99 workers; for 1958–60 average of male workers in establishments employing 10–99 workers. Figures in parentheses are related to male workers with high school education or better in establishments employing 10–99 workers.

e) W_8 represents an average of wage earnings of female laborers in the silk-reeling industry.

female farm workers was distributed as follows: manufacturing, 43.1 per cent; service industries, 30.5 per cent; and wholesale and retail, 18.8 per cent (M.A.F. 1962a, p. 27). As a matter of fact, the respective non-farm wage earnings necessarily involve an incentive to family outflow of expected successors in the postwar period. Assuming the expected successors have a high school education or better, the wage earnings in commercial establishments employing less than 100 workers, W_7 in Table 4, are higher than the supply price of the expected successor in family outflow P_1. Recent statistics indicate that in 1960, 45,000 expected successors out-migrated while 70,000 of them began commuting to non-farm occupations (M.A.F., 1965a, p. 178). Namiki estimates the recruitment rate of farm operators among the successors at 1.05 in 1950 and 0.54 in 1959 (Namiki, 1960, p. 35). This is quite a new development in the non-farm labor market which underlies the postwar decline in the numbers of farm households.

TABLE 5

Number of Farm Households and Farm Workers*

(Unit: 1,000)

Year	Total[a]	Farm house-holds without off-farm workers	Farm house-holds with off-farm workers	Farm workers
1920	5,485 (100)[b]	3,823 (69.7)	1,662 (30.3)	13,939
1925	5,463 (100)	3,811 (69.8)	1,652 (30.2)	13,941
1930	5,512 (100)	3,969 (72.0)	1,543 (28.0)	13,944
1932	5,552 (100)	4,042 (73.0)	1,509 (27.0)	13,868
1934	5,525 (100)	4,069 (73.6)	1,456 (26.4)	13,790
1936	5,505 (100)	4,100 (74.5)	1,405 (25.5)	13,711
1938	5,429 (100)	3,631 (66.9)	1,798 (33.1)	13,629
1940	5,390 (100)	3,697 (68.6)	1,693 (31.4)	13,549
1950	6,176 (100)	3,086 (50.0)	3,090 (50.0)	15,990
1955	6,075 (100)	2,125 (34.8)	3,950 (65.2)	15,410
1960	6,057 (100)	2,078 (34.3)	3,979 (65.7)	13,390
1965	5,665 (100)	1,218 (21.1)	4,446 (78.9)	10,856

* Data from *Major Statistics of Japanese Agriculture,* Kayō Nobubumi, ed. (Tokyo, 1958), p. 135, and from Ministry of Agriculture and Forestry, Bureau of Statistics and Survey, *Yearbook of Agricultural Statistics.*
a) Since the definition of farm household was changed several times during 1920–1966, the figures are not comparable over time. Most affected is the series of the number of farm households with off-farm workers.
b) Figures in parentheses denote percentages.

Turning to Fig. 2, the rate of outflow of male farm youth is represented by $\overline{Oq}$, and the estimate for the supply price of labor is P_1 for family outflow of the expected successor and P_2 for the individual outflow of the expected successor and individual and family outflow of the other sons. The relevant supply price of farm labor force at the margin is P_1, with P_1 seemingly lower than the comparable non-farm wage earnings of workers with a high school education or better. It can be easily seen that even a moving equilibrium is not attained in the process of the very rapid development of the non-farm labor market during the postwar period. In the non-farm labor market for farm operators, comparable non-farm wage earnings of unskilled laborers in construction and building are higher than the supply price of labor in the individual outflow of the operator, but are lower than the supply price in the family outflow of the operator. The wage earnings of female laborers in the textile industry are considerably higher than the supply price of female farm workers in individual outflow during this period. The large difference in wage earnings between the farm and the textile industry can hardly be described as a market disequilibrium unless the difference in quality of labor between female laborers in textile industry and female farm workers, who are relatively older and unskilled, is adequately taken into account. However, even taking this into account, we are still likely to find that the labor market is not in equilibrium over this period. Finally, we notice that the outflow of the labor force from farms is generally a very selective process with the young and better educated of the labor force migrating out. This feature of selectivity has become more prominent in the process of postwar economic growth.

In addition to the nationwide estimates of the supply prices of the labor of farm family workers for 1923–1960, the estimates on a regional basis are obtained for 1962–1964 in order to examine the equilibrium position in the non-farm labor market of the farm labor force. The supply price of labor in family outflow of expected successors (farm operators) of full-time farms of 0.5–1.0 ha. (2.0–3.0 ha. in Hokkaido) is estimated. The estimates of the supply price are assumed to be the lowest in the category of the supply price of labor of expected successors of full-time farms since the farms concerned fall in the smallest class of farm on which all the family workers can work. These estimates are given in Table 6.

TABLE 6

Estimated Supply Price[a] and Comparable Non-farm Earnings 1962–1964*

(Units: 1,000 yen)

Region	HKD[e]	TOH[e]	HOK[e]	KNT[e]	TOK[e]	KIN[e]	CHK[e]	SHK[e]	KYS[e]
$P_1{}^b$	389	385	408	465	489	509	370	392	327
$W_9{}^c$	248	214	210	263	301	309	279	219	207
$W_{10}{}^d$	319	327	334	401	386	419	366	329	406

* Supply price data from Bureau of Statistics and Survey, Ministry of Agriculture and Forestry, *Survey of Farm Household Economy by Economic Type of Farm,* and from National Council of Agriculture, *Report on Market Price of Paddy Field and Upland.*

Non-farm earnings data from Division of Labor Statistics and Research, Ministry of Labor, *Yearbook of Labor Statistics.*

a) The figures in Table 6 are expressed in 1963 prices, and in 1,000 yen per year.

b) P_1 refers to the supply price of labor of the expected successor in family outflow and is *equal to* the farm income of a full-time farm of 0.5–1.0 ha. size (2.0–3.0 ha. in Hokkaido) *minus* imputed land rental *minus* expected non-farm wage earnings of the other family members than family head *plus* imputed house rental *plus* expected future capital gains from farm land.

c) W_9 refers to the non-farm wage earnings of the family head of residential farms.

d) W_{10} refers to the non-farm salary earnings of the family head of residential farms.

e) HKD=Hokkaido; TOH=Tōhoku; HOK=Hokuriku; KNT=Kantō; Tok=Tōkai; KIN=Kinki; CHK=Chūgoku; SHK=Shikoku; KYS=Kyūshū region.

The lowest supply price of the family outflow of expected successors of full-time farms is higher than earnings in respective non-farm occupations in each region except Kyushu, as can be seen in Table 6. When we compare the supply price with labor earnings across regions, the supply price of labor of the expected successors in low income regions is lower than the labor earnings of comparable non-farm occupations in high income regions. There is much room for the inter-regional migration of farm workers, and the actual migration has been moving in that direction.

III. Concluding Remarks

In this study we have departed from the conventional concept of the supply price of labor in individual outflow and proposed a supply price of labor in terms of family outflow to take account of the cost of outflow on a family basis, the cost of closing out a farm, and the cost of leaving a village. In explaining the long-term behavior of the members of farm households and farm workers, the supply price of labor in family outflow of the expected successor has been proved to be the relevant parameter.

The rate of outflow of labor from the farm and the behavior of members of farm households are, of course, dependent on both supply conditions and the demand conditions in the non-farm labor market. In the present paper we have taken special interest in certain aspects of supply conditions which are often neglected. We have found that the supply price of labor of the farm family depends not only upon economic and institutional conditions within agriculture, such as the opportunity farm income and capital gains from land, but also upon conditions prevailing in non-agriculture, e.g., non-farm job opportunities for family members and security of employment. Insecurity of employment and low saleability of labor of family members in the non-farm sector lead to a high supply price of labor in the family outflow of expected successors. The scope is confined to an analysis of the non-farm labor market for the labor which occupies a comparable position to farm labor in terms of levels of skill and education. No doubt, a broader approach to human migration into different occupations of higher skills is also a promising field of study. We should not be surprised to see that the supply price of labor depends, indeed, upon the occupation which a worker strives for, reflecting different migration costs.

The central problem with which we have had to grapple is that a larger scale of outflow of the labor force from the farms has been associated with larger earning differences between farming and comparable non-farm occupations. The ratio of wage earnings in manufacturing to those of agriculture was 1.54 in the prewar period and 2.29 in the postwar period. Apart from cyclical fluctuations, if the non-farm labor market for farm workers were out of equilibrium, the increased labor force outflow would have occurred with a narrowing of the wage earnings differential. The fact was that a higher wage difference was needed to induce farm workers with higher migration costs to move from farming into the non-farm sector. Dispersion of industrial plants into rural areas in the postwar period may be regarded as an adaptive measure taken by industrialists to meet the above situation. The dispersion of industrial employment opportunities into rural areas leads to reduction in the cost of labor outflow from farms which tends to increase the non-farm supply of labor of farm family workers in individual outflow.

We may say that the non-farm labor market accessible to farm workers was functioning well since the direction and magnitude of the outflow of the labor force from farming to comparable non-farm occupations were consistent with the prediction based on a comparison of the supply price of labor in family outflow with the labor earnings of comparable non-farm occupations.[14] It is noteworthy that the higher level of outflow of labor of farm family workers in the postwar period is ascribed to a higher educational attainment of farm youth as well as rapid economic growth, dispersion of industrial plants and development of transportation facilities. The higher level of educational attainment[15] has particularly done much in broadening non-farm job opportunities and in improving work conditions such as stability of employment and the level of wage rates for farm youth.

---

[14] Minami runs a regression analysis of the supply function of the farm labor force in the non-farm labor market in a framework of simultaneous equations and finds the following results:

$$\log m_d = -.206 \log w_n + 10.366 \log (100 + g_n) - 19.399$$
$$\log m_s = 1.928 \log w_n - 2.428 \log w_a + 1.044$$

where m_d refers to non-farm demand for the farm labor force, m_s to the non-farm supply of the farm labor force, w_n to real wage earnings per employee in non-agriculture, w_a to the average of real wage earnings in agriculture, and g_n to the growth rate of real GNP in non-agriculture. The selected period is 1922–1961 (excluding 1939–1950). It is easily seen that wage parameters work well in the labor market. Elasticity with respect to w_n is 1.928 for the supply function and $-.206$ for demand. Professor Tanaka's view that the outflow of labor force from farms entirely depends upon non-farm employment opportunities can not be supported by the empirical data (Minami, p. 196).

[15] In addition to nine years of compulsory education, 60 per cent of farm youth had a high school education or better in 1962 (M.A.F., 1962a, p. 65). In 1935, only 35 per cent of rural youth had 11 years of school education or better (Nihon Nōgyō Nenkan Publishing Commission, 1958, p. 127).

REFERENCES

Abegglen, J. C. *The Japanese Factory: Aspects of its Social Organization.* Free Press, Macmillan, 1958.

Becker, G. S., "Investment in Human Capital: A Theoretical Analysis," *Journal of Political Economy,* LXX, No. 5 (October, 1962).

Bellerby, J. R. *Agriculture and Industry, Relative Income.* London: 1946.

Hemmi, K., "Constancy of the Farm Population (Nōka Jinkō no Koteisei)," *Japanese Economy and Agriculture (Nihon no Keizai to Nōgyō),* Tōbata and Ohkawa, eds., I, Tokyo: 1956.

Kayō, N. ed. *Basic Statistics of Japanese Agriculture (Nihon Nōgyō Kiso Tōsei).* Tokyo, 1958.

Kobayashi, K., "Outflow of Farm Population and Structure of Agricultural Surplus Population after World War II (Sengo no Nōka Rōdōryoku no Ryūshutsu to Nōgyō Kajōjinko no Senzai Keitai)," *Journal of Rural Economics (Nōgyō Keizai Kenkyu),* XXX, No. 4 (April, 1959).

——. *Employment Structure and Surplus Population in Agriculture (Shūgyō Kōzō to Nōson Kajōjinkō).* Tokyo: 1961.

Lewis, W. A., "Economic Development with Unlimited Supplies of Labour," *Manchester School of Economic and Social Studies* (May, 1954).

Mazumdar, Dipak, "Unemployment in Agriculture and Industrial Wage Rate," *Economica,* XXVI, No. 104 (November, 1959).

Minami, R., "Population Migration Away from Agriculture in Japan," *Economic Development and Cultural Change,* XV, No. 2, Part I (Jan. 1967).

Ministry of Agriculture and Forestry. *Survey of the Changes in Occupation of Members of Farm Households (Nōka Shūgyō Dōkō Chōsa).* 1958 and subsequent years.

——. *Farm Household Economy Survey (Nōka Keizai Chōsa).* 1921b and the subsequent years.

——. *Yearbook of Agricultural Statistics (Norin-shō Tōkeihyo)* 1920–1965.

Ministry of Labor. *Yearbook of Labor Statistics.* 1960.

Namiki, M., "Pattern of Outflow of Farm Population and Employment Structure (Nōka Jinkō no Idō Keitai to Shūgyō Kōzo)," *Disguised Unemployment in Agriculture (Nōgyō ni okeru Senzai Shitsugyō),* Tobata, ed., Tokyo: 1950.

——, "Growth of Industrial Workers and Farm Population (Sangyō Rōdōryoku no Keisei to Nōka Jinkō)," *Japanese Capitalism and Agriculture (Nihon Shihon-shugi to Nōgyō),* Tobata and Uno, eds., Tokyo: 1959.

——, "Recruitment Rate of Farm Population (Nōka Jinko no Hojuritsu)," *Nōgyō Sōgō Kenkyu,* XIV, No. 3 (July, 1960).

National Council of Agriculture (Zenkoku Nōgyō Kaigi). *Report of Market Prices of Paddy and Upland Fields 1965 (Denbata Baibai Kakaku Chōsa Hōkoku).* Tokyo: 1967.

Nihon Nōgyō Nenkan Publishing Commission. *1958 Yearbook of Japanese Agriculture (Nihon Nōgyō Nenkan).*

Nojiri, S. *Empirical Study of Farm Exodus (Nomin Rison no Jisshō Kenkyu).* Tokyo: 1942.

Ohkawa, K. *Measurements of Living Standards (Seikatsu Suijun no Sokutei).* Tokyo: 1953.

——. *Economic Analysis of Agriculture (Nōgyō no Keizai Bunseki)*. Tokyo: 1955.

S.B.P.M.O. (Statistics Bureau, Prime Minister's Office). *Handbook of Labor Statistics (Rōdō Tōkei Yōran)*. 1934.

——. *Family Income and Expenditure (Kakei Chōsa Hōkoku)*, Part II 1929a and Part IV 1929b, 1950–1960.

Shishido, H., "Farmers' Purchase Price Index (Kōnyūhin Bukkashisu no Suikei)," *Japanese Economy and Agriculture (Nihon no Keizai to Nōgyō)*, Tobata and Ohkawa, eds., Tokyo: 1959.

Showa-Dōjinkai ed. *Historical Analysis of Wage Structure in Japan (Wagakuni Chingin Kōzō no Shiteki Kōsatsu)*. Tokyo: 1960.

Sjaastad, Larry A., "The Costs and Returns of Human Migration," *Journal of Political Economy*, XX, No. 5, Part 2 (October, 1962).

Umemura M. *Wages, Employment and Agriculture (Chingin, Koyō, Nōgyō)*. Tokyo: 1961.

CHAPTER 10

AN ANALYSIS OF PART-TIME FARMING IN THE POSTWAR PERIOD[†]

TAKEO MISAWA

I. Significance of Part-time Farming in Japanese Agriculture

In the years immediately following the war, Japanese agriculture underwent great changes brought about as the result of the Land Reform. The Land Reform was regarded as a success; owner-farmer households became the dominant institution and a large number of farmers were freed from the heavy burden of rent payment. But, soon afterwards, it became evident that a fundamental problem of agricultural structure still remained unsolved. While the Land Reform had far-reaching effects in establishing the owner-farmer, it did little to create conditions favorable for the emergence of larger size holdings. Table 1 shows that no remarkable change had occurred in the distribution of agricultural holdings by size from the late 1930s to 1965, although some change in the relative importance of different strata seems to have been emerging since 1950. The number of larger size farms has been increasing, while smaller size farms have been decreasing, the dividing line between these two classes being about 1.0–1.5 ha. But in spite of this trend, in 1965 the average size of farms remained in the neighborhood of one hectare and showed little tendency toward any drastic increase.

The small size of holdings has served to severely limit the development of Japanese agriculture, particularly since about 1950 and the beginning of the period of rapid postwar growth. The remarkable increase in the number of part-time farms[1] in this period is asso-

[†] This article was originally written as part of the joint study on Economic Growth and Agriculture and appeared in *Rural Economic Problems*, III, No. 1 (May 1966). The present revised version was prepared for the Symposium, Agriculture and Economic Development, Japan's Experience. The author is grateful for valuable comments given by Professor Ohkawa and other participants in the symposium.

TABLE 1

Number of Agricultural Holdings by Size Class*

(Unit: 1,000)

Year	Total[a]	Below 0.3ha	0.3– 0.5ha	0.5– 1.0ha	1.0– 1.5ha	1.5– 2.0ha	2.0– 2.5ha	2.5– 3.0ha	Above 3.0ha	Others
1938	5,160	1,777		1,579	1,438		287		79	—
1947	5,702	1,399	1,018	1,813	910	351	181		29	1
1950	5,931	1,429	1,032	1,952	945	363	176		27	7
1955	5,806	1,268	1,006	1,955	981	376	132	48	30	10
1960	5,823	1,266	991	1,907	1,001	404	147	54	36	17
1965	5,466	1,131	954	1,762	945	407	156	59	41	11

* Data from the Ministry of Agriculture and Forestry, *Agricultural Statistics*.
a) Hokkaido and Okinawa are excluded.

ciated with a relatively low agricultural income, due to smallholdings and the difficulties involved in enlarging the farm size.

Non-farm job opportunities for farm people have existed since the prewar period, but it was not until the beginning of the war economy in the late 1930's that the non-farm labor market came to affect the employment structure of the farm household significantly in the sense that it gave rise to the prevalence of part-time farming. During the war the rapid growth of demand for labor in the munition and heavy industries which accompanied the decentralization of factories gave ample opportunities for the farm household in many parts of the country to change to part-time farming. After the recovery of the Japanese economy in the postwar period, part-time farms began to increase again, this time being caused by the increase of off-farm job opportunities within commuting distance of the farm. This increase in off-farm job opportunities was undoubtedly the result of the rapid economic growth since the 1950's. Table 2 and Fig. 1 show the increasing tendency toward part-time farming in Japan during the period 1938–1965.

---

[1] In this connection, it is necessary to note that in Japan part-time farming is defined on a farm household basis and not on an operator basis. In the statistics of the Ministry of Agriculture and Forestry, a farm is regarded as a part-time farm if any family member belonging to the farm household earns an off-farm income. Accordingly, a farm is full-time only if neither the operator nor any of his family members in the farm household is engaged in any off-farm occupations. Throughout this article the terms "part-time farming" and "full-time farming" are used in accordance with the Ministry's definition.

TABLE 2

Total Number^a of Farms and Part-Time Farms of Various Types*

(Unit: 1,000)

Year	1938	1941	1943	1947	1950	1955	1960	1965
Total farms	5,336	5,412	5,502	5,909	6,132	6,043	6,057	5,665
(%)^a	(100)	(100)	(100)	(100)	(100)	(100)	(100)	(100)
All part-time farms (%)	2,935 (54.8)	3,167 (58.5)	3,607 (65.6)	2,635 (44.6)	3,361 (54.8)	3,937 (65.1)	3,978 (65.7)	4,447 (78.5)
Category I part-time farms (%)^b	1,641 (30.6)	2,019 (37.3)	2,237 (40.7)	1,684 (28.5)	1,950 (31.8)	2,274 (37.6)	2,036 (33.6)	2,082 (36.8)
Category II part-time farms (%)^b	1,294 (24.2)	1,148 (21.2)	1,370 (24.9)	951 (16.1)	1,411 (23.0)	1,663 (27.5)	1,942 (32.1)	2,365 (41.7)
Part-time farms earning off-farm wage incomes (%)^c	1,278 (23.9)	1,753 (32.4)	2,373 (43.1)	1,558 (26.4)		2,360 (39.1)	2,680 (44.2)	3,622 (63.9)
Part-time farms earning off-farm regular wage incomes (%)						1,552 (25.7)	1,831 (30.2)	2,099 (37.0)
Category II part-time farms earning off-farm regular wage incomes (%)						748 (12.4)	956 (15.8)	1,258 (22.2)

* Data from the Ministry of Agriculture and Forestry, *Agricultural Statistics*.
a) Number of all farms in the respective year=100.
b) When a part-time farm earns a larger net farm income than off-farm income, it is classified as Category I part-time farm; in the reverse case, as Category II.
c) Wage incomes include all kinds of wages and salaries.

It should be noted here that the old series of agricultural statistics have underestimated the importance of part-time farming. According to the old statistical series,[2] the proportion of part-time farms in all farms was 33.1 per cent in 1938, but the new series which employed an exact definition of part-time farm has estimated the proportion in the same year to be 54.8 per cent. The divergence between the two estimates is impressive as is evident in Fig. 1.

[2] In the old *Agricultural Statistics,* a part-time farm was not clearly defined.

FIGURE 1
Percentages of Part-Time Farms of Various Types*

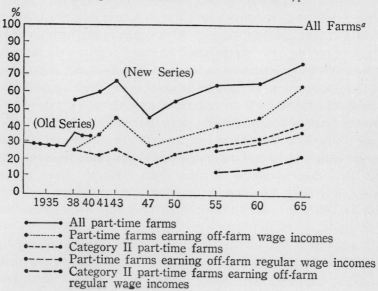

─────● All part-time farms
●·········● Part-time farms earning off-farm wage incomes
●─ ─ ─ ● Category II part-time farms
●─ ─ ─ ● Part-time farms earning off-farm regular wage incomes
●── ──● Category II part-time farms earning off-farm
          regular wage incomes

* Percentages are taken from Table 2.
a) Number of all farms=100.

Next, attention must be turned to the fact that the dominant type of off-farm occupation prevalent among farm people since the 1930s has been that of a wage- or salary-earner who resides on the farm and commutes by various means of transportation to his off-farm job. Farm households earning off-farm wage incomes have increased markedly, and part-time farms of this kind have been gaining ground even faster in the postwar period, except for the few years following the end of the war. It is also to be noted that in past years the Category II part-time farms, in which the total off-farm income exceeds the net farm income, have shown very large increases. The part-time farms with regular wage incomes from off-farm employment have also shown particularly large increases.

Although factors affecting such an increase in part-time farming may not be simple, the following can be said to be of great importance. First, the divergence in the income-forming potential between farming and off-farm occupations is important. The farmer's income from farming is apparently smaller than the non-farm regular laborer's income when compared to the average per qainfully employed person. As shown in Table 3, recent figures suggest that it has averaged only a little over 50 per cent of the income of non-farm laborers on a per capita basis. Second, for part-time farming to increase there must exist employment opportunities accessible to the farm population. In the prewar years, when the income disparity between the farmer and the urban laborer seemed great, part-time farming was not so conspicuous as in the postwar years, mainly because of the lack of off-farm job opportunities. However, the labor market surrounding the farm household has changed since the 1950's, and the industrialization of rural areas brought about by rapid economic growth has made a large number of farm people accessible to off-farm occupations which now fall within commuting distance.

In addition to the above, the change in the consumption pattern of the farm household has been of great importance to the increase of off-farm employment. Since World War II, most farm house-

TABLE 3

Comparison of Farmer's Income from
Farming and Regular Laborer's Income*

(Unit: 1,000 Yen)

Year	1962	1963	1964	1965
Farmer's income from farming[b]	263.7[a]	279.8	314.8	356.3
Regular laborer's income	479.5	492.4	555.6	604.0
Number of persons gainfully engaged:				
(1) in farming in the farm household[b]	2.00	1.95	1.91	1.84
(2) in non-farm jobs in the regular laborer's household	1.58	1.62	1.62	1.61
Income per person gainfully engaged:				
(1) in farming in the farm household	131.9	143.5	164.8	193.6
(2) in the non-farm regular laborer's household	303.5	303.9	342.9	375.2
Ratio (%) (1)/(2)	43.4	47.2	48.1	51.6

*   Farmer's income and gainfully engaged population data from the Ministry of Agriculture and Forestry, *Farm Household Economy Survey.*

Non-farm regular laborer's income data from Bureau of Statistics, Office of the Prime Minister, *Family Income and Expenditure Survey.*

a)   Income figures indicate averages per household.

b)   Hokkaido is excluded.

holds have been given incentives to change their pattern of consumption. Among the factors contributing to such a shift in consumption, most important are the increased contacts of farm people with urban ways of life. These contacts have been occasioned by the development of transportation facilities, the spread of means of mass communication, the move of factories and residences into rural areas and the increase of non-farm occupations and various other opportunities. Now that farm people have increasingly ample contacts with urban ways of life, they must be keenly aware of the consumption pattern of urban people and are strongly conscious of the disparity in the level of living between farm and non-farm households.

The change thus occasioned in the farm people's consciousness has brought about actual changes in the level and the pattern of consumption of the farm household. An analysis made by Ito and me indicates that there has been an increase in the average propensity to consume accompanied by a rise in the income level of the farm household in the postwar years as compared with the prewar period (Misawa and Ito, 1958). It may be assumed here that the "demonstration effect"[3] has affected the consumption of the farm household.

Such a change in consumption may possibly emerge irrespective of income improvement. But, in the process of consumption change, the divergence, if any, between income and consumption expenditure would induce the farm people to seek the means of correcting this disparity. The primary way for them to improve income would be sought naturally in farming. However, the effort of farmers in this direction is usually limited by the small size of holdings and the lack of opportunities for enlarging the scale of farming. Consequently, additional income must be, in most cases, sought outside farming. Thus, strong incentives towards part-time farming have resulted. Such a desire for farm people to raise their income level by means of off-farm occupations has been eventually met by the growth of a demand for labor having its origin in the industrialization of rural areas.

In this sense, it is to be noted that part-time farming has played a

---

[3] See Duesenberry, p. 27, and Nurkse, pp. 58–59.

dual role. First, it has operated as a motive force for changing the consumption pattern of farm households by introducing non-farm ways of life. Second, it has provided the means for farm people to earn additional income in order to overcome the discrepancy between income and consumption expenditure.

II. Per Capita Income and Consumption of the Farm and Non-farm Laborer's Households

It is evident from Table 4 that in recent years the average per capita income of family members of a farm household nearly approximates that of a non-farm regular laborer's household. In addition, there seems to exist a lag of about one year required for the farm household to reach the income level of the regular laborer's household. From these figures it may be assumed that, when com-

TABLE 4

Comparison of Per Capita Income of Farm Household and
Non-Farm Regular Laborer's Household*

(Unit: 1,000 Yen)

Year	1962	1963	1964	1965
Total income[a]				
Farm household[b]	523.7	581.8	669.7	760.7
Regular laborer's household	512.5	525.3	593.2	643.5
Number of family members				
Farm household	5.48	5.40	5.35	5.29
Regular laborer's household	4.20	4.20	4.16	4.13
Per capita income				
Farm household	95.6	107.7	125.2	143.8
Regular laborer's household	122.0	125.1	142.6	155.8
Relative level of per capita income of the farm household (%)				
in the same year	78.3	86.1	87.7	92.3
with 1 year's lag[c]		88.3	100.1	100.8
with 2 years' lag[c]			102.6	114.9

*   Non-farm regular laborer's household income data from Bureau of Statistics, Office of the Prime Minister, *Family Income and Expenditure Survey.*

Farm household income and the number of family members data from the Ministry of Agriculture and Forestry, *Farm Household Economy Survey.*

a) Income figures indicate averages per household.

b) Hokkaido is excluded.

c) Owing to the lack of continuous data, figures before 1962 are not adopted here.

pared on a per capita basis, the income of a farm household has a tendency to catch up with the income of a non-farm regular laborer's household, but after the passage of a small amount of time.

It is of interest to examine whether this feature varies in any way according to farm size differences. As can be seen in the 1964 data of Table 5, the equalizing tendency in per capita income seems to be prevalent in farms of all sizes although there are some differences in the magnitude of the time lag. The time lag is about one year, in the case of farms in Category II, which seem to be more attracted to off-farm occupations than to farming. It is also one year in the case of farms cultivating more than 1.5 ha. among those in Category I. However, it takes two years or more to close the income gap for the Category I farms with less than 1.5 ha. The length

TABLE 5

Relative Level of Per Capita Income of the Farm Household by Size of Holding, as Compared with That of the Non-Farm Regular Laborer's Household*

Year: 1964   (Unit: 1,000 Yen)

	Total income[a]	Number of family members	Per capita income[b]	Relative level of per capita income[b]		
				in the same year	with 1 year's lag	with 2 years' lag
				%	%	%
All farms	669.7	5.35	125.2	87.7	100.1	102.6
Category II farms[c]	612.9	4.73	129.6	90.9	103.6	106.2
Category I farms[c]	692.1	5.64	122.7	86.1	98.1	100.6
Category I farms						
0.1–0.5 ha	561.8	4.75	118.3	82.9	94.6	96.9
0.5–1.0 ha	616.7	5.28	116.8	81.9	93.4	95.7
1.0–1.5 ha	704.8	5.78	121.9	85.5	97.5	99.9
1.5–2.0 ha	789.8	6.24	126.6	88.8	101.2	103.7
Above 2.0 ha	963.3	6.78	142.1	99.6	113.6	116.4

* Total and per capita income data from the Ministry of Agriculture and Forestry, *Farm Household Economy Survey.*

a) Income figures indicate averages per household.

b) Per capita income of each farm class is compared with the per capita income of the average non-farm regular laborer's household as shown in Table 4.

c) Category I farms recently defined in the Farm Household Economic Survey include those farms which are regarded as agriculture-oriented and mostly cultivate more than 0.5 ha. Category II farms include those which occupy less than 0.5 ha., and are regarded as more interested in off-farm occupations than in farming.

of the time lag seems likely to depend, first, on the type of farm, particularly whether it is more agriculture-oriented or more interested in part-time farming and, second, on the size of the holding.

Now, turning our attention to the relative level of consumption expenditure, we will want to investigate the important aspect of the "demonstration effect." As shown in Table 6, the per capita consumption expenditure of a farm household has, in recent years, come to approximate that of the non-farm regular laborer's household. Such an approximating tendency in per capita consumption expenditure appears to be prevalent among farm households irrespective of the size of holding as shown in Table 7. It seems likely from Table 6 that per capita consumption expenditure of the farm household lags slightly behind the non-farm regular laborer's household. This time lag has recently shrunk to the point of disappearing altogether; apparently, the extent of the time lag is less for consumption than for income.

TABLE 6

Comparison of Per Capita Consumption Expenditure between Farm
Household and Non-Farm Regular Laborer's Household*

(Unit: 1,000 Yen)

Year	1962	1963	1964	1965
Total consumption expenditure[a]				
Farm household	457.6	514.1	582.2	652.5
Regular laborer's household	403.7	418.4	469.3	508.0
Per capita consumption expenditure[b]				
Farm household	83.5	95.2	108.8	123.3
Regular laborer's household	96.1	99.6	112.8	123.0
Relative level of per capita consumption of the farm household (%)				
in the same year	86.9	95.6	96.5	100.2
with 1 year's lag[c]		99.0	109.2	109.3
with 2 years' lag[c]			113.2	123.8

* Total and per capita consumption expenditure of farm household data from the Ministry of Agriculture and Forestry, *Farm Household Economy Survey*.

Total and per capita consumption expenditure of regular laborer's household data from the Bureau of Statistics, Office of the Prime Minister, *Family Income and Expenditure Survey*.

a) Consumption expenditure figures indicate averages per household.

b) For data regarding the number of family members per farm household refer to Table 4.

c) Due to the lack of continuous data, figures before 1962 are not adopted.

TABLE 7

Comparison of the Relative Level of Per Capita Consumption Expenditure
of Farm Household by Size of Holding and that of
Non-Farm Regular Laborer's Household*

	Total consumption expenditure 1,000 yen	Per capita[c] consumption expenditure 1,000 yen	Relative level of per capita consumption expenditure (%)[a]		
			in the same year	with 1 year's lag	with 2 years' lag
All farms[d]	582.2	108.8	96.5	109.2	113.2
Category II farms[b]	543.5	114.9	101.9	115.4	119.5
Category I farms[b]	598.7	106.2	94.1	106.6	110.4
Category I farms					
0.1–0.5 ha	522.1	109.9	97.4	110.3	114.4
0.5–1.0 ha	553.0	104.7	92.8	105.1	109.0
1.0–1.5 ha	605.1	104.7	92.8	105.2	108.9
1.5–2.0 ha	655.7	105.1	93.1	105.5	109.3
Above 2.0 ha	767.5	113.2	100.3	113.6	117.8

* Total and per capita consumption expenditure data from the Ministry of
Agriculture and Forestry, *Farm Household Economy Survey*.
a) The relative level is expressed respectively as a percentage of the per capita
consumption expenditure of the average non-farm regular laborer's household.
b) For the definition of Category I and Category II farms see footnote c of
Table 5.
c) For the number of family members within the above-mentioned farm categories, see Table 5.
d) Hokkaido is excluded.

From the data presented here it may be assumed that income and
consumption expenditure, both on a per capita basis, of farm households have risen in the past several years, lagging behind those of the
non-farm regular laborer's household by about one year. I offer this
comparison in order to emphasize the welfare aspect, in terms of per
capita income and consumption expenditure, in interpreting the
farm people's behavior with respect to income earning, and labor
allocation during the postwar period. The logic posed here is as
follows. First of all, the demonstration effect is postulated in explaining the relative level of per capita consumption expenditure of
the farm household which seems to follow that of the non-farm
regular laborer's household with a lag of about one year. Then, it
is assumed that income-earning opportunities are sought, largely
outside farming, by the farm people to make up for the deficiency

of income resulting from the shift in consumption. This, in effect, gives rise to the increased engagement of farm family members in off-farm occupations with higher income-forming potentials. Thus, part-time farming becomes prevalent.

TABLE 8

Comparison of Percentage Composition of Consumption Expenditure between Farm Household and Non-Farm Laborer's Household*

Year	1934–36 average		1964	
	Farm household	Non-farm laborer's household[c]	Farm household	Non-farm regular laborer's household
Per capita consumption expenditure (Yen)	115	219	108,822	112,817
Composition of consumption expenditure (%)[a]				
Total[b]	100.0	100.0	100.0	100.0
Food	44.5	37.7	36.3	39.5
Housing	6.7	16.0	16.1	11.4
Light and heat	5.0	4.8	4.5	4.4
Clothing	9.9	11.4	10.5	11.5
Others	33.9	30.1	32.6	33.2

* Farm household data for the prewar period from *Farm Household Economy Survey—The Reprinted Edition*, T. Inaba, ed., National Research Institute of Agricultrue (Tokyo: 1953).

The non-farm laborer's household data for the prewar period from *Family Income and Expenditure in the Postwar Japan*, Bureau of Statistics, Office of the Prime Minister (1956).

Farm household data for the postwar period from the Ministry of Agriculture and Forestry, *Farm Household Economy Survey*.

Non-farm laborer's household data for the postwar period from Bureau of Statistics, Office of the Prime Minister, *Family Income and Expenditure Survey*.

a) Indicates averages of all households.

b) There are differences in the method of sampling and in the specification of items between the prewar and postwar periods in the respective household groups. Therefore, the comparison may not be accurate.

c) In the case of non-farm laborer's household, no specification is made as to whether the occupation is regular or casual in the prewar surveys.

It is not an easy task to offer rigorous evidence to show how far the lives of farm people have been influenced by increased contact with urban ways of living. But as a rough measure, we have Table 8 in which the percentage composition of consumption expenditure of the average farm household is compared with that of the non-farm laborer's household for both the prewar and postwar periods. The percentage composition and the per capita level of consumption expenditure of the farm household seem to be more similar to those of the non-farm laborer's household in the postwar period than during the prewar years. The figures in the table suggest that the

TABLE 9
Relationship between Income, Consumption Expenditure, and the Extent of Off-Farm Occupations*   1964

	All farms[b]	Cate-gory II farms	Cate-gory I farms	Category I farms				
				0.1–0.5[ha]	0.5–1.0[ha]	1.0–1.5[ha]	1.5–2.0[ha]	Above 2.0[ha]
Income (Unit: 1,000 Yen)[a]								
Total	669.7	612.9	692.1	561.8	616.7	704.8	788.8	963.3
Farm	314.8	93.4	416.9	194.8	279.5	463.0	605.5	805.1
Off-farm	354.9	519.5	275.2	367.0	337.2	241.8	183.3	158.2
Consumption expenditure (Unit: 1,000 Yen)	582.2	543.5	598.7	522.1	553.0	605.1	655.7	767.5
Labor hours (Unit: hours)								
Total	5,174	4,284	5,583	4,667	5,232	5,860	6,113	6,271
Farm	2,869	1,145	3,662	2,387	2,899	4,119	4,751	5,176
Off-farm	2,305	3,139	1,921	2,280	2,333	1,741	1,362	1,095
Contribution of farm income to consumption expenditure (Unit: %)	54.1	17.2	69.6	37.3	50.5	76.5	92.3	104.9
Extent of off-farm occupation (Unit: %)								
in income	53.0	84.8	39.8	65.3	54.7	34.3	23.2	16.4
in labor	44.5	73.3	34.4	48.9	44.6	29.7	22.3	17.5

* Data from the Ministry of Agriculture and Forestry, *Farm Household Economy Survey*.
a) The figures represent averages per household.
b) Hokkaido is excluded.

consumption of the farm household has shifted in the postwar period due to the influence of urbanization. As a result of such changes in consumption, a wide divergence must have emerged between the farm household's consumption expenditure and the income from farming. Table 9 shows the extent of this divergence according to the size of farm and, further, how the divergence is remedied by means of part-time farming.

III. Preferences of the Farmer Affecting Farm Household Labor Allocation

For the analysis of labor allocation of a farm household, the farmer's preferences affecting this behavior must be taken into account. In this connection, three types of preference seem to be important.

A farm household possibly endeavors to raise its income level by opting for off-farm labor with its higher income-forming potential, provided the total amount of available family labor is unchanged. This may be termed the "substitution preference" in labor allocation. When we observe actual state of postwar Japanese agriculture, we cannot deny the existence of this type of preference among farmers.

Next, we perceive in the behavior of the farm-laborer a type of preference which aims at reducing the total amount of labor input, provided the income level is maintained. This preference for a withdrawal of labor becomes predominant when the farm household regards the achieved per capita income level as acceptable. I postulate that the standard of the acceptable income level which the farmer usually bears in mind is the per capita income of the non-farm regular laborer's household. This type of preference may be termed the "leisure preference." For the moment we lack any really precise measure for the leisure preference, but perhaps the per capita income and the participation rate (the proportion of the gainfully engaged to the total number of family members in the household) by category and by size class of farms of Table 10 may give us a rough idea of the withdrawal of labor with some relation to the per capita income level achieved.

The figures in the table seem to show an interesting point. Actu-

Table 10

Per Capita Income and Participation Rate* [b,c]   1964

	Non-farm regular laborer's household	All farms	Category II farms	Category I farms	Category I farms				
					0.1–0.5ha	0.5–1.0ha	1.0–1.5ha	1.5–2.0ha	Above 2.0ha
Number of family members[d]	4.16	5.35	4.73	5.64	4.75	5.28	5.78	6.24	6.78
Number of persons gainfully engaged	1.62	2.69	2.26	2.90	2.35	2.71	2.99	3.17	3.38
Participation rate (%)[a]	38.9	50.3	47.8	51.4	49.5	51.3	51.7	50.8	49.9
Per capita income (¥1000)	142.6	125.2	129.6	122.7	118.3	116.8	121.9	126.6	142.1
Relative level of per capita income (%)[d]	100.0	87.7	90.9	86.1	82.9	81.9	85.5	88.8	99.6

* Per capita income data from the Ministry of Agriculture and Forestry, *Farm Household Economy Survey* and Bureau of Statistics, Office of the Prime Minister, *Family Income and Expenditure Survey*.

a) The participation rate is the percentage of the gainfully engaged to the total number of family members in the household.

b) All figures indicate averages per household.

c) Hokkaido is excluded.

d) Refer to Table 5 for data regarding number of family members, per capita income, and the relative level of per capita income.

ally, as the data show, the participation rate of the farm household starts to decline when its per capita income reaches a level which is a little lower than the per capita income of the non-farm regular laborer's household. This suggests that the per capita income is accepted by the farm household, even though it is still lower than the income level of the laborer's household. This may be related to the fact that the participation rate is much higher in the farm household than in the non-farm regular laborer's household. But the point to be noted here is that the preference which gives rise to the withdrawal of labor becomes prominent when the farm household regards its per capita income to have reached a particular level, namely the income level acceptable to the farm household in comparison with that achieved by the non-farm regular laborer's household.

These two kinds of farmer's preference are the most important, but are not the only types of preference. Among the other subsidiary preferences, the one relating to holding agricultural land should not be neglected. The propensity to hold agricultural land as an asset seems to be conspicuous among our farm households because the land held is regarded as a means of stable employment, especially in depressed years, of security for the aged and the disabled, and of preserving asset value, especially when inflation is expected. With regard to such a propensity, we may assume that a part of family labor is retained in farming. If means that the holding of a particular acreage of agricultural land is in itself a factor affecting the labor allocation. This we may term the "asset preference." Although substitution and leisure preferences are major factors which affect the labor allocation of the farm household, the asset preference should be taken into account when interpreting recent development in part-time farming in Japan. These preferences will be considered when the subjective equilibrium positions are discussed below.

IV. An Approach to the Subjective Equilibrium Positions in Farm Household Labor Allocation

A diagrammatic approach is adopted here to ascertain the subjective equilibrium positions with respect to the labor allocation of a farm household between farm and off-farm occupations. For this, the following assumptions are made. First, it is assumed that a farm household seeks to attain a particular level of per capita income when determining the amount of labor input and its allocation between farm and off-farm occupations. It is also assumed that the per capita income and the participation rate of the non-farm regular laborer's household are most influential in determining the behavior of the farm household. We take it for granted that the size and the composition of the family are unchanged and the non-farm wage rates are given and constant during the time under consideration. Further, it is assumed that in farming there exist diminishing returns with respect to an increase in labor input and the income-forming potential of labor is generally higher in off-farm occupations than in farming.

Let us consider the labor allocation of a farm household in terms of Fig. 2. Take the amount of labor input in farming on the ordinate and that in off-farm occupations on the abscissa; then draw on the OXY-plane a number of iso-income curves each of which represents a specific level of per capita income of the farm household. Each of these income levels is realized by various combinations of labor input in farming and in off-farm occupations. These are indifference curves W_0, W_1, etc. We meet higher iso-income curves as we move on to the right, and according to the assumptions above, the curves must all be convex to the origin and steeper than 45° to the abscissa as seen in Fig. 2.

FIGURE 2
Subjective Equilibrium Positions

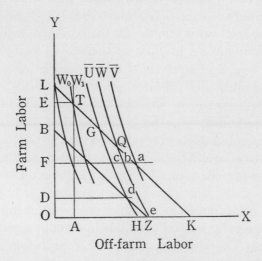

The available supply of family labor from the farm household is determined by the labor force of the family on the one hand and the participation rate on the other. It is assumed here to be OL or OK at the initial point in time under consideration. As OL is equal to OK, the straight line LK has a slope of 45° to both axes. Under these conditions, it is possible for the farm household to increase its per capita income by transferring a part of the family labor from farming to off-farm occupations. If the total amount of available supply of family labor were employed in farming, the per capita income represented by W_0 would be attained. However, suppose that a part of the available labor, for example, LE, is withdrawn from farming and transferred to off-farm occupations. That is to say, suppose that OA, which is equal to LE, is allocated to off-farm occupations and OE to farming, then a higher per capita income level represented by W_1 can be achieved as is evident in Fig. 2. In this way, the farm household can raise its per capita income level by increasing the extent of off-farm employment. We turn next to explain diagrammatically the pattern of behavior of a farm household with respect to labor allocation, taking into account the farmer's preferences. In so doing we would like to ascertain the subjective equilibrium points in the diagram.

To determine these equilibrium points, I postulate that the objective of employment of a farm household is to achieve the per capita income level being attained by the non-farm regular laborer's household. This income level is represented by one of iso-income curves $\overline{W}$ in Fig. 2. Therefore, if this objective were strictly pursued, the substitution of off-farm labor for farm labor would continue until point Q on the straight line LK, where the per capita income $\overline{W}$ is attained. After point Q is reached, it is probable that the farm household proceeds further on its growth path, seeking some subjective equilibrium position. Typically, there are two courses of the growth path after Q. One is the path on the straight line LK towards K. This path is taken when the farm household is interested in achieving an even higher per capita income level than the non-farm regular laborer's household without regard to the participation rate. This is the case in which substitution preference is dominant over leisure preference. The other is the path on the curve $\overline{W}$ towards Z. This path is traced when the farm household wishes to withdraw labor aiming at the reduction of the participation rate, keeping the per capita income level at $\overline{W}$. This is the case in which leisure preference is dominant over substitution preference.

Whichever path is taken, the asset preference comes to affect the labor allocation behavior of the farm household. I place particular emphasis on the asset preference because in postwar Japanese agriculture it seems likely to play an important role in determining subjective equilibrium positions of the farm household with respect to labor allocation. It seems to set limits on the substitution and withdrawal of labor. If OF in Fig. 2 is the amount of labor necessary to operate the farm at its normal intensity, the substitution and the withdrawal of labor must be affected significantly in retaining the amount of labor OF in farming. Thus, the subjective equilibrium position is possibly reached by the farm household at point a in the former case, and at point b in the latter. When the subjective equilibrium point a is chosen, the per capita income level $\bar{V}$ is realized.

Very often the per capita income level $\bar{U}$, which is lower than $\bar{W}$, is accepted by the farm household. This happens when the withdrawal of labor is urgently desired by the farm household, and therefore, leisure preference becomes predominant. In this case the path traced by the farm household is at first on the straight line LK to point G, where the per capita income level $\bar{U}$ is achieved. Then, after the per capita income level $\bar{U}$ is accepted by the farm household, it changes its direction and proceeds on the curve $\bar{U}$ towards H. Point c would be chosen by the farm household as the point of subjective equilibrium when farming of normal intensity is practiced. Point d, the intersection of the curve $\bar{U}$ with the straight line BZ which corresponds to the participation rate similar to that of the non-farm regular laborer's household, may also be a limiting case of the subjective equilibrium of the part-time farm. In this case the per capita income level $\bar{U}$ is accepted, and the participation rate is reduced until it reaches that level which is being realized by the non-farm regular laborer's household, but here farming is neglected. This happens when leisure preference is given first priority.

Point e, which is the same as point Z referred to above, represents the limiting case of the subjective equilibrium position of the farm household. The per capita income and the participation rate are both similar to those of non-farm regular laborer's household, and farming is completely deserted.[4]

As discussed here, the point of subjective equilibrium of the farm household is not uniquely defined. It seems to be determined by the relative importance of income, leisure, and farming to a particular farm household. The characteristic features of the typical cases discussed above are summarized in Table 11.

TABLE 11
Characteristic Features of Typical Cases
of Subjective Equilibrium Points

Subjective equilibrium point	Per capita income	Leisure	Farming
a	the first priority	neglected	normal intensity
b	equal to the non-farm	moderately desired	normal intensity
c	lower than the non-farm, but accepted	dominantly desired	normal intensity
d	lower than the non-farm, but accepted	the first priority	neglected
e	equal to the non-farm	equal to the non-farm	deserted

Thus, Japanese agriculture in the postwar period has been affected by the Land Reform, advances in technology, the increase in employment opportunities in the non-agricultural sectors and the increased contact with urban ways of life, all taking place under rapid economic growth. The agricultural community may no longer be deemed poor, at least in that the farm household is nearly realizing, even if with some time lag, the per capita income and also the per capita consumption expenditure being attained by the non-farm regular laborer's household (Tables 4–7). But, the efficiency of agriculture in terms of labor allocation is to be questioned. Though the farm household is realizing an economic position nearly comparable with that of the non-farm regular laborer's household, it is made possible mostly through part-time farming. There is still a wide divergence in the income-forming potential of farm and non-

---

[4] That the participation rate of the farm household becomes similar to that of the non-farm regular laborer's household at the point Z may be demonstrated as follows: Suppose that the off-farm wage rate of the farmer is the same as the wage rate of the non-farm laborer. Then take h, n, and y to be the number of family members, number of persons gainfully engaged, and the total income of the household, respectively. Finally, let 1 and 2 represent the farm and the non-farm, respectively. Then at point Z, $y_1/n_1 = y_2/n_2$, $y_1/h_1 = y_2/h_2$, therefore $n_1/h_1 = n_2/h_2$.

farm occupations as shown in Table 3. This in turn implies that an efficient labor allocation between sectors is beyond the capability of agriculture. In this sense, Japanese agriculture in the postwar period is a case to which Schultz's "efficient-but-poor" hypothesis[5] does not apply.

REFERENCES

Duesenberry, James S. *Income, Saving and the Theory of Consumer Behavior.* Cambridge: Harvard University Press, 1949.

Misawa, T., "An Analysis of the Allocation of Labor in Part-time Farming," *Rural Economic Problems,* III, No. 1 (May 1966).

Misawa, T. and Ito, Y., "Capital Formation and Capital Use in Japanese Agriculture, with Special Reference to the Effect of the Land Reform," *International Journal of Agrarian Affairs,* II, No. 4 (January, 1958).

Nurkse, Ragnar. *Problems of Capital Formation in Underdeveloped Countries.* Oxford: 1955.

Schultz, Theodore W. *Transforming Traditional Agriculture.* New Haven: Yale University Press, 1964.

---

[5] See Schultz, pp. 36–41.

CHAPTER 11

THE SUPPLY OF FARM LABOR AND THE "TURNING POINT" IN THE JAPANESE ECONOMY[†]

RYŌSHIN MINAMI

Introduction

This paper attempts to discover at what point in her long process of economic development Japan ceased to have available "unlimited supplies of labor." This point has been labeled in some economic development models the turning point.[1] Its timing is a controversial issue. W. A. Lewis, who originally set forth the concept and theory of the turning point, suggested that Japan would reach it sometime in the 1950's (Lewis, p. 29). J. C. H. Fei and G. Ranis, developing a more refined version of Lewis' theory, applied it to the Japanese economy and concluded that the turning point had already been reached by the end of World War I (Fei and Ranis, 1964b, p. 263). These findings were criticized by D. W. Jorgenson, who claimed that unlimited supplies of labor defined in the Lewis sense were not found even in the pre-World War I period (Jorgenson, pp. 59–60). On the other hand, among Japanese economists, Oh-

[†] This is a shorter version of the paper which was prepared when I was at the Economic Growth Center, Yale University (Center Discussion Paper No. 20 [1967]). Revision was made at the Institute of Social, Economic and Government Research, University of Alaska. I am indebted to some colleagues in these universities and in Hitotsubashi University. Thanks in the first place are due to Professor K. Ohkawa. The paper appeared, with slight revisions, in *The Quarterly Journal of Economics*, LXXXII, No. 3 (August, 1968). This work stems from earlier collaborations with Ohkawa, and some discussions appearing in this article are based on notes prepared jointly by Ohkawa and me. The analyses and conclusions contained here, however, are solely my responsibility. Also I am very much indebted to the comments by Professors A. Berry, D. L. Huddle, H. Kaneda, Hugh T. Patrick, and Mataji Umemura. And grateful acknowledgement is due to Mr. G. Saxonhouse and Professor A. R. Tussing for discussions and editing the English in this article.

[1] This is called "commercialization point" by J.C.H. Fei and G. Ranis (Fei and Ranis, 1964b, p. 202).

kawa in particular (Ohkawa, 1965a, p. 484), the view seems to be dominant that the turning point has occurred only since the end of World War II. That no systematic attempt has been made to date the Japanese turning point conclusively has tempted this author to propose the present paper. In Section I, some of the features of the economic transition in the vicinity of the turning point, derived from an idealized theory of the turning point, will be contrasted with available empirical evidence for Japan. This evidence has led the author to the conclusion that the turning point was passed sometime after the Pacific War. In Section II, the statistical evidence of Fei and Ranis and of Jorgenson, which supports their different conclusions, will be examined critically.

I. Statistical Findings

In Japan, the subsistence sector comprises almost the entire agricultural sector, as well as most small scale enterprises in non-agricultural industries. Unfortunately, however, statistics on the latter are quite poor. For this reason, we shall consider agriculture (or primary industry) as a proxy for the subsistence sector in the following discussion.

Changes in the Marginal Productivity of Labor in the Subsistence Sector

A necessary condition for the existence of an unlimited supply of labor is that in the subsistence sector the marginal productivity of labor is smaller than the subsistence wage rate.[2,3] A sustained increase in the former, therefore, will indicate that the turning point

[2] The subsistence level may be defined as the minimum price of labor supply, in the sense that laborers will not work if their wages are less than this level. Lewis' notion of the subsistence level is not identical with the concept used by the classical economists: Population increase is possible in the former case, and it is impossible in the latter case, if actual wages are equal to the subsistence level. In this sense, a Lewis-type theory of economic development is closer to Marxian theories than to classical economics. (Lewisian theory as well as Marxian theory deny the population principle. This principle is one of the most fundamental assumptions of the classical school.)

[3] It should be noted that the assumption of zero marginal productivity of labor is completely unnecessary. The marginal productivity can be positive, zero or negative. In this sense the concept of unlimited supplies of labor is quite different from the concept of disguised unemployment as established by Nurkse.

has been reached. It seems reasonable, then, to expect a discontinuity of a kind in the level of marginal productivity in the vicinity of the turning point.[4]

The marginal productivity of agricultural labor, as shown in Table I, seems to stagnate in the prewar period and to exhibit a high rate of increase in the postwar period.[5] The annual compound rates of growth, which are calculated by fitting a function log (productivity)$=a+b$ (year) to annual time series data, are 1.5 per cent[6] and 8.2 per cent[7] respectively for the periods 1874–1940 and 1950–1963. The big increase in the postwar period is a consequence in part of the unprecedented decrease in the number of agricultural laborers. Another important factor has been the upward shift in the marginal

---

[4] That the path of real marginal productivity will have this pattern, however, is not a strict implication of the theory of the turning point.

[5] Labor productivity should be measured in terms of labor hours or labor days. As we have no reliable statistics for working days covering both pre- and postwar periods, we must use man-years in our denominator.

[6] Strictly speaking, there is a kink around 1916: The annual compound rates of growth are 1.9 per cent and .75 per cent for the years before and after 1916. On the other hand, the annual growth rate of the capital labor ratio (fertilizer input per capita) is calculated as .62 per cent and .76 per cent (1.6 per cent and 2.0 per cent) respectively for the years before and after 1913–1917. Growth rates in the input ratios are somewhat higher in the years after 1913–1917. This means that the kink around 1916 cannot be explained by changes in the input ratios. Either of the following two factors might explain it. First, our series of agricultural output might be biased downward in the early years. This series was constructed relying mostly on the official statistics for agricultural output. According to Nakamura, these statistics show a strong downward bias in the early years (Nakamura, Ch. 2–4). Nakamura has made new estimates of real agricultural output, depending on three alternative assumptions on paddy rice yields. These assumptions, however, are quite arbitrary. Hence, I do not feel I can use the results of his estimation in the present analysis. Underestimation in my series, however, which is a revision of the old Hitotsubashi estimates criticized by Nakamura, may not be serious. Second, and more important, food imports from Taiwan and Korea expanded in the 1920's. These food imports, which satisfied most of the increase in demand for agricultural products after 1920, were supposed to have had an unfavorable impact on Japanese agriculture (The relation between retardation in agricultural productivity and food imports is of course, not quite so simple: the former is a cause as well as a consequence of the latter). This factor has been stressed by Ohkawa and Rosovsky (Ohkawa and Rosovsky, 1960, Sec. VI), and Johnston (Johnston, pp. 242–43).

[7] The annual compound rate of growth in average productivity of labor is 4.5 per cent for 1950–1963.

productivity curve, caused by the relative increase in non-labor inputs in agricultural production and/or the shifts in the production function resulting from technological progress. Measures of capital intensity and fertilizer input per capita in the same table show remarkable increases for the postwar years; their annual compound rates of growth are 4.9 per cent and 10.3 per cent respectively for 1948–1952 and 1958–1962. Comparable prewar growth rates are 1/8 to 1/6 as large. In the area of technological progress as well, a spurt may be found again in the postwar period (Ueno and Kinoshita, p. 44). In summary, the upturn in capital intensity, fertilizer input per capita and technological progress in the postwar years may well explain the spurt in labor productivity. The large increase in marginal productivity in the postwar period, especially after 1953, suggests that the turning point can be found during this period.

Changes in the Wage Rate in the Subsistence Sector

Under the condition of unlimited supplies of labor, the subsistence level determines the real wage rate in the subsistence sector. It is important to note, however, that in cases where the standard of living increases in accordance with changes in the institutional framework, the subsistence level may rise.[8] This makes it very difficult to identify the boundaries of the stage of unlimited supplies of labor in statistical series. That is, when there is a rising trend in the real wage rate, we cannot ascertain whether that increase comes from a change in the marginal productivity of labor or from an increase in the subsistence level itself. Rather than ignore wage data entirely, however, we shall assume in examining what evidence we have at our disposal, that while small increases in the real wage rate over time may be the result of changes in the level of subsistence, per-

---

[8] An increasing subsistence level was admitted even by classical economists: Ricardo claimed that the natural price of labor was dependent on "the quantity of food, necessaries and conveniences essential to him from habit" (Ricardo, p. 93). The quantity of necessities and conveniences increases in the course of cultural development (Concerning this, I am obliged to Professor Ryozaburo Minami). As long as we assume that the subsistence level increases independently of the increases in productivity in the subsistence sector, the concept of unlimited supplies of labor stands unaltered (Ohkawa and Minami, 1964, Sec. I and II).

sistent large changes quite likely mean that the stage of unlimited supplies has already ended.

TABLE 1

Marginal Productivity of Labor, Capital-Labor Ratio and Fertilizer Input Per Capita in Agriculture, 1934–1936 Prices (Yen)*

Year	(1) Marginal productivity	(2) Capital-labor ratio	(3) Fertilizer input per capita
1874	18	(Five-year averages)	
1880	21	315	17.9
1885	23	321	18.5
1890	27	328	18.8
1895	29	339	20.3
1900	30	346	21.9
1905	28	358	23.4
1910	34	378	28.4
1915	40	392	31.9
1920	43	402	35.8
1925	43	411	40.4
1930	46	430	45.0
1935	43	444	48.9
1940	47	451	52.8
1950	58	382	45.0
1955	93	455	82.1
1960	127	621	126.3
1963	162		

* Gross Value Added and Agricultural Price Index: Yamada's estimates (linked index) (Umemura et al., pp. 164, 182).
Labor Force: My estimates (Minami, 1966a, p. 278).
Output Elasticity of Labor, Prewar Period: A constant figure (.240), the estimate made by Ohkawa, is assumed for the entire period (Ohkawa, 1945).[9] This is the weighted average of output elasticities in rice production (.234) and in barley, naked barley and wheat production (.299). Weights used are their values of production. The former elasticity is the average of the figures for 1937–1939, and the latter, for 1940–1941. Cross-sectional data were used by Ohkawa to fit the Cobb-Douglas production function from which the elasticity estimates were taken. Output Elasticity of Labor, Postwar Period: Yuize estimated the output elasticities of labor by fitting cross-sectional data to Cobb-Douglas functions (Yuize, pp. 17–23).

	1952	1958	1960	1962
A	.4118[10]	.5110	.5396	.6018
B	.5618	.6972	.6977	.6478

Figures in line A are the estimates when the size of labor force is used as labor input.

Figures in line B are the estimates when labor hours are used. In this paper estimates A are adopted, because my concept of average productivity is defined in terms of the size of the labor force. For the years 1953–1957, 1959 and 1961, output elasticities are estimated by the method of linear interpolation. For the years 1950–1951 and 1963, they are obtained by extrapolation.

Gross Capital Stock: Umemura and Yamada's estimates (Ohkawa et al., pp. 154–55).

Fertilizer Input: Hayami's estimates (Umemura et al., pp. 186–87).

(1) Average productivity multiplied by the output elasticity of labor in agriculture. Average productivity is the value added gross of depreciation in agriculture, deflated by agricultural price index (1934–1936=1), and divided by the size of agricultural labor force.
(2) Gross capital divided by the size of labor force.
(3) Fertilizer input divided by the size of labor force.

The data which we use are Takamatsu's estimates of daily wages for day laborers in agriculture. These figures were compiled from the Agricultural and Commercial Statistics *(Nōshōmu Tōkei)* and the Statistics of Agricultural Employment *(Nōsaku Yatoi Chingin Hyō)* for the prewar period, and the Survey on Prices and Wages in Agriculture and Forestry *(Nōson Bukka Chingin Chōsa)* for the postwar period. Some problems exist concerning the reliability of the statistics. For the postwar years there is a good relationship between these data and the data calculated from other official statistics.[11] No such supplementary data are available for the prewar period.[12] Hence, we must assume a modicum of reliability for our data and use

---

[9] The assumption of constant output elasticity is simply the result of my having only one cross-section estimate of the production function for prewar agriculture. As there was little change in the organization of agricultural production for the prewar years (Ohkawa and Rosovsky, 1965, p. 67), my assumption may, in part, be justified.

[10] The original estimate by Yuize for this year is .6906 (Yuize, p. 17). In comparing this estimate with the A estimates for other years and the B estimates it seems that this estimate is not reasonable. Therefore, as a substitute for this, the figure .4118, being estimated by linking it with the figures in line B; that is,

$$.5110 \times \frac{.5618}{.6972} = .4118$$

is used in this paper.

[11] The ratios of the wages per day for male daily agricultural workers to the wages per day for temporary agricultural workers (both sexes), which are calculated in Appendix A, are quite stable for the entire period; 2.0, 1.9, 2.1, 2.1, 2.0, 2.2, 2.1, 2.2, 2.0, 2.1, 2.1 and 1.9 for the years from 1952 to 1963.

[12] It is not impossible to estimate labor income in agriculture as a residual from total agricultural income and to check my wage data with it. As is stated in Section II, the estimation for labor income is confounded with many problems.

them anyway. Another problem is the appropriateness of these data for the problem at hand. In Japan the majority of the agricultural workers are unpaid family workers. Wage workers, with whom these data are concerned, are only a small proportion of this labor force. We feel we can use these data, however, by assuming that the implicit wages of unpaid family workers are equal to or a constant proportion of the wages of daily workers. In Figure 1, the annual quotations for the wage rates of male workers are adjusted by two deflators, the consumer price index and the agricultural price index.[13]

FIGURE 1
Real Wage Rate in Agriculture; 1934-36 Prices*

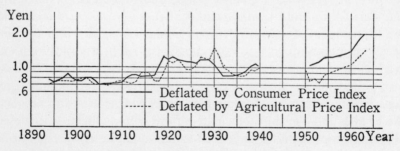

* Wage Rate: Takamatsu's estimates (*LTES*, VIII, p. 245).
Consumer Price Index: Noda's estimates (*LTES*, VIII, p. 134).
Agricultural Price Index: See Table 1.
a) For daily workers in agriculture—male only—per day.

Let us examine first the changes and the trend in wage rates deflated by the consumer price index (For a test of the subsistence wage theory, the consumer price index is a more appropriate deflator of the wage rate than the agricultural price index[14]). As far as the prewar years are concerned, the most striking change is a large swing in the years 1917–1931. A spurt in 1917–1918 was caused by an increase in demand for labor resulting from an accelerated increase in economic activity. From 1919 to 1931, on the other hand, Japan

---

[13] I use data for male workers only because (1) wage rates by sex are highly correlated with one another and (2) in my opinion the data are much better for male wages.

[14] Hansen, who analyzed Egyptian agriculture, used the cost-of-living index and the agricultural price index in the tests of the subsistence wage theory and of the marginal productivity theory respectively (Hansen, pp. 369–70).

experienced the longest period of general price decline in her modern economic experience. Nonetheless, because of downward rigidity in nominal wages,[15] combined with declining prices, the decrease in the real wage rate was not sharp until 1930. Thereafter there was a large decrease. (As a result of this large decline, the level of the real wage rate in 1932 was almost the same as that of 1916.) If we exclude the years of price decline (1919–1932) as an exceptional period in Japanese economic development, we find a rather constant trend in the real wage rate in the prewar years (1894–1939); the average annual compound rate of growth was .74 per cent.

On the other hand, for the postwar years, the reader will see at a glance a steady and substantial increase in the real wage rate. The annual compound rate of growth for the years from 1951 to 1963 is 5.0 per cent. This is about 6 times the growth rate of the prewar period. More importantly from the point of view of comparing the two periods, the real wage rate in postwar years shows a tendency to increase even in the recession years following 1961. This is not the case in the prewar years, when the real wage rate declined during such periods of price decline. The same observations may be made in the case of the wage rate series which has been deflated by the agricultural price index. Again the increase is small for the prewar period and very high for the postwar period, especially after 1953.[16] Following our criteria outlined earlier, the large increase in the real wage rate in agriculture since the end of World War II suggests that the turning point was passed only in the postwar years. In concluding this section, one problem remains to be answered. It concerns the large upward swing in the real wage rate during the period 1917–1919. Does this spurt mean that the turning point was reached during these years? It seems doubtful. In the extraordinary two or three year boom during and after World War I, it is quite correct to

---

[15] It seems to be difficult to acknowledge the downward rigidity in nominal wages in the labor surplus economy. In my opinion, however, the rigidity is not inconsistent with the hypothesis of unlimited supplies of labor.

[16] The annual compound rates of growth in the wage rate in agriculture deflated by agricultural price index are 54 per cent and 4.1 per cent respectively for 1894–1940 excluding 1919–1932, and for 1951–1963; (for 1953–1963, 5.7 per cent).

say that the labor supply became substantially less than infinitely elastic. But a situation approximating the phase of unlimited supplies returned with the subsequent downward phase of economic growth. Note here that the turning point should not be a swing phenomenon, but the inception of a long-term historical trend in the process of economic development. Hence, we do not believe that we can consider the turning point as having been passed in the 1917–1919 period. On the other hand, we do believe that the recent sharp increase in wages does constitute evidence that the turning point was passed in the postwar period; the sharp increase even in the recession years suggests that it is undoubtedly a trend phenomenon.[17]

Relationship Between the Wage Rate and Marginal Productivity in the Subsistence Sector

In the stage prior to the turning point, the real wage rate W is determined independently of the real marginal productivity of labor MP in the subsistence sector. Therefore, in estimating the linear equation $W = a + b\,MP$, coefficient b is expected to be zero. On the other hand, in the succeeding stage (stage of limited supplies of labor), where W is equal to MP, the expression above should show a good fit. Constant a should be zero; coefficient b should be unity. These are strict tests of the subsistence wage theory and the marginal productivity theory. However, these tests might be too rigid for our

---

[17] Here it may be of use to refer to the changes in wage differentials between agriculture and manufacturing. For the prewar period, as has been fully discussed by Taira, the ratio of manufacturing to agricultural wages increased and decreased respectively in the downward (1919–1931) and the upward swings (since 1932) of economic fluctuations (Taira, Sec. II). For the postwar period, however, it has continued to decrease even in the recession years since 1961, after a rather constant trend for 1951–1960. This is a new experience for Japan. (This point was called to my attention by Ohkawa.) In connection with this, the changes in the wage differential among enterprises by scale are also suggestive. In the ratio of total cash wage earnings for factories with 5–29 workers to the wage bill of factories with 500 or more workers: 43.6, 44.3, 46.3, 49.3, 57.0 and 58.1 for the years from 1958 to 1963, one can see a steady increasing trend for the entire period including recession years. Data is from the *Monthly Labor Statistics (Maigetsu Kinrō Tōkei)* (The Ministry of Labor, p. 328). The continuous decrease in the wage differentials between two sectors 1964, as well as among enterprises by scale may suggest that surplus labor in the subsistence sector has been disappearing (Ohkawa, 1965, p. 484).

purposes. In the first place, W and MP increase, as stated above, even in the stage of unlimited supplies of labor. Hence, in our time series data we might expect some correlation between them. Secondly, in the stage of limited supplies of labor, wage increases may lag somewhat behind productivity increases. Hence, even if they are not equal to each other ($a \neq 0$ and $b \neq 1$), marginal principle can hardly be rejected when there is a good correlation between them. Thirdly, there are problems of data. One problem involves the difficulty of estimating MP. MP is usually estimated as a product of the real average productivity and the output elasticity of labor. The former is rather easily obtained, but it is difficult to estimate the output elasticity. (In this article we could not help but assume a constant output elasticity over time for the prewar period.) One other difficulty involves the measurement of W and MP in comparable flow units. This problem arises because of the lack of reliable data on working days, working hours and so forth. Taking into consideration all these problems, it seems that to use a criterion which purported to make a very fine discrimination would be misleading. Hence, if we should find below that the correlation coefficient is much higher in a later period than in an earlier period, we will call the former period a stage of limited supplies of labor and the latter period a stage of unlimited supplies of labor.

Let us examine the relationship between the real wage rate and the marginal productivity of labor in agriculture. (The data are those which we used in Table 1 and Fig. 1.) For this test the wage rate deflated by the agricultural price index is a better index than the wage rate deflated by the consumer price index.[18] A coefficient of determination adjusted by degree of freedom, r^2, is calculated as .32 for 1894–1940. Excluding the years of price declines, 1919–1931, it becomes .56. And for 1951–1963[19] it is .94. This figure is extremely high compared with the estimate for the prewar years. This difference in the degree of correlation may suggest that the turning point was passed in the postwar years.[20]

[18] See Footnote 14.

[19] The year 1950 was omitted in this estimation, because the point of this year is far away from the regression line for the succeeding years.

[20] This test, however, is not free from two problems. The first is the possible influences of trends in the variables (This is incidental to any time-series analysis.) The second is the autonomous increase in the subsistence level. (Recall

Elasticity of Labor Supply to the Capitalist Sector

Before the turning point, the supply function of subsistence sector labor force facing the capitalist sector is given by the subsistence level. After the turning point, it is determined by the marginal productivity of labor in the subsistence sector. That is, the elasticity of labor supply with respect to the wage rate is infinite, and between zero and infinity, before and after the turning point, respectively. Noting the size of the labor force in the capitalist sector originally supplied from the subsistence sector by L and the wage rate in this sector by W, the elasticity η is defined as $\eta \equiv \dfrac{\dfrac{dL}{L}}{\dfrac{dW}{W}}$. Average elasticity can be obtained by estimating the parameters of the expression $\log L = a + \eta \log W$.[21] Examining the changes in such estimates of η might enable one to locate the turning point. Here again, however, there is a problem; as mentioned above, a part of the increase in W is caused by the increase of the subsistence level. Therefore the safest approach again may be to look for a large decline in η. Quite likely a large decline means that the economy is passing the turning point.

Here we substitute primary and non-primary industries respectively for the subsistence and capitalist sectors. That is, L is the non-primary labor force originally supplied from primary industry, and W is the wage rate in agriculture deflated by consumer price index. In Fig. 2 $\log L$ is regressed on $\log W$. The slope of this regression,

---

that the wage rate can rise with the increase in the subsistence level.) The first difficulty may be evaded by fitting the equation formulated on the basis of the first differences, as was attempted by Hansen (Hansen, p. 369). By so doing, however, the second cannot be avoided. To my mind, the best way may be to use cross-sectional data; this is attempted in Appendix A.

[21] In this discussion, the equality of the wage rate between two sectors is implicitly assumed. To make the model more realistic, a wage differential may be assumed. (This serves as the incentive continuously drawing labor from the subsistence sector to the capitalist sector.) Such a differential, if assumed as constant over time, however, does not alter the theory. In reality, the agricultural wage rate (a substitute for the wage rate in the subsistence sector) has a close relationship with the wage rate for female workers in the textile industry (perhaps the best index of the wage rate of unskilled laborers in the capitalist sector). The data for the latter are from my estimates (Minam i, 1966b).

the elasticity of labor supply from the primary to the non-primary sector, is not constant over the entire period covering the pre- and postwar years. The prewar years may be divided into sub-periods: The first sub-period is from 1894 to 1903, in which no significant relationship is found. For the second period, 1904–1918, the elasticity is calculated as .65. For the third period, 1919–1931, the elasticity is negative. Declining prices and the downward rigidity of nominal wage rate account for this negative value. The fourth sub-period, 1932–1939, shows a positive elasticity. Strictly speaking, this period should be divided in two, 1932–1936 and 1937–1939. The elasticity for the former period is 1.2; For the latter it is much smaller than this. For the postwar years, a kink in this regression occurs in 1960. Elasticities are 1.2 and 3.2 respectively for 1951–1960 and for 1961–1963. Excluding the periods 1919–1931 and 1937–1939 as exceptional (the former is a price-declining period and the latter is a wartime period), elasticity for 1961–1963 contrasts with the estimates, from .65 to 1.2, before 1960.[22] This kink may reflect the structural changes of the economy or the modernization of agriculture, both of which began in the postwar years and have been in progress up to the present day.

Changes in the Subsistence Sector Labor Force

As was already stated, a large increase in the marginal productivity of labor in the subsistence sector, one of the features of the turning point, comes from the shifts in the labor productivity schedule, and/or the declines in the number of laborers in this sector. Therefore we will consider large, sustained decreases in the subsistence sector labor force as additional evidence that the economy is approaching or has passed the turning point.

Again we use number of laborers in primary industry as a proxy for the subsistence sector labor force. The numbers shown in Table

---

[22] The elasticity of labor supply calculated and used here is not quite the same as the usual one defined in the text: The former is concerned with the labor supply, *gross* of retirements and deaths, from the primary to non-primary sector. (Our figure for L includes the number of retirements and deaths. See footnote for Figure 2.) The elasticity earlier defined refers to *net* labor supply. This may be one of the defects in our analysis. Note, however, that since our purpose is to examine the changes in behavior of labor migration, the elasticity used here may be defended.

FIGURE 2
Relation between the Number of Non-Primary Laborers Originally
Supplied from Primary Industry and Real Wage Rate in Agriculture*

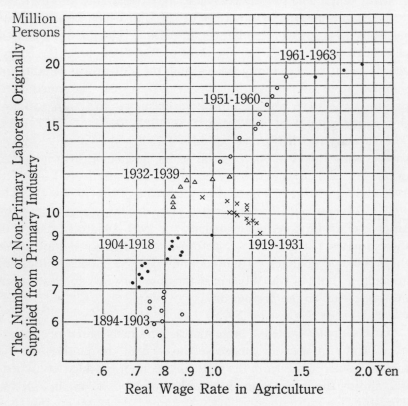

* Real Wage Rate in Agriculture (Deflated by consumer price index): Fig. 1.
Non-primary Laborers Originally supplied from Primary Industry: obtained by
substituting $L(0)$ and $dL(t)$ for 1879–1940 and 1949–64 into the equation $L(t)=$
$L(0)+ \sum_{t=1}^{t} dL(t)$. $L(0)$ is the figure for 1878 and for 1948 respectively. The former
is assumed to be equal to the total non-primary labor force; i.e., I assume non-
primary laborers in this point of time were all supplied from the primary sector.
The latter figure is assumed as 69 per cent of the non-primary labor force in this
year. The ratio is that of non-primary laborers originally supplied from the primary sector to total laborers in 1940. Considering the great changes in employment structure since the end of the war (1945), the estimation of $L(0)$ for 1948 is
one of the weakest points in my estimation of $L(t)$. For $dL(t)$, I assume that it
is equal to the annual net outflow of primary labor force (taken from Table 3);
that is, I neglect the retirements and deaths of the labor force originally supplied from primary industry, because I have no data for them.

TABLE 2

Labor Force in Primary Industry, Business Proprietors and
Family Workers*

(Unit: 1,000 Persons)

Population census and estimates				Labor force survey[a]			
Year	Primary labor force	Business proprietors	Family workers	Year	Primary labor force	Business proprietors	Family workers
1880	15,103			1948	16,950	9,420	12,430
1890	14,798			1950	18,430	10,110	12,970
1900	14,800			1952	16,890	10,120	12,950
1910	14,678			1954	16,190	10,140	13,540
1920	14,442	8,845	10,113	1956	16,150	10,480	13,240
1930	14,490	9,584	10,247	1958	15,200	10,310	12,410
1940	14,192	8,445	10,268	1960	14,490	10,330	11,510
1950	17,208	9,297	12,248	1962	13,690	9,810	10,940
1955	16,111	9,395	11,894	1964	12,510	9,750	10,250
1960	14,237	9,688	10,509				

* Population Census and Estimates, before 1920: Agriculture and Forestry, my
estimates (See Table 1.). Fishery; Hijikata's estimates (Yamada, p. 152). Hijikata
estimated fishery laborers since 1872, but the estimate for 1920 is larger than the
census figure for this year by 38 per cent. Therefore I have discounted all his
pre-1920 estimates by 38 per cent.

Population Census and Estimates, since 1920: Figures from the Population Census
(The Bank of Japan, p. 53).

Labor Force Survey: The Ministry of Labor, 1966, pp. 22–23.

a) For 1948–1952, fourteen or more years old. Since 1954, fifteen or more years
old.

2 indicate that the size of this labor force was strikingly stable for
the prewar years. Annual compound rates of growth are —.09 per
cent and —.11 per cent, respectively, for the periods 1880–1910 and
1910–1940. Rapid declines began only during the postwar years:
The rates of growth are —1.3 per cent and —2.5 per cent respectively for 1950–1955 and 1955–1960, if we rely on the Population
Census *(Kokusei Chōsa)* figures. Making use of a different series
available from the Labor Force Survey *(Rōdōryoku Chōsa)* on an
annual basis since 1948, it seems that the decline in the primary
industry labor force first began in 1951.[23] The main factor in these
declines is the increase in the rate of the shift of labor from primary
to non-primary industries. According to my provisional estimates
in Table 3, the net outflow of primary labor force in the

postwar period is more than four times as large as in the prewar years; the net outflow volumes are on the average 150 and 670 thousands, respectively, for the pre- and postwar periods.[24] This difference in the net outflow between the pre- and postwar periods is largely explained by the difference in the degree of economic activity in the non-primary industries.[25] For example, the annual compound rates of growth of real value added in these industries were about 4.8 per cent and 10.6 per cent respectively for the years 1910–1940 and 1950–1960.[26]

Business proprietors and family workers shown in the same table can be taken as an alternative proxy for the subsistence sector labor force; most business proprietors are, in fact, self-employed operators of farms or small-scale enterprises and hence can be considered to belong to the subsistence sector. According to the Population Census the number of business proprietors increased and decreased in 1920–1930 and 1930–1940, respectively. Through these periods, however, their number was rather constant, and in the postwar period, it increased to some extent. Annual compound rates of growth are −.23 per cent and .41 per cent respectively for 1920–

[23] The labor force in primary industry expanded by a large amount just after the end of the war because of a great flow of population back to rural areas. These workers began returning to the urban areas in large numbers, thus accounting for the initial decline beginning around 1951 in the subsistence sector labor force.

[24] My estimates for the net outflow of agricultural labor force seem to be biased upward for the postwar years. The net outflow of farm household population, which I have estimated, shows a much smaller difference between the pre- and postwar periods; the net outflow volumes are 360 and 800 thousands, and the net outflow rates are 1.1 per cent and 2.0 per cent respectively for the pre- and postwar periods (Minami, 1967, p. 186). The reason for the over-estimation of net outflow of agricultural laborers for the postwar period comes from my assumption that the natural rate of increase of labor force is the same for all sectors. Perhaps in the postwar period, it should be much lower for agriculture than for other sectors.

[25] I fully analyzed the relation between the population migration away from agriculture and economic activity (Minami, 1967).

[26] For the postwar period: National income by industry; estimates by the Economic Planning Agency (The Bank of Japan, pp. 44–45). Wholesale price index (as a deflator for national income); estimates by the Bank of Japan (The Bank of Japan, p. 77). For the prewar period: Real GDP; Ohkawa's estimates (Ohkawa, 1964, Table 3).

1940 and 1950–1960. With the Labor Force Survey we find a slightly increasing trend before 1957 and a decreasing trend thereafter. On the other hand, the Population Census data indicate that the number of family workers increased somewhat in the prewar period, and declined in the postwar years. Rates of growth are .08 per cent and −1.5 per cent in 1920–1940 and 1950–1960, respectively. The Labor Force Survey series, however, does not show a decreasing trend until 1956. In any case, it may be conclusively stated that the labor force in the subsistence sector began to decrease rapidly in the 1950's. This decrease, the result of a large increase in the demand for labor by the capitalist sector, is doubtless one of the major factors explaining the large increase in the marginal productivity of labor in the subsistence sector since the end of the war.[27]

TABLE 3

Net Outflow of Primary Labor Force*

(Annual averages for quinquennial years)

Period	Volume (1,000)	Rate (%)	Period	Volume (1,000)	Rate (%)
1881–1885	155	1.03	1921–1925	131	.89
1886–1890	156	1.05	1926–1930	125	.85
1891–1895	155	1.04	1931–1935	183	1.25
1896–1900	140	.95	1936–1940	152	1.40
1901–1905	154	1.04			
1906–1910	140	.95	1951–1955	760	4.58
1911–1915	137	.94	1956–1960	752	5.10
1916–1920	178	1.21	1961–1964	492	3.78

* My estimates. Net outflow of primary labor force, M, is the difference of the natural increase, N, from the actual increase, ΔL, in primary industry: $M \equiv N - \Delta L$. Now denoting the rate of natural increase in this sector as r; that is, $rN \equiv /L$, we obtain the relation $M \equiv rL - \Delta L \equiv L \ (r - \Delta L/L)$. Under the assumption that the rates of natural increase of labor force are equal among industries, r is equivalent to the rate of change of the total labor force. Substituting the figures for r, ΔL and L into the equation above, we can estimate the net outflow rate. Data used for the number of laborers is as follows: For the prewar period, my estimates for primary labor force (See Table 1) and the Hijikata's estimates for non-primary industries (Ohkawa et al., 1957, p. 145).

For the postwar period, the figures from the Labor Force Survey (The Ministry of Labor, 1966, p. 23).

[27] One may argue that the unprecedented decline in the birth rate since the end of the war might also have contributed to the decrease in surplus labor (e.g., Lewis, p. 29). The decline in the death rate since the war, however, has

Concluding Remarks

The statistical observations in this section perhaps suggest that:
(a) Both the marginal productivity of labor and the real wage rate in the subsistence sector have shown large increases since the end of World War II. Moreover, the correlation between them is seen to be quite close for this period.
(b) The large increase in labor productivity since the end of the war seems to be the result of accelerated shifts in the productivity schedule and unprecedented declines in the number of laborers in the subsistence sector.
(c) The shifts in the productivity schedule are caused by the increase in inputs other than labor, and/or technological progress.
(d) The decline in the labor force is on the whole due to accelerated shifts of labor out of the subsistence sector. This shift has been motivated by a large increase in the demand for labor in the capitalist sector.
(e) The elasticity of labor supply from the subsistence sector to the capitalist sector appears to have declined sharply around 1960.

From these results I incline towards the conclusion that the turning point was passed sometime during the postwar years. We cannot offer, however, a definite date for the turning point. One may observe that it occurred around 1953, because the real wage rate and the marginal productivity of labor in the subsistence sector are

---

kept the rate of natural increase of population in the 1950's as high as in the prewar period; the rate of natural increase is on the average 1.0 per cent, 1.2 per cent, 1.3 per cent and .9 per cent respectively for 1881–1910, 1911–1940, 1951–1955, and 1956–1960 (The Bank of Japan, pp. 12–13). As an index of labor supply to the whole economy, the production age population (the 19–59 year-old population) is superior to total population. This group's annual rate of growth has been 1.1 per cent, 1.5 per cent, 2.1 per cent and 1.9 per cent, respectively for 1880–1910, 1910–1940, 1950–1955, and 1955–1960 (Ohkawa et al., 1956, p. 127 and The Bank of Japan, p. 16). (Note that the largest rate of increase is recorded for the postwar period.) Clearly, structural changes in employment or the decline in surplus labor for the postwar years cannot be explained by the changes in total labor supply. The increasing demand for labor which has resulted from the unprecedented growth of the Japanese economy for these years is almost indubitably the proper explanation. In the near future, at which time the growth rate of production age population is expected to decrease, the demographic factor will begin to have an important role in the modernization of the Japanese labor market.

thought to have begun to rise steadily in that year. Another may insist that it is 1960 because the elasticity of labor supply kinks in 1960. Obviously neither date can be shown to be conclusively correct. In a sense this is quite natural, because the turning point, once put in historical perspective, is not a point of time, a certain day or a year, but rather should be defined as a span of years.

II. Examination of the Statistical Studies by Other Writers
Comments on Fei-Ranis' Conclusions

Fei and Ranis' 1918 turning point is based upon Umemura's findings of a sharp upturn in real wages in manufacturing around 1918 (Fei and Ranis, 1964b, pp. 263–64). This upturn is confirmed by new estimates (by nine industry groups and by sexes) which I made (Minami, 1966b). The average wage for all manufacturing and for both sexes deflated by the consumer price index shows an upward trend from 1905 until 1921. During this period, the upward trend accelerated as time passed, and was conspicuous for a number of years after 1916. The real wage stopped rising rapidly in 1921. Slight increases were registered after that year. The postwar years again show steady increases. In my opinion, however, the data by themselves are not sufficient to determine the date of the turning point. The data are average figures for males and females in many industries. The figures in Table 4 represent the ratios of average wage rates for both sexes and for nine manufacturing industry groups, calculated with variable weights, to average wages calculated under three alternative weighting assumptions: For Series A uses the 1909 sex weights, series B, the 1909 industry weights, and series C, the 1909 weights for both sex and industry groups. Each series shows an upward trend for the decade of the 1910's and for the years after 1925, during which time average wages for both sexes and all industries increased sharply. So the increase in average wages for both sexes and for all industries is partly the result of the structural changes of the labor force between sexes and among industry groups.

Here we should pay special attention to the changes in industrial structure. As we stated earlier, manufacturing industry in Japan is composed of a subsistence and a capitalist sector. Furthermore,

TABLE 4

Ratios of Average Wages with Variable Weights to Those with Constant
Weights in Manufacturing Industries*

(For the production workers in factories with
30 or more production workers only)

	1900	1905	1910	1915	1920	1925	1930	1935	1939
A	1.04	1.04	1.03	1.09	1.14	1.14	1.22	1.29	1.43
B	1.04	1.04	1.00	1.09	1.18	1.15	1.22	1.35	1.54
C	1.04	1.04	1.00	1.12	1.30	1.17	1.27	1.40	1.59

A: Ratio of the average of male and female wages with 1909 weights,
     for all manufacturing industries combined.

B: Ratio of the averages of wages of nine industry groups with 1909
     weights, for both sexes combined.

C: Ratio of the averages of wages of nine industry groups by sexes,
     with 1909 weights.

*   Wage Rates: Minami (1966b).
Weights: The number of production workers in the factories with 30 or more
workers taken from *Factory Statistics (Kōjō Tōkei Hyō)* for 1909.

following Ohkawa, the latter may be divided into two groups, according to their respective relationships with the subsistence sector
(Ohkawa, 1965a, p. 483). The first group, e.g., the textiles industry,
has a close relationship with this sector, in the sense that laborers
move smoothly between them, and as a result there is a tendency for
wage rates to equalize between them.[28] Capitalists in this sub-sector,
taking the institutionally determined wage rate as given, select the
most profitable input ratios. On the other hand, the second group,
e.g., big machinery, metal and chemical enterprises, does not have
this close relationship; labor does not move from the subsistence
sector to this sector,[29] and the wage level is determined almost independently of the subsistence wage. Technology in this sector,
mainly borrowed from developed countries, is most modern, and
the level of productivity is very high. The first group played an important role in the early stages of economic development in Japan;
the second group has grown since the end of World War I. (The

---

[28] See Footnote 21.

[29] It is known, however, that there is a relationship between these sectors;
sons of the laborers in the first group of the capitalist sector, originally supplied from the subsistence sector, are employed in the second group.

subsistence sector may not be covered in our series of wages inasmuch as wages are limited to factories with 30 or more workers.) Such changes in industrial structure may explain the upward trend in the figures in B and C, and at the same time show how dangerous it is to attempt to find the turning point by using the average wages for all manufacturing industries.[30]

Fei and Ranis consider their finding that the capital-labor ratio in non-agriculture ceased to show a decreasing trend since the end of World War I as additional evidence for a 1918 dating of the turning point (Fei and Ranis, 1964b, pp. 129–31). Some years ago Reubens made comprehensive comments on this aspect of Fei and Ranis' work (Reubens, 1964).[31] He also gave alternative estimates for the capital stock which indicated that no capital shallowing occurred between 1888 and 1928 (Reubens, p. 1056). In replying to this comment, Fei and Ranis revised their original estimates of the capital stock. In this new series, a turning point from capital shallowing to capital deepening appeared once again—this time, somewhat earlier, in the decade from 1893 to 1903 (Fei and Ranis, 1964a, p. 1064). The method of estimation used by Fei and Ranis, however, is too simple; they obtained their capital stock data by subtracting or adding an appropriate annual investment, as esti-

---

[30] Another problem in using the average wages for all manufacturing industries for this purpose comes from the more than proportional increase in skilled laborers: Their wages tend to increase faster than the subsistence wage. The concept of unlimited supplies of labor extends only to unskilled workers. The effect of changing composition of workers by age groups on the changes in average wages should also be considered. We do not have, however, sufficient data for wage rates by age groups covering long periods of the prewar. The data from the *Survey of Labor Statistics (Rōdō Tōkei Jitchi Chōsa)* are the exception. These data show that the nominal wage rate did *decrease* for all age groups and for all industry groups for the price-declining periods, 1924–1927 and 1927–1930. During the former period, the average figure for all groups increased by 1.4 per cent per year (Nihon Rōdō Undō Shiryō Iinkai, pp. 296–97).

[31] Shallowing in capital intensity in the capitalist sector is not a necessary implication of the theory of unlimited supplies of labor. (In equation (1) of Appendix B, the growth rate of the capital-labor ratio, $G(K/L)$, can be positive, zero or negative depending on the sign of H_L.) In this respect Fei and Ranis and Reubens all agree (Fei and Ranis, 1964a p. 1063; and Reubens, p. 1053). For this reason we did not examine changes in capital intensity in non-agriculture when I attempted to find the turning point. Also see the comments by Watanabe (Watanabe, fn. 6).

mated by Rosovsky, from a benchmark capital stock figure obtained from the National Wealth Survey *(Kokufu Chōsa)* in 1930. Rosovsky's figures as a whole had first been deflated by them using Ohkawa's non-agricultural price index. On the other hand, the capital intensity in non-primary industry shown in Table 5 depends on new estimates of capital stock by Ishiwata. These are rather comprehensive estimates covering many specific items of the capital stock. According to this series, no capital shallowing occurred in any period with the exceptions of 1883–1887 to 1888–1892. These data include, however, tertiary industry, in which subsistence enterprises are dominant. We have no data for manufacturing industries alone.[32] As a substitute, horsepower of prime movers per worker in manufacturing industries is shown in the same table. This series shows an upward trend, not decreasing in any period. To my mind,

TABLE 5

Capital-Labor Ratio in Non-Primary and Horsepower of Prime Movers
Per Worker in Manufacturing Industries*

Period	Capital-labor ratio[a] (Yen)	Horsepower per worker[b] (10^{-3} Horsepower)	Period	Capital-labor ratio[a] (Yen)	Horsepower per worker[b] (10^{-3} Horsepower)
1878–1882	575		1908–1912	949	77
1883–1887	590		1913–1917	1,148	136
1888–1892	572	10	1918–1922	1,462	284
1893–1897	634	20	1923–1927	1,681	459
1898–1902	720	20	1928–1932	1,937	588
1903–1907	786	36	1933–1937	2,124	801

   * Gross capital stock: Ishiwata's estimates (*LTES*, III, pp. 160, 162).
Horsepower: My estimates (*LTES*, XII, p. 223).
Labor force for non-primary and manufacturing industries: Hijikata's estimates (Ohkawa et al., 1957, p. 145).
   a) Gross capital stock in 1934–1936 prices divided by the size of labor force (Residential construction is excluded in capital stock) for non-primary industries.
   b) Horsepower of prime movers divided by the size of labor force for manufacturing industries.

---

[32] Ishiwata has also presented a provisional estimate for the capital stock in manufacturing industries. Although Watanabe has used this estimate (Watanabe, p. 296), the assumptions by which Ishiwata has derived these figures from his estimates for non-primary industry as a whole are so untenable as to render the former estimates unacceptable for use in this paper.

therefore, capital intensity in the capitalist sector as a whole has continued to increase throughout the process of economic development in Japan.[33]

Comments on Jorgenson's Conclusions

Jorgenson, developing two kinds of theories of economic development, classical and neo-classical, introduced the following hypotheses (Jorgenson, pp. 54–58).[34] In the classical theory, (1) the real wage in agriculture remains constant, (2) the agricultural labor force declines absolutely, (3) labor productivity remains constant in non-agriculture, (4) the rates of growth in output and employment increase in non-agriculture, and (4) the capital-output ratio falls in non-agriculture. In my opinion, however, these hypotheses, with the exception of (1), are not strict implications of the theory of unlimited supplies of labor.[35] Therefore, in this article, we will examine the statistical test in the light of hypothesis (1) only. Jorgenson estimated real labor income per capita in agriculture by deducting rents for tenants from total agricultural income. Having found that income per capita tended to increase from 1878–1882 until 1913–1917

---

[33] The increasing trend in the capital-labor ratio is consistent with my conclusions that the turning point was in the postwar period; theoretically, it is not inconsistent with the concept of unlimited supplies of labor (See footnote 31). The increasing trend may be explained in part by (1) the increase in the subsistence wage level and (2) a continuously increasingly tight labor market for skilled workers. Recall also that (3) in the highly modernized manufacturing enterprises, which mainly used a technology borrowed from outside the economy, the capital-labor ratio has been determined somewhat independently of the relative factor prices.

[34] Before examining these hypotheses, Jorgenson surveyed and criticized the statistical work on the existence of zero marginal productivity of labor attempted by other scholars (Jorgenson, Sec. II). This discussion is not really relevant for the question of the appropriateness or inappropriateness of the unlimited supplies of labor concept (See footnote 3).

[35] For hypothesis (2): The direction of changes in the agricultural labor force depends on many variables; the natural rate of increase of population, the rates of technological progress in agriculture and non-agriculture, the propensity to save in both sectors, and so forth. For hypothesis (4): This is not independent from the assumption of a *constant* rate of technological progress: The rates of growth of output and employment in non-agriculture can remain constant or decrease depending on the changes in the rate of technological progress. For hypotheses (3) and (5); these come from the special production function assumed by Jorgenson, i.e., the Cobb-Douglas function with neutral technological progress (See Appendix B).

(Jorgenson, p. 54),[36] he concluded that the concept of unlimited supplies of labor was inapplicable (Jorgenson, p. 60).[37]

Prior to Jorgenson's work, Umemura attempted the same estimation in a more precise way and for a longer period. According to his series of five-year moving averages for 1885–1936, real labor income per capita increased from the beginning of his series until 1902. The upward trend begins once more in 1923 after tending towards constancy for the first two decades of this century (Umemura, 1961, p. 85). These kinds of estimations do have some problems. One is data; if it is true that there are some underestimations in agricultural output in the early years, then real labor income per capita is somewhat underestimated. Perhaps the increase before 1913–1917 in Jorgenson's estimates and those before 1902 in Umemura's estimates may be explained partly by this factor.[38] Another more basic problem is the estimation procedure[39]; agricultural income is composed of five components: rents, wages for wage earners, implicit wages for unpaid family workers, profits and interests. Under the assumptions, rents=rents for tenancy, and profits+

---

[36] The real disposable income per worker in agriculture estimated by Gleason shows a steady increase since 1883–1887 up to 1933–1937. He obtained the disposable income figures by subtracting direct taxes on agriculture and gross agricultural investment from net income produced in agriculture (Gleason, p. 414). Note, however, in the first place that his figures are not a direct index for labor income as they contain incomes from rents and interests. (The disposable income per capita is equal to the labor income per capita only if the labor income is all consumed and the incomes from rents and interests are all saved and invested.) Moreover, the agricultural output statistics on which Gleason bases his estimates may be downward biased (See footnote 38).

[37] In support of this conclusion, one might suggest the well-known violent competition for workers in the cotton spinning industry in the late Meiji and early Taisho periods. This competition was, however, for trained workers and resulted from temporary regional disequilibria caused by lack of information (Tussing, p. 74). Tussing, who comprehensively studied the labor force and wages for this industry in Yamanashi Prefecture for these periods, concluded that the supply of labor for non-agriculture was elastic (Tussing, p. 79).

[38] The data of agricultural output used by Gleason, Jorgenson and Umemura were taken from the old Hitotsubashi estimates (Ohkawa et al., 1956 and 1957). On the other hand, the data used in this paper are from the revised Hitotsubashi estimates (*LTES*, IX). Underestimations in agricultural output have been corrected to some extent in the new estimates.

[39] This was pointed out by Umemura himself in his correspondence to me.

interest=0, we can estimate labor income (that is, total of wages for wage earners and implicit wages) by deducting rents for tenancy from agricultural income. Dividing labor income by the number of laborers, labor income per capita is obtained. This method of estimation has some defects. First, implicit wages might lag behind the market wage rate. Second, rents for tenancy should be equal to the total of rents and interest. Third, the profits might not necessarily be zero; depending on economic situations, they could be positive or negative. Labor income per capita may be a good index in the sense that it covers all agricultural workers including unpaid family workers. Considering, however, that we have no reliable data for profits, interests and so forth, I am sure that the agricultural wage rate which was used in my analysis is superior.

REFERENCES

Bank of Japan. *Hundred-Year Statistics of the Japanese Economy (Meiji Ikō Honpō Shuyō Keizai Tōkei)*. Tokyo: 1966.

Fei, J.C.H., and Ranis, G., "Capital-Labor Ratios in Theory and in History: Reply," *American Economic Review*, LIV (Dec. 1964), pp. 1063–69.

———. *Development of the Labor Surplus Economy: Theory and Policy*. Illinois: 1964.

Gleason, A. H., "Economic Growth and Consumption in Japan," *The State and Economic Enterprise in Japan*, W. W. Lockwood, ed., New Jersey: 1965, pp. 391–444.

Hansen, B., "Marginal Productivity Wage Theory and Subsistence Wage Theory in Egyptian Agriculture," *Journal of Development Studies*, II (July, 1966), pp. 367–405.

Johnston, B. F., "Agricultural Development and Economic Transformation: A Comparative Study of the Japanese Experience," *Food Research Institute Studies*, III, No. 3 (Nov. 1962), pp. 223–76.

Jorgenson, D. W., "Testing Alternative Theories of the Development of a Dual Economy," *The Theory and Design of Economic Development*, I. Adelman and E. Thorbecke, eds., Baltimore: 1966, pp. 45–60.

Kaneda, Hiromitsu, "Substitution of Labor and Non-Labor Inputs and Technical Change in Japanese Agriculture," *Review of Economics and Statistics*, XLVII (May, 1965), pp. 163–71.

Lewis, W. A., "Unlimited Labour: Further Notes," *Manchester School of Economic and Social Studies*, XXVI (Jan. 1958), pp. 1–32.

Minami, Ryoshin. *Estimates of Long-Term Economic Statistics of Japan since 1868 (Chōki Keizai Tōkei)*, Kazushi Ohkawa, Miyohei Shinohara and Mataji Umemura, eds., XII: *Railroads and Electric Utilities (Tetsudō to Denryoku)*, Tokyo: 1965.

——, "Estimation of Daily Wages in Manufacturing Industries in Prewar Japan: A Note," Yale University, Economic Growth Center, Discussion Paper No. 12, mimeo. (Oct. 1966).

——, "Estimation of Employment in Agriculture and Forestry, 1872–1940 (*Nōringyō Shūgyōsha-Sū no Suikei,* 1872–1930)," *The Economic Review (Keizai Kenkyū),* XVII (July, 1966), pp. 275–78.

——, "Population Migration Away from Agriculture in Japan," *Economic Development and Cultural Change,* XV, NO. 2, Part I (Jan. 1967).

Ministry of Labor. *History of Labor Economy in the Postwar: Source Book (Sengo Rōdō Keizai Shi: Shiryō Hen).* Tokyo: 1966.

——. *White Paper on Labor: Analysis of the Labor Economy (Rōdō Hakusho: Rōdō Keizai no Bunseki).* Tokyo: 1964.

Nakamura, James I. *Agricultural Production and the Economic Development of Japan, 1873–1922.* Princeton: Princeton University Press, 1966.

Nihon Rōdō Undō Shiryō Iinkai. *Historical Statistics of Industrial Relations in Japan (Nihon Rōdō Undō Shiryō),* X: *Volume of Statistics (Dai Jukkan: Tōkei Hen).* Tokyo: 1959.

Ohkawa, Kazushi, "Agriculture and Turning Points," *Developing Economies,* III (Dec. 1965), pp. 471–86.

——, "Economic Growth in Japan: Basic Statistical Tables," (Working Paper Prepared for SSRC Project, mimeo., 1964).

——. *Theory and Measurement of Food Economy (Shokuryō Keizai no Riron to Keisoku).* Tokyo: 1945.

—— and Minami, Ryoshin, "The Phase of Unlimited Supplies of Labor," *Hitotsubashi Journal of Economics,* V (June, 1964), pp. 1–15.

——, Noda, T., Takamatsu, N., Yamada, S., Kumazaki, N., Shionoya, Y., Minami, R. *Prices (Bukka), Estimates of Long-Term Economic Statistics of Japan since 1868,* VIII, K. Ohkawa, M. Shinohara, and M. Umemura, eds., Tokyo: Toyo Keizai Shimposha, 1967.

——, Ishiwata, S., Yamada, S., Ishi, H. *Capital Stock (Shihon Sutokku), Estimates of Long-Term Economic Statistics of Japan since 1868,* III, K. Ohkawa, M. Shinohara, and M. Umemura, eds., Tokyo: Toyo Keizai Shimposha, 1966.

——, Shinohara, M., Umemura, M., Ito, M., Noda, T. *The Growth Rate of the Japanese Economy (Nihon Keizai no Seichō-Ritsu).* Tokyo: 1956 (in Japanese).

——. *The Growth Rate of the Japanese Economy since 1878.* Tokyo: Kinokuniya, 1957.

—— and Rosovsky, H., "A Century of Japanese Economic Growth," *The State and Economic Enterprise in Japan,* W. W. Lockwood, ed., Princeton: Princeton University Press, 1965, pp. 47–92.

—— and Rosovsky, H., "The Role of Agriculture in Japanese Economic Development," *Economic Development and Cultural Change,* IX (Oct. 1960), pp. 43–67.

Reubens, E. P., "Capital-Labor Ratios in Theory and in History: Comment," *American Economic Review,* LIV (Dec. 1964), pp. 1052–62.

Ricardo, D. *The Works and Correspondence of David Ricardo.* P. Sraffa, ed. Cambridge: 1951.

Taira, Koji, "The Inter-Sectoral Wage Differential in Japan, 1881-1959," *Journal of Farm Economics,* XLIV (May, 1962), pp. 322-34.

Tussing, Arlon R., "The Labor Force in Meiji Economic Growth: A Quantitative Study of Yamanashi Prefecture," *Joural of Economic History,* XXVI (Mar. 1966), pp. 59-92 (reproduced as chapter 8 in this volume).

Ueno, H. and Kinoshita, S. *Model of Economic Growth in Japan (Nihon Keizai no Seichō Moderu).* Tokyo: 1965.

Umemura, Mataji. *Wages, Employment and Agriculture(Chingin, Koyō, Nōgyō).* Tokyo: 1961.

——, Yamada, S., Hayami, Y., Takamatsu, N., and Kumazaki, M. *Agriculture and Forestry (Nōringyō), Estimates of Long-Term Economic Statistics of Japan since 1868,* K. Ohkawa, M. Shinohara, and M. Umemura, eds., IX, Tokyo: Toyo Keizai Shimposha, 1966.

Watanabe, Tsunehiko, "Economic Aspects of Dualism in the Industrial Development of Japan," *Economic Development and Cultural Change,* XIV (Apr. 1965), pp. 293-312.

Yamada, Yūzō. *Comprehensive Survey of National Income in Japan (Nihon Kokumin Shotoku Suikei Shiryō).* Tokyo: 1951.

Yuize, Yoshihiko, "Estimation of Aggregate Production Functions of Agriculture *(Nōgyō ni okeru Kyoshiteki Seisan Kansu no Keisoku)*," *Quarterly Journal of Agricultural Economy (Nōgyō Sōgō Kenkyū),* XVIII (Oct. 1964), pp. 1-53.

APPENDIX A: Cross-Sectional Test of
the Marginal Productivity Theory

Data are available from the Survey of Farm Household Economy *(Nōka Keizai Chōsa)* for the postwar period. The daily wages for temporary workers are obtained as the annual wage payments divided by the working days per year multiplied by eight, the assumed figure for working hours per day. The average productivity of labor is calculated by dividing gross value added per year by total labor input per year in terms of adult-man-day equivalent in agricultural production.[40] These statistics are calculated for ten agricultural regions and for six scales of operation of farm household;[41] under .3, .3—.5, .5—1.0, 1.0—1.5, 1.5—2.0 and over 2.0 *chō*[42] for every other year since 1952. Therefore, we have 10×6=60 (10×5= 50, for 1952–1956) samples for each year. Dividing these samples into two groups; A, the farms of under 1.0 *chō* and B, the farms of over 1.0 *chō,* and regressing the wage rate for temporary workers, under the assumption that it is equivalent to that for permanent workers, on the average productivity of labor, we obtain the coefficients of determination[43] adjusted by the degree of freedom as follows:

	1952	1954	1956	1958	1960	1962
A	.179*	.054	.164*	.405**	.310**	.170*
B	.251**	.232**	.421**	.611**	.689**	.593**

Note first that all coefficients are statistically significant at the 5 per cent level, with the exception of the figure for A in 1954. Second, coefficients are larger for B than for A in every year. Third, there is an increasing trend in the figures for B. Fourth, the trend in B seems to be influenced by economic fluctuations; for the boom years of 1952 and 1960, the coefficients of determination are at peaks, and for the recession years of 1954 and 1962 they reach troughs. Now, if we assume that the output elasticity of labor is

---

[40] These procedures are from Kaneda (Kaneda, p. 165).

[41] See footnote 4.

[42] For the years 1952–1956, the data is tabulated by five scales of operation; under .5, .5–1.0, 1.0–1.5, 1.5–2.0 and over 2.0 *chō* (One *chō* is 2.45 acres).

[43] One and two asterisks mean that the coefficients of determination are significant at the 5 per cent and 1 per cent significance levels respectively.

constant among regions and over scales of operation for each year, we may deduce from these findings the following conclusions: First, the wage rate in postwar agriculture has been determined according to the level of marginal productivity. The relationship is, however, much clearer for the large-scale farms than for the small-scale ones and has been becoming tighter gradually. In other words, the modernization of agriculture has begun in the large-scale farms and is steadily progressing. Modernization, on the other hand, has been delayed on small farms. Second, the correspondence of the wage rate to marginal productivity is much closer in boom-times than in recession periods. This implies that labor supply tends to become less elastic when the demand for labor increases rapidly and vice versa.

APPENDIX B: Mathematical Examinations of the Changes in the Capital-labor Ratio, Labor Productivity and the Capital-output Ratio

Assume a general production function in the non-agriculture sector, which satisfies the conditions of constant returns to scale and diminishing returns to all inputs; $Q=f(K, L, t)$, where Q, K, L and t denote total output, capital stock, labor force, and time. From this function Fei and Ranis obtained the equations: $G(Q)=\phi_K G(K)+\phi_L G(L)+J$, and $G(f_L)=\dfrac{\phi_K}{\sigma} G(K/L)+H_L$, where $G(\;\;)$ is the growth rate of a variable in parenthesis, ϕ_K and ϕ_L are the output elasticities to capital and labor respectively ($f_K K/f$ and $f L_L/f$), J is the intensity of innovation (f_t/f), f_L and f_K are the marginal productivities of labor and capital respectively, σ is the elasticity of substitution ($f_K f_L/f_{LK}$), and H_L is the time rate increase of f_L(f_{Lt}/f_L). Assuming that the wage rate is constant over time[44] and equal to the marginal productivity of labor, say, $w=\overline{w}=f_L$, from the two equations above, the following relations are obtained:

$$G(K/L)= -\frac{H_L}{\phi_K}, \tag{1}$$

$$G(Q/L)= -\sigma H_L+J. \text{ [45]} \tag{2}$$

Subtracting (2) from (1), we get

$$G(K/Q)=\sigma\left(1 - \frac{1}{\phi_K}\right)H_L-J. \tag{3}$$

Equations (1), (2), and (3) show the conditions of the changes in capital-labor ratio (K/L), average productivity of labor (Q/L) and capital-output ratio (K/Q). If we specify a production function of the Cobb-Douglas type ($\sigma=1$) with neutral technological progress

---

[44] A general presentation of the unlimited supplies of labor is $G(w)= \overline{G}(w)$, where $\overline{G}(w)$ is an exogenous variable. The condition, $w=\overline{w}$ or $\overline{G}(w)=0$, in the text is the special case.

[45] Marglin introduced the equation of $G(Q/L)$ under the assumption of neutral technological progress (Jorgenson, pp. 65–66). Our mathematical development here is much more general in the sense that we do not assume neutrality in technological progress.

$(H_L = J)$,[46] these equations become,

$$G(K/L) = -J/\phi_K \tag{1}'$$

$$G(Q/L) = 0 \tag{2}'$$

$$G(K/Q) = -J/\phi_K \tag{3}'$$

This is the basis of Jorgenson's assertion that the capital-labor ratio and the capital-output ratio decrease,[47] while average labor productivity remains constant in the classical model.

---

[46] Neutral technological progress in the Hicksian sense is expressed as $H_L = H_K$, where H_K is the time rate of increase of f_K. Substituting this into the relation, $J = \phi_L H_L + \phi_K H_K$, which was obtained by computing f_t from $Q = f_K K + f_L L$ (Fei and Ranis, 1964b, p. 109), we get $J = H_L = H_K$.

[47] We have $G(K/L) = G(K/Q) < 0$. That is, the growth rate of the capital labor ratio is equal to that of the capital-output ratio in the Jorgenson model (This is the reason why he called the decreasing capital-output ratio *capital shallowing,* which was originally defined as the decreasing capital-labor ratio by Fei and Ranis). Under the general assumptions, however, this is not true (See equations (1) and (3) in the text).

PART IV

PART IV

CHAPTER 12

PRIMARY PRODUCT EXPORTS AND ECONOMIC DEVELOPMENT: THE CASE OF SILK

KENZŌ HEMMI

I. Problem

One of the major issues in economic development of developing countries is whether dependence on the export of one or a few primary products tends to promote or retard the economic development of these countries. It has been asserted that, through various multipliers, linkages, and demonstration effects, such primary-product exports act positively. Thus, a number of economists have stressed the importance of primary-product exports, such as wool in the case of Australia, in launching the modern economic development of the countries concerned. Yet, judging from the developmental policies present-day developing countries are pursuing, the predominant attitude in these countries is one of distrust of dependence on primary-product exports. One of the reasons for this distrust may lie in the fact that the successful cases of economic development dependent on one of a few primary-product exports consist mainly of those of newly settled countries, and not of stagnant and densely populated countries. It is believed that the profitability of primary production depends on favorable natural resource endowment, and that, among the stagnant and densely populated countries, it is rather difficult to find instances in which expanding exports of primary-products have played an important role.

Although some evidence indicates that there were changes in the Japanese economic condition in the latter half of the Tokugawa period, it is safe to say that the Japanese economy of the period was that of a stagnant, densely populated country. In spite of this situation the silk exports played a crucial role in the early stage of Japanese modern economic development.

The purpose of this paper is to show how important silk, including cocoon production in agriculture, was in launching modern Japanese economic development (Section II), and how it was possible to increase silk and cocoon production in densely populated rural Japan (Section III).

II. Measurement of the Contribution of Silk to Japanese Economic Development

An extremely simple method of measuring the contribution of silk to the Japanese economic development is to confine the analysis to the field of agriculture, and to measure the share of sericultural production in the total value of agricultural production at current prices. Unfortunately, there is no reliable data over time on costs of production by farm product. It is also impossible to estimate value added by sericultural production over the years. However, there is no doubt that in producing sericultural products of a certain value, a larger value of intermediate inputs is needed than in the case of producing the same value of agricultural output in general. Therefore, figures in Column A of Table 1 overestimate the importance of sericulture.

The second measurement (Column B, Table 1) is also confined to the field of agriculture. The figures in this column are the percentage share of the increase in sericultural production in the increase in total value of agricultural production at current prices in the same period. We ignore again the problem of accounting for non-factor inputs. The third measurement shown in Column C of the same table is a hypothetical one. During the period under consideration, there was keen competition between mulberry and the group of dryland crops termed *mugi*—wheat, barley, naked barley, oats and rye (Nasu, p. 20). It is reasonable to assume that if mulberry had not been planted at all, *mugi* would have occupied the same area. Therefore, the *net* contribution by sericultural production to total agricultural production in a given period must be "increase in sericultural production in a period less the hypothetical increase in

TABLE 1

Contribution of Sericultural Production to Total
Agricultural Production at Current Prices

Period[a]	A[b] Share of sericultural production in total value of agricultural production (%)	B[b] Share of increase in sericultural production in increase in total value of agricultural production (%)	C[c] Net contribution of sericultural production to increase in total value of agricultural production (%)
1874/75 –1876/80	5.5	8.4	8.5
1876/80 –1881/85	7.5	16.6	7.1
1881/85 –1886/90	8.7	—[d]	—[d]
1886/90 –1891/95	8.6	13.6	11.4
1891/95 –1896/1900	9.9	9.7	7.5
1896/1900 –1901/05	9.8	11.4	9.2
1901/05 –1905/10	10.1	15.1	12.3
1906/10 –1911/15	11.2	7.4	3.2
1911/15 –1916/20	10.4	18.2	15.4
1916/20 –1921/25	14.4	30.2	30.3
1921/25 –1926/30	16.2	—[d]	—[d]
Average	10.2	14.5	11.7

a) The basis for calculating A is the former of the two quinquennials in a period.
In the case of calculating B and C, the difference between the first and the second
half of the period is used. For example, sericultural production in 1876/80 and in
1881/86 was 141 million yen and 190 million yen respectively, and the total value
of agricultural production in the same respective periods was 1,883 million yen
and 2,178 million yen. Therefore, B for 1876/80−1881/85=(190−141)÷(2178−
1883)×100=16.6.

b) Values of sericultural and of agricultural production at current prices are
taken from *LTES,* IX.

c) Value of *mugi* (wheat, barley, naked barley, oats and rye) production is taken
from *LTES,* IX. Acreage under mulberry is taken from *LTES,* III. Acreage under
mugi is taken from Ministry of Agriculture and Forestry (1953).

d) Both the total value of agricultural production and the value of sericultural
production at current prices decreased from 1881/85 to 1886/1890.

mugi production on the same acreage as was needed by mulberry for sericulture in the same period" divided by the increase in total agricultural production in the same period.[1] This hypothetical calculation is shown in Column C.

As is shown in Column A, the share of sericultural production in the total value of agricultural production increased steadily from 5.5 to 16.2 per cent during the period under consideration, the average being 10.2 per cent. On the other hand, as shown in Columns B and C, both the share of the increase in sericultural production in the increase in total value of agricultural production and the net contribution of sericultural production to increase in total value of agricultural production did not show any marked upward trend. The averages were 14.5 per cent and 11.7 per cent, respectively. The difference between these two figures is the contribution by *mugi* to the increase in total value of agricultural production. The conclusion that can be drawn from Table 1 is that the contribution by sericultural production to the increase in the total value of agricultural production in the period ranges from 14.5 per cent to about 10 per cent. During the same period the annual rate of growth of total Japanese agricultural production was about 1.8 per cent to about 2.0 per cent at constant prices. Therefore, the annual rate of growth of Japanese agricultural production contributed by sericultural production may be said to have ranged between 0.3 and 0.2 per cent. These figures are not insignificant, though not particularly spectacular.

Turning our attention next to the process of reeling silk from cocoons, we find that only extremely scanty information is available concerning this process. The cost of cocoons was 79 per cent in 1879 and 77 per cent in around 1912 of the total production costs in silk reeling factories (excluding fixed costs such as depreciation of building and machinery) (Yamaguchi, 1966, p. 43). Within the remaining 21 or 23 per cent, the largest item was wages paid including board, while costs of fuel, packing materials and others were very insignif-

---

[1] The contribution in Column C is somewhat overestimated as it was not possible, because of lack of data, to make allowance for summer crops such as sweet potatoes that might be planted on the same acreage after *mugi* was harvested.

icant. Almost all workers in the silk reeling factories during this period were from farm families, and one may reasonably assume that wages paid by the factories contributed to the increase in off-farm income of farm families. I assume for the entire period under consideration a constant ratio of 100 to 15 between the current price value of cocoons produced and the amount of wages received by farm families from the factories. If we assume that 30 per cent of the value of sericultural products came from inputs of non-farm origin, the ratio of value added by sericultural production to the amount of wages received by farm families from the factories becomes 100 to 20. The figures mentioned in the preceding paragraph become 0.36 to 0.24. As will be seen presently, in value terms, 60 to 80 per cent of silk produced was exported as raw silk. Moreover, as costs of weaving silk into silk fabrics and those of processing the latter are not known, I shall refrain from examining these processes. It should be noted, however, that there was a large difference in value terms between raw silk not exported and silk fabrics as shown in Table 2. Thus the figures in Table 2 do stress the importance of the weaving industry.

TABLE 2
Production of Silk and Related Goods, 1874*

(in 1,000 Yen)

Commodities	Amounts produced	Percentages of total manufac- tured goods
Raw silk (A)	6,165	5.5
Floss silk (B)	220	0.2
Silk fabrics (C)	4,581	4.1
Silk fabrics (cotton mixtures) (D)	1,379	1.2
Silk not exported[a] (E)	1,233	1.1
(A+B+C+D)−E	11,121	9.9
Total manufactured goods	111,892	100.0

* Yamaguchi (1956), pp. 14–5.
a) Calculated on the assumption that 80 per cent of raw silk produced was exported.

Turning now to the contribution made by the silk industry to the industrialization of the Japanese economy, we find that the silk industry played a key role at the beginning of Japanese industrialization.

As given in Table 2, raw silk production occupied 5.5 per cent of the total production of all manufactured industries in 1874. The most important manufactured item in the same year was alcoholic beverages (16.8 per cent), followed by cotton textiles (9.7 per cent), while the fourth position was occupied by soy sauce *(shoyu)* (Yamaguchi, 1956, p. 14). The silk industry as a whole occupied 9.9 per cent of the total manufacturing industries as shown in Table 2. It must be noted further that both the production of alcoholic beverages and that of *shoyu* were based not on modern, but on quite traditional techniques, thus playing minor roles in the launching of modern industries in Japan. Even cotton textile production was on the traditional basis relative to silk production as will be seen shortly. Therefore, it is reasonable to conclude that the silk industry was the largest among modern industries at that time, and that the development of the silk industry played a key role in the early industrialization of Japan.

If we characterize a modern factory as one using mechanical power and a large number of workers, Table 3 shows the importance of the silk industry in early modern Japanese factories, although its importance declined over the years. In using Table 3 for our present purpose, however, some caution is necessary. For example, the average size of the machinery and chemical factories might have been larger in terms of capital invested, or in some other terms, than that of the textile factories, since the textile industry might have been more labor intensive than the other industries. Nevertheless, the importance of the silk industry in the initial period and the subsequent decline of its relative position are both remarkable. We may state that the silk industry was a training school for Japanese industrialization and an important market for products of other manufacturing industries which were not yet competitive in the world market during this period. It must be noted in this context that almost all primary products are really semi-manufactured, and that it is almost impossible to develop a country's primary product exports without efficient processing or manufacturing capacity. The increase in primary product exports means the development of capacity for

Number of Factories and Factory Workers*

Year	Total number	Share of Each Industry							
		Textile			Machinery, including transport equipment	Chemical	Food and drink	Others
		Total	Silk	Cotton				
Number of factories using mechanical power								
1886	405	77.0%	71.0%	4.9%	2.7%	4.9%	4.2%	11.2%
1891	971	66.5	58.3	4.2	4.0	6.5	10.2	12.8
1897	2,950	70.8	64.0	2.5	5.6	4.5	6.4	12.7
1902	2,991	62.8	53.4	4.9	8.3	8.3	8.4	12.2
1906	4,656	59.6	48.1	4.8	9.6	8.1	9.8	12.9
1909	6,723	58.8	35.6	1.8	10.9	6.5	10.9	12.9
1914	10,334	55.5	23.9	1.2	11.0	8.2	10.7	14.6
1919	17,653	48.1	16.1	1.4	15.8	11.0	10.1	15.0
Number of factory workers employed in factories using 10 or more workers[a]								
1886	99,405	35.0	26.9	3.0	2.9	13.3	0.8	48.0
1891	108,336	66.5	40.8	21.3	4.6	4.0	2.2	22.7
1897	439,549	51.9	25.1	14.2	5.3	10.5	9.1	23.2
1902	498,891	54.0	25.9	15.7	6.9	16.5	6.1	16.5
1906	612,177	53.2	24.6	14.1	9.7	10.3	8.1	18.7
1909	692,221	64.0	26.7	15.0	7.9	9.5	9.4	9.2
	(508,177)	(70.1)	(34.4)	(20.2)	(9.5)	(6.5)	(6.9)	(7.0)
1914	814,042	60.9	23.8	15.3	10.8	10.3	7.2	10.8
	(715,026)	(67.5)	(29.6)	(17.4)	(11.6)	(8.4)	(4.1)	(8.4)
1919	1,390,942	57.1	20.4	14.6	16.3	11.7	5.4	9.5
	(1,271,951)	(58.8)	(22.0)	(16.0)	(17.3)	(10.8)	(4.1)	(9.0)

* Furushima, p. 284.

a) Except for 1891, factory workers include those employed in factories not using mechanical power. Figures in parentheses are only those factory workers employed in factories using mechanical power.

TABLE 4

Contribution of Silk and Related Goods Exports
to Total Merchandise Exports

Period[a]	A[b] Share of silk and related goods exports in total merchandise exports (%)	B[b] Share of increase in silk and related goods exports in increase in total merchandise exports (%)
1868/70		
−1871/75	61.0	—
1871/75		(25.6)[c]
−1876/80	44.5	44.8
1876/80		
−1881/85	44.6	46.2
1881/85		
−1886/90	45.0	48.8
1886/90		
−1891/95	46.5	41.6
1891/95		
−1896/1900	44.4	25.4
1896/1900		
−1901/05	36.6	43.7
1901/05		
−1906/10	39.4	33.4
1906/10		
−1911/15	37.5	7.2
1911/15		
−1916/20	29.2	31.8
1916/20		
−1921/25	30.9	—
1921/25		(156.5)[d]
−1926/30	45.7	19.8
Average	42.1	38.4[e]

a) The basis for calculating A is the former of the two quinquennials in a given period. In calculating B, the difference between the former period and the latter period is used. (See also Note a to Table 1.)

b) Silk and related goods includes raw silk, cocoons, waste silk, dupion, peignes, spun silk yarns, and various kinds of silk fabrics (including cotton mixtures). Goods processed further such as shirts made of silk are excluded. All figures are calculated from Tōyōkeizai Shimpōsha (1935).

c) During this period the value of exports of silk and related goods decreased. The figure in parentheses was calculated from the differences between 1868/70 and 1876/80.

d) During this period the value of total merchandise exports decreased. The figure in parentheses was calculated from the differences between 1916/20 and 1926/30.

e) The figures in parentheses were used, and both 44.8 and 19.8 were not used.

processing raw materials. The development of the Japanese silk industry seems to furnish a powerful case for those who advocate industrialization via primary product exports.

The importance of primary product exports in the economic development of developing countries is largely due to the fact that these exports are their main source of foreign exchange earnings. Silk was, of course, very important as a source of foreign exchange earning in Japan as shown in Table 4. If we include tea and other farm products, farm product exports occupied 85 per cent of the total Japanese exports during 1868–72 and continued to be more than half of the total exports until toward the end of the nineteenth century. However, it should be noted that while tea ceased to be a major export item before the end of the nineteenth century,[2] the exports of silk and related goods continued to be of major importance for quite a long time.

As seen from Table 4, the average share of silk and related goods in total merchandise exports is larger than their average share in the increase in total merchandise exports, and both of these shares declined during this period. It was shown that sericultural production increased its importance in total agricultural production (Table 1), while the silk industry exports decreased in importance in the total merchandise exports (Table 4). Among the silk industry exports, both cocoon and silk-worm egg exports decreased in importance, while the exports of silk fabrics increased in importance (Table 5).

TABLE 5
Composition of Silk and Related Goods Exports*

Period	Cocoons, silk eggs, waste silk, dupion and peignes (%)	Raw silk (%)	Spun silk yarns and silk fabrics, including cotton mixture (%)	Total (%)
1868–70	38	61	0	100
1871–75	26	73	0	100
1921–25	3	83	14	100
1926–30	2	83	15	100

* Tōyōkeizai Shimpōsha (1935).

---

[2] The volume of tea exports did not decline until 1917. However, the total value of Japanese exports increased very rapidly during this period, and tea lost its position as a major export item (Tobata and Kawano, p. 137).

After World War I, silk was in keen competition with rayon, and raw silk came to be used in producing stockings rather than silk fabrics. Had there been no competition with rayon, the percentage of processed silk exports in total silk industry exports might have increased much more than it actually did. If raw silk had not found a new outlet in stocking production, on one hand, the total value of silk industry exports might not have increased as rapidly as it did, but on the other hand the percentage of processed silk exports in the total silk industry exports might have increased even more than it actually did. At any rate, the change in composition of silk and related goods exports might have been more remarkable than the actual change shown in Table 5. We can reasonably conclude that there was a strong potential for silk exports to shift from raw materials to semi-manufactured silk. The drive to increase the share of semi-manufactured silk in the total silk exports contributed to the maintenance of the importance of silk exports in the total Japanese merchandise exports.[3]

III. Conditions Favorable to Silk Production in Rural Japan

Before going into those favorable conditions in rural Japan which made possible the rapid increase in silk production and exports as shown in the preceding section, I will mention briefly the international circumstances and the conditions in non-agricultural sectors, notably factors influencing the availability of capital.

Until about 1880 Japanese silk was exported mainly to Europe. Afterwards the exportation to the United States became relatively more important. At the end of the nineteenth century 60 to 70 per cent of Japanese silk exports were destined to go to the United States. Therefore, the rise or fall of the silk manufacturing industry in the United States was one of the most important factors determining Japanese silk exports. In 1864 the United States imposed a very high import duty on silk textiles in an effort to encourage the development of the domestic silk industry. However, it was soon

---

[3] It has been emphasized that Japan's industrialization was facilitated by its ability to take advantage of elastic supplies of machinery imported from abroad even though it did not rely heavily on foreign capital imports. See, for example, papers by Tsuru (1963) and Berrill (1963). The success in expanding silk exports was, of course, an important factor in making this possible.

proven that the establishment of sericultural production and of a silk reeling industry was not economical, and the United States government decided to import raw silk. American raw silk imports increased from 3.4 million lbs. in 1884 to 7.8 million lbs. in 1894, and then to 16.4 million lbs. in 1904. Subsequently they amounted to 25.5 million lbs. in 1914, and more than 50 million lbs. in and after 1922.[4] This steady increase reflects both the rapid economic growth and the high income elasticity of demand for silk in the United States. The major exporters of raw silk to the United States in the nineteenth century were Japan, China, Italy and France, among which the keenest competition existed between China and Japan. On one hand, Italian silk was superior in quality to the Japanese, but slightly more expensive than the Japanese. On the other, Japanese silk was superior in quality to the Chinese, but slightly more expensive than the Chinese. Japanese silk could so meet American demand both in quality and price that while it was 47 per cent of the total American silk imports during the 5 years from 1896 to 1900 it came to occupy 66 per cent of the total during the 5 years from 1910 to 1914. Between the price and the quality considerations price was more important in gaining a competitive position.

Rayon production in the United States increased steadily after World War I. In 1914 it was 2.4 million lbs., but in 1922 it was 24.1 million lbs. In 1927 it increased to 75.5 million lbs., while raw silk imports in the same year were 72.7 million lbs. Because of the competition with rayon the rate of increase in raw silk imports became lower after 1920. Although the main disadvantage of silk was its sharp price fluctuations while the price of rayon remained stable, because of the quality difference between these commodities rayon could not be a substitute for silk in all its uses. Especially, in manufacturing stockings as it required glossiness and durability in the raw materials, silk easily won in competition with rayon. Thus a new and expanding market for silk was found in stocking manufacturing. If there had been no such new outlet, the importance of silk exports in the total Japanese merchandise exports would have been

---

[4] All figures are from U.S. Department of Commerce, p. 145. The same text is used in quoting rayon production figures in the next paragraph.

much less after the 1920's. In this connection it should be mentioned that World War II, "by cutting off raw silk imports, delivered a decisive blow to silk consumption and gave the synthetic fabrics an opportunity to establish themselves in the consumer's taste" (Humphrey, p. 31). In part this was the result of continuous improvements in artificial fibers and by the development of new ones such as nylon. It is to be mentioned also that as early as 1916 the United States raw silk users tried to encourage raw silk production in China, India and other oriental countries in order to weaken the monopolistic position of Japan in the world silk market (Hayakawa, pp. 324–5).

Among the conditions in the non-agricultural sectors of Japan which favored the development of silk industry, the supply of capital was most important. The silk industry was able to attract a reasonable share of the capital funds available, and since techniques of reeling remained rather simple and traditional the capital requirements were not unduly large. In Japan raw silk is classified into two categories: raw silk produced by the traditional reeling method, called *zaguri* and raw silk produced by mechanical reeling methods called *kikaiseishi*. However, of the total 666 mechanical reeling factories using 10 or more workers in 1879, the number of those using steampower was only four, the number of those using a water wheel was 552 and the remaining were driven by human power. Moreover, the reels used in the mechanical reeling factories, while termed mechanical, did not differ greatly from those used in the *zaguri* factories; they were merely a slightly improved version of the same.[5] The Tomioka Reeling Factory, a demonstration factory established by the Government in 1873, was quite modern and served as a training center, but there was no association between the number of women workers sent by each prefecture for training there and the number of mechanical reeling factories subsequently established in each prefecture (Furushima, p. 237). This suggests that the technical element might not be crucial, and in fact leading

[5] Furushima, p. 226. It should be understood that the *kikaiseishi* in this period was quite different from that in the recent years, and was more like the *zaguri* in later years. Silk by *kikaiseishi* has almost always been of higher quality than that by *zaguri* and the price of *kikaiseishi* silk has almost always been higher than that of *zaguri silk*.

experts in one traditional sericulture prefecture investigated the reason why the number of mechanical reeling factories did not increase rapidly; and their conclusion was that the main reason was not lack of technical knowledge, but lack of capital (Furushima, p. 233).

Generally speaking, the *zaguri* factories were operated mainly by silk cocoon producers themselves, while the managers in *kikaiseishi* factories did not engage in sericultural production but bought cocoons from sericulturalists. In the latter case, *urikomidonya,* who bought raw silk from local middlemen and sold it to silk exporters, financed the local middlemen. In the former case, *urikomidonya* financed either the local middlemen or the silk reeling factories. In the early Meiji period when Japanese merchants were not familiar with the exporting business, silk exporters were mainly foreign companies such as Siber Brenwald & Co., H. Siber, Jardin Matheson, and Ulysse Pilla & Co. Although they were in a somewhat monopsonistic position, there was generally keen competition among the many *urikomidonya.* In the later Meiji period several Japanese trading companies, such as Mitsui, increased their business in silk exporting. Moreover, some *urikomidonya* established fairly large-scale mechanized factories around 1890. The point to be stressed is that sharp competition dominated the reeling process and the marketing process from the silk producing region to the export ports and competition among exporters was also keen.

Why was this keen competition possible? The answer is the sufficient supply of capital for this profitable activity. Until about the early 1880's there was no difficulty in finding capital for increasing silk production. Traditional financing methods, such as discounting bills, expanded. As noted earlier, faced with increasing demand for silk from foreign countries, Japanese silk production increased very rapidly especially after the latter half of the 1880s, and the amount of capital available from traditional sources could not match this increase in production. From then on financing either by means of advance payment to the silk reeling factories or to *zaguri* farmers' cooperatives, or by means of discounting promissory notes issued by the silk reeling factories, or by other new means dominated. The most important fact to be noted in this connection is that those local banks and state banks *(kokuritsu ginkō)* which financed the silk industry received loans from the Bank of Japan.[6] The state banks were established in about 1878 in an effort to encourage Japanese industrialization, and these banks were expected to mobilize potential savings in the traditional sector of the Japanese economy for the development of the modern sector. However, faced with the shortage of total domestic mobilizable savings and with the very rapid Japanese economic development, these banks, after ten years of operation, began to depend on loans from the Bank of Japan for a part of their operation. This latter bank was established in 1882 and began to issue its notes in 1885. We call this type of loan the "Meiji over-loans" (Yoshino, pp. 174–5). These "Meiji over-loans" encouraged not only the development of the silk industry, but also the development of many other industries.

It is difficult to evaluate the magnitude of the loans that supported the expansion of the silk industry because of inconsistencies in the available data. As an indication of the order of magnitude of bank financing, it has been reported that such financing amounted to 25 to 30 million yen in 1907 (Yamaguchi, 1966, p. 31). Sericultural production in the same year amounted to 192 million yen.

Government action to set up "model factories" in the silk industry and to control the quality of raw silk and silkworm eggs were also of considerable importance. Before 1880 the government effort was concentrated on quality improvements. Already in 1868 the government had established an Inspection Office of Silkworm Eggs and Raw Silk *(Sanranshi kiito aratame dokoro)* in an effort to improve their quality as both were very important export items in this period. This institution was the predecessor of the Raw Silk Inspection Office *(Kiito kensa jo)*. In 1870 two Western-type silk reeling factories were established under government sponsorship. The raw silk produced by the *zaguri* method of reeling before 1870 was for the exclusive use of factories producing Japanese silk apparel, which demanded a different quality of raw silk from that demanded by the European textile factories. The Tomioka Silk Reeling Factory, established in 1872, was a government demonstration factory and trained many women workers. Under the programs

---

[6] In writing this part the author owes very much to Yamaguchi (1966).

encouraging employment of former *samurai (Shizoku jusan jigyo)* the government supplied a fairly large amount of capital to the former *samurai* to encourage the establishment of silk reeling factories modeled after the Tomioka factory. Many of these were not successful, however, because of insufficient working capital and other problems.

Finally, it is necessary to consider two interrelated phenomena that were of great importance in the development of sericulture and the rapid increase of silk production: one is the technological progress that took place and the other is the relative profitability of sericulture for farmers. The remarkable technical progress in sericulture, which was also important from the viewpoint of Japan's agricultural development, was a result of government action in the fields of research, education, and extension and of innovative activity by individual farmers, specialized producers of silkworm eggs, and firms in the silk industry.

In 1881 courses pertaining to sericulture were introduced in some primary schools, and two years later they were introduced in some agricultural schools too. In 1884 a Silkworm Disease Research Station *(Sanbyo shikenjo)* was established. This was the predecessor of the sericultural colleges which were established in Tokyo in 1896 and in Kyoto in 1898. The next major step was the establishment in 1911 of the Silkworm Variety Improvement Station *(Gensanshu seizojo)*. This later became the National Sericultural Experiment Station whose contribution to the development of new sericultural techniques was most remarkable.

The striking expansion of sericulture is evident in the rapid increase in the mulberry area and the spectacular expansion of cocoon production. According to the official statistics of the Ministry of Agriculture and Forestry, the index of mulberry area, with 1881–1890=100, increased to 176 in 1891–1900, 234 in 1901–1910, 307 in 1911–1920, and 371 in 1921–1930. The corresponding changes in the index of cocoon production were: 172, 263, 470, and 714 (Johnston, p. 230). There may be some overestimation of the growth rate because of underestimation of cocoon production for earlier years. And yet there is no doubt that the rate of increase in cocoon yield was high as compared with other competing crops. For example, cocoon yield per hectare increased from 205 kilograms in 1889, by which time the statistics had become more or less reliable, to 333 kilograms in 1910; the average annual rate of increase during these 21 years is 2.33 per cent—a rate which is considerably higher than that of rice yield.

So far as the farmers' behavior was rational (and we believe that it was), this record of expansion suggests the relative profitability of sericulture. It is desirable, however, to examine such direct evidence as is available. The usual concept of "profitability" needs to be qualified in this context. An important factor was that the development of sericulture made possible an increase in cash income through fuller utilization of labor within the traditional organization of production in farm households with surplus labor, a character-istic of densely populated rural Japan. During the early period sericulture was largely confined to "spring rearing" and most co-coons were harvested in June. The Japanese farmer was particularly short of cash at that season of the year, so that additional cash income became available at an especially opportune time. Moreover, the period of peak labor requirements for cocoon production is very short, just one week, and therefore this additional activity could be incorporated into the farming calendar without undue interference with other enterprises.

We can show roughly the relative profitability of sericulture in terms of gross farm values of output per unit area. The farm value of sericultural products per *tan* (approximately equal to one-tenth of a hectare) was 30 yen in 1899 and 34 yen in 1915, fluctuating within the range of 25 and 44 yen between those two years. Sub-sequently it increased very rapidly up to 148 yen in 1919 along with the rise in cocoon prices due to World War I boom. The farm value of rice per *tan* in 1899, on the other hand, was 14 yen and that of wheat or barley, both of which were dryland crops and also the main winter crops in paddy fields, was 8 or 9 yen in the same year. Mulberry was cultivated on dryland fields, so that even allowing for the additional value of summer crops, sericulture was far more profitable than other dryland farming in 1899. Even compared with rice cultivation combined with winter crops in paddy fields, which was generally the most profitable combination of enterprises at that time, sericulture was more profitable in 1899. However, in the ensuing years as the relative price of rice rose, its farm value per *tan* increased and amounted to 35 yen in 1912, which was equal to that of sericulture in that year, while the farm value of wheat or barley in the same year was 13 yen.[7] Consequently, between 1912 to 1915, sericulture became less profitable and the acreage of mulberry cultivation did not increase. This period was, however, of short duration, and following World War I sericulture became more profitable and the acreage of mulberry cultivation began to increase again.

It is to be noted that, although the price of cocoons was not unfavorable as compared with the prices of other agricultural commodities in general during the nineteenth century, it became unfavorable during the period between 1900 and 1920 (*LTES,* IX pp. 156–158). This change in the relative price certainly had an adverse effect on the profitability of sericulture. The important point, however, is that almost throughout the entire period under review, the fundamental factor that maintained the relative profitability of sericulture was not so much a favorable price for cocoons as it was the rapid and sustained progress of technology in this particular sector. In our view, expansion of the raw silk industry and accordingly the improvement of its competitive power in international trade depended heavily upon the technological progress in sericulture. In fact, it is an outstanding example of a situation in which the semi-factoral terms of trade moved much more favorably than the commodity or barter terms of trade.

This is not the place to describe this historical process of technical change in detail but its major aspects deserve special attention. Sericulture technology involves three major interrelated but separate processes of production: first, production of silkworms; second, production of cocoons by rearing silkworms; and third, production of mulberry leaves to feed the silkworms. First of all, the creation and diffusion of improved silkworms was essential for expanding this industry and this was successfully done in the early years of Meiji. The traditional silkworms raised by farmers varied widely and changed from year to year. As the requirement for higher

---

[7] These figures are from Nasu, pp. 24–25.

quality and uniformity of cocoons became more severe, there first appeared some concentration on certain indigenous varieties and then foreign varieties were introduced. In 1898, Taguchi established a sericultural research institute. Using imported silkworm eggs of outstanding varieties from France and Italy, he succeeded in breeding excellent varieties in 1903–04. Toyama demonstrated cross-breeding for practical purposes and improved F_1 hybrids became available beginning in 1912 (Ogura, pp. 541ff.). These facts suggest that the diffusion of improved varieties based on scientific methods only became possible at the end of the initial phase; therefore, a wide diffusion of the selected indigenous varieties must have been the principal response to the need for cocoons of better and more uniform quality. The government recognized the importance of quality improvement and enacted a law to curb the production of raw silk of inferior quality. However, there must have been strong incentives for farmers to shift to better varieties because of sizable premiums paid for them.[8]

Next, the invention and diffusion of "summer-fall rearing" *(kashū-san)*, i.e., the rearing of an autumn as well as a spring crop of cocoons, must be mentioned as an important technological development. As mentioned above, the spring rearing was conventional in the early years and farmers could raise cocoons only once a year. Introduction of summer-fall rearing was of great importance in enabling fuller utilization of family labor and in avoiding too much concentration of labor demand at the spring peak of labor requirements. (Labor demand for sericulture competes with the requirements for rice, wheat, and barley in the spring.) Technically this method was invented as early as 1875. According to official statistics, the ratio of summer-fall crops to that of spring crops increased from 5.5 per cent in 1886 to 14.6 per cent in 1895 and to 32.3 per cent in 1905. It should also be mentioned that various seemingly minor inventions and improvements in the traditional

---

[8] Efficiency in the silk industry was enhanced by the introduction of more economical and better controlled methods of producing silkworm eggs. Egg production came to be increasingly concentrated in a limited number of specialist firms; this process became a major factor in later years and forms another notable aspect of technological advance regarding silkworm production.

methods of rearing silkworms were in aggregate of considerable importance. To mention just one example, the method of controlling temperature was improved successively. The traditional "cool rearing" was first shifted to "warm rearing" and then a "combined method" of cool and warm rearing was invented by a progressive farmer, and this became the standard method following tests carried out at the government experiment station. Technological advance in these various aspects of sericulture contributed to increasing both the efficiency and stability of cocoon production.

Lastly, technological progress in mulberry cultivation also draws attention. Better cultural practices, varietal improvements, and higher rates of fertilization contributed to heavier production of mulberry leaves. In addition, the feeding value per unit area of mulberry was augmented by the introduction of better methods of gathering and feeding leaves. For example, methods were devised to reduce losses from excessive drying of the young mulberry leaves while also avoiding silkworm losses from diseases that thrive under high humidity. In later years even a labor-saving method such as "branch feeding" *(jōsōiku)* was introduced.

In conclusion, it should be emphasized that without this technological progress in the three related processes of production in sericulture, the relative profitability of sericulture and accordingly the rapid expansion of the silk industry could not have taken place. Expansion was also favored by the fact that the supply of capital to the processing and distributing sectors was reasonably satisfactory and those sectors were quite competitive. Thus the possibilities opened up by the growing demand for silk in foreign countries were transmitted to the sericulturalists. The combined effect of all these factors was to maintain the profitability of sericulture as compared to alternative crops—especially dryland crops—produced in Japan.

IV. Concluding Remarks

In Section II, three facts were made clear: (1) sericultural production contributed considerably to the increase in total value of Japanese agricultural production, (2) the increase in silk exports was accompanied by the development of domestic processing or manufacturing, and (3) silk was very important as a source of foreign exchange earnings in Japan for a fairly long period. Thus, there is no doubt that the exportation of silk played a crucial role in the early stage of Japanese economic development, and that Japanese experience presents a case for economic development via primary product exports. As was clear in Section III, growing world demand for silk made it possible for Japan to expand silk production and exports at a rapid pace. Fortunately, the Japanese silk industry was blessed with a sufficient supply of capital, quite competitive during the period under consideration, and price incentives played an important role from the level of sericulturalists to the point of export shipment. Even more important, with the help of the government, mainly in the fields of research and education, there was continued improvement in the level of skill and technological knowledge that made possible remarkable increases in productivity in the sericulture industry.

REFERENCES

Berrill, Kenneth, "Foreign Capital and Take-off," *The Economics of Take-off into Sustained Growth,* W. W. Rostow, ed., 1963.

Furushima, Toshio. *Growth of Japanese Agriculture and Industry (Sangyo Shi).* 1966.

Hayakawa, Naose. *Japanese Silk Industry and American Silk Weaving Industry (Hompo Sanshigyo to Beikoku Kengyo).* 1920.

Hirschman, Albert O. *The Strategy of Economic Development.* 1958.

Humphrey, Don D. *American Imports.* 1955.

Johnston, Bruce F., "Agricultural Development and Economic Transformation: A Comparative Study of the Japanese Experience," *Food Research Institute Studies,* III, No. 3 (1962).

Ministry of Agriculture and Forestry. *Historical Statistics of Food and Agriculture, 1868–1953* (Norinsho, *Norinshi Ruinen Tokeihyo, 1868–1953),* 1953.

Nakamura, James I. *Agricultural Production and the Economic Development of Japan, 1873–1922.* Princeton: Princeton University Press, 1966.

Nasu, Hiroshi. *Land Utilization in Japan-Sericulture (Hompo Tochi Riyo no Kenkyo—Soen no Bu).* 1933.

Ogura, Takekazu. *Agricultural Development in Modern Japan.* Tokyo: [Japan FAO Assn., 1963.

Ohkawa, K., Ishiwata, S., Yamada, S., Ishi, H., *Capital Stock (Shihon Sutokku), Estimates of Long-Term Economic Statistics of Japan since 1868,* III, K. Ohkawa, M. Shinohara, and M. Umemura, eds., Tokyo: Toyo Keizai Shimposha, 1966.

Tobata, Seiichi and Kawano, Shigeto, eds. *Structural Change of Agriculture in the Expanding Economy (Nihon no Keizai to Nogyo-Kozo Bunseki).* 1956.

Toyo Keizai Shimposha. *Foreign Trade of Japan, A Statistical Survey (Nihon Boeki Seiran).* 1935.

Tsuru, Shigeto, "The Take-off in Japan, 1868–1900," *The Economics of Take-off into Sustained Growth,* W. W. Rostow, ed., 1963.

Umemura, M. Yamada, S., Hayami, Y., Takamatsu, N., and Kumazaki, M. *Agriculture and Forestry (Nōringyō), Estimates of Long-Term Economic Statistics of Japan since 1868,* IX, K. Ohkawa, M. Shinohara, and M. Umemura, eds., Tokyo: Toyo Keizai Shimposha, 1966.

United States Department of Commerce. *Historical Statistics of the United States.* 1861.

Yamaguchi, Kazuo ed. *History of Japanese Industrial Finance—Silk Reeling Industry (Nihon Sangyo Kinyushi Kenkyu—Seishi Kinyu Hen).* 1966.

——. *Study of Economic Situation in Early Meiji (Meiji Zenki Keizai no Bunseki).* 1956.

Yoshino, Toshio. *History of the Bank of Japan (Nihonginkō Seido Kaikakushi).* 1962.

CHAPTER 13

DEVELOPMENT OF LONG-TERM AGRICULTURAL CREDIT†

YUZURU KATŌ

I. Introduction

The credit institutions which took care of long-term agricultural credit in the prewar period were private joint-stock banks. Since World War II, however, government corporations or special accounts of the national budget have become the long-term credit institutions for agriculture. This contrast between the prewar and postwar periods may give us the impression that drastic changes have occurred in the institutions of long-term agricultural credit. In fact, the process of change was not so drastic. This paper will show that (1) the private joint-stock banks in the prewar agricultural credit field were not purely private banks but special semi-government banks which were, on the one hand, given privileges by the government, and, on the other hand, were under its strict control, and (2) these banks were continuously being transformed into ordinary commercial banks insofar as they were increasingly run on a profit-making basis. Thus, instead of a drastic change, we conclude that the credit provision for agriculture has shifted gradually from private funds to government funds in the prewar period.

Although no attention is paid to traditional credit or short and intermediate term credit in this paper, these types of credit played important roles in the growth of agricultural production. (For a discussion of the dominant role of traditional credit in the early Meiji era, the reader is referred to Asakura and Nakamura, pp. 155–174; for short and intermediate term credit, to Ito, pp. 163–195 and Kato, pp. 13–19).

† I would like to acknowledge with gratitude the comments received from K. Ohkawa, B. F. Johnston, J. Nakamura, O. Sacay, T. W. Schultz, A. Tang, S. Ishikawa, V. Ruttan, and S. C. Hsieh.

II. Secular Improvements in Agricultural Credit

The oldest systematic survey of farmers' debt in Japan is the 1912 survey of the Ministry of Finance. Table 1 shows the balance of debt by the interest rate in 1912 and 1964 with the burden of the interest rate on the farmer being mitigated over these 50 odd years. Improvement is remarkable especially in the field of long-term credit, although the term breakdown of farm debt in 1912 was not available. Comparing the balances of long-term and intermediate debt by type of lender, it is notable that the shares of agricultural cooperative associations and of special banks or government loans increased and those of money lenders and of individuals decreased (Table 2). The fall of interest rates is connected with such changes in lender shares, although interest rates charged by each type of lender also decreased.

TABLE 1

Balance of Farmers' Debt by Rate of Interest*

(Unit: %)

	Less than 10%	10–15%	15–20%	20% and more	Inaccurate	Total
1912[a]	35.2	44.9	15.6	4.3		100.0
1964[b] Long-term and intermediate	95.9		3.5		0.6	100.0
Short-term[c]	37.3	59.9	1.1	0.2	1.5	100.0

 * Data from Ministry of Agriculture and Forestry, *Handbook of Agricultural and Forestry Finance (Nōrin Kinyū Binran)* (1953), and Ministry of Agriculture and Forestry, *Farm Household Fund Situation Survey (Nōka Shikin Dōtai Chōsa)* (1965).

 a) Calculated using balance of debt.

 b) Calculated by using borrowings. Balance of debt by rate of interest is not available.

 c) Short-term rate of interest is contracted on a daily basis; therefore, the figures are not exactly fitted to the classification in the above column.

Although we would expect long-term rates of interest generally to be higher than short-term rates of interest, Table 1 shows that long-term and intermediate rates of interest were far lower than the short-term rates of interest in 1964. This is due to long-term and intermediate credit administered by government provided either by public funds or cooperative funds which are subsidized and guar-

TABLE 2

Balance of Farmers' Debt by Type of Lender*

(Unit: %)

Lender	1912	1964	
		Long-term and intermediate	Short-term
Special banks and government loan	10.3	30.5	2.2
Other banks	17.6	0	3.9
Insurance companies	0.1	1.2	0
Cooperative	2.9	41.2^a	
associations		15.8^b	75.5^b
Money lenders	20.3	0	0
Pawn shops	1.3	0	0
Merchants	1.7	0	1.8
Mutual loan associations	8.4	0	2.5
Individuals	35.9	4.0	11.7
Others	1.6	7.3	2.4
Total	100.0	100.0	100.0

* Data from Ministry of Agriculture and Forestry, *Handbook of Agricultural and Forestry Finance (Nōrin Kinyū Binran)* (1953), and Ministry of Agriculture and Forestry, *Farm Household Fund Situation Survey (Nōka Shikin Dōtai Chōsa)* (1965).

a) Loans administered by government.

b) Loans not administered by government.

anteed by government or government-sponsored institutions to compensate for risk. However, government financial institutions did not exist, and agricultural cooperative associations were not so powerful in 1912 as today. The enlightened lenders to agriculture of that time were the special banks such as the Hypothec Bank of Japan, the Prefectural Agricultural and Industrial Banks, and the Hokkaido Development Bank which were different from ordinary commercial banks. These were long-term credit banks which issued long-term debentures and supplied long-term credit mainly to agriculturalists on the mortgage of paddy fields, upland fields, forests, salt fields, etc. Interest rates on their loans were far lower than those of other lenders, and their provision of credit at low rates of interest served to cut down the level of interest rates of other lenders (Table 3). It can be said that the establishment of these long-term credit banks marked the beginning of improvements in agricultural credit.

TABLE 3
Interest Rates on Loans Secured by Real Estate
(Selected Years: 1912–1940)*

(Unit: %)

Year	Individuals	Ordinary commercial banks	HBJ[a]
1912	11.40	9.30	7.50
1916	11.66	8.50	7.40
1921	11.52	11.10	7.80
1926	11.74	10.80	7.70
1930	11.35	9.60	7.20
1935	10.40	8.20	6.50
1940	8.92	5.90	5.60

* Data from Bank of Japan, *Hundred-year Statistics of the Japanese Economy* (*Meijiikō Honpō Keizai Tōkei*), 1966, pp. 260–1.
a) Hypothec Bank of Japan.

III. Special Banks to Promote Development

When Japan opened her doors to the outside world and took her first step towards modern economic development, she tried to introduce Western technology and institutions and planned to achieve rapid economic development in order to catch up with the West. To this end the government used to guide, to protect and to intervene in industries. Special banks were established by specific acts prescribing their specific aims as financial organs which were to provide the credit necessary for the pursuance of policies for industrialization *(shokusan kōgyō seisaku)*. While, on the one hand, the government gave them privileges such as subscription, subsidies and the issue of debentures, on the other hand, it severely regulated their business operations. The names of the special banks established by 1918 and their years of establishment are as follows: Yokohama Specie Bank (Yokohama Shōkin Ginkō), 1880; Bank of Japan (Nippon Ginkō), 1882; Hypothec Bank of Japan (Nippon Kangyō Ginkō), 1897; Prefectural Agricultural and Industrial Banks (Nōkō Ginkō), 1897–1900; Bank of Taiwan (Taiwan Ginkō), 1899; Hokkaido Development Bank (Hokkaidō Takushoku Ginkō), 1899; Industrial Bank of Japan (Nippon Kōgyō Ginkō), 1902; Bank of Korea (Chōsen Ginkō), 1911; and Korea Development Bank (Chōsen Shokusan Ginkō), 1918.

The banks for agricultural credit were the Hypothec Bank of Japan (HBJ), the 46 Prefectural Agricultural and Industrial Banks (PAIB's), and the Hokkaido Development Bank (HDB). The government guaranteed the HBJ a subsidy for dividends which did not exceed 5 per cent of the paid-in capital for 10 years after its establishment and allowed it to issue bonus-bearing debentures, a privilege that was not allowed to any other bank.[1] The central government granted the prefectural governments funds which were to be used for subscriptions to PAIB's on the stipulation that it not exceed one third of their paid-in capital. PAIB's were exempted from paying dividends to the capital of prefectural governments for 5 years following their establishment. The PAIB's were authorized to issue debentures while receiving deposits as was the case with the HDB. The HDB's capital was subscribed by the government until it exceeded one million yen, for 10 years after its establishment dividends to government capital were exempted, being later added to reserves. But in contrast to this operational leeway, all these banks were obliged to obtain government approval when they intended to revise their articles, to open new branch offices, to change the maximum loan rate of interest, to pay dividends, and to issue debentures. The government appointed directors, dispatched comptrollers, and could at any time order these banks to present their records for government inspection.

Many of the institutions mentioned above were established in the 1896–1902 period of national euphoria that followed Japan's victory in the Sino-Japanese War (1894–1895) and served to stimulate economic development. For example, the number of companies increased from 2,104 in 1894 to 8,612 in 1902, and their paid-in capital increased from 148 million yen in 1894 to 879 million yen in

---

[1] In order to provide long-term agricultural credit with low rates of interest, the bank must issue debentures with low rates of interest. The bonus-bearing debenture was adopted for such a purpose. The lucky debenture holder received a bonus determined by lot; individuals who were prone to gamble were induced to purchase such a debenture. However, the government prohibited gambling except for horseracing at that time. Therefore, the government permitted only HBJ and no other bank to issue such debentures. The rate of interest on the HBJ loans has been far lower than that on loans of the other banks, although the HBJ loan was of far longer term than that of the other banks (See Table 3).

1902; likewise, the number of banks increased from 864 in 1894 to 2,323 in 1902. In comparison with both previous and subsequent periods, the growth in the number of companies and their paid-in capital was remarkable during the years 1894–1902 (Table 4). The foundation of agricultural policy was also set in this period with principal agricultural legislation being enacted as follows: the Silk Worm Eggs Inspection Act (1897), the Forest Act (1897), the Agricultural Society Act (1899), the Fertilizer Regulation Act (1899), the Land Improvement Act (1899), the Livestock Growers Associations Act (1900), and Industrial Cooperative Associations Act (1900) (Higashiura, p. 151).

TABLE 4

Growth of Number of Companies and their Paid-in
Capital (Selected Years: 1886–1910)*

Year	Number of companies	Paid-in capital	Number of banks
1886	1,655	91^a mil. yen	357
1894	2,104	148	864
1902	8,612	879	2,323
1910	12,308	1,481	2,144

* Bank of Japan, *Hundred-year Statistics of the Japanese Economy (Meijiikō Honpō Keizai Tōkei)*, pp. 194, 325.
a) Figure of 1889.

Several of the special agricultural credit banks that were established in the 1896–1900 period were first proposed at much earlier dates. The first special agricultural bank was proposed in 1881 by Matsukata, Minister of Internal Affairs at that time and later Minister of Finance. He advocated the establishment of three types of banks: a central bank, a development bank, and savings banks. The central bank was to re-discount only short-term paper held by commercial banks. The development bank was to specialize in long-term loans to agriculture and industry while commercial banks were to specialize in short-term loans. Savings banks were to specialize in mobilizing small personal savings and it was this type of development bank which later served as a prototype of the HBJ. The Prefectural Agricultural and Industrial Banks appeared first in government thinking, concerning the banking system around 1890, but their establishment was postponed until after the Sino-Japanese War period for the following reasons: First, the Japanese economy had suffered from serious inflation just after the Meiji Restoration, particularly following the Satsuma Rebellion in 1877. Matsukata established a central bank and pursued a deflationary policy through measures such as the redemption of inconvertible paper money and a balanced budget. Redemption of inconvertible paper money ended in 1886, and the price level was re-stabilized at that of 1880. Business activity was again stimulated resulting in a subsequent rise in the price level. In order to prevent inflation and to encourage capital formation it was decided that the long-term debentures of these banks should be purchased with savings which were, prior to the establishment of the bank, judged to be inadequate. Second, the government did not have enough funds to subsidize these banks. In August 1895, Matsukata presented to the government his opinion *(Zaisei Ikensho)* on the policy to guide the postwar management of the national economy in which he proposed to establish the HBJ and PAIB's again. After the Sino-Japanese War a part of the indemnity from China, amounting to some 360 million yen, was appropriated for the HBJ subsidy and the PAIB's subscriptions (HBJ, 1953, pp. 121–2).

IV. Activity of Special Banks and Their Gradual Transformation

The post-Sino-Japanese War policy for "managing the national economy" *(sengo keiei)* had a different character than that of the policy for industrialization in the period immediately following the Meiji Restoration *(shokusan kōgyō)*. Under the *shokusan kōgyō* policy, the government enjoyed a wide range of prerogatives which even allowed it to intervene in industrial decision making. However, under the *sengo keiei* policy, the government was more restrained and confined its direct guidance and intervention to military and heavy industries such as iron and steel and munitions. Industries which were able to stand on their own feet obtained freedom from the direct control of the government.[2]

Generally speaking, businessmen wanted more freedom and

hesitated to borrow funds under the strict supervision of government in the period following the Sino-Japanese War (HBJ, 1953a, p. 123). Therefore, these special banks were established not as government-owned but as joint-stock banks, even though they were not of a strictly private nature. Because they had obtained privileges from the government and were under its strict control as mentioned before, they could better be called semi-government banks, although legally speaking, they were established as private banks. This decision was also influenced by the fact that a considerable number of landlords who were men of wealth and of intelligence in the rural districts had been interested in agriculture and had acted as entrepreneurs by providing capital to their tenants playing a leading role in land improvement projects and in conferences where improved techniques were introduced and discussed. At the same time, increases in the efficiency of agricultural investment were sought through the adoption of modern agricultural technology such as variety improvement, application of fertilizer, and land improvement. We might recall that raw silk and tea were major export items of that period, and even rice was exported.[3]

Such being the situation, it was believed that joint-stock banks would provide enough agricultural credit from real estate mortgages if organized as described above and that the extension of such agricultural credit would increase agricultural productivity. In fact, however, the ratio of the balance of agricultural loans to the balance of total loans tended to decline as shown in Table 5. In other words, these agricultural credit banks which were established as such by specific bank acts shifted their focus towards non-agricultural projects and preferred non-agricultural loans to agricultural loans.[4] It

[2] Under the shokusan kōgyō policy initiated in about 1880, the government used to transfer businesses it owned to private companies since it appeared that the businesses had the ability to stand on their own feet. Such transfers were also due to a deflation policy begun in the same year. Representative industries in which many firms were transferred to private companies were textiles, marine transportation, and mining (HBJ, 1953a: pp. 56–61).

[3] Rice was exported up to the 1888–1892 period.

[4] According to Table 5, the share of the balance of agricultural loans in the total balance of loans was already as low as about 50 per cent in the case of the HBJ and 69 per cent in the case of the PAIB's in 1910. The reasons are as follows: First, the purpose of these banks was to provide credit for formation of

TABLE 5

Ratio of Balance of Agricultural Loans^a to Balance of
Total Loans (Selected Years: 1910–1945)*

(Unit: %)

Year	HBJ	PAIB's
1910	47.2	69.0
1915	50.1	67.3
1920	34.3	51.4
1925	34.1	41.5
1930	41.4	42.8
1935	41.2	37.9
1940	35.4	
1945	7.3	

* Data from Ministry of Agriculture and Forestry, *Handbook of Agricultural and Forestry Finance (Nōrin Kinyū Binran)* (1953).

a) Agricultural loans include loans to farmers, agricultural companies, land-improvement associations, agricultural cooperative associations, agricultural societies, and livestock grower's associations.

was widely recognized that hypothec credit based on the mortgage of rural real estate was not always agricultural credit, and funds which were mobilized from the mortgage of rural real estate were often appropriated for non-agricultural purposes.

There were three main reasons for these unforeseen results: First, the rate of growth of non-agricultural industries was much more rapid than that of agriculture. The share of agricultural income (including income from forestry and fisheries) in national income decreased from 48.0 per cent in 1896 to 35.9 per cent in 1918 as the role of the city was increasing in the process of economic development. The ratio of population in the cities which had more than

capital for agriculture and industry. It should be noted that industry in those days was not modern manufacturing industry but ancillary cottage industry in rural districts. In this connection it should be noted that raw silk and tea were the leading export goods in the early stages of Japanese economic development. Second, the textile industry suffered seriously in 1898 due to the depression which followed the Sino-Japanese War, and the government tried to rescue textile companies. This task should be pursued by industrial banks; however, the Industrial Bank of Japan was not established yet. Therefore the government ordered the HBJ to provide rescue loans to such industries. Since these loans were of huge amounts and were on a long-term basis, the shares of agricultural loans were lower in the early days of HBJ (See Appendix, Table 2) (HBJ, 1953a, pp. 180–186).

50,000 inhabitants to total population increased from 9.4 per cent in 1898 to 16.5 per cent in 1918. Consequently, the demand for urban real estate loans increased very much. According to the original acts which regulated the HBJ and PAIB's, these banks were to be restricted to loans for investment in agriculture or in ancillary industries. However, the movements against such restrictions gained power, and these restrictions were finally removed with the amendment of these acts in 1911.

Second, these joint-stock banks were run on a profit motive basis and preferred non-agricultural loans to agricultural loans. This was in part due to the fact that agricultural borrowers were scattered and located far from bank offices. Furthermore, the average size of these loans was relatively small, and therefore, the cost of lending per unit of loanable funds was higher than that of non-agricultural loans. Also, the agricultural loan entailed greater risk because agricultural prices and output were less stable.

Third, the landlords, i.e. the men of wealth who were the real agricultural entrepreneurs, gradually became rentiers in the process of economic development. The more they engaged in non-agricultural activities, purchased stock or debentures, deposited money in commercial banks, and were interested in political problems, the less they used the funds for the purpose for which they were borrowed. The increase in the number of companies and banks as shown above depended much on the capital of these landlords. Consequently, funds continued to flow out of agriculture into the non-agricultural sector. For example, when the HBJ began to supply credit in 1897, it decided not to approve applications for loans under 10,000 yen.[5] The bank adopted this policy as a means of risk aversion, since it felt that loans to peasants were more risky than those made to landlords and/or rich owner-operators. But at the same time the bank expected that landlords who were able to borrow such large amounts of money would naturally invest in agriculture. As a matter of fact, the average size of loans exceeded

---

[5] The maximum amount of secured loans of the bank was two thirds of the appraisal value. Generally speaking, the appraisal value of the security was about two thirds of the market price of the security. Since the price of paddy fields was about 1,500 yen per hectare, borrowers were obliged to mortgage about 15 hectares of paddy field in order to borrow 10 thousand yen.

this amount, but tended to decrease over time (Table 6). However taking into account that at that time farmers were tenants or owner-operators of small farms and that the landlords were becoming rentiers, it is doubtful that loans of such size were used for real investment in agriculture.[6]

TABLE 6

Average Size of Agricultural Loans of HBJ

(Selected Years: 1897–1907)*

(Unit: 1,000 yen)

End of f.y.	Direct loans	Indirect loans[a]
1897	31.2	
1902	17.2	1.7
1907	12.0	1.4

* Hypothec Bank of Japan, *History of the Hypothec Bank of Japan (Nippon Kangyō Ginkōshi)* (1953), p. 216.
a) Loan of HBJ entrusted to PAIB.

Such being the case, the necessity of providing unsecured credit to peasants who had either no land or only smallholdings of their own and to their associations (such as land improvement associations and industrial cooperative associations, the forerunner of agricultural cooperative associations) was recognized by the government. Although the HBJ, PAIB's and HDB had granted unsecured loans to municipal governments, irrigation associations and other groups of peasants[7] from the time of their establishment, the total balance of these loans had remained relatively small in comparison with hypothec loans (Table 12 below). As mentioned above,

[6] In 1908, 50 per cent of total paddy field and 40.4 per cent of upland field were cultivated by tenants. The ratio of the number of owner-operators to the total number of farmers was 33.3 per cent, that of part owner-operator, part-tenant 39.1 per cent, and that of tenant 27.6 per cent. The ratio of the number of landowners who owned less than 1 hectare to the total number of landowners (including landowners who did not cultivate alone) was 72.2 per cent and only 0.9 per cent of landowners who owned more than 10 hectares. (Ministry of Agriculture and Commerce, 1918, pp. 1 and 3)
[7] At the time of establishment of the PAIB's, the Industrial Cooperative Associations Act was not yet enacted. Therefore, the PAIB's in each prefecture also served as industrial cooperative associations. They were able to grant unsecured loans to groups of peasants whose membership exceeded 20 and whose debt was guaranteed jointly.

the Land Improvement Act was enacted in 1899 and revised in 1909 in order to promote the establishment of land improvement associations, and the Industrial Cooperative Associations Act was enacted in 1900 with a large number of these associations being established throughout the country. Since these were the organizations of cultivators, the necessity of providing them with sufficient unsecured credit was widely recognized.

TABLE 7
Dispersion of Interest Rates[a] by District
(Selected Years: 1892–1921)*

(Unit: %)

	1892	1897	1902	1907	1912	1916	1921
Loan on deeds							
Banks in Tokyo	9.20	11.90	12.05	12.78	12.05	12.05	13.18
All banks, average	14.09	13.91	13.91	11.50	11.21	10.91	13.69
Absolute differences	4.89	2.01	1.86	1.28	0.84	1.14	0.51
Discounts							
Banks in Tokyo	12.05	11.64	11.86	11.68	12.78	10.59	14.60
All banks, average	14.42	14.78	14.34	11.53	11.32	10.77	12.70
Absolute differences	2.37	3.14	2.48	0.15	1.46	0.18	1.90

* Data from Bank of Japan, *Hundred-year Statistics of the Japanese Economy (Meijiikō Honpō Keizai Tōkei)* (1966), pp. 260–1.
a) Highest rate of interest.

On the other hand, the number of banks increased rapidly in those years. Since almost all of them were commercial banks, they served to absorb funds from rural areas and then channel these funds into the cities (Kato, 1966). The resulting dispersion of the loan rates of interest was remarkable (Table 7), and agriculturalists and representatives of rural interests scored this disparity in the credit situation with the postal savings system chosen as the target of their criticism. Postal savings offices were government institutions and were established in every city, town and village; they received the deposits of people who hesitated to deposit money in banks because of the small size of their accounts and their distance from the banking offices. The deposits of the postal savings offices were held in the Deposit Bureau of the Ministry of Finance and were used mainly for purchasing government bonds (Table 8). Although

TABLE 8

Sources and Uses of Deposit Bureau Funds

(Selected Years: 1894–1924)*

(Unit: Million yen and %)

	End of fiscal year	Postal savings deposits	Other deposits	Reserves and Miscellaneous	Total	As reference	
						Deposits of all banks	Deposits of all ordinary banks
Sources	1894	24(82)	2 (8)	3 (10)	30(100)	134	49
	1905	55(63)	20(23)	12(14)	88(100)	974	693
	1917	462(77)	63(10)	77(13)	603(100)	5,146	3,233
	1924	1,137(69)	279(17)	238(14)	1,656(100)	10,232	8,093
	1931	2,773(81)	356(10)	293 (9)	3,422(100)	11,093	8,269

	End of fiscal year	Government securities and loans to government	Local Government securities	Public corporation bonds and bank debentures	Securities of foreign countries	Deposits and cash	Total
Uses	1894	23(79)	—	—	—	6(21)	30(100)
	1905	39(44)	—	3 (4)	34(39)	11(13)	88(100)
	1917	126(21)	16 (3)	162(27)	190(31)	108(18)	603(100)
	1924	498(30)	195(12)	580(35)	170(10)	210(13)	1,656(100)
	1931	1,515(44)	645(19)	1,000(29)	18 (1)	241 (7)	3,422(100)

* Ministry of Finance, *History of Development of Financial Institutions (Kinyū-kikan Hattatsushi)* (1949,) pp. 414–7, Bank of Japan, *Hundred-year Statistics of the Japanese Economy (Meijiikō Honpō Keizai Tōkei)* (1966), pp. 194, 199, 201.
a) Numbers in parentheses indicate percentage.

postal savings deposits of any one person were small, the total amounted to a huge sum. The ratio of the balance of postal savings deposits and other deposits of the Deposit Bureau to the balance of deposits of all ordinary banks was 53.1 per cent in 1894 and was 10.8 per cent in 1905 (Table 8). It was estimated by the Ministry of Posts and Telecommunication that about 30 per cent of the deposits of the postal savings office was from agriculturalists (Table 9).

In response to this situation, the Deposit Bureau of the Ministry of Finance began to purchase debentures carrying low rates of interest of the HBJ, PAIB's, and HDB and from 1909 ordered these banks to grant unsecured loans at considerably lower rates of

TABLE 9

Shares of Postal Savings of Agriculturalist in Postal Savings
(Selected Years: 1897–1907)*

	Number of deposit account holders (1,000)			Postal savings deposits (1,000 yen)		
	Agriculture (1)	Total (2)	(1)/(2)	Agriculture (1)	Total (2)	(1)/(2)
Mar. 1897	374	1,273	29.4	8,577	28,251	30.4
Mar. 1902	654	2,402	27.2	7,199	27,971	25.7
Mar. 1907	2,145	7,414	28.9	20,598	79,956	25.8

* Data from Postal Savings Bureau of the Ministry of Posts and Telecommunication, *Outlines of Postal Money Orders and Savings Banks (Yūseishō Yūbinkawase Chokin Jigyō Gaiyō)* (Dec. 1897), p. 81; (May 1903), p. 104; (Apr. 1908), p. 120.

interest than the market rate[8] to land improvement associations, industrial cooperative associations, fishermen's associations, Forest Grower associations, and Livestock Grower associations. This was a tied loan of the government and was called Ordinary Funds for Local Areas *(Futsu Chihō Shikin)*.[9]

Using this government fund, the government tried from that time to promote the provision of unsecured, low-interest credit to cultivators to establish an infrastructure for agriculture. Since the original idea about the business of these agricultural credit banks was to absorb private funds from the capital market and to provide

[8] The rate of interest on this loan was far lower (about 1–3 per cent lower in the case of the HBJ) than that on the properly secured loans of these banks. Since the postal savings bank was a government institution, people had much confidence in it. Therefore, people used to deposit there at rates of interest lower than the market rate. In addition, the administration costs of the postal savings bank had until 1924 been covered by an appropriation from the General Account of the National Budget; therefore, this loan was a subsidized, low interest loan.

[9] The rules of utilization of these funds were established in 1909. From 1909 these funds were supplied continuously. From 1923 extraordinary Funds for Local Areas *(Tokubetsu Chihō Shikin)* were supplied in case of emergencies such as earthquake, flood, frost, and other disasters. It was also supplied year by year during and after the agricultural depression in the 1930's as relief loans such as loans for purchase of fertilizer, loans for refunding high interest rate bearing debts, etc. This was also supplied through subscription to bonds of municipal governments and debentures of special banks (Ministry of Agriculture and Forestry, 1953, p. 5; Ministry of Finance, 1949, p. 413).

secured credit to landlords, we can say that the principle of agricultural credit policy had been revised.

The balance of agricultural loans of the special agricultural banks expanded largely thanks to these government funds. Taking again the HBJ as an example, we can show to what extent the principal, unsecured agricultural loans depended on government funds (Appendix, Table 1). If we break down the balance of total loans into secured loans, the shares of the balance of agricultural loans were far higher in unsecured loans than in secured loans (Appendix, Table 2). In the case of secured loans, the funds supplied were mainly obtained from the general capital market by issuing debentures. Therefore, it is not erroneous to say that the ratio of the balance of agricultural loans to the balance of total loans of these banks would have decreased more if the Deposit Bureau had not purchased the special debentures carrying low rates of interest of these banks. Such being the situation in the functioning of the long-term agricultural credit banks in the prewar period, we could say, with some exaggeration, that government funds were used for agricultural loans and private funds for non-agricultural loans.

The share of the balance of unsecured loans in the balance of total loans of those banks tended to increase. Since unsecured loans based on government funds were often used by the government as one of the relief measures in rural areas, the loans increased rapidly in depression years such as 1920, 1927 and especially in the 1930s (Table 10).[10]

Turning briefly to the liability side of these banks, we see that the

---

[10] Until 1937 the accumulated amount of loans of the Ordinary Fund for Local Areas was about 420 million yen, and that of the Extraordinary Fund of Local Areas was about 1,350 million yen. The dominant part of both funds has been within the jurisdiction of the Ministry of Agriculture and Forestry. The balance of loans of both funds within jurisdiction of the Ministry of Agriculture and Forestry was about 360 million yen at the end of July of 1936. The balance of agricultural loans of special banks was 381 million yen, 209 million yen, and 76 million in the case of the HBJ, PAIB's, and HDB, respectively, by the end of F.Y. 1936. The balance of loans of Agricultural Cooperative Associations (short-term credit institutions for agriculture) was about 1,048 million yen at the end of F.Y. 1936. The relative weight of government funds was quite large as shown by the above figures (Ministry of Agriculture and Forestry, 1953 pp. 6, 211, 227, 232, and 236).

TABLE 10

The Ratio of the Balance of Unsecured Long-Term Loans to the Balance
of Long-term Loans of HBJ (Selected Years: 1911–32)*

(Unit: 1,000 yen)

	Balance of Long-term unsecured loans (1)	Balance of long-term loans (2)	$(1)/(2) \times 100$
1911	32,976	132,777	24.8%
1917	61,781	223,769	27.6
1920	103,520	328,139	31.5
1924	191,147	693,455	27.6
1927	250,932	800,963	31.3
1930	343,192	1,062,182	32.3
1931	343,786	1,077,862	31.9
1932	364,475	1,122,376	32.5

* Data from Hypothec Bank of Japan, *Statistics of the Hypothec Bank of Japan* (*Nippon Kangyō Ginkō Tōkei Shiryō*) (1953), pp. 22, 33.

shares of special debentures (*Tokushū Saiken*)[11] in total debentures tended to increase up to the 1930's. Although shares of all debentures in total outside capital tended to decrease, that of borrowings from the Deposit Bureau and the deposits from the public tended to increase through the whole prewar period (Appendix, Table 3). Here we can see the process of transformation of the special debenture banks into ordinary deposit banks, a tendency that was particularly remarkable in the period after 1937. Consequently, the share of short-term loans in total loans increased, and investment in securities (chiefly government bonds) and deposits with the Deposit Bureau and other agencies increased (Appendix, Table 4). Such changes in the balance sheet corresponded to the rapid decrease in the share of agricultural loans in total loans as shown in Table 5.

The focus of economic policy was on the encouragement of munitions industries during the war (1937–45). In this period the special bank which played the central role was not the hypothec banks but the Industrial Bank of Japan, and the HBJ, PAIB's and HDB were assigned by the government to auxiliary roles. With the remarkable increase of short-term loans, both the commercial and industrial loans of these banks increased rapidly. However, these

[11] See note to Appendix 3.

loans were chiefly made to small and medium size businesses that played a supporting role in wartime production. At the same time, these banks were asked to absorb floating purchasing power both through deposits and debentures, to purchase government bonds in order to prevent wartime inflation and to redeposit in the Deposit Bureau and other agencies.

FIGURE 1

Farmers Disposable Income and Per Capita
Consumption 1924-41 at Current Prices*

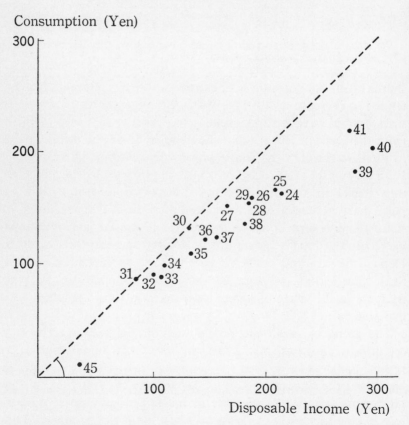

*   Data from Ministry of Agriculture and Forestry, *Farm Household Economy Survey* (*Nōka Keizai Chōsa*), 1925-1942.

FIGURE 2
Farm Household Income and Investment[a]
in Farms (1924-41 at Current Prices)*

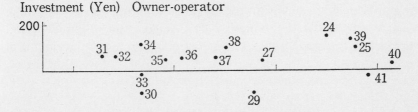

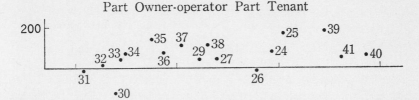

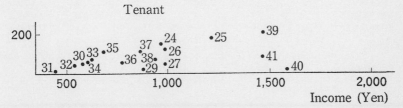

Income (Yen)

* Data from Ministry of Agriculture and Forestry, *Farm Household Economy Survey (Nōka Keizai Chōsa)*, 1925-42.
a) Figures of investment in 1928 were not available.

As the government tried to maintain food production and to collect as much of the produce from the farmers as possible, the relative prices of agricultural products, and therefore the nominal incomes of farmers, increased. However, the consumption of farmers and their investment in agriculture were stable during wartime. This is due to certain characteristic features of peasant economy as well as to the shortage of consumption goods and of agricultural equipment caused by an economic policy which favored the allocation of production resources to munition industries (See Figures 1 and 2.). In this situation, these agricultural banks absorbed surplus funds from agriculture and poured them into the non-agricultural sector either by granting loans directly or by purchasing government bonds and depositing them in the Deposit Bureau and other places. Some of the statistical evidence relating to these organs for "pumping up" funds is shown in Table 11. Comparing the period of the post-World-War-I depression (1921–33) and the wartime period (1938–45), the share of sales of *tai-ken* debentures[12] in agricultural prefectures, as well as the amount of total issues of the debentures, increased remarkably during wartime.

TABLE 11
Issues and Purchases of *tai-ken* Debentures by Type of Prefecture*

(Unit: million yen and %)

Period	Industrial prefectures[a]	Agricultural prefectures[b]	Total	Industrial prefectures[a]	Agricultural prefectures[b]	Total
	(mil. yen)	(mil. yen)	(mil. yen)	(%)	(%)	(%)
1921–1933	278.9	125.2	404.1	69.0	31.0	100.0
1938–1945	166.7	544.8	711.5	23.4	76.6	100.0
1897–1945	601.3	733.0	1,334.0	45.1	54.9	100.0

* Data from Hypothec Bank of Japan, *Statistics of the Hypothec Bank of Japan (Nippon Kangyō Ginkō Tōkei Shiryō)* (1953), pp. 64–9.
a) Tokyo, Osaka, Kyoto, Aichi, Kanagawa, Hyōgo, Fukuoka.
b) Rest of the country.

V. The Post World War II System of Long-Term Agricultural Credit

As shown in the preceding section, special banks for agriculture were being transformed into ordinary banks and into banks for non-agriculture ever since the time of their establishment. In fact, one could say that they had already become ordinary banks in 1950 through the abrogation of the acts by which they had been established.[13]

The reasons for this change were as follows: First, these banks could not have issued long-term debentures due to hyper-inflation

---

[12] See note to Appendix 3.
[13] 46 PAIB's had merged in the HBJ over four rounds, 1921–23, 1927–30, 1934–36, 1944; therefore only two special banks, that is, HBJ and HDB, remained in the field of long-term agricultural credit.

which occurred shortly after the war. Second, banks could not own agricultural land due to the land reform, since they were not themselves cultivators. Although granting loans on the mortgage of agricultural land was not prohibited, the government had the right to purchase land at official, cheap prices when it was foreclosed and no cultivator offered to purchase it. In addition, rent rates have been officially set at far lower levels in the postwar period than that in the prewar period. In the prewar period, when competitive rent rates had been maintained at high levels due to the stiff competition for agricultural land, the amortization of the landlords' debt was secured by either the high level of rent or the landlord's profit from non-agricultural investment. In the postwar period, when the landlord had been done away with and rent rates had been set by the government at low levels, it was not profitable for banks to grant hypothec loans to peasants. Third, the special banks were judged as undesirable by the occupation authorities, since they had added a certain militaristic flavor in their role as promoter of rapid economic development. Special banks were on the verge of deciding whether they would remain as debenture-issuing banks without the said privileges which had been given to them by the government or to become deposit banks. Under these circumstances, both HBJ and HDB were transformed into ordinary banks (HBJ, 1953, pp. 729–824).

However, promotion of food production was of the utmost importance following World War II. Population had increased due to increases in the birth rate and the return of people from the colonies, but food production decreased due to the wartime disinvestment in agriculture and to the frequent occurrence of disasters. At the same time, the number of people trying to find jobs in the agricultural sector had increased because of the great dislocation of the industrial sector.

The role of the government in public investment in agriculture has become more important in the postwar period as shown in Table 12. However, the financial burden on the peasants and their organizations has still been high. Taking note of the demise of both the landlords and special banks which had acted as promotors of investment in the prewar period, the Rehabilitation Finance Corporation, the Aid's Counter-part Funds and the Central Cooperative Bank for Agriculture and Forestry moved in to supply the long-term credit. Since their business in the field of long-term agricultural credit was provisional, the total balance of long-term agricultural loans was small. Therefore, a strong and permanent system to take care of the supply of long-term agricultural credit was required (Agriculture Forestry and Fisheries Finance Corporation, pp. 22–35).

TABLE 12

Public Investment^a in Agriculture and its Sources of Funds*

(Unit: 100 Million yen and %)

	Central government	Local government	Land-lords	Peasants and peasant organizations	Total
1934–1936	29.8		62.7	59.5	152.0
(average)	(19.6)		(41.3)	(39.1)	(100.0)
1953–1955	117	76		61	254.0
(average)	(46.1)	(29.9)		(24.0)	(100.0)

* Data from Ministry of Agriculture and Forestry, *White Paper on Agriculture and Forestry (Nōrin Hakusho)* (1957), p. 12.

a) Public works and private investment administered by government at 1934–36 producers goods prices.

In 1951, the Special Account for Agriculture, Forestry, and Fisheries Finance was set up as the forerunner of the present Agriculture, Forestry, and Fisheries Finance Corporation established in 1953. Its funds are from the General Account and the Industrial Investment Special Account, but are also borrowed from the Trust Fund Bureau Special Account[14] and the Post Office Life Insurance and the Postal Annuity Special Accounts. It makes loans on a long-term basis for the establishment and maintenance of owner-operators, for land improvements, whose installation is to be used jointly, and for public regulation of tree cutting, etc. With regards to the provision of credit to settlers of newly cultivated lands, the Special Account for Settlement Finance was established

---

[14] The Deposit Bureau was transformed into the Trust Fund Bureau in 1951.

in 1946, and its funds are now taken from the General Account and the Trust Fund Bureau.

So far we have explained the important role of government institutions in the field of long-term agricultural credit in the postwar period. Their overwhelming share in the long-term and intermediate debts of farmers was shown previously in Table 2. In comparison with this postwar situation, the joint-stock banks had taken care of long-term and intermediate agricultural credit in the prewar period. Therefore it seems to us that the postwar situation differs from the prewar situation with substantial changes occurring between these two periods. As explained in preceding sections, however, the government has been playing an important role in the field of long-term agricultural credit since the 1900's when the modern agricultural credit system was set up in Japan.

Although intermediate credit is not the main subject of this paper, a few points merit attention. We could say with only slight exaggeration that there was no demand for this type of credit, important for the introduction of machinery, livestock and related equipment, in the prewar period. Since there was plenty of underemployed labor in rural districts and land-saving and labor-intensive techniques such as the improvement of varieties, heavy application of fertilizers, and land improvement were the dominant techniques employed, there was no considerable demand for agricultural machinery in the prewar period. In addition, since income per capita was low, there was no considerable demand for livestock products in the prewar period. However, the introduction of machinery and livestock in agricultural production has been remarkable in the postwar period as a result of the rapid out-flow of labor from agriculture and the changes in food patterns that have accompanied rapid economic growth. Consequently, as the problems of supply of intermediate agricultural credit have mounted, the role of government in this field has become increasingly important. This type of credit is supplied mainly by the agricultural cooperative credit system (Kato, 1966) and supplemented by other financial institutions such as commercial banks and mutual banks. Although the funds absorbed by deposits in these organs are in this case not governmental but private, the government plays an important role through subsidies and the guarantee of debt[15] (Table 2). The rate of increase of such agricultural credit provided by the Agricultural Modernization Fund *(Nōgyō Kindaika Shikin)* which is administered by the government has been larger than that of credit which is not administered by the government; the former tends to substitute for the latter. The flow of private funds into the non-agricultural sector from the agricultural sector through the agricultural cooperative credit system is shown in Appendix Table 5 (Kato, 1966).

VI. Summary and Conclusion

The long-term credit banks for agriculture were set up as financial organs for agricultural development during 1896–1900. They were not ordinary banks but special banks which were given privileges by the government such as the subscription of capital, issue of debentures, and subsidies for dividends which enabled them to provide longer-term credit at lower rates of interest than could ordinary banks.

They were none the less not treated as government corporations. They were established as private joint-stock banks on the premise that only such a free enterprise system would allow the landlords to fulfill their role as the entrepreneurs in agriculture. Agricultural development was thought possible if these banks could absorb private funds through issuing debenture and then provide long-term credit on a paying basis to landlords on mortgages of paddy field, upland field, forests, etc. However, with the rapid growth of the non-agricultural sector, the landlords tended to become rentiers, and the share of agricultural loans in total loans of these banks tended to decline. Secured loans to landlords were not always used for capital formation in agriculture, but often used for non-agricultural investment. Therefore, in 1909 the government began to furnish funds to these banks in order to provide unsecured loans

---

[15] For example, the rate of interest of the Agriculture Modernization Fund is 6 per cent in 1967; however, the cost of cooperative funds is estimated as 9 per cent by the government. Therefore, the government subsidizes as much as 3 per cent of this fund for the cooperative associations. When a borrower could not pay to the lender, the Prefectural Agricultural Credit Insurance Associations *(Nōgyō Shinyō Kikin Kyōkai)* would pay up to 80 per cent of the amount to the lender on behalf of borrower.

for land improvement, cooperative associations, and municipal government, thus revising the principle of agricultural credit policy, Since that time it can be said, although somewhat of an exaggeration, that the special banks channeled private funds absorbed from the general capital market to non-agriculture and government funds to agriculture. During the whole of the prewar period, the banks themselves tended to change into ordinary and non-agricultural banks.

Land reform, inflation, and the policy of the occupation made it necessary for these banks to be converted into ordinary commercial banks following World War II. However, a new perpetual financial system for long-term agricultural credit was required to handle the urgent problems of promoting food production and job opportunity in agriculture. The present financial organs for long-term agricultural credit, that is, the Agricultural Forestry and the Fisheries Finance Corporation and the Special Account for Settlement Finance were established as government financial organs, and government funds have been supplied to agriculture through these organs.

A superficial contrast between joint-stock banks in the prewar period and government institutions in the postwar period would give us the impression that a drastic change has occurred since the war. However, scrutinizing the functioning of the long-term credit banks for agriculture in the prewar period, they appear as semi-government banks which only serves to further emphasize the dominant role played by the government in the field of long-term agricultural credit ever since the 1900's.

REFERENCES

Agriculture Forestry and Fisheries Finance Corporation. *10 Years of Agriculture, Forestry and Fisheries Finance Corporation (Norin Gyogyō Kinyū Kōko Jūnenshi)*. Tokyo: 1965.

Asakura, Koichi. *History of Japanese Financial Structure in Early Meiji Era (Meiji Zenki Nippon Kinyū Kōzōshi)*. Tokyo: 1961.

Bank of Japan. *Hundred-year Statistics of the Japanese Economy (Meijiikō Honpō Keizai Tōkei)*. Tokyo: 1966.

Higashiura, Syōji. *Introduction to Japanese Agriculture (Nippon Nōgyō Gairon)*. Tokyo: 1937.

Hypothec Bank of Japan. *History of the Hypothec Bank of Japan (Nippon Kangyō Ginkōshi)*. Tokyo: 1953.
——. *Statistics of the Hypothec Bank of Japan (Nippon Kangyō Ginkō Tokei Shiryō)*. Tokyo: 1953.
Ito, Yuzuru. *Economic Development and Agricultural Finance in Japan (Keizai Hatten to Nōgyō Kinyū)*. Tokyo: Tokyo Daigaku Shuppankai, 1962.
Kato, Yuzuru, "Mechanism for the Outflow of Funds from Agriculture into Industry in Japan," *Rural Economic Problems* (Dec. 1966).
Ministry of Agriculture and Commerce. *Thirty Third Statistical Yearbook of the Department of Agriculture and Commerce (Daisan Jūsanji Noshōmu Tōkei-hyō)*. 1918.
Ministry of Agriculture and Forestry. *Handbook of Agricultural and Forestry Finance (Nōrin Kinyū Binran)*. 1953.
——. *Farm Household Fund Situation Survey (Nōka Shikin Dōtai Chōsa)*. 1965.
——. *Farm Household Economy Survey (Nōka Keizai Chōsa)*. 1925–42.
——. *Annual Report on Agricultural and Forestry Finance (Nōrin Kinyū no Dōkō)*. 1966.
——. *White Paper on Agriculture and Forestry (Nōrin Hakusho)*. *1957*.
Ministry of Finance. *History of Development of Financial Institutions (Kinyū Kikan Hattatsushi)*. Tokyo: 1949.
Ministry of Posts and Telecommunication. *Outlines of Postal Money Orders and Savings Banks (Yūseishō Yūbinkawase Chōkin Jigyō Gaiyō)*. 1897, 1903, and 1908.
Nakamura, James I. *Agricultural Production and the Economic Development of Japan, 1873–1922*. Princeton; Princeton University Press, 1966.

APPENDIX

Appendix: TABLE 1

Ratio of Balance of Deposit Bureau Funds to Balance of Principal
Unsecured Loans of HBJ (Selected Years: 1911–1931)*

(unit: %)

End of F.Y.	Loans to industrial associations	Loans to land improvement associations
1911	81.4	39.8
1917	77.4	64.5
1920	85.8	88.0
1924	69.1	60.6
1927	73.9	50.3
1931	67.6	58.4

* Data from Division of Investigation of the Hypothec Bank of Japan, unpublished worksheets.

Appendix: TABLE 2

Ratio of Balance of Agricultural Loans[a] to Balance of Total Loans of
HBJ (Secured and Unsecured Loans), (Selected Years: 1897–1945)*

(Unit: %)

End of F.Y.	Total[b]	Secured[c]	Unsecured[d]
1897	39.9	29.6	95.4
1902	45.9	45.6	47.5
1907	50.1	58.0	40.3
1911	46.8	39.0	51.9
1917	51.2	39.2	69.2
1921	34.6	25.5	50.7
1923	36.8	28.2	53.7
1927	41.4	29.8	59.8
1931	46.0	36.4	60.3
1937	41.1	32.8	65.9
1941	36.3	28.1	67.8
1945	9.5	19.5	6.2

* Data from Hypothec Bank of Japan, *Statistics of the Hypothec Bank of Japan*
(*Nippon Kangyō Ginkō Tōkei Shiryō*) (1953), pp. 32–7.

a) Including loans to forestry and fisheries.

b) Balance of total agricultural loans / Balance of total loans.

c) Balance of secured agricultural loans / Balance of total secured loans.

d) Balance of unsecured agricultural loans / Balance of total unsecured loans.

Appendix: TABLE 3
Balance of Outside Capital of HBJ (Selected Years: 1907–45)*

(Unit: %)

Year	Sho-ken[a] debenture	Tai-ken[b] debenture	Tokushu[c] saiken debenture	Borrowing from deposit bureau	Deposit	Total
1907	71.6	—	28.4	—	—	100.0
1911	36.8	34.7	26.9	—	1.6	100.0
1917	46.0	25.6	24.5	—	3.8	100.0
1921	49.0	15.9	27.2	—	8.0	100.0
1923	49.3	25.6	24.0	—	10.1	100.0
1927	30.2	25.5	33.7	—	10.6	100.0
1931	24.6	22.7	40.5	0.2	12.1	100.0
1937	29.0	24.4	22.2	4.1	20.3	100.0
1941	26.9	24.4	16.6	1.7	30.5	100.0
1945	6.9	21.7	3.1	5.9	62.4	100.0

* Data from Hypothec Bank of Japan, *Statistics of the Hypothec Bank of Japan* (*Nippon Kangyō Ginkō Tōkei Shiryō*) (1953), pp. 56–9.
a) Bonus-bearing debenture. Its face value was small and was purchased mainly by individuals.
b) Face value of *taiken* was of large sum and carried no bonus. It was purchased mainly by institutional investors such as banks, insurance companies, trust companies and others.
c) Special debenture purchased by Deposit Bureau of the Ministry of Finance.

Appendix: TABLE 4
Principal Assets of HBJ (Selected Years: 1897–1945)*

(Unit: %)

Year	Long-term loans	Short-term loans	Securities	Deposits	Miscel- laneous[a]	Total
1887	13.7	—	9.6	1.7	75.0	100.0
1907	54.0	—	0.6	30.8	14.6	100.0
1911	79.5	0.5	0.5	13.1	6.4	100.0
1917	77.0	1.1	5.4	10.4	5.1	100,0
1921	79.8	4.4	1.7	5.8	8.3	100.0
1923	81.0	1.8	2.1	5.9	9.2	100.0
1927	77.3	1.5	4.4	9.4	7.4	100.0
1931	79.7	2.0	4.7	7.7	5.9	100.0
1937	69.6	2.7	7.1	7.7	12.9	100.0
1941	42.1	2.1	6.6	34.1	15.1	100.0
1945	21.4	18.7	6.7	32.5	20.7	100.0

* Data from Hypothec Bank of Japan, *Statistics of the Hypothec Bank of Japan* (*Nippon Kangyō Ginkō Tōkei Shiryō*) (1953), pp. 96–7.
a) Unpaid-in capital, debentures of PAIB's, call loans, land and buildings, etc.

Appendix: TABLE 5
Agricultural Cooperative Credit System, Consolidated
Balance Sheet End of F.Y. 1964*

(Unit: 100 million yen)

Loans to affiliated members	11,073	Agricultural co-ops deposits	19,314
Marketing, supply and equipment utilization account		Non-affiliated	
appropriations	1,575	members' deposits	3,135
Cash and miscellaneous	1,079	Debentures	2,054
AFFFC^a trusted funds	2,943	AFFFC^a trust funds	2,927
Total	16,670	Capital and	
	(56.8%)	miscellaneous	1,917
Loans to ancillary industries	2,685		
Other loans to non-affiliated members	472		
Loans to financial institutions	5,428		
Deposits in non-affiliated financial institutions	1,571		
Securities	2,521		
Total (Surplus funds)	12,677		
	(43.2%)		
Grand total	29,347	Total	29,347
	(100.0%)		

* Data from Ministry of Agriculture and Forestry, *Annual Report on Agricultural and Forestry Finance (Nōrin Kinyū no Dōkō)* (1966), p. 71.
a) Agriculture Forestry and Fisheries Finance Corporation.

CHAPTER 14

SAVINGS OF FARM HOUSEHOLDS

Tsutomu Noda[†]

I. Introduction

The aim of this paper is to undertake a comparative analysis of the saving behavior of farm and workers' households in an attempt to explain their behavior functionally. We already have several international comparisons of the saving ratios, which facilitate explanation of the high aggregate saving ratio in Japan. The average gross domestic saving ratio in Japan, as a proportion of total national income, was estimated to be 34 per cent during the years 1956–1963. This was considerably higher than the corresponding figure of 18 per cent for the United States, 17 per cent for United Kingdom and 20 per cent for France.[1] The main components of

---

[†] I have benefited from the critical comments of T. W. Schultz, K. Ohkawa, O. Sacay, T. Shinohara, M. Shinohara and other symposium participants. I wish to express my thanks to F. Egaitsu, now at Tokyo University, for his helpful work on an earlier draft. Any errors that still remain are, of course, my sole responsibility.

[1]

	Net savings			Depreciation allowances, etc.	Gross domestic saving
	Personal	corporate	government		
Japan	11	5	7	11	34
Netherlands	8	5	5	10	28
W. Germany	9	2	7	9	27
Canada	5	3	2	12	22
Belgium	8	2	—	10	20
France	5	3	3	9	20
U. S. A.	5	2	2	10	18
U. K.	3	5	2	8	17

* Data for Japan from Economic Planning Agency, *Annual Report on National Income Statistics* (1967); and the data for other countries from United Nations, *Yearbook of National Accounts Statistics* (1965).
a) Data for Japan is given in terms of fiscal years.
b) All the figures in this Table represent percentages of gross national product of the respective countries.

352

this high gross savings ratio of 34 per cent for Japan were in net terms 11 per cent for personal savings, 7 per cent for governmental savings and 5 per cent for corporate savings, all these ratios being higher for Japan than for the above-mentioned countries. We should note in particular the high ratio of personal savings since it played an important role in the development of the Japanese economy.

Some economists emphasize that the high personal saving ratio in Japan has been brought about by the large proportion of independent proprietors' incomes in personal income. This argument assumes that the independent proprietors' propensity to save should be higher than the workers' propensity to save. If so, it follows that farmers and non-farm proprietors' savings must be higher than the savings from workers' income[2] and that the saving ratio of non-farm proprietors' income and that of independent farm households should be higher than those of workers' households.[3]

Although the question of the validity of the above assumptions is in itself interesting and important, I will largely confine myself here to a comparison of farmers' savings with workers' savings. More specifically, I will first present a brief critical review of the previous studies of saving functions in order to clarify the problems which exist (Section II). Second, I shall offer my own analysis of saving behavior in farm households (Section III). Finally, I shall present a brief summary of the previous two sections.

The reader should be aware that the analysis here will be concerned largely with postwar phenomena; the prewar situation will be discussed only briefly. For the purpose of my analysis, I depend solely upon the data of family budget surveys. With Table 1 and Fig. 1 and 2, an overall picture of saving-income relation based on these data is presented for farm households and workers' households. National income statistics do not provide the necessary information because personal savings and personal income data are not broken down into employees, farm, and non-farm proprietors. In this study I shall use Japanese family budget surveys which

---

[2] For example, our estimates (Noda ond Egaitsu, 1965, p. 10) indicate that in 1963 the share of non-farm proprietors' savings ond of farm households in total savings were about 40 per cent and 20 per cent, respectively.

[3] Until quite recently, no reliable data was available for verifying these assumptions except through indirect estimation.

TABLE 1
Net Saving Ratio by Household Type*^a

Year	Farm household[b]		(per annum)	Workers' household		(per month)
	Income (1,000 yen)	Saving (1,000 yen)	Saving ratio (%)	Income (1,000 yen)	Saving (1,000 yen)	Saving ratio (%)
1951	280	24.6	8.8	18.9	0.4	2.0
52	306	22.6	7.4	23.0	1.0	4.4
53	317	17.8	5.6	26.2	1.5	5.8
54	312	10.6	3.4	26.6	2.0	7.4
55	336	30.2	9.0	27.9	2.6	9.2
56	324	14.3	4.4	29.5	3.5	11.8
57[c]	347	19.8	5.7	31.1	3.9	12.5
58	357	25.0	7.0	33.3	4.2	12.6
59	377	30.9	8.2	35.4	4.9	13.9
1960	410	43.5	10.6	37.7	5.6	14.9
61	435	45.2	10.4	39.7	6.6	16.5
62	474	65.4	13.8	41.7	6.7	16.2
63	502	67.8	13.5	43.0	6.8	15.7
64	555	81.6	14.7	46.3	7.8	16.8
65	577	91.1	15.8	46.1	7.7	16.8

* Farm household data for the period 1951–56 from R. Hasebe's, "Estimation of Consumption Function for Farm Households," *Keizaigaku Kiho*, IX (Nos. 3 and 4, Rissho University), and for the period 1957–65 from the Ministry of Agriculture and Forestry, *Survey of Farm Household Economy*.

Worker's household data from the Bureau of Statistics, Office of the Prime Minister, *Annual Report on Family Income and Expenditure Survey*.

a) Income and Saving for both households showed at 1960 prices deflated by both consumer price indices.

b) Farm household's figures are based on annual data for averages of all prefectures, and workers on monthly data for averages of cities of over 50 thousand population.

c) In 1957, there was a big change in survey methods for the Survey of Farm Household Economy. Mr. Hasebe's figures were used to revise the bias in these two periods.

provide us with information about various types of incomes and savings based on both time-series and cross-section data.

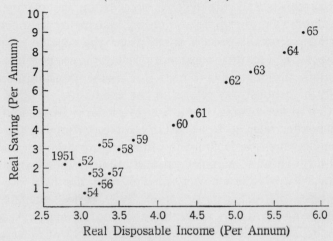

FIGURE 1
Income and Saving of Farm Households*
(unit: ten thousand yen)

* Data from Table 1, Columns 1 and 2.

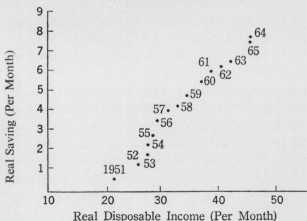

FIGURE 2
Income and Saving of Workers' Households*
(unit: thousand yen)

* Data from Table 1, columns 4 and 5.

II. Review of Previous Savings Function Studies

Farmers

The characteristics of the saving behavior of farm households differ from those of other social classes.[4] These differences may be related to the following three features, one technical and the other two substantial: (a) the size of farms on the average is too small (about 1 ha.) to apply accounting systems to farm activities, (b) farmers generally receive some wage-type income as well as farm income and (c) their consumption patterns are peculiar in that they retain agricultural products for home consumption. The difficulty of problem (a) relates to the evaluation of costs in the estimation of net-income. In the Survey of Farm Household Economy (hereafter referred to as SFHE), some portions of the saving for farm activities are included in family saving although the direct costs for agricultural management and other business expenses are estimated. By evaluating such savings with the help of certain assumptions, my earlier paper (Noda, 1959, p. 112) suggested that income-saving ratios were lower than the usual estimates. According to this calculation, the income-savings ratios for farmers were lower than for workers in both the postwar and prewar periods. We are also faced here with the problem of how to handle capital depreciation. For example, it is doubtful whether the traditional farm activities in Japan can be accounted for adequately with the modern concepts of depreciation although the SFHE has mechanically employed straight-line depreciation methods in their calculation. On the other hand, Kawaguchi and Hasebe (Kawaguchi, 1961; Hasebe, 1959) obtained their savings functions by using gross concepts for both income and saving.

The decreasing proportion of agricultural receipts in farm household income, item (b), is one of the noteworthy developments in postwar farming. The rapid growth of the Japanese economy has enlarged the income differentials between urban and rural areas, and, as a result, farmers have tended to engage in non-agricultural employment. The reduced number of their labor hours spent on the farm is compensated for by mechanizing the methods of cultivation.

---

[4] For example, Shinohara (1958, p. 222) pointed out that in 1951–56 the saving function of farm households fitted the semi-Duesenberry type and that of workers' household fitted the Keynesian type.

The SFHE results indicate this tendency. The percentage of agricultural income in total household income has declined from 67.5 per cent in 1950 to 42.7 per cent in 1965. Thus an analysis of change in the income-composition of farmers is more important than in the case of urban workers. The simplest classification is that of dividing the household income into agricultural and non-agricultural income. Kubo and Murakami (Kubo and Murakami, p. 16) suggested a hypothetical consumption function using this classification for the cross-section data:

$$C_t = \alpha \tfrac{1}{2}\left(Y_t^A + Y_{t-1}^A \right) + \beta Y_t^W + \gamma \qquad (1)$$

where Y^A is agricultural income, Y^W is non-agricultural income, and Y_{t-1}^A denotes the effects of the time lag on the income-consumption relationship due to the year-to-year fluctuations of agricultural income. This classification of income introduced several theoretical complications into the stability of income, structure, and motives of earnings vis-a-vis consumption behavior. The time-series analyses which take into account changes in income composition are few. However, a consumption function by farm size may give a hint as to the solution of this problem because the decreasing trend of the percentage of agricultural income in total household income is much more marked in small-scale farms than in large-scale farms. The statistical analyses by Kawaguchi and Hasebe confirmed that a linear, Keynesian-type function was the best in a time-series analysis (1951–58) for small-scale farms (farms smaller than 0.5 ha.); however, a Duesenberry-type function proved better for large-scale farms. Mizoguchi (Mizoguchi, p. 16) also obtained consistent results in his 1950–61 time-series studies by farm size and by regions.

Finally, the consumption of agricultural products retained for self-consumption, item (c), should be examined. Farmers in Japan are accustomed to products such as rice and vegetables which are necessary for maintaining their standard of living. Small farm households, in particular, still retain a large portion of these products for self-consumption *(hanmai-noka)*. Thus, the percentage of products retained for self-consumption in total food consumption expenditure was 70 per cent in 1955, and diminished on an average to 45 per cent in 1965. Consequently, a study of consumption patterns for products retained for self-consumption is necessary for any analysis aimed at forecasting income-consumption ratios. For this reason, two kinds of consumption functions are proposed: one which relates total income and money expenditure and another which relates money income and money expenditures (Ito, p. 99). Computations along these lines resulted in a higher correlation between total income and total expenditure. The problem has been solved, however, only in a preliminary sense, and more rigorous theoretical and empirical analyses should be developed in the future.

The above analysis has not completely solved the problem of how to treat these three characteristics of Japanese farmers. However, a synthesis of these will be attempted in the following to obtain a better consumption (saving) function for the farm household and to explain the differences in consumption patterns between workers and farmers.

Workers

National income statistics show that the income-consumption ratio decreased during 1951–56. Therefore, the linear Keynesian type consumption function,

$$C = a + b^Y \tag{2}$$

where C is consumption, Y is income and a and b are positive constants, seems to fit the income-consumption relation for Japanese workers best. Shinohara (Shinohara, 1962, p. 217) tried to explain this tendency using the prewar real income level of urban workers. He assumed that the real income level in the surveyed period was still lower than in the highest prewar level. Thus, he assumed that the income-saving ratio would stop increasing after the real income level recovered its prewar peak. Then a Duesenberry-type saving function,

$$S_t / Y_t = a + b\left(\frac{Y_t - Y_0}{Y_t}\right) \tag{3}$$

where Y_0 is the highest previous income, was assumed to describe the fundamental behavior of workers; this function also can explain the behavior of farmers in this period. The income-saving ratio of workers stopped increasing in 1956–58, but after 1959 began to increase again, having recovered its prewar income level around

1955. Thus, improved types of saving functions will be necessary for this later period.

Studies which have employed the liquid assets effect should be examined, but the Family Income and Expenditure Survey (FIES) of the Bureau of Statistics, Prime Minister's Office, does not contain figures for stocks of liquid assets before 1959. Shinohara has derived some interesting results by calculating the ratio of deposits to national income (Marshallian K) as an approximation for workers' savings; however, even in 1960 the ratio was still lower than the highest prewar level. As a result of this finding, he speculated that the income-saving ratio would stop increasing after the ratio recovered its prewar level. Since 1959, the Survey of Saving Behavior has been available, and a time-series analyses can be used to explain these complicated results. The cross-section analyses using the data of this survey substantiates Tobin's hypothesis for explaining the difference of propensity to save by urban occupational groups (Noda and Egaitsu, 1965, p. 14).

Workers' incomes are classified by sources of origin: (1) Y_1-regular income of the household head, (2) Y_2-other income of the household head, e.g., transitory and subsidiary job income, (3) Y_3-income of other household members, (4) Y_4-income from self-employment and (5) Y_5-other income. Of course, the major part of income is derived from Y_1 while bonus receipts largely account for Y_2. These amounts are determined nearly in proportion to the basic wage or salary among workers; however, the proportion fluctuates according to the company's profit or general economic condition every year. Y_3 is not so important in family budgets, except in the lower income class. Y_5 consists of returns from assets, social security benefits, gifts, and remittances. Shinohara (Shinohara, 1962, p. 236), defining Y_2 and Y_4 as the "income of transitory nature," pointed out the increase of their percentages in disposable income since 1951; he considered this to be responsible for the increasing income-savings ratio. However, in spite of the increase of these percentages from 1961 to 1962, the income-saving ratio has since stopped increasing. By pooling the time sequences of the "quintile group data" of the FIES for 1951–62, Mizoguchi (Mizoguchi, 1964, p. 53) also examined the increase of income-savings ratio on the basis of the increasing percentage of transitory income and the constancy of the consumption-permanent income ratio. In this case, Y_1 was considered the main index of consumption behavior because its portion was the most stable. He found that the consumption-permanent income ratio not only remained nearly constant in the time series for each income group, but that their levels were very similar between different income groups. However, the ratio of the lowest income group showed a downward trend, and its level was higher than that of other income groups. That is to say, this group's behavior could be explained by relative income effects. The income-saving ratio of other income groups, from the second to fifth, could best be determined by the portion of Y_1 in the total. The saving ratio of urban workers as a whole, excepting the lowest income group, might have increased according to the decreasing Y_1-total ratio. After the survey schedules of FIES were controlled by family type, Obi and Sano (1962) and Ozaki (1962) made cross-section analyses based on similar principles. They found the marginal propensities of different incomes to consume by sources of origin and by family type. For example, the marginal propensity of the household head to consume was found to be larger than that of other household members. From the above, it is clear that the savings ratio in Japan is a product of complex effects as pointed out by different hypotheses.

Prewar Research

Largely due to the unreliability of the basic data, the studies of savings functions in the prewar period are relatively weak, especially the time-series analyses. The official national income statistics leave much to be desired; the Survey of Farm Household Economy and the urban Family Budget Survey probably contain upward and downward biases respectively in household incomes and expenditures the size of the samples was much smaller than in the postwar sampling surveys.[5] With these reservations the following deserve mentioning. Although the Survey of Farm Household Economy of the prewar period underwent two major revisions in 1924 and 1931, we can still get a reasonable fit by the use of a Keynesian-type savings function. Ito (Ito, p. 97), Shinohara (Shinohara, 1958, p. 250) and Kurabayashi (Kurabayashi, p. 317) estimated the savings functions for farm households of the prewar period using a Keynesian function for the SFHE time-series data. For example, the consumption functions for 1924–41 are estimated by Ito as follows:

$$C = 42.98 + 0.515\ Y; \quad R^2 = 0.97,$$

where C and Y are the nominal per capita consumption expenditure and per capita pre-tax income, respectively. In his estimates, the average cultivated land per household is taken to be 1.22 ha. in order to provide continuity to the SFHE data. According to the above equation, the marginal propensity to save is 0.48. If only cash expenditures and cash income are considered,

$$C_c = 24.95 + 0.414\ Y_c; \quad R^2 = 0.99.$$

In this regard, it can be further noted that over the period 1921–36 Shinohara and Kurabayashi also found good fits for a linear function. According to Shinohara's estimates the marginal propensity to save was, with some revisions, 0.817 for 1921–23, 0.601 for 1924–30, and 0.452 for 1931–36.

We also have some meaningful cross-section studies of savings functions for the prewar period. The Family Budget Survey for September 1926 to August 1927, of the Cabinet Statistics Bureau was the largest scale survey of its kind taken in the prewar period,[6] on the basis of which Shinohara has derived the following consumption function estimates by occupational group:

Salary earners:	$C = 12.30 + 0.812Y;$	$R^2 = 0.99$
Wage earners:	$C = 18.49 + 0.711Y;$	$R^2 = 0.99$
Farm households:	$C = 37.87 + 0.599Y;$	$R^2 = 0.94$

The order of magnitude of the marginal propensity to save is

---

[5] The samplesizes of the prewar Survey of Farm Household Economy, in 1921–23 was about 100, in 1924–30 was about 200, and in 1931–41 was about 300 (number of total farm household was about 5.5 million). According to SFHE data, the average cultivated land per household was about 1.7 ha. for 1921–30 and about 1.24 ha. for 1931–41. However, the national average was 1.05–1.09 ha. in this period. Thus, the prewar SFHE data have an upward bias in the household economy. On the other hand, the Family Budget Survey of the Cabinet Statistics Bureau is limited mainly to incomes lower than middle class and households who live in rented houses. In this case we can say the survey probably contained a downward bias in household income and expenditures.

[6] The number of households surveyed was 7,220 of which 1,575 were salary earners' households, 3,210 wage earners, and 670 farm households.

greatest for farmers followed by wage earners, and then by salary earners. This prewar ordering is also maintained in the postwar period[7] which may be due to the higher transitory component in the measured farmer's income. In other words, the instability of agricultural incomes, which are more entrepreneurial in character and which are subject to the changes in harvests, make for a higher marginal propensity to save. In addition, the stability of the farmer's consumption is also an important factor in accounting for the above results.

III. Savings Behavior of Farm Households
Concepts of Savings and Income

The concepts of savings and income in the SFHE data can be explained as follows:

(1) Net disposable income (Y_d^n) = Net agricultural income

(Y_a^n) + Net non-agricultural income (Y_{na}^n), including pensions—Taxes (T).

(2) Gross disposable income (Y_d^g) = Y_d^n + Depreciation charges due to farm operation (D_a) + Depreciation charges due to non-farm business (D_{na}).

(3) Y_d^n —Consumption excluding depreciation charges of housing (C^n) = Net savings (S^n) + Depreciation charges of housing (D_h).

(4) $Y_d^g - C^n$ = Gross savings (S^g)

(5) $S^g = Y_d^n + D_a + D_{na} - C^n$
$= S^n + D_h + D_a + D_{na}$

---

[7] According to our estimates (Noda and Egaitsu, 1965, p. 10) we found the following savings function using FIES time-series data for 1951–64:

$$S = 3,424 - 1,747N + 0.2478Y + 845D; \quad R^2 = 0.99,$$
$$\quad\quad (447) \quad\quad (0.014) \quad\; (160)$$

where S and Y are real saving and real income, N is number of families, and D is a dummy variable (wage earners, households is 1, salary earners, O). The coefficient of D is significant, and it is clear that the propensity to save for wage earners' households is higher than that of salary earners' households. These differences may be explained by the liquid assets hypothesis (Noda and Egaitsu, 1965, p. 10).

= (Increase of deposits) + (Increase of other liquid assets) + (Gross investment of the real assets) — (Increase of liabilities),

Here we will take gross to include depreciation charges, and in dealing with the SFHE, S^n can be thought of as the "surplus of farm household economy" *(Nōka keizai yojyo)*. Thus, savings here is the difference between disposable income and consumption; furthermore, an increase in net worth or in the deposits outstanding is included in savings.

Savings Functions of Average Farm Households

The first step of our study is the application of linear Keynesian and modified Duesenberry (equation 3) savings functions using recent SFHE time-series data employing gross and net saving, respectively. Savings functions were estimated for each farm size class with the aid of 1952–62 time-series data. Some discontinuity produced by the survey data may not be of serious significance because of our use of time-series data for each farm size.

TABLE 2
Correlation Coefficients of Farmers' Saving Functions, 1952–1962*

		Keynesian-Type Function				
		-0.5^{ha}	$0.5-1.0^{ha}$	$1.0-1.5^{ha}$	$1.5-2.0^{ha}$	2.0^{ha} —
Net saving	Tohoku	.92	.87	.91	.77	.74
	Kinki	.93	.74	.67	.75	.44
Gross saving	Tohoku	.75	.95	.96	.95	.93
	Kinki	.95	.81	.81	.79	.61

		Duesenberry-Type Function				
		-0.5^{ha}	$0.5-1.0^{ha}$	$1.0-1.5^{ha}$	$1.5-2.0^{ha}$	2.0^{ha} —
Net saving	Tohoku	.27	.58	.88	.96	.51
	Kinki	—	.55	.34	.45	—
Gross saving	Tohoku	.58	.88	.61	.87	.02
	Kinki	.05	.41	.32	.05	.10

* Data from the Ministry of Agriculture and Forestry, *Survey of Farm Household Economy*, 1952–1962.

[8] The Tohoku district in northern Japan is the representative area for a single crop (especially rice), and the average cultivated area is larger than the national average. The Kinki district (in central Japan) is a double crop area, and the land is cultivated for commercial crops.

We will first attempt to find the fit for the savings functions for the Tohoku and Kinki districts[8] of Japan. Table 2 shows the correlation coefficients of equations for farm size by districts. Savings functions of both types were fitted for 1952–62 data. As Table 2 shows, we obtained relatively high coefficients of correlation for the gross data and for the linear Keynesian equation. However, the fit for the Kinki district function shows, excluding farms of less than 0.5 ha., a low coefficient of correlation—less than 0.8. Because this may be explained by the severe changes of employment structure in this region, it can be said that the Keynesian-type functions fitted well in all groups for time-series. Differences of parameters clearly exist between each group; however, we cannot judge to what extent these are reflections of saving level differences.

Next, we will fit the following savings function, using the 1957–62 SFHE time-series data prefectural averages, in order to clarify the differences in saving propensities for each group; the effects due to differences in composition of income will then be introduced. The data was obtained by pooling the time-sequence and cross-section data for 6 years and for 6 farm size groups with income and savings being defined gross of depreciation. We obtain the following Keynesian-type savings equation:

$$S = -78.7 - 7.9013N + 0.4835Y, \qquad (4)$$
$$ (3.06) \quad\;\; (0.0228)$$
$$R^2 = 0.9846, \quad d = 1.26,$$

where S is real saving, Y real disposable income, N number of household members, R^2 the coefficient of determination, and d the Durbin-Watson statistic. However, this equation has neglected the inter-group differentials of parameters, so that even an extremely high correlation between saving and income may yield a low Durbin-Watson statistic owing to the serial correlation of residuals. Therefore, we have inserted a dummy variable for farm size ($D=1$ for farms less than 0.3 ha, $=2$ for 0.3–0.5 ha, $=3$ for 0.5–1.0 ha, $=4$ for 1.0–1.5 ha, $=5$ for 1.5–2.0 ha and $=6$ for 2.0-ha) and also the dummy variable for the year ($D=1958$–1962).[9] The equations are as follows:

$$S = 381.5 - 83.974N + 0.1873Y + \sum_{i=2}^{6} \alpha_i D_i \qquad (5)$$
$$ (11.55) \quad\;\; (0.0502)$$
$$R^2 = 0.9938, \quad d = 2.18$$

$$S = -58.1 - 15.057N + 0.5405Y + \sum_{j=1958}^{1962} \beta_j D_j \qquad (6)$$
$$\quad\; (6.33) \qquad (0.0495)$$
$$R^2 = 0.9834, \quad d = 1.20$$

These equations suggest that there is a significant difference of parameters among size groups; yearly differences, however, are not significant. Thus, determining the inter-group differentials of propensity to save, we will next want to introduce the effect of income composition to explain the inter-group propensity differences. Here we have three income categories: agricultural income–Y_0, non-agricultural income–Y_1, and Pensions minus Taxes, Y_2. Taking note of the fact that the value of Y_2 is negligible and its parameter is relatively insignificant[10] we have the following equations:

$$S = 169.7 - 45.762N + 0.5226Y_0 + 0.2023Y_1 - 0.3602Y_2 \qquad (7)$$
$$\qquad\quad (4.02) \qquad (0.012) \qquad (0.029) \qquad (0.181)$$
$$R^2 = 0.9964, \qquad d = 2.31$$
$$S = 186.0 - 47.103N + 0.5388Y_0 + 0.213Y_1 - 0.2793Y_2 \qquad (8)$$
$$\qquad\quad (3.94) \qquad (0.012) \qquad (0.026) \qquad (0.170)$$
$$R^2 = 0.9968, \qquad d = 2.53$$

In equation (7), Y_0 includes non-agricultural business income, rent, and interest income, and Y_1 implies salary and wage income only; however, in equation (8) this income was included in Y_1. Furthermore, depreciation is included in Y_0 for both equations. In order to check whether the equations fit or not, we have made an extrapola-

---

[9] As a first step, the data were obtained by pooling the time-sequence and cross-section data in order to avoid multi-collinearity. However, we still have the serial correlation of residuals in equation (4). The dummy variables can be used to eliminate serial correlation effects. The dummy variables for farm size and for year can explain the inter-group and time effects. Our estimates assume that in this case the time-series is dominant.

[10] The composition of income of farm households changed year by year in the postwar periods. Income composition between agricultural and non-agricultural income, using SFHE data, is as follows:

	agricultural income	non-agricultural income
1951	69%	31%
1955	67	33
1960	50	50
1965	44	56

The declining tendency in agricultural income may be responsible for the changes in consumption (savings) behavior of farm households.

tion test for three equations (4), (7), and (8). Equation (4) shows estimation biases compared with the other two equations; furthermore it tends to underestimate the actual values before 1959 and overestimate after 1960 (See Table 3). Compared with equation (4), the extrapolated value of equations (7) and (8) show only small errors, and the bias of the residuals was not as large. Although we still have the problem of a large under-estimation in 1953, we may conclude tentatively that the differences in propensity to save by farm size are mainly explained by differences in income composition.[11]

Full-time and Part-time Farms

It should be very interesting to construct a savings function for farm households depending on the extent of engagement in farm pursuits[12] and compare this with the saving behavior of workers' households. We would expect those households engaged in part-time farming to be more likely be affected by the demonstration effect of urban consumption behavior, thus showing a mixed consumption behavior pattern. We do not have time-series data for full-time and part-time farm households. The Farm Household Cost of Living Survey (attached survey of the SFHE), however, gives information cross-tabulated by income classes and by full- and part-time groups for three years (1960, 1962, and 1963).

Because we cannot use the concept of gross savings (as this survey lacks data relating to farm management procedures, especially the treatment of depreciation), the following cross-section estimates for

---

[11] The SFHE definitions used before 1963 were as follows. "Full-time farm household" refers to the households whose members engage exclusively in agriculture. "Part-time farm household" refers to those households in which one or more members was engaged in other subsidiary occupations. This definition is different from the standardized definitions used by both the Ministry of Agriculture and Forestry and the World Agricultural Census which is as follows: "Part-time farm household" refers to households whose household head or heir is engaged in non-agricultural occupations for over 60 days in a year and earns more than 100 thousand yen per annum from such an occupation. Those farm households which do not fulfill this criterion are referred to as full-time farm households. After 1964, however, SFHE adopted these definitions.

[12] There is no one method by which adjustment can be made in differences in prices between rural and urban areas. Hence, we assumed the price level of rural districts to be 80 per cent that of urban districts.

TABLE 3
Test of Savings Functions of Farm Households*

Year	Actual[a] (1,000 yen)	Function (4)		Function (7)		Function (8)	
		Estimated (1,000 yen)	Difference (%)	Estimated (1,000 yen)	Difference (%)	Estimated (1,000 yen)	Difference (%)
1953	63.1	51.3	−18.7	45.9	−27.3	48.2	−23.6
54	60.9	50.2	−17.6	52.6	−13.6	56.2	−8.0
55	86.8	66.0	−24.0	77.5	−10.7	81.2	−6.5
56	65.9	58.7	−10.9	68.3	+3.6	70.3	+6.7
57	59.7	54.7	−8.4	59.6	−0.2	59.1	−1.0
58	67.1	61.3	−8.6	65.3	−2.7	66.1	−1.5
59	74.4	72.1	−3.1	74.2	−0.3	74.9	+0.7
60	88.8	89.6	+0.9	90.1	+1.5	89.6	+0.9
61	101.9	106.6	+4.6	103.0	−1.1	102.3	+0.4
62	120.5	125.6	+4.2	122.7	−1.8	122.6	+1.7
63	127.9	141.8	+10.9	127.1	−0.6	127.9	0.0

* The original data are the same as for Table 1.
a) Actual figures of savings are taken by the Farm Household Economy Survey as an average of all prefectures, gross of depreciation, and at 1960 prices.

1960 and 1963 are therefore given in net terms:

$$1960: \quad S=330.6-103.2N+0.6773Y+81.7D \qquad (9)$$
$$(36.7) \quad (0.1432) \quad (6.1)$$
$$R^2=0.92, \qquad d=1.5$$
$$1963: \quad S=121.3-14.6N+0.4753Y+ 5.6D \qquad (10)$$
$$(19.5) \quad (0.045) \quad (10.8)$$
$$R^2=0.99, \qquad d=1.3$$

where N is the number of family members, Y is disposable income, and D is a dummy variable for the full-time farm household. According to equations (9) and (10), under the net saving concept, a high propensity to save is implied for full-time farmers rather than for part-time farmers. It may be noted that if we could estimate a gross savings function, this trend might appear even more distinctly.

Levels of Savings Ratios: Farm Households and Workers' Households

If the high savings ratio of independent proprietors can be explained by the instability of income, savings for investment purposes, etc., the savings ratio of farm households should not be much lower than that of non-farm proprietors at the same income levels. Let us, therefore, compare the saving ratio between farm and workers' households with similar real income levels. Because the data for non-farm proprietors is not of the same quality, there are several reservations which should be noted in the above comparisons.[13] First, the concept of household disposable income, especially the evaluation of farm capital depreciation, has an important influence on farmers' disposable income. There is no single objective standard for the evaluation of depreciation and the evaluation methods taken by the SFHE introduce over-estimation of depreciation for the following two reasons: (1) the net increments of fixed assets in each year for farm households show negative values, notwithstanding large increases in machinery investment; (2) in the SFHE income accounts straight-line depreciation has been used for assets which are still in use, although completely written off. Thus, we can see that depreciation has an upward bias compared to real cost. The above, being essentially the status of the depreciation problem for

---

[13] The standard level of income is the income of an average farm household as in SFHE, and I compared it earlier for the same income level of workers using FBS data (Noda, 1959, p. 113).

both gross and net concepts, we will now want to turn our attention to the fact that the number of household members in a farm household is usually larger than that of a worker's. In order to compare the saving ratios of both households, we adopt a method in which savings functions for workers' households of a given number of family members are compared with the farm household savings function of a similar number of family members. Next, the workers' hypothetical savings are estimated from their savings function using the value of a farmers' income for a family of similar size. Then, we compare the estimated workers' savings and actual farm savings.

TABLE 4

A Comparison of Savings Ratios by Farm Size*

(Unit: %)

	Family members	Farm household[a]		Workers' household[b]	
		Net saving ratio	Gross saving ratio	Net saving ratio	Gross saving ratio
0.1–0.3 ha	4.67	10.7	15.8	12.7	13.0
0.3–0.5	5.17	8.8	15.4	12.4	12.9
0.5–1.0	5.65	7.9	18.3	11.8	12.8
1.0–1.5	6.30	9.5	22.1	12.2	13.6
1.5–2.0	6.91	12.3	26.1	13.9	15.5
2.0–	7.66	14.9	28.8	16.4	17.7

* The original data are the same as for Table 1.

a) The figures for farm households are the actual values mentioned in the of Survey Farm Household Economy. The actual values were calculated by pooling the data for 1957–62 and the results can be found in "Table of Farm Size" in the Survey. In this calculation the following equations were used: Net Income=Disposable Income; Gross Income=Net Income+Depreciation of Farm management; Savings=Income−Family Consumption Expenditures; Gross Savings=Net savings+Depreciation of dwelling.

b) Savings ratio of workers' household were estimated from the saving functions by worker's family size using the incomes of farm households with corresponding family sizes.

Saving function by family size of worker's household are as follows:

4 members: $S = -4681 + 0.2662\ Y$
$R^2 = 0.99,\quad d = 1.3$
5 members: $S = -5175 + 0.2589\ Y$
$R^2 = 0.97,\quad d = 1.4$
6 members: $S = -5750 + 0.2597\ Y$
$R^2 = 0.97,\quad d = 1.6$
7 members: $S = -7282 + 0.2760\ Y$
$R^2 = 0.98,\quad d = 2.1$
8 members: $S = -7883 + 0.2789\ Y$
$R^2 = 0.93,\quad d = 2.0$

Table 4 shows the results of our comparison under the above assumptions with the figures for farm households representing actual SFHE values. For the net savings ratio, workers' households show slightly higher figures, but in the case of the gross savings ratio, farm households show higher figures, the differences increasing considerably in the upper classes. In the preceding section we have stated that the group differences in savings ratios can be explained by the differences in income composition between gross agricultural income and wage and salary income. However, strictly speaking, these differences appear to arise due to differences in the treatment of depreciation.

TABLE 5

A Comparison of Saving Ratios of Office and Non-Office Workers

(Unit: 1,000 yen)

		Actual[a] (Urban)	Estimated[b]		
			(1)	(2)	(3)
Non-office worker's household	Family members	4.34	—	—	—
	Income	290.6	—	—	—
	Saving	39.0	36.7	88.3	130.6
Office worker's household	Family members	4.35	—	—	—
	Income	413.8	—	—	—
	Saving	59.6	61.8	135.3	195.5

* Data for actual urban savings from F. Egaitsu's, "Estimating Savings Functions from Farm Household Survey Data (Nōka no Chochiku Kansu to Chochiku Ritsu)," *Nōgyō Keizai Kenkyū,* XXXVII, No. 1 (1965), p. 41.

The Estimated savings ratios are based on the information collected by the author.

a) The figures for the actual savings represent an average savings of all city workers' households during the years 1957–62.

b) Estimate (1) assumes that income is due, exclusively, to non-agricultural pursuits; Estimate (2) assumes that 55 per cent of the total income is due to agriculture; and Estimate (3) assumes that all income is due, exclusively, to agriculture. Finally, estimated savings is an average of the results which are introduced by equations (7) and (8) on p. 17.

On the basis of equations (7) and (8), we have found distinct differences in the marginal propensity to save between agricultural, wage and salary income, and non-agricultural business income. Can these differences be explained by the differences in the propensity to save between workers' households and farm households? We can estimate hypothetical farm savings, substituting the number of household members and income into equations (7) and (8); in this case we neglect the pensions and gifts (Y_2) and assume that the price differential is 100:80 between urban and rural districts. As Table 5 indicates, the savings ratios calculated on the assumption that farm incomes are solely from wage and salary incomes do not seem to exhibit any great differences compared to those of workers' households. However, the savings ratios are more than 40 per cent if we assume that farm household income is composed solely of agricultural income. These findings suggest that there is an element of proprietorship in the saving behavior of workers' households and private proprietors' households. This also is in line with the fact that private proprietors showed a saving ratio of over 30 per cent.

Finally, I shall make a few remarks on the saving ratios of farm households and workers' households of the prewar period. Although the family budget surveys have some sample bias as mentioned above, this is not a defect inherent in the data itself. Therefore, it may be useful to compare the time-series saving ratios for both family types in terms of the same level of income. According to the Survey of Farm Household Economy and the Family Budget Survey, the net saving ratios for farm households and workers' households of the same income level are as follows:[14]

	Farm (%)	Worker (%)
1926	2.0	10.1
1932	9.3	7.9
1934	13.7	8.1
1937	15.9	10.7

[14] Shinohara (1967, pp. 24–28) suggested a savings function using this classification on the time series and cross section data. His computations resulted in a higher marginal propensity to save for agricultural incomes in comparison to non-agricultural incomes. For the purposes of computation he used the time series for all prefectures for the period 1953–61. But, when he computed the time series after breaking down the incomes according to size and classes, he found that the marginal propensity of agricultural incomes to save was higher than that of non-agricultural incomes in the case of farms of small size, and vice-versa in the case of farms of large size. He arrived at the same results after applying similar methods to the cross-section data. These findings, it should be noted, have a close resemblance to our findings which were obtained by pooling the time-series and cross-section data.

From the above we note that the saving ratio of farm households is higher than that for workers for 1932–1936. However, the opposite was the case in 1926. It seems difficult to draw any definite conclusion regarding the levels of saving ratios between farm and workers' households in the prewar period.

III. Summary

With respect to the savings behavior of farm households we found the following four points:

1.   A good fit can be obtained by use of a Keynesian-type gross savings function for the postwar years since 1952. We have found that there are clear differences in propensity to save by farm size groups when we pool both time-series and cross-section data.

2.   Using the pooled data, the differences in propensity to save by size groups are explained by the different composition of income. The marginal propensity to save from agricultural income appears higher than that from non-agricultural income if we use gross savings. It also show that the propensity to save for full-time farmers is higher than for part-time farmers.

3.   The ranking by the relative magnitude of the marginal propensity to save is: farmers (among farmers, full-time farmers, and then part-time farmers); wage earners; and salary earners. This order is also found in prewar Japan as may be expected from the permanent income hypothesis and is due to the entrepreneurial character of farming and the instability of agricultural output.

4.   It seems difficult to say anything definite about a comparison of average levels of savings ratios between farm households and urban workers' households, using net concepts. But if we make comparisons on the basis of the same level of income between them, we find that the saving ratio tends to be almost the same, using net concepts. The farmers' savings ratio, however, is much higher, especially in large scale farms, when gross concepts are used. This is due to large differences in capital depreciation allowances.

REFERENCES

Egaitsu, F., "Estimating Savings Functions from Farm Household Survey Data (Noka no Chochiku Kansu to Chochiku Ritsu)," *Nogyo Keizai Kenkyu,* XXXVII, No. 1 (1965).

Hasabe, R., "Estimate of Consumption Function for Farm Households (Noka Shohi Kansu no Keisoku ni tsuite)," *Keizaigaku Kiho,* Rissho Univ., IX, Nos. 3, 4 (1959).

Ichioka, K., "On Saving Behavior of Farm Families (Noka Setai no Chochiku Kodo)," *Nogyo Sogokenkyu,* National Research Inst. of Agriculture, Ministry of Agriculture and Forestry, XIV, No. 3 (1960).

Ito, Y. *Economic Development and Agricultural Finance (Keizai Hatten to Nogyo Kinyu).* Tokyo: Tokyo Daigaku Shuppankai, 1962.

Kawaguchi, H. *Analysis of Saving Structure (Chochiku no Kozo Bunseki).* Chiho-ginko Kyokai, 1961.

Kubo M. and Murakami, Y., "On Consumption Patterns of Farm Economy (Noka Keizai ni okeru Shohi Pattern no Doko)," *Fabian Kenkyu,* Fabian Association, XI, Nos. 5, 10; XII, No. 7 (1961).

Kurabayashi, Y., "An Estimate of Saving Functions for Agriculture (Nogyo ni okeru Chochiku Kansu no Suikei)," *Structural Analyses of Japanese Economy (Nihon Keizai no Kozo Bunseki),* I. Nakayama, ed., I, 1954.

Mizoguchi, T. *Statistical Analysis of Consumption Function (Shohi Kansu no Tokeiteki Bunseki).* Tokyo: Iwanami Shoten, 1964.

——, "An Analysis of Farmers' Consumption Function in Japan (Noka Setai Shohi Kansu no Ichi Bunseki)," *Hitotsubashi Review,* Hitotsubashi Univ., L, No. 2 (1963).

——, "International Comparison of Saving Behavior by Occupational Groups (Shokugyobetsu Chochiku Kodo no Kokusai Hikaku)," *Hitotsubashi Review,* Hitotsubashi Univ., LII, No. 1 (1966).

Noda, T., "On the Saving Behavior of Farmers (Noka no Chochiku Kodo)," *Keizai Kenkyu,* Inst. of Economic Research, Hitotsubashi Univ., VII, No. 2 (1959).

——and Egaitsu, F., "Consumption Structure and Propensity to Save: Study on Family Type (Shohi Kozo to Chochiku Seiko—Setai Ruikeibetsu Bunseki—)," *Keizai Bunseki,* Economic Research Institute, Economic Planning Agency, No. 15 (1965).

——, "Saving Ratio by Family Type: A Study of Family Budget Data (Kakei Chochiku Ritsu no Setai Ruikei Betsu Bunseki)," *Kikan Rironkeizaigaku,* Toyo Keizai Shinposha, XVII, No. 1 (1966).

Obi, K. and Sano, Y., "Income Compositions and Marginal Propensity to Consume (Shotoku Bunpu to Genkai Shohi Seiko)," (mimeographed), Institute of Statistical Research, 1962.

Ozaki, I., "Changes of Income Compositions and Their Effects on Consumption Behavior (Kinrosha Kakei ni okeru Shotoku Kozo no Henka to Shohi Kodo)," Institute of Statistical Research, 1962, mimeographed.

Shinohara, M. *The Consumption Function (Shohi Kansu).* Tokyo: Kinokuniya Shoten, 1958.

——. *Growth and Cycles in the Japanese Economy.* Tokyo: Kinokuniya, 1962.

——, "Savings Behavior of the Farm Household," Far Eastern Meeting of Econometric Society (June, 1967), mimeographed.

Yuize, Y., "Farmers' Consumption Functions by Their Main Farm Products (Gyotaibetsu Noka no Shohi-Kansu)," *Nōgyō Sogokenkyu,* National Res. Inst. of Agriculture, XV, No. 2 (1961).

CHAPTER 15

EFFECTS OF THE LAND REFORM ON CONSUMPTION AND INVESTMENT OF FARMERS†

SHIGETO KAWANO

The present paper will examine the epochal change in postwar Japanese agriculture brought about by the Land Reform as well as its economic implications centering in consumption and investment of farmers. For reasons noted below, the analyses focus on the period 1951–54.

Theoretically speaking, it is difficult to isolate the effects of the Reform because the condition of "other things being equal" is difficult to maintain for economic and social phenomena. In the case of the Land Reform, major changes had been in progress between the pre- and post-Reform period, such as inflation and the drastic increase in population due to the return of Japanese in large numbers from abroad. Hence, to examine the short-run effects of the Reform, it would be most desirable to compare the periods just before and after the Reform. Unfortunately, due to the paucity of accurate statistical data for these periods, I have had to resort to two periods as far apart as 1934–36 and 1951–54 (excluding 1953) for purposes of comparison. The prime reason for the choice of the above periods is that reasonably satisfactory statistical data are available from the Farm Household Budget Survey by the Ministry of Agriculture and Forestry of Japan which makes it possible to analyze in a comparative manner the effects of the Reform on farmers' propensity to consume and invest.

I. The Pre-Reform Land Tenure System

The land tenure system in Japan was radically changed by the Land Reform implemented just after World War II which also had

---

† An earlier version of this paper was published under the title "Economic Significance of the Land Reform in Japan" in *The Developing Economies*, III, No. 2 (1965).

a profound effect upon the distribution of agricultural income, the consumption level of farm families, and agricultural investments. In order to see how this change was effected, we must first examine the land tenure system which prevailed before the Reform, in particular, its basic features and its agricultural implications.

The land tenure system in Japan is characterized not only by the extremely small acreage of agricultural land available per farm family, as is common in the case of most Asian countries, but also by a larger ratio of cultivated land and a smaller ratio of pastures and stock-farms to total agricultural land. Although the total acreage of Japan's agricultural land in 1956 was only 6,040,000 cho,[1] that is, 1.05 cho per farm family, the ratio of cultivated land to the total amounted to 18 per cent, a marked difference from the world average of about 30 per cent. This seems to indicate the extremely intensive use of limited farm land.

Farm lands in Japan consist of paddy and upland fields which in 1955 accounted for 56.5 per cent and 43.5 per cent, respectively, of the total acreage under cultivation. Most of the substantial and longer-range investment has been made in paddy fields in the form of irrigation, drainage, and land improvement. Consequently, its productivity is on the average much higher than that for upland, and the price of paddy field was about 1.8 times higher than that of upland throughout the period from the 1930s to the Reform.

This led to the increased drive to purchase rice fields for profit as well as investment in opening up new rice fields. Large holdings were more often seen in paddy land than in the case of uplands. From research conducted in 1941, we can get a picture of land-holding just before the Reform. In the case of paddy field owners, the proportion of those who owned more than 2 chō among all paddy field owners was 4.7 per cent in number and 36.4 per cent in aggregate acreage, both being far larger figures than in the case of upland owners for whom the figures were 2.3 per cent and 26.1 per cent, respectively. Among the large owners, paddy field owners and upland owners alike, were those who owned as much as 1,500 chō of farm land. On the whole, however, family farming was operated

---

[1] 1 chō equals 2.45 acres.

on a small scale as represented by the above-mentioned average of 1.05 chō of agricultural land per family.

These conditions naturally led to the extensive establishment of landholdings not cultivated by owners, namely, tenanted lands. The ratio of tenanted land to the aggregate acreage of paddy fields and uplands combined had been 45 per cent or so almost continuously from about 1910. In 1941, 53.2 per cent of paddy fields and 37.7 per cent of upland were tenanted lands, with those regarded as true tenant farmers accounting for about 28 per cent of the total number of farmers. The general features of the landowner-tenant relations before Reform were as follows:

(1)   Tenancy agreements were seldom made in written form, and consequently, in most cases, no terms except the amount of rent were expressly specified; not even the period of tenancy was provided for in the contract so that an "indeterminate tenancy," so to speak, was dominant, making landowner-tenant relations unstable.

(2)   The tenant's right to compensation for investment made on the land upon termination of a contract was not established.

(3)   Because a tenancy contract was made not for a certain farm unit but for each parcel of land comprising only 0.05 cho or so, the level of rent was drastically pushed up by competition until there was no profit retained in tenant farm management. The payment of rent was made in several forms, such as fixed rent in kind, rent in kind payable in cash,[2] fixed rent in cash, and crop-sharing. As shown in the following table, the ratios for the different forms of rent, in terms of the acreage of tenanted land, were 65.7 per cent for fixed rent in kind, 13.0 per cent for rent in kind payable in cash, and 20.5 per cent for rent in cash. In spite of these figures, it does not seem that there were substantial differences in the rent burden according to type of payment. More precisely, in the case of paddy fields, rent in kind and rent in kind payable in cash, which is essentially the same as the former, were predominant, rent payment in cash being hardly practiced. However, in the case of ordinary uplands, mulberry farms and orchards, 50 per cent or so of the total number of contracts were covered by rent in cash. Apparently, this

---

[2] Rent to be paid in cash equivalent of a certain amount of crops valued at the time of payment.

lead us to think that in the latter case the burden of farm rent was relatively light, and the tenant's position as a cultivator was more secure, but, in fact, this was not always true. Rent payment in a certain quantity of rice was convenient not only for tenants, but also for landowners, small landowners in particular, for it constituted the provisions of the latter, and it was because of this convenience that rent in kind was prevalent in the case of paddy fields. On the other hand, the predominance of rent in cash for other categories of farm land is due to the fact that the products of the land for which rent was paid were industrial crops, and this form of rent was more convenient for both payers and payees.

Accordingly, the burden of rent in cash, which is stable in respect to the amount to be paid by tenants, fluctuated considerably over time, if not for the crop year concerned. Thus, rent in cash was not necessarily more stable in character or smaller than a rent in kind which fluctuates with the price of the produce. On the other hand, it can be said that rent in kind and rent in kind payable in cash tend to offset in some degree, even within the period of a contract, the effect of changes in the amount of economic rent caused by fluctuations of the price of produce (subject to adjustment corresponding to these fluctuations). Thus, long-term investments by tenant farmers on their tenanted land were generally hard to make, restricting the capital intensity of tenant farming. Illustrating the above situation, the per *tan* (0.1 chō) yield of a given crop was lower on tenanted land than on owner-cultivated land, and perennial crops such as mulberries and fruits were mostly grown on owner-cultivated land. According to the government statistics for 1929, the only survey taken before the Reform showing the ratios of owner-cultivated and tenanted land, the ratios of tenanted land in the total acreage of paddy fields, upland, mulberry farms, orchards, and tea plantations were 55.2 per cent, 43.6 per cent, 31.9 per cent, 26.0 per cent, and 24.4 per cent respectively (See Table 2). Note that in the case of perennial crop cultivation, the ratio of tenanted land is remarkably small when compared with the case of paddy field or upland cultivations. This is presumably due to the fact that unstable tenancy terms, combined with the scanty means of tenant farmers, generally prevented tenant farmers from making such long-term investments.

TABLE 1
Distribution of Tenanted Land by Form of Rent*

	Total	Paddy field	Upland	Mulberry farm	Orchard	Tea plantation	Others
Total acreage of tenanted land (chō)	2,620,585	1,665,254	795,995	121,477	26,375	8,543	2,941
Rent in kind (%)	65.68	86.43	29.71	29.29	24.27	21.27	50.23
Rent in kind payable in cash (%)	13.03	12.39	12.11	25.91	19.9	17.11	23.49
Rent in cash (%)	20.48	0.56	56.98	44.80	51.50	59.87	25.87
Crop-sharing and other forms of rent (%)	0.81	0.62	1.20	—	4.44	1.75	0.41
Total (%)	100	100	100	100	100	100	100

* Data from the Farm Land Bureau, Ministry of Agriculture and Forestry, *Statistics concerning Problems of Farm Land (Nōchi Mondai ni kansuru Tōkei Shiryō)* (Tokyo, 1952).

As a result, infrastructure investments in paddy fields were made exclusively by landowners with tenant farmers taking to fertilizer investments, the returns on which can be recovered in a short period. This is counted as a cause for the development of a fertilizer-intensive agriculture of a type rarely seen elsewhere in the world.

TABLE 2

Ratios of Owner-Cultivated Land and Tenanted Land
by Categories of Farm Land*

(Unit:%)

	Owner-cultivated land	Tenanted land
Paddy field	44.8	55.2
Upland field	56.4	43.6
Mulberry farm	68.1	31.9
Orchard	76.1	26.0
Tea plantation	75.6	24.4

* Data from Bureau of Statistics, Office of the Prime Minister, *Report of the 1929 Agricultural Survey (Showa 4 Nen Nōgyō Chōsa Kekka Hōkoku)*.

II. The Land Reform

The Land Reform produced a drastic change in the structure of Japanese agriculture; during the two years from 1945 to 1947 a total of about 2 million cho of paddy fields and uplands were transferred from the hands of landowners to tenant farmers. The ratio of tenanted land to the total acreage under cultivation was reduced from 45 per cent to 10 per cent, and the ratio of tenant farmers to the total number of farmers decreased from 28 per cent to 5 per cent (See Table 3).

TABLE 3

Ratio of Tenanted Land to Total Farm Land and Ratio of Tenant
Farmers to Total Farm Families*

	Before the reform (as of Nov. 23, 1945)	After the reform (as of Aug. 1, 1950)
Total acreage under cultivation (chō)	5,155,697	5,200,430
Acreage of tenanted land (chō)	2,368,233	524,683
Ratio of tenanted land (%)	45.9	10.1
Ratio of tenant farmers (%)	28.4	5.1

* Data from the Farm Land Bureau, Ministry of Agriculture and Forestry, *Report on the Results of Farm Land Release Program (Nōchi no Jisseki Chōsa)* and *27th Statistical Yearbook of the Ministry of Agriculture and Forestry (Dai 27ji Nōrinshō Tōkeihyō)*.

This reform implied roughly three things. First, it aimed simply at the establishment of owner-farmers. In other words, it not only brought about an increase in the acreage of owner-cultivated land and in the number of owners as well, but it caused a change in property distribution, leading thereby to an equalization of property. Tenanted lands were transformed into owner-cultivated lands by the transfer of land in the following categories: all of the tenanted lands belonging to non-resident landowners, the portion in excess of the national average of 1 chō of tenanted lands in the hands of resident landowners and the portion exceeding the national average of 3 chō of owner-cultivated land. This measure was enforced in such a way as to keep the price of expropriated land unchanged in the course of violent inflation so that as a consequence tenant farmers increased their land holdings virtually without bearing any financial burden. Specifically, the average purchase price of expropriated land per 0.1 chō was 760 yen for paddy field and 447 yen for upland field. These are the owner farmer's revenue prices[3] derived on the basis of the price of rice purchased by the government from landowners in 1945 which stood at 55 yen per koku.[4] These prices were low enough, being only about one-third of the prices calculated on the basis of the producer's price of rice at that time which stood at 150 yen per koku. With the rapid advance of inflation after that time, the producer's price of rice rose further to 1,750 yen per koku in 1947. Hence, if calculated on this basis, the purchase price of farm land in terms of rice fell as low as 0.5 koku which in turn means that, with approximately half the amount of rent being paid in kind before the Reform, tenant farmers could readily pay for the price of the land they purchased from landowners.

Thus, the liberation of tenanted land transferred the ownership of landed property from non-resident and resident landowners to tenant farmers with almost no compensation for landowners. It had the effect of bringing about an equalization of property ownership within the rural community and at the same time of

---

[3] This denotes the highest possible price of land and is so calculated as to make possible an annual profit of 4 per cent for the agricultural enterprise and to enable the landowners to receive a rental almost equal to the yield of government bonds.

[4] 1 koku equals 4.9629 bushels.

increasing the property of resident farmers as a whole since it deprived non-resident landowners of all their landholdings.

Secondly, the Land Reform tightened legal regulations concerning the terms and conditions of tenancy and thereby strengthened the position of tenant farmers. More specifically, it aimed at stipulating the minimum period of tenancy; that is, it intended to remove the anxiety of tenant farmers due to indeterminate tenancy and at the same time to stabilize their farming program by assuring them of a minimum tenancy term of three years. It stipulated the tenant farmer's right to compensation for the investment he made on the land he cultivated, and finally it standardized various forms of rent payment in cash as well as controlling the amount of rent. According to the Farm Land Law which has legalized these regulations, the maximum rental rate is prescribed as 25 per cent of the production value of the main crop in the case of paddy field, and as 15 per cent of the production value of all crops in the case of upland.

Thirdly, the Land Reform brought the rental level under strict control and restricted the transfer of ownership of land between farmers or between farmer and non-farmer. Because rent is stipulated as a certain amount of money for each plot of land in spite of inflation, the level of the rental rate dropped to about 7 per cent of the production value of rice yield—remarkably low when compared with the rental rate before the Reform which had been about 50 per cent of the per acreage yield of rice as rent in kind. On the other hand, the ownership of land by non-residents was of course forbidden, and the purchase of land on too large a scale or in excessively small units leading to fragmentation was forbidden.

III. Effects of the Land Reform on Consumption and Investment

If the above were the main features of the Land Reform, what then were its economic effects, especially on consumption and investment among farmers?

It must first be noted that in the course of this Land Reform, small-scale landownership and small-scale farm management conspicuously increased. The number of farm families increased from 5,697,948 in 1946 to 6,176,419 in 1950, an increase of 8.4 per cent.

In this process, the number of farmers operating more than 2 chō of farm land decreased while those operating less than 2 chō rapidly increased. The increase is particularly remarkable among marginal farmers who operate less than 0.5 chō of farm land (Table 4). It must of course be taken into account, in this connection, that these changes were brought about under pressure of such difficult postwar problems as the rapid inflow of repatriates and food shortages in urban areas. Nevertheless, there is no denying the fact that these changes were motivated mainly by the expropriation of farm land formerly leased by landowners without imposing extra burdens on the cultivators and the consequent establishment of owner-cultivators.[5]

TABLE 4

Changes in the Number of Farming Families by Operation Scale*

	Number of families in 1946	Number of families in 1950	Number increased or decreased	Rate of increase or decrease(%)
Total number of farming families	5,697,948	6,176,419	+478,471	+8.4
–0.3 chō	1,293,759	1,471,872	+178,113	+13.8
0.3–0.5	939,349	1,050,469	+111,120	+11.8
0.5–1.0	1,785,640	1,972,925	+187,285	+10.5
1.0–2.0	1,336,871	1,339,536	+2,665	+0.2
2.0–3.0	211,260	207,845	−3,415	−1.6
3.0–5.0	77,130	76,928	−202	−0.3
5.0–	50,693	48,442	−2,251	−4.4
Others	3,246	8,402	+5,156	+158.8

* Data from the Ministry of Agriculture and Forestry, *27th Statistical Yearbook of the Ministry of Agriculture and Forestry (Dai 27ji Nōrinshō Tōkeihyō).*

[5] At this point I wish to answer several questions raised by Prof. Dantwala in his comment on my paper. He was amazed at the smoothness with which the transfer of ownership to tenants and reduction in rents were effected during 1945–47, a time when employment in agriculture increased at an unprecedented annual compound rate of 1.76 per cent, thereby reversing the previous long term declining trend (See Chapter 7 by Umemura). Prof. Dantwala wanted to find out the reason why black marketing in the leasing of lands did not emerge in spite of such severe pressure of population on land. I think that the reasons why a black market did not emerge in the case of Japan are twofold: First, the existence and pressure of the Allied Occupational authorities was a decisive factor enabling the thorough implementation of the Reform in spite of unfavorable circumstances. Second, we should take note of the strong attitude of the Japanese people, especially in the rural areas, to adhere to laws and government regulations.

Other things being equal, the equalization of landownership will elevate the income level of ex-tenant farmers in that it enables those farmers to acquire for nothing, so to speak, an extra income from the land previously held by landowners. It may also elevate the level of average agricultural income of the farmers as a whole. This is quite probable, if not certain, in spite of the fact that the number of farm families increased by 8.4 per cent, when we consider that revenue from land ceased to accrue to non-resident landowners while the collection of farm rent by resident landowners for their unexpropriated land was restricted by the farm rent regulation.

The increased average income standard will, as a matter of course, result in a higher average consumption level. However it is also important to study what effect the equalization of income will have on the change of the average propensity to consume. From the viewpoint of those who attach importance to the demonstration effect caused by the high consumption level of large income earners, the weakening of this effect due to the equalization of income will work as a restraint on the propensity to consume. On the other hand, according to the view that the equalization of income will change the fixed ideas of farmers as to their consumption and accordingly promote consumption in rural communities, the equalization of income will, on the contrary, raise the average propensity to consume. In reality, however, there are various conditions other than land reform in and outside the rural community that affect consumption, and besides, no ready material is available on the change in propensity to consume brought about by the Reform. Hence, it is difficult to reach an exact conclusion on this problem.

If we choose a certain scale of farm land operation (before the Reform for 1934–1936, 1.24–1.32 chō, and after the Reform for 1951, 1952, and 1954, 1–1.5 chō) and compare the economic situations of farm families with regard to disposable income, consumption, and saving per member of a family, the following observations can be made (See Table 5).[6]

---

[6] The year 1953 was dropped from our analysis because it was a year of bad crops, particularly in the case of rice, making it unsuitable for the purposes of comparison. For this comparative study we are much indebted to the paper by Takeo Misawa and Yuzuru Ito (Misawa and Ito, 1958), although the figures obtained by us are a little different from those in the above paper.

TABLE 5

Disposable Income, Consumption, and Saving per
Member of a Farming Family*

(Unit: %)

| | 1934–1936 | | | | 1951, 1952, 1954, Average | |
| | Owner-farmers | | Tenant farmers | | | |
	Yen	%	Yen	%	Yen	%
Disposable income	141.50	(100)	103.15	(100)	147.59	(100)
Consumption	115.40	(81.6)	91.62	(88.8)	136.81	(92.7)
Saving	26.10	(18.4)	11.53	(10.2)	10.78	(7.3)

    * Disposable Income data (1934–36) from the Ministry of Agriculture and Forestry, *Survey of the Farm Household Economy.*

    1951, 1952, 1954 average figures from *Reprinted Survey Report on Farm Household Economy Survey (Fukkokuban Nōka Chōsa Hōkokusho),* T. Inaba, ed. (Tokyo, 1951, 1953, 1954).

    Adjustment to base year prices based on the prewar data from Research Section, Economic Planning Agency, *General Statistics of Japanese Economy (Keizai Yōran).*

    (1) 1953 being a lean year, figures for this year have been excluded.

    (2) Adjustment to 1934–36 constant prices were made according to the Farm Families' Purchase Index.

    (3) Disposable income for 1934–36 was calculated according to the following formula:

        Disposable income=(Income of farm family)−(Public charges and interests on debts included in household expenditures).

The per capita disposable income of owner-farmers increased slightly from 141.50 yen in the years before the Reform to 147.59 yen in the years after the Reform. The consumption rate increased remarkably from 81.6 per cent to 92.7 per cent and the saving rate showed a sharp decrease. In the case of the tenant farmers who are comparable to the above owner-farmers in respect of farming scale, disposable income increased from 103.15 yen to 147.59 yen against which the consumption rate rose from 88.8 per cent to 92.7 per cent while the saving rate declined from 10.6 per cent to 7.9 per cent. In money terms, in the case of owner-farmers, against a rise of 6 yen in disposable income, consumption increased by 21 yen, and saving decreased by 14 yen. In the case of tenant farmers, against an increase of 44 yen in the disposable income, consumption increased by the same amount, and saving neither increased nor decreased.

After the Reform, an average of as much as 90 per cent of the farm land under management by farm families was converted to owner-cultivated land, while owner-farmers in prewar years owned as much as 90 per cent of their farming land. Therefore, the above comparison based on Table 5 is tantamount to a comparison of the change in economic situation between those owner-farmers who used to be tenant farmers at the same farming scale before the Land Reform and those farmers who have been owner farmers at the same farming scale through all the years before and after the Reform.

Then, it follows that in the case of tenant farmers, disposable income increased by approximately 43 per cent largely because the Land Reform granted them the amount of former landowners' rental income, and all the increased income was spent on consumption. In the case of owner-farmers, against only a 4 per cent increase in disposable income, the expenditure for consumption increased as much as 19 per cent. Table 6 indicates the rates of increase of farm household expenditures calculated by expenditure item. What draws our attention in this table is the unusually large figures for owner-farmers. While it is well known that the real income level of the farmers as a whole in the pre-Reform period was rather lower than in the post-Reform period, the income elasticity was lower in the former than in the latter. Thus we find that a large-scale shift in the farmers' propensity to consume took place after the Reform, and more important, this shift was particularly large in the case of owner-farmers. It is difficult to discern the extent to which these changes can be attributed to Land Reform alone. In my opinion, the only thing that can be concluded in this regard is that the addition of rental income enabled the ex-tenant farmers to raise their consumption level without eating into the absolute amount of previous annual saving and that it expedited the rise in the propensity to consume of farmers as a whole. Accordingly, in the case of owner-farmers who had to frequently draw from their past savings, the increased propensity to consume is presumed to have entailed considerable difficulties. The reason why it was nevertheless achieved is, in my opinion, that the large-scale rise in the consumption level of ex-tenant farmers induced a similar rise in the case of owner-farmers—a sort of "demonstration effect."

Viewed differently, however, this would mean an increase in

TABLE 6

Rates of Increase of per Capita Income and Consumption Among
Farm Family Members *

(Unit: Yen)

	Owner-farmer		Tenant-farmer	
	141.50–147.59		103.15–147.59	
Per capita disposable income[a]	(1934–1936)	(1951, 52, 54)	(1934–1936)	(1951, 52, 54)
Household expenditure		+4.31		+1.14
Food and drink		+8.39		+1.04
Lighting, heating, and power		+4.98		+1.26
Clothing		+9.60		+2.48
Education and culture		+19.81		+6.33
Housing, furniture, and utensils		+21.90		+4.11

* Data from the Ministry of Agriculture and Forestry, *Survey of the Farm Household Economy.*
a) Per capita income is adjusted to base year (1934–36) prices.

TABLE 7

Increase in Expenditure Per Member of Farm Families
between 1934–1936 and 1951–1954 (excluding 1953)*

(Unit: Yen)

	1934–1936		1951, 1952 and 1954^a	Increases		Rates of increase (per cent)	
	Owner-farmer	Tenant-farmer		Owner-farmer	Tenant-farmer	Owner-farmer	Tenant-farmer
Household expenditure	115.40	91.62	136.81	21.41	45.19	18.55	49.32
Food and drink	51.39	48.24	69.93	18.54	21.69	36.08	44.84
Lighting, heating, and power	5.70	4.48	6.92	1.22	2.44	21.40	54.46
Clothing	11.44	7.81	16.16	4.72	8.35	41.26	106.91
Education and culture	4.45	2.21	8.24	3.79	6.03	85.17	272.85
Housing, furniture, and other utensils	7.70	5.40	14.95	7.25	9.55	94.16	176.85

* Data from the Ministry of Agriculture and Forestry, *Survey of Farm Household Economy*.

a) Postwar expenditure figures are adjusted to base year (1934–36) prices.

domestic demand and an expansion of the home market for consumer goods. Table 7 shows the increase in principal items of per capita farm family expenditure. The increase in household expenditures for both owner and tenant farmers are shown as 19 per cent and 50 per cent, respectively, during the period under review. It can be easily supposed that such increases in family expenses of farmers should have been part of the cause for the shortage in consumer goods, especially in food, which extended from 1945 to the early 1950's. It would also partly account for the fact that the government had to enforce controls on prices and quantities of food grains, based on a system of food delivery and rationing, as a necessary follow-up to the Land Reform. While food price control was apparently meant to control farm incomes, the control of food quantities through delivery was directed at limiting the farmers' consumption of food.

What effect, then, did the Land Reform have on investment in agriculture? It would follow from what has already been discussed that, other conditions being equal, it should promote long-term and fixed capital investment. As a means of shedding additional light on this point, let us examine the changes in the expenditures for physical inputs in agriculture per farm household and in its ratio to gross income per household as shown in Table 8. For it can be

TABLE 8
Ratio of Expenditures on Physical Inputs to Gross Farm Income*

	1934–1936		1951, 1952 and 1954[a]
	Owner-farmer	Tenant farmer	
A. Gross farm income per household (Yen)	1,138.06	1,063.35	1,093.16
B. Material cost per household (Yen)[b]	263.00	225.86	298.31
B/A (%)	23.11	21.24	27.28
Agricultural income per member of family (Yen)	129.20	79.62	119.13

* Data from the Ministry of Agriculture and Forestry, *Survey of the Farm Household Economy*.

a) Adjusted to 1934–36 (base year) prices.

b) Physical inputs expenditure in 1934–36 represents farm management outlay minus farm rent, interest on debt and other liabilities, while in 1951–54 (excluding 1953) it represents only the farm management outlay.

assumed that if fixed and long-term capital investment increase, the gross farm income per household should also rise. Both the amount of such expenditures and its ratio to the gross farm income of the average owner-farmer were higher than those of tenant farmers before the Land Reform. After the Reform, this expenditure, as well as the ratio for owner farmers, tended to increase further. These expenditures consisted mainly of fertilizers, feeds, agricultural chemical and depreciation allowances for animal stocks, crops, farming machines, implements and building facilities and did not include depreciation allowances for land improvement investment. If the last item were to be included, the expenditures incurred by owner farmers would increase still further.[7]

As regards the effect of fixed and long-term capital investments by farmers on labor productivity, no consistent data and material are available, but comparing per-capita-agricultural income before and after the Land Reform, we notice a decline following the Reform. Therefore, this may be said to indicate roughly that, although the Land Reform encouraged fixed and long term investments in agriculture, it was not accompanied by a rise in productivity, at least in the early 1950s.

Furthermore, the ratio of the income from farming of owner-farmers to their total earnings (agricultural income plus non-agricultural earnings), as well as the ratio of their agricultural income to their total disposable income, showed a marked decrease as seen in Table 9. This income pattern of a smaller fraction of total income coming from agricultural income supplemented by a larger fraction coming from non-agricultural earnings became similar to the pre-Reform income pattern of tenant farmers, even if, in absolute value terms, the total or disposable income level of the former was a little higher than that of the latter. Moreover, as is indicated by Table 9, the number of post-Reform farming family members is

---

7. Prof. Dantwala pointed out that expenditure on physical inputs should be broken down into its long-term (farming machines) and short-term (fertilizers, seeds) elements. This breakdown could not be done because of data limitations. However, we can point out the tendency of increase in long-term investment with the help of other associated data, for instance, that of the increase recorded in the number of agricultural machines and implements during this period.

TABLE 9

Agricultural, Non-Agricultural, and Disposable Incomes Per Household*

	1934–1936		1951, 1952, 1954 average
	Owner-farmer	Tenant farmer	
A. Agricultural income (Yen)[a]	834.84	514.63	830.14
B. Non-agricultural income (Yen)[ab]	140.48	146.21	241.01
C. Total (Yen)	975.32	660.84	1,071.15
D. Disposable income (Yen)	914.31	672.91	1,025.56
A/C (%)	85.60	77.84	77.50
A/D (%)	91.31	76.48	80.95

* Data from the Ministry of Agriculture and Forestry, *SFHE*.

a) Agricultural income in 1934–36 represents agricultural income plus various farm incidence and liabilities; Non-agricultural income is equal to side incomes plus non-agricultural liabilities and other domestic work incomes (minus gifts).

b) Non-agricultural income in 1951 may include incomes from gifts and relief, but these have not been excluded because of difficulty in so doing.

larger than that of both owner and tenant farmers before the Reform so that the disposable income per member of the household did not increase in absolute value from pre-Reform years to the same extent as did household income.

The raising of the farm income level through the redistribution of land ownership may be supposed to have so affected the post-Reform farmer's income as to bring about a decrease in labor hours per farm household head, but sufficient, consistent data are not available to confirm this. According to pre-Reform and prewar data, disposable income per farming family member used to differ between owner and tenant farmers, provided the scale of farming in terms of acreage under cultivation was the same, but their labor hours did not necessarily differ to the same extent. Table 10 shows that, for owner and tenant farmers both cultivating 1.3 chō of land, annual average per-capita-disposable income for the period between 1934 and 1936 was 141.50 yen for the former versus 103.15 yen for the latter. Although this reveals a great income gap between the two, the total annual labor hours per head, inclusive of both farming and non-farming work, for the same period of time, was 1,156 hours for the former and 1,152 hours for the latter. In time series too, as well as in annual averages, no discernible trends are noted to the contrary. A comparison between farmers in the "First category,"

Table 10

Per-Capita-Disposable Income and Labor Hours of Farm Families*

	Owner-farmer		Tenant farmer	
	Disposable income (Yen)	Labor hours[a] (Hours)	Disposable income (Yen)	Labor hours[a] (Hours)
1934	126.07	1,191	92.79	1,143
1935	143.64	1,138	99.63	1,134
1936	154.79	1,139	117.02	1,179
Average	141.50	1,156	103.15	1,152

* Data from *Reprinted Survey Report on Farm Household Economy Survey
(Fukkokuban Nōka Chōsa Hōkokusho)*, T. Inaba, ed., Tokyo.
a) Labor hours represent the annual total of labor hours involved in farming,
side jobs, etc.

which comprised farmers cultivating more than 70 per cent of the
average cultivated acreage per household of those farmers surveyed
by the Ministry of Agriculture and Forestry (as shown in Table 11),
and those in the "Second category," which consisted of those other
than the first category farmers (that is, a comparison between farmers with different scales of farming), does not show any differences
either. Labor hours of tenant farmers in the second category were
slightly less than those of the first, to be sure, but considering the
fact that the number of working members within the family was
smaller in the case of the former, labor hours per working member
of the family may be regarded as more or less the same, regardless
of the scale of farming or size of disposable income. It would follow,
then, that no great income effect was felt in the labor supply of
farmers, at least over a short period of time, either because of
technological conditions in agriculture or because of customary
practices in rural communities. Therefore, even in the case of the
post-Reform owner-farmers who were formerly tenant farmers
whose disposable income increased greatly after the Land Reform,
their augmented income would not be expected to push down the
labor supply because of the aforementioned inelastic labor supply.
This is even less so in the case of pre-Reform owner-farmers whose
disposable income barely increased as a result of the Reform. Thus,
we may conclude that, so far as the farmers with a farming scale of
between 1.24 and 1.32 chō of land are concerned, their labor supply

TABLE 11

Per-Capita-Disposable Income and Labor Hours of Two Categories of Farm Families*

| | "First category" farmer [a,b] | | | | "Second category" farmer [a,b] | | | |
| | Owner-farmer | | Tenant farmer | | Owner-farmer | | Tenant farmer | |
	Disposable income (Yen)	Labor hours (Hours)	Disposable income (Yen)	Labor hours (Hours)	Disposable income (Yen)	Labor hours (Hours)	Disposable income (Yen)	Labor hours (Hours)
1934	126.80	1,192	93.88	1,138	123.44	1,182	81.99	1,162
1935	144.77	1,141	102.78	1,173	141.18	1,135	91.88	1,037
1936	154.74	1,151	124.87	1,227	154.68	1,085	96.78	1,056
Average	142.10	1,163	107.18	1,179	139.77	1,134	90.23	1,085

*   Data from *Reprinted Survey Report on Farm Household Economy Survey (Fukkokuban Nōka Chōsa Hōkokusho)*, T. Inaba, ed.
a) Areas under cultivation by first and second category farmers are 1.43–1.53 cho and 0.82–0.92 cho respectively.
b) Those actually employed in farming as a proportion to the total number for family members in the "First category" owner-farmer and tenant farmer categories were 0.59 and 0.59 respectively, while the ratios in the "Second category" owner-farmer and tenant-farmer categories were 0.59 and 0.55 respectively.

did not appreciably decrease as compared with pre-Reform years.[8]

When farm rents are under control, it is considered that the gap between the controlled rent and a competitive rent is capitalized and forms a sort of premium. However, this transaction is not permitted in Japan. As a result, rent control may possibly have resulted in the wasteful tillage of both owned and rented farm lands for farm lands necessarily have to be undervalued because of these controls. Moreover, since competitive rent cannot operate openly, comparisons between different fields of farming with respect to earning power tend to become difficult; thus, an effective utilization of land is hampered. The gaps between various fields of farming in respect to the amount of remuneration brought by a day of family labor, including the portion payable as rent, tend to widen. Thus, criteria for rationally allotting capital and labor become obscure.

If the rent is undervalued in the name of rent control, it may conversely bring about a high valuation of the remuneration of family labor while restrictions on purchase of farm lands in the name of farm land control may so affect the mobility or allotment of labor that it may tend to stay in the same old field of farming. This seems to be proved partly by the fact that both agricultural and disposable incomes per member of farm households with 0.5–1.0 chō of land are nearly equal to, or even less than, those of households cultivating under 0.5 chō of land. As is seen from Table 12, the net property

---

[8] In this connection, the following table shows that the changes in disposable and agricultural incomes per farm household member in 1951, 1952, and 1954 and those in both total and family labor hours per head of the same household in the same years are not found to be related to each other.

Per Capita Income[a] and Labor Hours of Farm Household with Farming Scale of 1.0–1.5 chō*

	Disposable income (Yen)	Agricultural income (Yen)	Family labor hours (Hours)	Total labor hours (Hours)[b]
1951	133.41	112.06	—	—
1952	146.21	118.07	881.13	999.18
1954	163.15	127.25	884.59	998.01

* Data from *Reprinted Survey Report of Farm Household Economy Survey* (*Fukkokuban nōka chōsa hōkokusho*), T. Inaba, ed., Tokyo.
a) Incomes are in 1934–36 prices.
b) Total hours do not include those of the members having side jobs as permanent employment.

per member, of a household in the 0.5–1.0 chō category is, taking the average for the 1952–1954 period for which relevant data are available, 30 per cent larger than that of households in the class under 0.5 chō. The opposite is the case with respect to farm income and disposable income. This is probably because the farmers in the latter class depend more on sidework in the form of permanent employment, with the resultant higher hourly income, than the former category farmers. Such differences must have arisen from circumstances which prevented the farmers in the 0.5–1.0 chō category from allotting their labor to subsidiary jobs. The very reason for this must lie in the low evaluation of rent which conversely causes an evaluation of the remuneration of family labor at a higher level than the competitive wage together with the tendency on the part of the farmers to overvalue their farm labor in the present against the future difficulty of land purchase. The inability or difficulty for farmers in the 0.5–1.0 chō category to allot their labor to a permanent employment in side-jobs may also have arisen from their family composition.

TABLE 12

Per Capita Net Property, Labor Hours, and Income of Farm Family*

	Net property^a (Yen)	Labor hours^b (Hours)	Income (Yen)	Disposable income^a (Yen)
0.5 chō	105,812	650.34	42,003	42,308
0.5–1.0	141,143	919.07	41,937	41,894
1.0–1.5	177,453	998.60	46,710	45,575

* Data from the Ministry of Agriculture and Forestry, *Farm Household Economy Survey (Nōka Keizai Chōsa Hōkoku)* (1954).
The figures are an average of 1952 and 1954.
a) Net property, income and disposable income are in 1952 constant prices.
b) Labor hours do not include those of the members having side jobs as permanent employment.

In the final analyses, rent control, as well as the control of the transfer of lands, has very possibly hampered an effective and rational utilization of land by farmers, regardless of their farming scale, including those in the under 0.5 chō category. Table 13 shows a comparison of farm labor hours both per capita and per acre, agricultural income per head and productivity between 1952 and

TABLE 13

Farm Labor Hours and Incomes by Scale of Farming *

Chō	Farm labor hours (Hours)				Farm income (Yen)[a]						Ratio of farm income to total income (%)		Disposable income per member of household (yen)	
	Per capita		Per acreage		Per capita		Per acreage		Per labor hour					
	1952	1954	1952	1954	1952	1954	1952	1954	1952	1954	1952	1954	1952	1954
-0.5	503.06	459.93	713.56	631.77	13,919	14,793	19,743	20,320	27.67	32.16	36.50	32.25	38,422	46,194
0.5-1.0	782.95	744.08	627.87	572.37	25,671	27,469	20,658	21,130	32.90	36.92	64.91	62.18	39,463	44,324
1.0-1.5	881.13	884.59	498.94	481.02	34,992	37,731	19,814	20,517	39.71	42.65	78.51	77.20	43,330	48,385

* Data from the Ministry of Agriculture and Forestry, *Farm Household Economy* (*Nōka Keizai Chōsa Hōkoku*) (1952 and 1954).
a) Incomes are based on constant (1952) prices.

1954 and also between different scales of farming. From this table, the following observations may be made. With the exception of the 1.0–1.5 chō category, per capita labor hours show a steady decrease, especially in the under 0.5 chō category. A corresponding decrease is seen in labor hours per acre, but the rate of decrease is lower than in per capita labor hours, regardless of the scale of farming. As a result, agricultural incomes per head, per acre and per hour register an increase for all scales of farming, the rate of increase in each of these being higher the smaller the scale of farming. At the same time, the ratio of the agricultural income to total earnings is declining due to the relative increase in side-job incomes. Accordingly, the disposable income per head shows a higher rate of increase than that of the per capita agricultural income, but the rate of increase is higher in smaller scale farming.

We may now conclude from the foregoing that the increase in per capita income was brought about chiefly by the increasing earning power of land and the increased opportunities for non-agricultural employment and to a lesser extent by the decreased volume of labor input in agriculture which accompanied the increase in the earning power of farm land. The increase in income, however, is greater for smaller scale farming. As a result, the gaps between different scales of farming with respect to farm and disposable incomes per capita decreased markedly, although great differences still persist in hourly farm incomes. This, of course, is a reflection of the controls on the transfer of farm lands. If such transfers remained free, productivity would not be affected so much by differences in the scale of farming as may be indicated by Table 12 which shows that there is not much difference in disposable income per labor hour between first and second category farmers before the Land Reform, as long as the acreage of landholding or leased land was the same.

IV. Concluding Remarks

In the foregoing discussion, we have studied how the Land Reform influenced consumption, savings, investment, and productivity in the agriculture of Japan up to 1954. It has been made clear that the Reform stimulated a marked rise in propensity to consume, but that its effect on productivity via an increase in agricultural investment was still rather feeble. Moreover, the control of farm land transfer and rent control had rather negative effects on land use so that a rational allotment of capital and labor for their profitable utilization was hampered. At one time after the war the average income level of farmers was thought to have risen to such degree that it exceeded that of the non-farming population. This was when the redistribution of income through the Land Reform made itself felt around 1950. Since then, however, the income disparity between the agricultural and non-agricultural sectors has again turned against the former. The Land Reform must be counted as a contributing factor in the sense that it has not helped much in raising productivity in agriculture.

CHAPTER 16

LONG-TERM CHANGES IN FOOD CONSUMPTION PATTERNS IN JAPAN

Hiromitsu Kaneda[†]

Introduction

There have been many conspicuous changes in Japanese life
during the century that has elapsed since the beginning of the modernization process in the late 1860's. Although less marked than
many, the changes in food consumption patterns are of considerable
importance.

It is the purpose of this paper to trace the changes that have taken
place in the patterns of food consumption as reflected in the changing relative importance of various food groups, and to investigate
the inter-relationship between aggregate food consumption and
changes attendant to economic development. As much as available
data permit, the present study aims at relating changes in food consumption patterns to those of real income, urbanization, relative
prices and consumers' "tastes." The basic approach adopted is
similar to that of many studies available on the demand side of food
markets, in analyses of household expenditures, and in estimation of
consumption functions of various commodities. Some new statistical
procedures used in the paper are explained in detail in the Appendix.

The period of about 90 years covered in this study is divided into
three parts depending on the sources of data used for analyses: (1)
1878–1922, for which I rely mainly on the most recent estimates by

† I would like to thank Professor B. F. Johnston and Professor K. Ohkawa for their constant encouragement and valuable suggestions during the
course of this study. Without their help this study would not have been completed. I am deeply indebted also to Professor M. Shinohara and Dr. S. Yamada
for providing me with their data. The research contained in this paper was
carried out during my tenure as visiting research staff economist at the Economic Growth Center, Yale University, 1966–67.

This is an abridged version of my article of the same title in *Food Research
Institute Studies,* VIII, No. 1 (1968).

Saburo Yamada; (2) 1921–1940, for which I depend on Miyohei Shinohara's estimates as well as official statistics of the Ministry of Agriculture and Forestry; and (3) the postwar years, for which the quality of the official data, as well as the quantity, is unquestionably superior to those of the prewar years. It is inevitable in a study of this kind that disparities and divergencies appear in different sets of data. The problem is particularly acute among the estimates of consumption pertaining to the earlier periods. Attempts will be made to examine the consistency of available sets of data and to reconcile such divergencies whenever adjustments are possible.

I. Food Consumption Patterns: 1878–1922

"Many scholars and Japanese government officials have warned against the uncritical use of Japanese government statistics of the Meiji period" (Nakamura, 1965, p. 249). However, lacking alternative sources of data and supplementary information to correct such errors that exist in government statistics, scholars based their estimates of income and rates of growth of agriculture on the available official statistics without correction for errors. Since the publication of James I. Nakamura's essay (Nakamura, 1965), and subsequent book (Nakamura, 1966), however, the use of government statistics for the early years of Japan's modernization has been effectively discouraged.

That Nakamura has been successful in marshalling generally convincing evidence for discrediting the government statistics of the Meiji period does not mean that his alternative estimates of the level and the growth rate of agricultural production provide us with correct sets of data upon which we can rely.[1] Indeed, the controversy surrounding the growth of Japanese agriculture during the early period is not so much about Nakamura's critical examination of the

---

[1] Nakamura's basic proposition is that land tax evasion practices "caused a significant understatement of agricultural production during the Meiji period." The author himself acknowledges that "precise corrections are impossible because what is being attempted, in effect, is to measure the extent of tax evasion for which the responsible parties could scarcely have been expected to leave records" (Nakamura, 1965, p. 250).

His estimates are based on two quinquennial indices (1873–1877 and 1918–1922) of area planted and those of yield per unit area.

available official data as about the alternative estimates that can be offered under the circumstances. In view of the inevitable disputes over estimates constructed for this period, in this section I shall first examine Nakamura's estimates along with those on agricultural production more recently made available by Saburo Yamada (Umemura, 1966).

TABLE 1

Agricultural Products Available for Consumption Per Capita,
Some Recent Estimates, Five-Year Averages, 1878–1922*

Year	Total agricultural products		Rice	
	Nakamura-Noda	Yamada-Noda	Nakamura-NNKT	Yamada-NNTK
	(1)	(2)	(3)	(4)
	(In 1934–36 prices)		(In kilograms)	
1878–1882	51	39	177	137
1833–1887	52	42	175	142
1888–1892	52	44	175	145
1893–1897	54	46	175	138
1898–1902	57	51	175	149
1903–1907	60	55	179	162
1908–1912	61	58	170	159
1913–1917	63	63	167	163
1918–1922	68	68	173	173

* Sources: (1) Nakamura's implied total agricultural production from his "Corrected Index of Total Agricultural Production," under the assumed paddy rice yields of 1.6 and 1.95 *koku* for the five-year periods 1878–1882 and 1918–1922, respectively. Quinquennial average values in 1934–1936 prices were derived on the basis of Yamada's estimate of total agricultural output for 1918–1922. To this were added quinquennial averages of net agricultural imports and net inventory adjustment by Noda (Noda, 1956) deflated by the linked index of agricultural deflators from Ohkawa, et al. (in 1928–1932 prices) (Ohkawa, 1957) and from the "Ohkawa Series" (in 1934–1936 prices). See footnote 4, p. 403.
(2) Yamada's estimates of total agricultural production in 1934–1936 prices plus Noda's estimates of net agricultural imports and inventory adjustment in 1934–1936 prices deflated as above.
(3) Nakamura's implied rice production from his "Corrected Index of Rice Production," under the assumed paddy rice yields of 1.6 and 1.95 *koku* (for 1878–1882 and 1918–1922). Quinquennial averages were derived on the basis of Yamada's estimate of rice output for 1918–1922. To this average series were added quinquennial averages of net imports of rice from (Kayo, 1958: Table K-a-1) (referred to as NNKT above).
(4) Yamada's estimates of rice output plus quinquennial averages of net imports of rice from (Kayo, 1958: Table K-a-1).
The population data were obtained from Bank of Japan (1966, Table 1).

Columns 1 and 2 in Table 1 show quinquennial averages of agricultural products available for consumption per capita for the period between 1878 and 1922. The figures are in constant prices based on Nakamura's and Yamada's estimates of agricultural production, both adjusted on the basis of Tsutomu Noda's data to take account of net imports of agricultural products and changes in inventories (Noda, 1956). It is clear that the growth rate of agricultural products available for consumption is significantly less for the former than for the latter estimates. It is not surprising that this is so because Nakamura assumes (uses as one of his supporting arguments) that consumption of foods in terms of calories grew at about the same rate as population. Presumably, a part of growth in the value of agricultural products available for consumption per capita is attributable to shifts in consumption from less preferred food items (which are cheaper relatively in terms of calories) to preferred food items. This is a well-known empirical phenomenon observable in many countries (including currently underdeveloped countries) and, as later analyses show, in Japan itself.

In order to examine more closely the above presumption, quinquennial average quantities of rice available for consumption per capita were estimated from two sources. The estimated quantities are given in Columns 3 and 4 in Table 1. It is indeed remarkable that according to the Nakamura estimates there is stability, if not decline,[2] in the per capita quantity of rice over some forty years. Even if the assumption is correct that there was no change in per capita intake of calories, it should be expected that the composition of food would change during a period of (real per capita) income growth and, therefore, that per capita consumption of rice should increase at the expense of other "inferior" starchy staples. There is no question that rice has always been the most preferred among various starchy food products in Japan. Hence, the presumption of substitution among food, as suggested by the increase in per capita value of agricultural output shown in Column 1, should be reflected in an increase of rice consumption. This, however, is not what

---

[2] The computed figures show a slight decline over the years. If the population in early Meiji is underestimated, however, the decline in per capita availability is only apparent.

Column 3 shows.[3] On the contrary, the estimates by Nakamura are tantamount to the supposition that rice consumption has zero elasticity with respect to income (on a per capita basis). This is a doubtful proposition and, in turn, casts doubt on the assumptions involved in his estimating procedures. Since, however, there is no hard evidence to negate the implied zero income elasticity of rice consumption, for the period in question, it seems reasonable to take Nakamura's estimates of total agricultural production as the very minimum of the possible estimates of output growth in agriculture.

Under the assumption of stable relative prices, demand for agricultural products grows at a rate approximately equal to the income elasticity multiplied by the growth rate of per capita real income plus the rate of population growth. This familiar relationship can be expressed as follows:

$$\frac{\dot{D}}{D} = \frac{\dot{N}}{N} + \eta\left(\frac{\dot{Y}}{Y} - \frac{\dot{N}}{N}\right)$$

where D denotes demand (in real terms) for agricultural products,

[3] One possible counterargument may be that substitution of foods took place among various food groups, such as among starchy staples, animal protein foods, and other "protective foods" (i. e., those that are rich in vitamins and other nutrients), rather than among individual items within each of the food groups. But I find it hard to believe that this process could continue for forty years without changes in the composition of each major food group.

Another possible argument may be made on the basis of Seiki Nakayama's estimates. The Nakayama estimates can be used to show that: of the total calories derived from starchy staples over the period in question, the percentage attributable to rice remained rather stable; that derived from barley first increased and returned to the original level; and the percentage of miscellaneous cereals declined, while potatoes increased their relative importance.

Per Cent of Calories Attributable to Starchy Food Items*

Years	Rice	Barley	Miscellaneous Cereals	Potatoes	Total Starchy
1878–1882	69%	21%	6%	5%	100%
1898–1902	64	24	5	8	100
1918–1922	67	21	3	9	100

* Computed from Nakayama, 1958, p. 25.

Since Nakayama's data are based on government statistics without the benefit of recent revisions, I am skeptical of their reliability. It is a fair presumption that there would be greater underestimation of output of commodities other than rice than that of rice itself in the early Meiji period. I believe that the actual contribution by barley and potatoes was greater than the figures indicate.

N and Y population and real income, respectively, and η is the income elasticity of demand, and where dots indicate change in the variable over a unit period (See Appendix). It suggests a rough, but simple, measure of income elasticity of demand for agricultural products during the period under study.

By combining national income produced in non-agricultural sectors from Ohkawa (1957), together with Yamada's estimates of value-added in agriculture, the quinquennial average levels of national income were obtained for the period 1878–1882 through 1918–1922. Similarly, by adding Ohkawa's non-agricultural income and the values of agricultural income implied by Nakamura's estimates of total agricultural production, a second quinquennial series of national income estimates was constructed.[4] On the basis of these quinquennial data, then, along with those used in Table 1, the

---

[4] In want of established national income estimates compatible with the two agricultural series used here, I resorted to the following method of procuring the rough estimates:

(1) *Yamada-Ohkawa National Income Quinquennial Estimates*

S. Yamada's estimates of value-added in agriculture (1934–1936 prices) plus estimates of national income in non-agriculture by Ohkawa (1957) (in current prices) deflated by the index constructed by linking non-agricultural deflators from the same source and aggregate deflators (in 1934–1936 prices) from the *SSRC Project, Economic Growth in Japan, Basic Statistical Tables* (mimeo.), which is known as the "Ohkawa Series" at the Economic Research Institute at Hitotsubashi University.

(2) *Nakamura-Ohkawa National Income Quinquennial Estimates*

Nakamura's implied total agricultural production was obtained from his "Corrected Index of Total Agricultural Production," under the assumed paddy rice yields of 1.6 and 1.95 *koku*, on the basis of Yamada's estimates of total agricultural output (in 1934–1936 prices) for 1918–1922. This series was adjusted by Yamada's estimates of current inputs in agriculture (in 1934–1936 prices) to give national income produced in agriculture. Final estimates were obtained by summing this series and the Ohkawa non-agricultural income described above.

As Nakamura points out in his monograph, in the Meiji period there is a possible undermeasurement of income produced in non-agricultural sectors as well. I made no adjustment for this factor in the calculations above.

If indeed there is an undermeasurement of income produced in non-agricultural sectors, the growth rates of national income used here are overestimated. Moreover, the use of national income rather than personal income in this context implicitly assumes that corporate savings as a per cent of national income did not change. Although relevant data are not presently available, it is quite unlikely that this was the case.

following annual growth rates in real terms were computed for the forty-year period:

Population	
The Bank of Japan Estimates	1.0%
National Income Produced	
Nakamura-Ohkawa Estimates	3.2
Yamada-Ohkawa Estimates	3.8
Agricultural Products Available for Consumption	
Nakamura-Noda Estimates	1.7
Yamada-Noda Estimates	2.4
Agricultural Food Products Available for Consumption[5]	
Nakamura-Noda Estimates	1.4
Yamada-Noda Estimates	2.1
Rice Available for Consumption	
Yamada-NNKT Estimates	1.6

If these growth rate estimates are approximately what the actual rates were, and if the terms of trade between agricultural products and other commodities remained rather stable during these years, the implied, rough, income elasticities of demand for agricultural products may be derived from the relationship discussed above. These estimates of income elasticity for the period 1878 to 1922 are as follows:

Agricultural Products Available for Consumption	
Nakamura-Noda Estimates	.32
Yamada-Noda Estimates	.50
Agricultural Food Products Available for Consumption[6]	
Nakamura-Noda Estimates	.18
Yamada-Noda Estimates	.39
Rice Available for Consumption	
Yamada-NNKT Estimates	.21

---

[5] The quinquennial averages were constructed by subtracting non-food products in agriculture (such as, industrial crops, green manure and forage crops, sericulture and straw products) from the two estimates of total agricultural production. These data were added to the series of imports of agricultural food products (obtained by subtracting imports of cotton from total agricultural imports) used by Noda (1963).

[6] Considerable difference between the elasticity values for agricultural products and agricultural food products reflects a more rapid growth of output of the sericulture and tea export sectors.

According to Yamada's estimates of output of starchy staples (in 1934–1936 prices, not adjusted for imports), production of this food group grew at the annual rate of 1.4 per cent during the forty year period. This implies an income elasticity of demand for this food group of about .14.

These are, no doubt, crude estimates. Given the degree of uncertainty associated with the data used, however, it does not seem advisable to employ sophisticated estimating procedures on them. Nonetheless, comparison of the present estimates with those previously obtained by other scholars seems to be in order. The following are some of the well-known estimates:[7]

Products	Source	Years Covered	Income Elasticity
Agricultural Products	Noda (1956)	1878–1917	.74
		(1913–1937)	(.26)
Agricultural Food Products	Noda (1956)	1878–1921	.63
		(1922–1937)	(.23)
Agricultural Products	Noda (1963)	1878–1917	.82
		(1915–1937)	(.36)
Agricultural Food Products	Noda (1963)	1878–1917	.59
		(1915–1937)	(.18)
Starchy Staple Food	Nakayama (1958)	1878–1922	.38
		(1918–1942)	(−.27)

It is clear that for the period in question the present estimates of income elasticities are very much smaller than those given in the tabulation above. Evidently, the discrepancy between the two sets of estimates can be attributed to two causes, namely, (1) the significant upward revision of the levels of agricultural output during the early years embodied in the two sources used here, and, as its consequence,

---

[7] All the estimates were derived on the basis of constant-price aggregates, except for Nakayama's starchy-staple-food estimate which was aggregated on the basis of calories. In the present estimates rice only is in terms of weight. All the above estimates were based on the time-series regression of demand (per capita in logarithms) on real income (per capita in logarithms). Mathematically, this is the same as the present procedure.

Sources: Noda (1956); Nakayama (1958); Noda (1963).

(2) a similar revision of the levels of national income for the early years (thus reducing its estimated growth rate) in the present data. The more interesting aspect of the present estimates, however, is their relative proximity to the estimates pertaining to the second interval of years (given in parentheses) in the tabulation above.

For some time the drastic change in income elasticities around 1920 apparent in the tabulation has intrigued many Japanese and foreign scholars. What exactly happened in the years around the First World War? What factors account for such a change? These were some of the questions asked without ever being answered to satisfaction. The present results indicate that the drastic change alleged to have occurred may have been only illusory. Since the present estimating procedure does not yield the statistics for making judgment on the computed elasticities, and since the previous estimates by Noda and Nakayama are not helpful in this regard,[8] it is not possible to say whether or not the difference between the present estimates pertaining to the first forty-year period and the previous estimates for the second is statistically significant. It is reasonable to state, nevertheless, that the change in the elasticities around 1920 does not seem to have been as drastic as was believed previously. Given the expectation of decline in the values of elasticities during the ordinary process of economic growth, there is nothing strange about the phenomenon. The only relevant questions seems to be in regard to a task for empiricists to lop off years in order to choose certain periods in preference to others.[9] If Nakamura is right in theorizing that undermeasurement of production persisted until about 1920 (although Yamada thinks that the date should be

---

[8] Both authors do not give the standard errors of the coefficients estimated, nor do they give Student's t-ratio and R-squares, to say nothing of the Durbin-Watson statistic. Although this is not to discredit their estimated values entirely, there is no denying that the practice imposes severe limitations on interpretation of their results.

[9] It is well known that in the case of cross-section data, the characteristics of the group sampled are of crucial importance in interpreting measured elasticities. Similarly, in the case of income elasticities measured from time-series data, the characteristics and, particularly, the length of the period covered are of crucial importance. If Milton Friedman's permanent income hypothesis is accepted, it should be expected that measured elasticities are larger the longer the period covered (Nerlove, pp. 103–109).

advanced to around 1890), we have no alternative but to choose 1920 as the year for dividing the two periods.

The data used in the present study (Yamada-Ohkawa national income in 1934–1936 prices and the Bank of Japan population figures) yield 155 yen as an estimate of per capita national income for 1918–1922. At the average foreign exchange rate between the U.S. dollar and the Japanese yen prevailing in 1934–1936 (in New York), this figure is equivalent to $45 per year. Although the yen figure will be more than $45 at the U.S. price levels in recent years (say, double or triple the 1934–1936 prices), the level of per capita income is still low. The striking part of the story of Japanese food consumption is that the elasticities estimated, .2 to .4, are rather low at this meager level of per capita income. In recent years "accepted" values of income elasticity for food have ranged around .6 and .7 for poor countries whose per capita income is roughly comparable to Japan's in the 1920s.[10] Granted that a part of the explanation can be found in (1) the exclusion of transport, storage, retail and other marketing components of food values and in (2) the exclusion of marine products in the present data, I am inclined to think that the main reason must be sought elsewhere. That Japanese income elasticities in the early years of development were so low implies that the Japanese did not change their food consumption patterns greatly as they became wealthier. People were content to eat basically the same kind of food that they used to eat when they were poorer, although there were gradual changes in the relative composition of food and some occasional improvements in processing and other services. It is my contention that, in fact, food consumption patterns in Japan did not undergo any sudden, drastic change in the years preceding World War II.

II. Food Consumption Patterns: 1909–1940

According to Kuznets' calculations of the share of food in private consumption expenditures, on the basis of the data in Ohkawa (1957), the food share in total consumer expenditures declined markedly—from over 75 per cent in 1878–1882 to less than half of

---

[10] See, for example, Kaneda and Johnston (1961); Houthakker; and Clark and Haswell (1964).

that level in the 1930's (Kuznets). Upon examining these calculations Kuznets found three interrelated aspects of the trends in the food share: (1) the extremely high level of the share until World War I; (2) the striking decline from that level to the 1930s and even to the 1920s; and (3) the "very sharp character of the break" in the decline of this share between the prewar and the postwar (W.W.I) periods. Besides raising serious questions regarding the data he had used, Kuznets urged further scrutiny and explanation of the trends and expressed hope for research being undertaken by Japanese scholars.

According to Shinohara's data, recently made available (Shinohara, 1967), the share of foods in private consumption expenditure declined from 66 per cent in 1878–1882 to around 50 per cent in the 1930s.[11] This is what one could have expected. Given the growth of expendable resources per capita, the rise in the level of living would be reflected in a decline of this proportion. Although the absolute amount of food expenditures rises (per capita), mainly because demand shifts from less preferred foods, alternative uses of the consumer's budget for goods and services other than foods become relatively more important.

Far more interesting and quite revealing are the figures presented in Table 2. The picture presented by the table is unmistakable. The share of starchy staples in total food expenditure declines steadily from the level of around 56 per cent to 44 per cent during the course of the years. On the other hand, the relative importance of animal proteins and other foods (among which are such "protective" foods as fruits and vegetables) rises, the former rising more rapidly than the latter. The story is exactly the same when it is cast in terms of calories derived from these food groups. In terms of both food expenditure and calorie "intake," protein-rich animal foods increase their relative importance over the years.

In an international comparison of dietary patterns, M. K. Bennett

---

[11] Shinohara's estimates are based on the "commodity-flow" approach of measuring consumption expenditure. He starts with output (in quantities) and arrives at net food supply after adjusting for changes in inventories, net exports, wastage, non-food uses, etc. The net food supply figures are used to estimate food expenditure by applying appropriate price data (prices on farm—where a part of the supply is consumed—and retail prices).

found a rather close inverse relationship between the fraction of total calories derived from the starchy staples and the level of per capita income (Bennett, pp. 214–222). This decline of the "starchy staple ratio" as incomes rise reflects the tendency of people to consume increasingly large quantities of meat, dairy products, and other relatively costly foods as enlarged purchasing power allows them to modify their dietary pattern. Among the starchy staple foods there is also a tendency for people to shift away from consumption of sweet potatoes, barley, naked barley, and other miscellaneous cereals, while consumption of rice increases its relative importance. This phenomenon can be seen clearly in the following tabulation:

TABLE 2

Composition of Food Consumption, by Major Food Groups, 1911–1940*

Years	Starchy staples[a]	Animal proteins[b]	Other foods	Total[c]
	Food expenditure per capita (In 1934–1936 prices)			
1911–1915	35.0	5.5	21.9	62.4
	(56.0)	(8.8)	(35.1)	(100.0)
1916–1920	36.6	7.7	24.0	68.3
	(53.5)	(11.2)	(35.2)	(100.0)
1921–1925	35.4	10.5	27.8	73.8
	(48.1)	(14.3)	(37.6)	(100.0)
1926–1930	34.5	10.8	30.1	75.3
	(45.8)	(14.3)	(39.9)	(100.0)
1931–1935	33.4	11.7	31.0	76.0
	(43.8)	(15.4)	(40.8)	(100.0)
1936–1940	33.9	13.6	30.1	77.5
	(43.7)	(17.5)	(38.8)	(100.0)
	Calories Per Capita Per Day			
1911–1915	1765	40	232	2037
	(86.6)	(2.0)	(11.4)	(100.0)
1921–1925	1807	47	269	2123
	(85.1)	(2.2)	(12.7)	(100.0)
1931–1935	1711	72	272	2055
	(83.3)	(3.5)	(13.2)	(100.0)

* Computed from Shinohara.

a) Starchy staples include: rice, barley, naked barley, other cereals, sweet potatoes, white potatoes, wheat flour, starch, and noodles.

b) Animal proteins include: meat, milk, eggs, fish, shellfish, and other marine products.

c) Expenditure total excludes beverages and tobacco. Calorie total excludes canned (and bottled) foods as well as beverages.

In parentheses are percentages of the total.

The Share of Starchy Staple Foods in Total Calorie "Intake"
(Selected Periods, Japan: 1911–1935)[12]

Years	Rice	Barley	Naked Barley	Misc. Cereals	Potatoes	Wheat Flour and Starch	Noodles
1911–1915	65.6	6.4	7.8	2.7	1.6	.5	2.1
1921–1925	68.1	4.6	5.6	1.8	1.3	.6	3.1
1931–1935	69.3	3.4	4.7	1.7	.9	.7	2.6

The decline in the consumption of these "inferior" starchy staples is a reflection of the shift of emphasis on the part of consumers from food calories per se to higher culinary satisfaction.[13]

In regard to animal protein food, it is accepted that Japanese people began to eat meat and dairy products only after the Meiji Restoration (1868). In the traditional diets animal protein came mainly from fish and shellfish. The rise in consumption of meat and dairy products during the period under review was rather modest, however, when put in terms of absolute quantities. Not until after World War II, and quite recently, did expenditure and calorie contribution claimed by meat and dairy products exceed those of fish and shell fish. Then, even in the late 1950's, per capita consumption of meat amounted to only 5–6 kilograms (11–13 lbs.) per year.

Measured Income Elasticities of Demand for Food; the Interwar Years

According to Shinohara's data, over the period of 25 years between 1911–1915 and 1936–1940, total private consumption expenditure (per capita in 1934–1936 prices) increased at the annual rate of some 1.6 per cent while per capita food expenditures rose at .6 per cent per year. Moreover, the latter category increased at about .4 per cent when measured from 1921–1925, whereas per capita real expenditures increased at the rate of approximately 1 per cent per year. This suggests, of course, a crude income elasticity (taking "total expenditure" as the proxy variable) of .3 or .4 for food demand during the interwar years.

---

[12] Computed from net food supply data in Shinohara. Calorie figures were taken from FAO (1954).

[13] Barley and naked barley are pressed flat and mixed in rice and then boiled, when the latter is not available in sufficient quantities. In other words, these grains are inferior substitutes for rice in the Japanese diet.

During these years the composition of total food expenditure underwent noticeable changes. As was seen in Table 2, the share of starchy staples dropped from 48 to 44 per cent, that of animal proteins rose from 14 to 18 per cent, and the share of other foods remained rather stable at 39 per cent of the total food expenditure. In other words, a drop of 4 percentage points in the share of starchy staples was taken up by the rise of the same amount in the share of animal proteins. It is evident that the substitution of the animal proteins group for starchy staples took place, as expected, even during the years in which the total calorie "intake" did not show a significant response to the income growth.

Examining the movements of the prices and aggregate real expenditures of these two food groups during the period between 1910 and 1940, we find that the real expenditures (per capita) on these food groups did not show much fluctuation around the respective trends. It becomes apparent also that the prices of the two major food groups moved almost in parallel, implying that the relative prices of the two groups were rather stable.[14]

On the basis of the data presented in Table 2, we observe that over the period between 1921–1925 and 1935–1940 per capita real expenditure on starchy staples declined at a rate of .2 per cent, that on animal proteins increased at 1.7 per cent, and per capita expenditure on other foods rose at .5 per cent per annum. Given that the relative prices of these food groups were more or less stable, these growth rates immediately translate themselves into crude income elasticity estimates (since the annual growth rate of per capita real consumption expenditure was about one per cent). Thus, the implied income elasticities are —.2, 1.7, and .5 for starchy staples, animal proteins, and other foods, respectively. The indication is that as a food group, starchy staples are "inferior" foods, whereas animal proteins are "preferred" items. Although we cannot tell with confidence how much change in per capita expenditure on starchy staples takes place in response to a 1 per cent increase in real income per capita, we can reasonably say that the change would

---

[14] Price indices were constructed by dividing the current-price expenditures (aggregated over commodities in the group) by the constant-price expenditure (similarly aggregated) for each group.

not be in the upward direction. It is to be noted that these crude elasticity estimates compare well with those formerly derived by Noda and Nakayama for the interwar years.[15]

Among various household expenditure surveys carried out during the interwar years, only a few are easily available for general use today. Four household expenditure surveys were chosen here for the purpose of supplementing the elasticities estimated above. Although all the surveys chosen relate to incomes and expenditures of urban workers' households, differences are inevitable among those survey records in the concepts and procedures used in collecting and classifying the data. The lack of parallelism is not too serious, however, if we confine ourselves to analyses of large aggregates.[16]

Using total household expenditure per capita instead of recorded income of the household, income elasticities were computed by the method of ordinary cross-section regression of food expenditure per capita on total consumption expenditure per capita (both in logarithms). Because of the nature of the data, observations entering into the regression were weighted according to the number of households represented in each class average. The resulting measured elasticities are given in the second panel of Table 3 along with their respective standard errors in parentheses. Most regressions show

---

[15] See the preceding section, p. 396. The estimates pertaining to the interwar period are given in parentheses.

[16] Each survey covers over 1200 urban workers' households. The sample households are classified into several income classes, whose monthly average incomes and expenditures are available for analysis. Some characteristics of the surveys are listed below.

Selected Surveys of Average Monthly Income and Expenditure,
Urban Workers' Households, 1921–1936*

Survey period	Sample size	Number of classes	Persons per household	Total consumption expenditure (In current yen)
1921 (March)	1,212	13	4.8	76.6
1926–1927	4,785	9	4.2	102.2
1931–1932	1,517	7	4.1	76.3
1935–1936	1,673	7	4.1	80.1

* Weighted averages over the classes. From: Ohuchi, 1958. pp. 302–307.

an excellent fit as expected: the coefficients of determination are all above .90. The starchy staples group (here only cereals are included) is atypical in this regard, except for the 1931–1932 survey whose coefficient of determination is a respectable .85.

TABLE 3

The Shares of Major Food Groups in Total Household Expenditure and Measured Income Elasticities of Urban Workers' Households*

Period of survey	Food total	Starchy staples^a	Animal proteins^b	Other
Share in total expenditure (Food expenditure)				
1921 (March)	38.0	17.6	7.6	12.8
		(46.3)	(20.0)	(33.7)
1926–1927	30.2	14.2	5.2	10.8
		(47.0)	(17.2)	(35.8)
1931–1932	26.9	10.2	5.0	11.7
		(37.9)	(18.6)	(43.5)
1935–1936	31.1	14.2	4.9	12.0
		(35.7)	(15.7)	(38.6)
Measured income elasticities				
1921 (March)	.494	.216	1.182	.477
	(.052)	(.075)	(.146)	(.064)
1926–1927	.386	−.021^c	.943	.657
	(.018)	(.027)	(.024)	(.019)
1931–1932	.347	−.105	.753	.582
	(.027)	(.016)	(.096)	(.035)
1935–1936	.329	−.016^c	.824	.545
	(.024)	(.024)	(.052)	(.059)

* "Average Monthly Income and Expenditure of Urban Workers' Households," 1921 (March), September 1926–August 1927; September 1931–August 1932; September 1935–August 1936 (Ohuchi, pp. 302–307).

The figures in the first panel, "Share in Total Expenditure," are the weighted averages of the classes represented.

The figures in parentheses in the second panel are standard errors of estimates.

a) Include cereals only.

b) Include meat, dairy products, eggs, and fish.

c) Not significantly different from zero at 5 per cent.

It is quite remarkable that the cross-section estimates are so consistently close to the crude estimates from the time-series estimates. Ignoring the data for 1921, the measured income elasticity of demand for all foods falls in the range between .3 and .4. Interestingly enough, too, their values decline over the years. The same seems to be the case for the measured elasticities of starchy staples, zero to —.1, and of animal proteins, which are around 1 to .8.

According to L. Juréen's calculation, income elasticities for some prominent food groups at varying income levels can be expected to be as follows:

Prewar Income Elasticities at Varying Income Levels, Juréen's Data[17]

Income Per Capita in 1934–1938 U.S. Dollars	Animal Foods (excluding fish)	Cereals	Total Food in Constant Prices
35 dollars	.79	.03	.47
50	.73	—.10	.42
75	.64	—.23	.37

Recent estimates by Ohkawa and his associates put per capita national income in 1934–1936 at about 210 yen. This is equivalent to about U.S. $61 in 1934–1936.[18] Some interesting observations emerge when the income elasticities calculated here are contrasted with those "predicted" empirically at similar income levels by Juréen.

Juréen's international data were limited to observations relating to European countries. Necessarily, therefore, the exact content of his food groups, such as animal foods and cereals, is different from the ones relevant to the Japanese dietary patterns during the interwar period. Nevertheless, at the per capita income level of U.S. $ 61 the elasticity value of between 1 and .8 for animal foods is rather higher than that expected from Juréen's calculation. Moreover, the present estimates of Japanese elasticity for cereals falling between zero and —.1 is also high. That is to say, in regard to each food group, the estimated Japanese income elasticities correspond to those "expected" for countries with much lower per capita income than Japan actually had in the interwar years. Since the relative weights of these food groups in the Japanese and the European diets are very much different (i.e., the relative share of cereals is much higher in the Japanese diets), it is not surprising to observe that the present estimate of income elasticity for all foods turns out lower than indicated from Juréen's table.

---

[17] The data are from Juréen (p. 9); the figures are taken only for the lower income levels contained in Juréen's table.

[18] See Juréen above for the method used for conversion.

Again, Japanese income elasticity for all foods was much lower than most international data indicated. Put another way still, this means that Japanese food consumption patterns in the prewar period were such that changes in food demand in response to income growth were very much like those in countries where per capita incomes were higher than in Japan. Japanese did not change their dietary habits as much as other peoples (Europeans) did when they became richer. The Japanese behaved as though they were richer at a per capita income level which was actually low. One implication of this behavior in regard to food consumption seems rather clear: it provided Japanese industries with the growing domestic markets for their products.

III. Food Consumption Patterns: the Postwar Years

The violent disruption in the general process of Japan's economic growth brought forth by World War II and its aftermath is quite evident in the economic statistics of the time. The indicators of food consumption patterns are no exception. The ratio of food expenditure in total consumption expenditures (the so-called Engel ratio) jumped up to a very high level once again, after having declined steadily since Japan's modernization. The starchy staple ratio was again at about 87 per cent, a substantial portion of which represented starchy roots and "inferior" cereals. The apparent intake of food calories and proteins declined as domestic production decreased and the quantity of emergency food supplies brought in by the occupation authorities was substantially below the prewar levels of food imports.

As expected, along with the reconstruction of food collection and distribution systems and the gradual recovery of food production, the indicators showed steady improvement in the years following the disaster. The food rationing covering cereals and starchy roots was gradually relaxed: rationing of sweet potatoes was abolished in December, 1949, and that of barley in June, 1952 (Kayo, 1958, p. 353). The 1955 crop of rice greatly eased the supply shortage and the per capita ration of this last item in the rationing system was increased to the extent that rice control lost much of its significance.

Over the five-year period between 1934 and 1938, per capita real national income (in 1934–1936 prices) ranged from about 200 yen to 230 yen. During the postwar period per capita real income, in prewar prices, rose from about 180 yen in 1951 to about 470 yen in 1964. The prewar level of real income was reached around 1954–1955 when the figures once again registered between 205 and 230 yen in 1934–1936 prices. It is not at all surprising, therefore, that we find the return of food consumption patterns to the prewar level around these years. As with other indicators of general economic activity, the middle of the 1950s witnessed the return of food consumption to the peak levels attained in the prewar period.

It is indeed interesting, however, to note that the Engel ratio remained still high, relative to the comparable prewar period, its value attaining the prewar level only after the mid-1950s.[19] It appears that this phenomenon cannot be explained easily without examining rather closely non-economic factors as well as income and price situations.

Such an explanation must emphasize: (1) massive exposure of Japanese people to the influences of "foreign consumption patterns";[20] (2) the rapid acculturation of these influences through mass communication media; and (3) the inauguration in 1947 of a school lunch program (with emphasis on bread and milk). These factors, along with the rise in the purchasing power of the population, enabled Japanese to change their dietary pattern considerably. The increases in consumption of meat and dairy products, white potatoes, and wheat are cited as a clear indication of this trend. The increase in per capita consumption of oils and fats, too, is suggested as collaborating evidence reflecting the changes in cooking methods. Frying as an increasingly popular form of food preparation, as well as use of oil in salad dressing, mayonnaise, and other

---

[19] The Engel ratios for the selected years are as follows:

	1933–1937	1946–1950	1951–1955	1956–1960	1961–1965
A/B:	49.9%	84.5%	53.4%	46.9%	39.9%

(A: private cons. exp. foods, B: private cons. exp. total)

Sources: Shinohara; Bank of Japan (1966); Economic Planning Agency (1967).

[20] Used as an antonym of "indigenous consumption patterns" (Rosovsky and Ohkawa, P. 476).

shortening, reflects the gradual shift from dependence on boiling and broiling with traditional condiments such as *shoyu* (soy sauce) and *miso* (bean paste). The nature of demand for the starchy staples has undergone a radical change. Just as wheat in the form of bread has become increasingly familiar as a substitute for rice, whereas in the prewar period it was an inferior substitute as the major ingredient in noodles, white potatoes have come to be regarded as something decidedly different from sweet potatoes which go better with dishes of Western origin.[21]

Moreover, rapid urbanization of Japanese life, not only in the usual sense of the shift of population from rural to urban areas, but in the sense of all that modern urban life and technology connote, has helped in shaping new food consumption patterns. Electric appliances, such as refrigerators, ovens, toasters, and other kitchen implements (to say nothing of gadgets such as automatic rice cookers), technologically expand the range of feasible methods of food preparation and their variety. Rural and urban acceptance of these items, as well as the popular use of processed foods, attests to the continuing change. In recent years, furthermore, increasing affluence of the Japanese economy has permitted imports of exotic foods in increasing amounts along with imports of such essential food items as grains (for food and feed) and meat and dairy products.[22]

---

[21] Changes in the calories (per capita per day) contributed by some of these commodities are as in the following:

Years	Rice	Wheat	Naked Barley	Barley Miscellaneous Cereals	Sweet Potatoes	White Potatoes	Oils Fats	Milk, Eggs, Meat	Fish
1931–1935	1319	132	137	33	119	19	20	23	36
1951–1955	956	246	179	13	109	41	50	37	62
1961–1964	1074	245	42	8	39	35	140	130	73

Sources: Kagaku Gijutsuchō (1962); Ministry of Agriculture and Forestry, (1950–1964).

[22] Before 1960, the annual cost of imported foodstuffs ranged between $700 million and $800 million. Since 1960, however, the rise in the imports of food has been conspicuous. In 1963 total food imports were approximately $1.5 billion, an increase of 39 per cent over the preceding year. Following are the commodities which contributed most to this rise in the value of food imports: sugar and molasses (accounting for 30 per cent of the increase), wheat and soy beans (each 8–9 per cent), sesame seeds, bananas, corn and meats (each 5–6

These socio-cultural and technological changes have had a profound impact on Japanese food consumption patterns. In contrast to the prewar period when food consumption patterns were changing rather slowly, the postwar period calls for a radically different approach and methods of analysis. The assumption of stable "tastes," which may have been tolerable in the prewar analyses, cannot be reasonably maintained. In a study published elsewhere, I have explicitly incorporated the possible shifts in "tastes" into analyzing the postwar data (Kaneda, 1968). In this study let us trace some of the significant changes in the postwar food consumption patterns with familiar and more conventional methods of analysis.

TABLE 4

Net Food Supply in Calories Per Capita Per Day, Selected Years*

Years	Total food	Starchy staples[a]	Animal proteins[b]	Other
1934–1938[c]	2,050cal.	1,605cal.	54cal.	391cal.
1948–1950	1,910	1,660	71	179
1951–1953	1,930	1,500	93	337
1954–1956	2,070	1,548	107	415
1957–1959	2,170	1,472	136	462
1960–1962	2,230	1,524	175	531
1963–1964	2,298	1,500	221	577
	Per cent of total calories			
1934–1938	100.0	78.3	2.6	19.1
1948–1950	100.0	87.9	3.7	9.4
1951–1953	100.0	77.7	4.8	17.4
1954–1956	100.0	74.8	5.2	20.1
1957–1959	100.0	72.4	6.3	21.3
1960–1962	100.0	68.3	7.8	23.8
1963–1964	100.0	65.3	9.6	25.1

* Sources: United Nations, F.A.O., *Food Supply, Time Series* (Rome, 1960). Japan, Ministry of Agriculture and Forestry, *Nōrinshō Tōkeihyō (The Statistical Tables of the Ministry of Agriculture and Forestry)*, various annual editions.
Note: Total food does not include calories derived from beverages.
a) Include cereals and potatoes.
b) Include meat, eggs, milk, and fish.
c) I cannot reconcile a substantial difference between this set of figures for 1934–1938 and those of Table 2 (the second panel) pertaining to 1931–1935.

per cent), and coffee and cocoa (each 3 per cent). Imports of meat registered the largest increase as a single item in 1963, rising by 160 per cent over the preceding year. Foods accounted for 23 per cent of total imports in 1964.

Measured Income Elasticities of Food Demand, the Postwar Years

Table 4 presents net food supply in terms of calories contributed by major food groups (on a daily per capita basis) during the postwar years as contrasted to the prewar peak levels in 1934–1938. Judging from the starchy staple ratio, the prewar level of food consumption was recovered around 1951–1953. The recovery of total calorie "intake" from all sources, however, had to wait until about 1954–1956 to reach the prewar peak levels. Nonetheless, judging from protein consumption, the prewar level was regained around the end of the 1940's. The divergence in these recovery dates is clear evidence of the change in food consumption patterns from the prewar to the postwar period. In view of the historical predominance of starchy staples in the Japanese diets, I shall choose 1951 as the starting point in the study of the postwar period.

For the annual observations on food expenditure and total expenditure covering 1951 through 1964 the following (two-stage least squares) regression model was adopted:

$$v_t = \alpha + \beta M_t + e,$$

where, specifically, v is per capita food expenditure (including beverages and tobacco) in real terms, M is per capita real personal consumption expenditures total, and where per capita real national income is used as the instrumental variable.[23] The instrumental estimates with and without logarithmic transformation of observations yield the following:

$$v_t = 6.239 + .380 M_t, \qquad R^2 = .947 \text{ and } D-W = .524$$
$$\quad (2.011) \ (.027)$$
$$\log v_t = .096 + .808 \log M_t, \qquad R^2 = .998 \text{ and } D-W = 1.567$$
$$\quad (.042) \ (.011)$$

Strictly speaking, comparison of the two equations cannot be made solely on the basis of R^2s. However, on grounds of homoscedasticity as well as the Durbin-Watson statistics, it seems that the second

---

[23] For the rationale of using the instrumental variable, see Liviatan (1961), pp. 336–362.

The sources of the data used are as follows:

Expenditures: Japan, Economic Planning Agency, *Annual Report on National Income Statistics, 1966*. It is not possible to separate food expenditure from expenditures on beverages and tobacco.

Population: Bank of Japan, *Hundred-Year Statistics of the Japanese Economy*.

equation is superior to the first. Nonetheless, evaluating the elasticity at the point of the mean in the first equation, we obtain .809 as the income elasticity for expenditure on food. This value compares very well with the estimate from the second equation, where the value is .808.

Because it is not possible to separate expenditure on food from those on beverages and tobacco in the data source as given, it is essential to adjust for this factor in order to arrive at the income elasticity of demand for food items only. On the basis of the data on expenditures on food, beverages, and tobacco provided separately for the seven-year period between 1958 and 1964, the income elasticity of demand for beverages and tobacco can be estimated. It is not surprising that the estimated value of this elasticity is quite high at about 1.56. Since in 1958 the expenditures on these "non-food" items occupied 13 per cent of the total of the food, beverage, and tobacco expenditures, we multiply 1.56 by .13 and subtract this product from the income elasticity estimated by the use of the equation above. The resultant income elasticity estimate (adjusted for the proportion of food) is .69 for expenditures on food *per se*.

Given that the service (processing and marketing) components of food expenditure are higher in the postwar years, and that these components grow more rapidly in response to income rises than demand for foods valued at the farm level, it is noteworthy that the elasticity estimated for the period is significantly higher than those computed for the prewar periods. The higher income elasticity of food demand should be interpreted as indicating that the Japanese are not content to eat the same kinds of foods as they used to before World War II. Their food consumption patterns are changing together with the rapid income growth. However, because the aggregate income elasticity is a product of many influences working on the aggregate economy besides the variables formally accounted for in the regression equation, further scrutiny of the changes in the aggregate economy is necessary in order to interpret its meaning correctly. It is, of course, impossible to do justice to the full range of factors that determine the aggregate income elasticity. Some of these have already been mentioned earlier in this section. In addition, the patterns of income distribution, occupational composition of the population, and the geographic distribution of the population are all relevant factors. Here we shall focus on only one of these factors.

Granted that Japan's agricultural sector employed only 26 per cent of the total labor force in 1964 and, hence, that urban workers are more important in influencing aggregate food demand today, a study of Japanese food consumption patterns cannot be complete without examining also the rural patterns of food consumption. The sizable movement of people from rural to urban areas has been in progress since the beginning of the modernization process, bringing forth a decline in the agricultural labor force relative to the urban counterpart. However, as is well known, only after the end of World War II and during the 1950s did an absolute decline in the agricultural labor force begin. Recently it has been decreasing at about 4 per cent per annum. In the first place, such a rapid change in the geographic distribution of the population has a large impact on the pattern of aggregate demand, if in fact there are differences in urban and rural consumption patterns. Secondly, significant changes in the patterns of income distribution (as a result of the movements of people from rural areas to improve their income positions) influence the aggregate consumption patterns. For instance, if an average income rise in a given economy were mainly the result of an improvement in the level of the lower income groups, food demand would be expected to increase more rapidly than otherwise. Thirdly, movements of rural people to urban areas would be further expected to increase the aggregate elasticity of food demand as new arrivals in cities improve their income positions and begin to emulate urban consumption patterns. Although it is difficult to measure satisfactorily, there is no denying that some or all of these factors contributed to the rise in the aggregate Engel ratio and the aggregate income elasticity. On the basis of these observations I shall focus my attention on urban workers' households and farm households during the period from 1952 through 1962.

Table 5 identifies the variables and their definitions used in the remainder of this section. The sources of the data are given also in the table. For farm households, the expenditures are for family members only and exclude those attributable to hired hands. For

TABLE 5

List of Variables and Their Definitions*

Variables	Name	Definition
N_t	Persons per household	Not adjusted for sex, age, or other attributes
Y_t	Real total expenditure	*For Farm Households:* Total of household living expenditures, *kakei-hi,* including value of barter transactions, imputed value of home consumption of products, depreciation as well as cash transactions. Deflated by the rural cost of living index (1957=100). *For Urban Households:* Total of household living expenditures, defined as *shohi-shishutsu* in the source, including cash expenditures only. Deflated by the all-urban cost of living index (1960=100).
D_{it}	Real expenditure	Deflated by p^r_{it} or p^u_{it}, where the scripts refer to the *i-th* component of the rural or urban cost of living index at year *t*, respectively. $i=1$—Total Food Expenditure. 2—Expenditures on starchy staples, including cereals and starchy roots for farm households, but including cereals only for urban workers, households. 3—Expenditures on meat, milk, eggs, and fish. 4—Expenditures on other food items.

* Sources: Japan, Ministry of Agriculture and Forestry, *Nōka Keizai Chōsa Hōkoku* (*The Report on the Farm Household Economy*), annual editions, 1952 through 1961. For prices: Japan, Ministry of Agriculture and Forestry, *Nōson Bukka Chingin Chōsa Hōkokusho* (*The Report of Prices and Wage Rates in Farm Villages*), 1962.

For urban data: Japan, Office of the Prime Minister, *General Report on the Family Income and Expenditure Survey: 1946–1962* (Tokyo: 1964).

each of the five scales of operation, classified according to the farm's operating acreage, district averages are the cross-section observations over ten years from 1952 through 1961. Data were drawn from ten agricultural districts out of eleven in Japan, excluding northernmost Hokkaido. For urban households, the data refer only to workers' households (blue-collar and white-collar, public as well as private employees). The sample households are classified into quintile groups according to money income. For this set of data, the cross-section observations are quintile-group averages over the ten year period between 1953 and 1962.

It is quite clear from Table 6 that the high growth rates of per capita real incomes in both urban and rural sectors are amply reflected in the substantial (and rapid) reduction in the respective Engel ratios over the years. Moreover, on the average, the Engel ratio for urban workers' households is lower than that for farm households in any selected year. This is in part a reflection of higher per capita monthly incomes enjoyed by the urban workers' households. Because the rural expenditures on starchy staples include

TABLE 6

Percentages of Total Household Expenditure Devoted to Food Groups of Urban Workers' Households and Farm Households, Selected Years*

Year	Food	Starchy staples[a]	Animal proteins[b]	Other
		Urban workers' households		
1953	44.2%	16.0%	8.6%	19.6%
1957	41.5	14.1	8.8	18.5
1961	37.2	10.3	8.8	18.0
		Farm Households		
1953	48.8	25.8	1.9	21.1
1957	48.1	24.6	2.3	21.3
1961	41.5	19.4	2.6	19.5
	Per cent of total food expenditure			
	Urban Workers' households			
1953	100.0	36.2	19.5	44.3
1957	100.0	34.0	21.2	44.8
1961	100.0	27.6	23.7	48.4
		Farm households		
1953	100.0	52.9	3.9	43.2
1957	100.0	51.1	4.8	44.1
1961	100.0	46.7	6.3	47.0

* Sources: Same as in Table 5.
Note: Figures are weighted averages of the cross-sectional groups.
a) Including cereals and starchy roots for farm households, but including cereals only for urban workers' households.
b) Including meat, dairy products eggs, and fish.

starchy roots, while the urban counterpart does not, it may not be immediately obvious that the share of starchy staples in total expenditure is lower in the urban sample. However, this becomes evident when the shares from the two samples are closely examined. In regard to the share of animal protein foods, the picture is essentially the same. The urban levels of food consumption are unquestionably higher than those in rural areas.

For the cross-section data for selected years the logarithmic regression equation used in the time-series analysis was adopted. The logic of this method is comparable with the instrumental estimation because money income, or its proxy, is used as the instrumental variable in grouping the sample. The resulting estimates of income elasticities are given in Table 7.

TABLE 7

Measured Income Elasticities Based on Household Budget Surveys of Urban Workers' Households and Farm Households, Selected Years*
(in parentheses are the standard errors of estimate)

Year	Food	Starchy staples[a]	Animal proteins[b]	Other
		Urban workers' households		
1953	.481	.196	.750	.590
	(.015)	(.032)	(.012)	(.017)
1957	.456	.062	.773	.602
	(.011)	(.012)	(.032)	(.018)
1961	.472	.075	.700	.585
	(.004)	(.012)	(.008)	(.012)
		Farm households		
1953	.529	.466	1.117	.412
	(.036)	(.080)	(.220)	(.084)
1957	.531	.363	1.156	.507
	(.044)	(.089)	(.181)	(.069)
1961	.529	.159[c]	1.087	.720
	(.040)	(.091)	(.136)	(.072)

* Source: Same as in Table 5.
Note: Estimates were derived by weighted logarithmic regressions: observations were weighted according to the number of households represented in each group.
a) For workers' households including cereals only.
b) Include meat, dairy products, eggs, and fish.
c) Not significantly different from zero at 5 per cent.

As in the case of the share of food expenditure in the total, here also the measured elasticities for all food, starchy staples, and animal proteins are smaller for the urban sample than for the farm sample. The indications are that in response to income rises the farm households would expand expenditures on food groups relatively more than the urban households, although, strictly speaking, the differences do not appear to be statistically significant in most cases. This urban-rural comparison strongly suggests a tendency for farm households to emulate the consumption patterns of urban households.

Looking at the results for the urban households and comparing them with the measured income elasticities for urban samples in the prewar years (Table 3), we observe close similarities of the elasticities in both prewar and postwar years. In fact, the differences between the urban and the rural households in the postwar years are more pronounced than those of the urban households between the prewar and the postwar years.[24] Because of the increase in the relative share of animal proteins and other food groups the postwar elasticity for total food tends to be higher than the prewar one. However, if each food group is taken separately, the differences are slight. The geographic shifts of the population, changes in the technological and institutional framework of food consumption, and the unprecedented rapidity and dynamism of the economic growth, which brought forth these changes, are more important in determining the aggregate consumption patterns in the postwar years. The comparison of the cross-sectional elasticities between the two periods tends to reinforce this contention.

IV. Conclusions

The present study indicates that the income elasticity of demand for food remained rather low in Japan until after the end of World War II. Bearing in mind the uncertainties associated with the data

---

[24] Two factors should be noted here. There is a problem of the upward bias in the samples of urban workers' households in the prewar family budget surveys. It is suspected that this is particularly serious for those prior to the 1926 survey. Furthermore, strictly speaking, the price effects in the postwar years cannot be ignored. The relative prices of foods in the postwar years show a clear upward trend. Especially pertinent to the discussion here is that the relative prices of animal proteins and of the other food group show a distinct increase among foods.

used for the earlier periods, we may offer some of the implications of this study.

The income elasticities estimated at .3 or .4 for food during the years between 1878 and 1922 and also during the years between 1922 and 1940 mean that the drastic change in the Japanese patterns of food consumption alleged to have occurred around World War I may be an illusion. Because of the progress in industrialization after World War I, the patterns of food consumption in the urban areas underwent some considerable changes.[25] The aggregate patterns, however, remained rather stable, and the changes that took place were moderate and gradual.

The relatively low elasticities estimated for the periods prior to World War II imply that the Japanese did not change greatly their food consumption patterns as they became richer. The Japanese behaved as though they were richer at per capita income level which was actually low. Consequently, Japanese food consumption patterns on the aggregate level were very much like those of countries where income levels were higher: changes in food demand in response to income growth were relatively small.

In my judgment here is a remarkable aspect of the story of Japan's economic development. As agricultural production grew slowly, in any case less rapidly than previously believed,[26] people's food consumption habits also changed slowly. There was no pressing and

---

[25] Ohkawa estimates that the income elasticities for demand for rice in the 1931–1939 period were —.2 to —.4 for salaried workers and zero to —.2 for wage workers, indicating that cereals became "inferior" goods during these years. With regard to rural consumption, Ohkawa estimates income elasticities for rice to be .3 for the owner-cultivators and .6 or .7 for the tenant farmers in 1936 (Ohkawa, 1945).

[26] According to the two well-known estimates by Johnston and by Ohkawa, agricultural production grew at the annual rate of 1.9 and 2.4 per cent in the Meiji period. Nakamura's estimates reduce it to 1.0 per cent (Nakamura, 1965 p. 138):

Yamada's estimates used in this paper indicate an annual growth rate of 1.8 per cent for the period between 1878–1882 and 1918–1922.

It is to be noted, however, that the growth rate of 1.8 per cent is relatively high in comparison with the experience of other economically advanced countries in their early phases of development, especially when the comparison is on a per capita basis.

persistent demand for large quantities of imported foods, except for rice and sugar. Nor were there sudden, pressing demands (and the market justification) for a radical transformation of agriculture in order to cultivate and raise "preferred" foods (for example, wheat, meat, and dairy products) in which Japan lacked natural advantage. Indeed, the terms of trade between agricultural products and other products seem to have remained more or less stable during the early period. And the slow change in food consumption patterns materially "contributed" to economic development by freeing foreign exchange earnings from the necessity of massive food imports and making it possible to finance imports of other essential goods and services. Just as it can be said that a rapid development of agricultural production "contributes" to the development of an entire economy, it can be stated that small import contents and slow changes in food consumption patterns "contribute" to the same cause by compensating for even slow development in agricultural production. In this regard also it is to be noted that the slow changes in food consumption patterns "contributed" to high rates of savings and "enabled" the Japanese to purchase (and become important sources of demand for) products of the domestic industrial sector.

The structural transformation of the Japanese economy in the 1950's was reflected in the beginning of the absolute decline in the agricultural labor force and in the emergence of highly sophisticated industrial complexes in Japan. This transformation coincides with the radical changes in food consumption patterns of Japanese people. As the level of income grew rapidly, the institutional and technological framework of Japanese life in general also changed rapidly. Under these circumstances, a drastic transformation took place in methods of food preparation and in patterns of food consumption. The income elasticity of demand for food increased to about .5 or .6. These indicators of food consumption remained high long after the peak prewar levels of income had been recovered.

This study indicates that the geographic shifts of the population and the changes in the technological and institutional framework of food consumption played vital roles in determining Japanese food consumption patterns in the postwar years. The rural emulation of the urban consumption patterns is expected to continue for some time, as in most other aspects of life.[27] At the same time the urban consumption habits seem to be moving more rapidly toward the Western pattern than in any other period in Japan's economic history.

REFERENCES

Bank of Japan. *Hundred-Year Statistics of the Japanese Economy.* Tokyo: 1966.

Bennett, M.K. *The World's Food.* New York: 1954.

Clark, C. and Haswell, M. R. *The Economics of Subsistence Agriculture.* London: 1964.

Food and Agriculture Organization of the United Nations. *Food Composition Tables for International Use.* Rome: 1954.

———. *Food Supply, Time Series.* Rome: 1960.

Houthakker, H. S., "An International Comparison of Household Expenditure Patterns Commemorating the Centenary of Engel's Law," *Econometrica* (Oct., 1957), pp. 532–551.

Japan Economic Planning Agency. *Annual Report on National Income Statistics, 1967.* Tokyo: 1967.

Japan, Kagaku Gijutsu Cho, "Food Resources," *Nippon no Shigen (Japan's Resources),* Tokyo: 1962, pp. 490–538.

Japan, Office of the Prime Minister. *General Report on the Family Income and Expenditure Survey, 1946–1962.* Tokyo: 1964.

Japan, Ministry of Agriculture and Forestry. *Norinsho Tokeihyo (Statistical Tables of the Ministry of Agriculture and Forestry),* various annual editions 1950–1964/65.

———. *Nōka Keizai Chōsa Hōkoku (Survey of Farm Household Economy),* various annual editions. 1952–1961.

———. *Nōson Bukka Chingin Chōsa Hōkokusho (The Report of Prices and Wage Rates in Farm Villages).* 1962.

Juréen, L., "Long-Term Trends in Food Consumption: A Multi-Country Study," *Econometrica,* XXIV (Jan. 1956), pp. 1–21.

Kaneda, Hiromitsu and Johnston, B. F., "Urban Food Expenditure Patterns in Tropical Africa," *Food Research Institute Studies* (Nov. 1961), pp. 229–275..

———, "Long-Term Changes in Food Consumption Patterns in Japan 1878–1964," *Food Research Institute Studies,* VIII, No. 1 (1968).

Kayo, Nobufumi, ed. *Nihon Nōgyō Kisotōkei (Basic Statistics of Japanese Agriculture).* Tokyo: 1958.

Kuznets, Simon, "Notes on Consumption: Trends in Level and Structure," paper presented at International Conference on Economic Growth—Case Study of Japan's Experience, Tokyo: 1966, mimeographed.

Liviatan, Nissan, "Errors in Variables and Engel Curve Analysis," *Econometrica* (July, 1961), pp. 336–362.

---

[27] For a more detailed study of urban-rural contrasts in food consumption patterns and that of changes in preferences for foods see Kaneda, pp. 21–6.

Nakamura, J. I., "Growth of Japanese Agriculture, 1875–1920," *The State and Economic Enterprise in Japan, Essays in the Political Economy of Growth,* W. W. Lockwood, ed., Princeton: Princeton University Press, 1965, pp. 249–324.

———. *Agricultural Production and the Economic Development of Japan, 1873–1922.* Princeton: Princeton Univ. Press, 1966.

Nakayama, Seiki, "Shokuryō Shōhi Suijun no Chōki-Henka ni tsuite (Long-Term Trend of Food Consumption in Japan, 1878–1955)," *Nōgyō Sōgo Kenkyū* (Oct. 1958), pp. 13–37.

Nerlove, Marc. *Distributed Lags and Demand Analysis.* U.S.D.A. Agriculture Handbook, No. 141 (June 1958).

Noda, Tsutomu, "Nosan-Butsu Juyo no Chōki Henka to Shotokudanryokusei (Long-Term Changes in Demand for Agricultural Products and Income (Elasticities)," *Nippon no Keizai to Nōgyō,* S. Tohata and K. Ohkawa, eds., Tokyo: 1956, pp. 159–174.

———, "Juyo to Boeki no Chōki-Henka (Long-Term Changes in Demand and International Trade)," *Nihon Nōgyō no Seichō Bunseki,* K. Ohkawa, ed., Tokyo: 1963.

Ohkawa, Kazushi. *Shokuryō Keizai no Riron to Keisoku (Theory and Measurement of the Food Economy).* Tokyo: 1945.

———, Shinohara, M., Umemura, M., Ito, M., Noda, T. *The Growth Rate of the Japanese Economy Since 1878.* Tokyo: Kinokuniya, 1957.

Ohuchi, Hyoe. *Nihon Keizai Tōkeishū, Meiji, Taishō, Shōwa (Collected Statistics of the Japanese Economy for Meiji, Taishō, and Shōwa Periods).* Tokyo: 1958.

Rosovsky, Henry and Ohkawa, Kazushi, "The Indigneous Components in the Modern Japanese Economy," *Economic Development and Cultural Change* (April, 1961), pp. 476–497.

Shinohara, Miyohei. *Choki Keizai Tokei, VI, Kojin Shohi Shishutsu (Estimates of Long-Term Economic Statistics of Japan Since 1868, VI, Private Consumption Expenditures).* Tokyo: 1967.

Solow, R. M., "Technical Change and the Aggregate Production Function," *Review of Economics and Statistics* (Aug. 1957), pp. 312–320.

Umemura, M., Yamada, S., Hayami, Y., Takamatsu, N., and Kumazaki, M. *Agriculture and Forestry (Nōringyō), Estimates of Long-Term Economic Statistics of Japan since 1868,* IX, K. Ohkawa, M. Shinohara, and M. Umemura, eds., Tokyo: Toyo Keizai Shimposha, 1966.

APPENDIX:
A Note on Growth in Demand for Agricultural Products

Under the assumption of stable relative prices, demand for agricultural products grows at a rate approximately equal to the income elasticity multiplied by the growth rate of per capita real income plus the rate of population growth. Strictly speaking, however, this familiar relationship must be further qualified.

Let D denote demand (in real terms) for agricultural products, N and Y population and real income respectively, and t denote the shift of the function over time. Then, under the assumption of stable relative prices,

$$D = f(N, Y; t).$$

Assuming that changes in tastes are autonomous and shifts over time of the demand function above can be expressed by a multiplicative term $A(t)$, we obtain,

$$D = A(t)F(N, Y).$$

Differentiating this expression with respect to time, we get (after dividing by D)

$$\frac{\dot{D}}{D} = F\frac{\dot{A}}{D} + A\frac{\delta F}{\delta N}\frac{\dot{N}}{D} + A\frac{\delta F}{\delta Y}\frac{\dot{Y}}{D} ,$$

where dots denote the time derivatives.

Since

$$A\frac{\delta F}{\delta N} = \frac{\delta D}{\delta N} \text{ and } A\frac{\delta F}{\delta Y} = \frac{\delta D}{\delta Y} ,$$

by substituting

$$\varepsilon = \frac{\delta D}{\delta N}\frac{N}{D}\left(\text{that is, } \frac{\delta D}{D}\frac{N}{\delta N} = \frac{\delta D}{D}\bigg/\frac{\delta N}{N}\right) \text{ and}$$

$$\eta = \frac{\delta D}{\delta Y}\frac{Y}{D},$$

we obtain

$$\frac{\dot{D}}{D} = \frac{\dot{A}}{A} + \varepsilon\frac{\dot{N}}{N} + \eta\frac{\dot{Y}}{Y}.$$

It is clear that ε is the elasticity of demand with respect to population and η is the familiar income elasticity. The equation states that the growth rate of demand for agricultural products is the sum of shifts over time of the function, the population elasticity multiplied by the growth rate of population and the income elasticity multiplied by the rate of real income growth.

If, for the sake of simplicity, we were to neglect the shift factor altogether (assume that "tastes" remain the same), the growth rate of demand for agricultural products may be projected by the use of the two elasticities and the growth rates of population and real income. It should be noted here that any kind of shift in the function is regarded as change in tastes. Thus defined, tastes may include: (1) the economy's preferences and habits with respect to consumption; (2) patterns of income distribution; (3) the degrees of urbanization; (4) stages of development of marketing, transportation, and processing of agricultural products, etc. Moreover, if we impose a condition that the elasticity of demand with respect to population, ε, is $(1-\eta)$, i.e., the demand function postulated is homogeneous of degree one (there are no economies of scale in consumption/demand), then we have the simplified relationship stated in the text.

The technique of derivation is essentially the same as that used by Solow (1957).

PROGRAM OF THE CONFERENCE

July 3

Morning: Chairman: T.W. Schultz

Paper: Y. Hayami and S. Yamada, "Agricultural Productivity at the Beginning of Industrialization"

Discussants: A. M. Tang and J. I. Nakamura

Afternoon: Chairman: S. C. Hsieh

Papers: (1) S. Sawada, "Effects of Technological Change in Japanese Agriculture: 1885–1960"
(2) K. Tsuchiya, "Economics of Mechanization in Small Scale Agriculture"

Discussants: (1) V. W. Ruttan
(2) C. Nakajima and G.S. Tolley

July 4

Morning: Chairman: J. H. Park

Paper: M. Umemura, "Agriculture and Labor Supply in the Meiji Era"

Discussants: B. F. Johnston and Y. T. Wang

Afternoon: Chairman: K. Ohkawa

Papers: (1) Y. Masui, "Supply Price of Labor of Farm Family"
(2) T. Misawa, "Farm Economy and Part-time Farming in the Postwar Period"

Discussants: (1) O. Tanaka
(2) J. H. Park

July 5

Morning: Chairman: T. Misawa

Papers: (1) Y. Kato, "Development of Government-Administered Long-Term Agricultural Credit"
(2) T. Noda, "Savings of Farm Households"

Discussants: (1) J. I. Nakamura and O. Sacay
(2) J. Shinohara and O. Sacay

Afternoon: Chairman: K. Janlekha

Paper: H. Kaneda, "Long-Term Changes in Food Consumption Patterns in Japan: 1878–1964"

Discussants: M. Shinohara and V. W. Ruttan

July 6
  Morning: Chairman: B. F. Johnston
            Paper: K. Hemmi, "Primary-Product Exports and
                       Economic Development"
            Discussant: G. S. Tolley
  Afternoon: Chairman: G. S. Tolley
            Papers: (1) S. Kawano, "Economic Significance of
                       the Land Reform"
                       (2) Y. Yuize, "Econometric Model of Agri-
                       culture in Japan"
            Discussants: (1) Y. T. Wang
                       (2) Y. Maruyama and A. M. Tang

July 7
  Morning: Chairman: A. M. Tang
            Paper: B. F. Johnston, "Agriculture and Economic
                       Development in Japan: Its Relevance to the
                       Developing Nations"
            Discussants: S. Ishikawa and K. Janlekha
  Afternoon: Chairman: V. W. Ruttan
            Paper: K. Ohkawa, "Phases of Agricultural Deve-
                       lopment and Economic Growth; A Sum-
                       mary Discussion"
  General Comments: T. W. Schultz.